APPLYING THE CANON IN ISLAM

SUNY Series, Toward a Comparative Philosophy of Religions
Paul J. Griffiths and Laurie L. Patton, editors

APPLYING THE CANON IN ISLAM

The Authorization and Maintenance of Interpretive Reasoning in Ḥanafī Scholarship

Brannon M. Wheeler

State University of New York Press

Published by
State University of New York Press, Albany

Printed in the United States of America

For information, address State University of New York Press,
State University Plaza, Albany, N.Y. 12246

Production by Marilyn P. Semerad
Marketing by Theresa Abad Swierzowski

Library of Congress Cataloging-in-Publication Data

Wheeler, Brannon M., 1965–
Applying the canon in Islam : the authorization and maintenance of interpretive reasoning in Ḥanafī scholarship / Brannon M. Wheeler.
p. cm. — (SUNY series, toward a comparative philosophy of religions)
Includes bibliographical references (p.) and index.
ISBN 0-7914-2973-3 (alk. paper). — ISBN 0-7914-2974-1 (pbk. : alk. paper)
1. Islamic law—Interpretation and construction. 2. Islamic law--History. 3. Hanafites—History. 4. Authority—Religious aspects--Islam. I. Title. II. Series.
LAW <ISLAM 7 Wheeler 1996>
340.5'9—dc20 96-10615
CIP

10 9 8 7 6 5 4 3 2 1

Contents

List of Illustrations

Foreword

Brannon Wheeler's work is the first in-depth treatment of the philosophical and practical significance of commentarial practice for a community constituted largely by such practice. This is the series' first book-length treatment of what we take to be an extraordinarily important topic for philosophers of religion, especially those with comparative interests.

Most religious communities generally have made and make the composition and use of commentaries their principal discursive practice; they have used it to define themselves, to construct and defend the knowledge they take to be important, and to transmit such knowledge to new generations. The composition of commentaries has served as a vehicle for catechesis, polemics, exegesis (of course), canon fixation, and systematic thought. Jonathan Z. Smith's hope that scholars of religion would begin to turn their attention to commentary and exegesis has gradually begun to be realized, especially in the work done by John Henderson, Jeffrey Timm, and Laurie Patton;[1] and yet, in spite of its central importance to religious communities, insufficient work has yet been done to make the idea of commentary usable as a focus for comparative work (compare the amount of attention given to categories such as "myth" or "ritual") or to analyze the philosophical implications of commentary composition.

Wheeler takes some important steps in both directions. Although his work is not essentially comparative, focusing as it does on a single commentarial tradition within Islam (that of the early Ḥanafī school), the way in which he treats this tradition suggests some categories for thinking about commentary that will be useful for future work in this area. Specifically, Wheeler shows how the commentarial practice of Ḥanafī exegetes made the authority of the texts upon which they commented (principally the Qur᾽ān) dependent, in the end, on the exegetical practice of the community, rather than making the authoritativeness of the community's commentarial practice derive from a prior and independent authority possessed by the Qur᾽ān. This move calls into question some stereotyped views of the nature of Qur᾽ānic authority for Islamic interpretive communities; and it should prompt future studies of commentary to ask how the authority of the work commented on is related to that of the commentator.

Wheeler's attention to the details of the patterns of reasoning used by the Ḥanafī exegetes (the derivation of principles by induction from a body of authoritative texts together with their interpretations, followed by the quasi-deductive application of these principles to cases) suggests some interesting philosophical questions. Is it typical, or inevitable, that a community of commentarial practice will justify its deliverances in the way the Ḥanafī exegetes do? What conceptual resources are available to the members of such a community for the adjudication and resolution of intracommunity interpretive disagreements? And how is such a community likely to meet challenges from without as to the validity of its practice as a way of discovering and defending knowledge?

We are delighted that Brannon Wheeler's work is appearing in the series. It is our hope that it will be of use both to Islamicists with specialized interests in the history of exegesis and to comparativists hoping to understand better the philosophical and practical implications of composing and using commentaries.

Paul J. Griffiths
Laurie L. Patton
Summer 1995

Acknowledgments

For academic support, I would like to acknowledge my four advisors: Fred Donner, Frank Reynolds, Widad Kadi, and Jonathan Z. Smith. Part of the research for this study was supported by a Goldsmith Scholars Fellowship for study in Jerusalem during the Summer of 1989. I have also enjoyed the support of colleagues at Macalester College during the 1991–1992 year, at Earlham College during the 1992–1993 year, and at Vanderbilt University during the 1993–1994 and 1994–1995 years. A long-gone version of Chapter 4 was presented at the twenty-fifth annual MESA conference in Washington, D.C., in November 1991, where I received helpful criticism. I would like to thank Kevin Reinhart in particular for his thoughtful comments. A revised version of Chapter 1 was presented at the AAR conference in November 1992, at which time many encouraging remarks were made that helped me in my final version. Substantial revisions were made to Chapters 3 and 4 thanks to comments and insights I received from the Islamic law group at the American Oriental Society meeting in Madison, Wisconsin, in March 1994. My thanks also go to Carl Ernst, long-time friend and *nāṣiḥ,* whose helpful comments on the revised manuscript I received earlier this year. It should also be mentioned that, having not yet acquired my own Ḥanafī library, the interlibrary loan staff at Vanderbilt University, and the libraries that agreed to loan the many multivolume sets, made much of what is in these pages possible for me. Finally, but not least, I want to thank my wife Deborah and sons Jeffry and Zachary for their support of a person whose temperament while writing is little better than that of the Terminator.

Note on Conventions

In the following pages, Arabic words are transliterated according to the standard used in the *International Journal of Middle East Studies,* except that the tā marbūṭa ö is indicated with "ah" in the final, nonconstruct position. Arabic terms are italicized on the first occurrence but not subsequently. Arabic terms included in square brackets [ ] are not italicized. They are meant for the reader of Arabic, to indicate key Arabic terms being translated in the body of the text. All dates, unless otherwise indicated, are Hijrī dates.

Introduction

In recent years interest has developed in the notion of "canon" and, in particular, how the authority of a given canon depends upon its traditional interpretation.[1] This is, in large part, due to a shift in the perspective and goals of the study of religion. Inverting the notion that the use of the canon to support a particular traditional agenda is a degenerate form of religion, Jonathan Z. Smith asserts that the salient feature of religion is its preoccupation with the interpretation of certain texts.

> [T]he radical and arbitrary reduction represented by the notion of canon and the ingenuity represented by the rule-governed exegetical enterprise of applying the canon to every dimension of human life is that most characteristic, persistent, and obsessive religious activity. It is, at the same time, the most profoundly cultural, and hence, the most illuminating for what ought to be the essentially anthropological view point of the historian of religion and a conception of religion as human labor.[2]

This is a critique of the view of religion that privileges the "original" text contained in a canon over what is considered to be a later rationalization of this text's meaning.[3] The study of religion, Smith argues, is about how different people conceive of and practice the interpretive reasoning that allows them to apply a relatively fixed range of things to their changing circumstances.

The following is a study of how a particular conception of canon is used by Ḥanafī fiqh scholarship to perpetuate a certain tradition of interpretation. In Ḥanafī fiqh scholarship, and to some extent sunnī Islam in general, the revelation contained in the text of the Qur'ān is interpreted through the medium of the sunnah to indicate the contents of the sharī'ah. The sharī'ah is the "definition of practice," how certain aspects of everyday life are to be practiced according to the model provided by the canon.[4] Much of classical Ḥanafī scholarship is devoted to the discussion, both in practical and theoretical terms, of how the canonical authority of the Qur'ān and the sunnah is predicated upon their interpretation as represented in the opinions of certain second century authorities. This study is an attempt to explain, for a limited case, how certain forms of interpretive reasoning are authorized and maintained through the manipulation of canonical authority. The Ḥanafī case shows that the notion of canon is best understood as a device to promote the pedagogic agenda of those who use certain texts to represent the authority of the past.

I

The explication of the Ḥanafī case builds upon the understanding of canon put forward by Smith, especially his contention that the conception of a given text's canonical authority is dependent on the application of that text to a particular set of circumstances. Smith exemplifies this point in his account of Ndembu divination.[5] According to Smith, the Ndembu diviner applies a "canon" of twenty-four fixed objects to a client's situation, first selecting a few of the objects by shaking the basket, interpreting the selected objects according to a range of meanings fixed by public convention, and matching the meanings to the client's particular condition.[6] Smith shows that, only in relation to a given set of practical circumstances, has the canon communicative value or functions as a message to clients.

> [A] canon cannot exist without a tradition and an interpreter. That is to say, without the public lexicon [langue] and the explicit engagement in application [parole], the closure of canon would be impossible.[7]

For Smith, a certain set of objects becomes canonical when it is applied to a particular situation by the interpretive ingenuity of an individual exegete through the medium of the public meaning of those objects. The interpretation of the "canon" of objects by the diviner is what makes these objects authoritative in the first place. The objects themselves might be found anywhere, but are considered canonical in the context of the Ndembu divination because of how they are manipulated by the diviner. Without knowing both the fixed range of meanings and the particular condition of the client, an outside interpreter of the objects could come to an understanding of the objects themselves but would not then be interpreting them as the Ndembu canon. For Smith, the objects become significant and thus canonical only when their general meaning, known from "local" knowledge,[8] is matched, through the interpretive ingenuity of the diviner, to the client's condition, the specific circumstances of which are known by questioning the client.

Smith contributes to an understanding of canon by emphasizing that a text's authority is not predicated on some inherent semantic value of its contents. The significance of a canon depends on its being interpreted according to a traditional, established mode of interpretation. There is no meaning that is not imputed to the canon by the exegete through the medium of this established interpretation. Unfortunately, Smith does not go far enough in exploiting the example of Ndembu divination to show the dependence of a canon upon its application. Smith's interpretation, in its privilege both of the objects as a fixed set of things and of the fixed range of meanings given to the objects, gives the impression that, in the Ndembu case, the canon is already "closed" at the time of its application.

A closer examination of the Ndembu case, as it is described by Victor Turner, shows that it is not the closure of the canon that requires exegesis but rather the exegesis that closes the canon. The "canon" per se is never closed but that portion of the canon that is to be applied to a particular case is fixed with its application.

> The diviner keeps a set of from twenty to thirty objects of various shapes, sizes, and colors in a round basket with a lid. When he divines he places these objects in a round, flat, open basket [lwalu] of the type used by women to winnow millet, shakes them and throws them up so that they form a heap at the far side of the basket. He examines the top three or four objects, individually, in combination, and with reference to their relative height in the heap.[9]

It is evident from Turner's description that the canon of objects used by a particular diviner is not fixed in number nor in type.[10] In theory, one might argue that the Ndembu canon would consist of all the objects ever put in divination baskets by all diviners. But what if there were an object that was used by only a few diviners or an object was used by many diviners but that rarely or never came to the top of the heap? What makes something canonical is not that it is a given object, but rather that it is considered to be part of a set of things from which applications are drawn according to certain local considerations.[11] All the objects ever used are not necessarily employed by a given diviner, nor are the objects that do not come to the top of the heap significant except as a reference to the relative height of the objects on top. Of the range of objects available, only those selected by the diviner by shaking the basket are pertinent to the client. Put in the basket, a particular collection of objects is more relevant than the larger range of objects outside of the basket but less relevant than the few objects selected by the diviner by shaking, and even less relevant than the diviner's interpretation of the selected objects.

Turner's description evinces that it is the range of meanings traditionally attributed to certain objects that mediates between the Ndembu canon and its application. Certainly, an object, even if it is in a given diviner's basket, is not considered to be canonical unless it has an interpretation associated with it by the agreement of other diviners. The individual diviner must "communicate" the canon of objects through the "language" of the established interpretations to ensure that his clients will listen to him. No set interpretation exists for each object. Rather, what Turner describes is an established method of interpretation that yields a certain, relatively fixed range of meanings attached to certain objects in certain combinations and in certain circumstances. The individual diviner must adhere not to a specific meaning but to this particular method of interpretation. Otherwise, the individual diviner would be making up his own canon by using objects in an unrecognized fashion.[12] The canon is "open" in the sense that no particular object must be used, but "closed" in the sense that it is limited to the range of objects that have, at the time of their application, an established mode of interpretation.

This established interpretation is itself fixed only by usage. The range of meanings attributed to a given object are several, open to debate among diviners, and often distinguished from one another by technical divinatory knowledge.[13] This choice of different meanings is, in part, probably because an unpopular conclusion by a diviner can result in the death of the diviner.

> The diviner had to make a sound appraisal of the balance of power between rival factions interested in the death [of a relative of one faction] who were present at the public gathering. If he did not, and gave an unpopular verdict, he was likely to be in some danger himself. Many diviners sought the protection of a chief and performed near his capital village. But I have been told of several diviners who despite such protection were speared to death by angry kin of the persons declared to be sorcerers [by the diviners].[14]

The choice of established meanings available to the individual diviner is also expanded to include previously unprecedented interpretations derived from the recurrent appearance of a given object in certain configurations with other items.[15] This means that how the objects were applied to particular cases historically determines in part how the objects are to be applied in present cases. The authoritative interpretations of objects is established through a kind of professional evolution within the discipline devoted to this type of divination, developed through the application of the canon to changing social circumstances.

It is not as though the inherent authority of the canon is transferred to a particular application by the ingenuity of the individual diviner in mastering the limits of the canon. Rather, the authority of earlier applications, used as precedent established by how diviners traditionally interpret the canon to mediate between tribal disputes, authorizes both the specific conclusions of a given diviner and the objects this diviner uses to reach these conclusions (see Figure I.1).

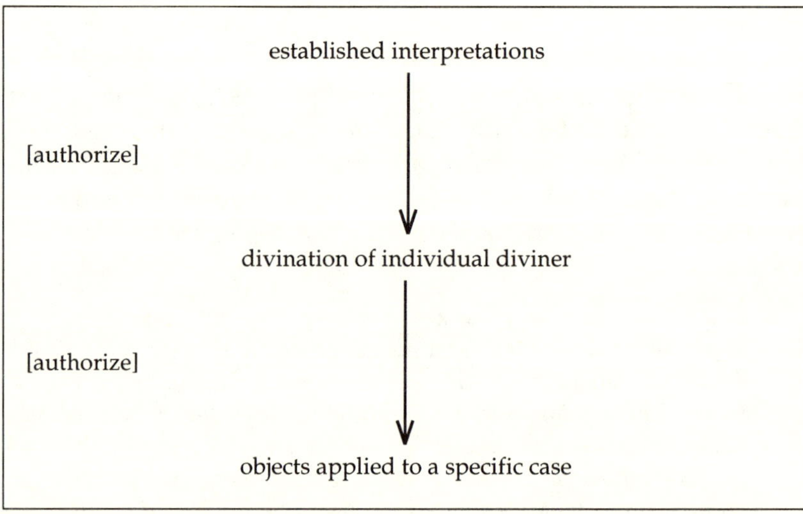

Figure I.1. Showing how the authority of the established interpretations authorizes the divination of the individual diviner, which, in turn, authorizes the objects applied to this specific case.

The established interpretations both delimit the contents of the canon and allow for the broader application of those contents. In theory, the "first" diviners, by their specific application of certain objects to particular circumstances, authorized the collective "canon" of objects they used and established a range of traditional interpretations of those objects. Subsequent diviners, by interpreting objects in accordance with the first diviners' application of those objects, authorized their own applications of the objects. Future diviners must not only acquire a basket of objects, but must undergo an apprenticeship with an accomplished diviner.

During this apprenticeship, the future diviner is taught the range of established interpretations for certain objects that are only then, after having been defined, given to the apprentice to interpret.[16] The apprentice must undergo a type of preprofessional training to learn the technical knowledge required to practice divination. Turner reports that this knowledge is guarded from the general public by this process of apprenticeship.[17] The apprentice must pay a high price in goods, and in some cases to undergo bodily mutilation, similar to that experienced in other rites of initiation, to a practicing diviner to secure his apprenticeship.[18] The apprentice learns from a practicing diviner who, in turn, learned as an apprentice from a practicing diviner of the previous generation. In this way, a certain tradition of interpretation is maintained through pedagogic means. By limiting the significance of the objects to how earlier generations of diviners interpreted them, divinatory apprenticeship makes the authority of later diviners' applications dependent upon the authority of earlier applications. The authority of the objects is accessible to the diviner only through the medium of previous generations.

This focus upon the established interpretations as the source of the objects' authority demonstrates how the scope of what is considered "canonical" extends beyond the "original" corpus of objects.[19] The objects acquire their authority relative to their application through the medium of established interpretations, but the objects also must be made to apply to changing circumstances, unforeseen by the precedents established by earlier applications.[20] To be authoritative, later applications of the objects must be shown to be consistent with the established interpretations, but because the later circumstances are different, the diviner must determine which interpretation from the range he knows is apt.

> Here the vagueness and flexibility of the referent series of each symbol leave him free to make a detailed interpretation of the symbol configuration which corresponds to the

> diagnosis he is making of the state of relationships between his clients and the deceased and between the living kin concerned in the matter.[21]

The contents of the canon and the range of interpretations traditionally attached to those contents do not determine the diviner's conclusions. Rather, the diviner must use his own analysis of the current circumstances to delimit which interpretations, out of those made possible by the contents and established interpretation, apply to the case at hand.

Mediating between the circumstances of the client and the established interpretations, the diviner establishes a *chidimbu,* or an interpretation of the object as it applies to his client's circumstances through the medium of the established interpretations.[22] This interpretation is arrived at by the diviner's induction of a general principle from the circumstances surrounding the application of the established interpretations and from that general principle deduces an interpretation applicable to the circumstances of his client.[23] This principle or meeting point of the various referents is arrived at when the diviner is able to show how the established interpretation of the basket's contents jibe with his client's circumstances. The diviner compares the circumstances of his client to the different circumstances to which the different established interpretations of the given object are applicable to determine which circumstances associated with an established interpretation are most analogous to the circumstances of his client. In doing so, the diviner extends the meaning of a given object to a novel case, but more important, he extends the authority of the established interpretations. In this sense, divination is not about interpreting the objects in the basket but rather about determining a link between the different variables applicable to a given case, linking past precedent to present circumstances. The diviner does not work to overcome the limitation of the canon but rather attempts to limit the various possible interpretations available to him so that the canon applies to the case at hand.[24]

By using this sort of interpretive reasoning, the diviner is not primarily occupied with the application of the objects but rather with the manipulation of the traditional interpretation of the objects. The application of the canon, in Ndembu divination, entails that the locus of interpretation is the range of established interpretations rather than the objects themselves. In effect, the established interpretations must be "overcome" for the objects to be both authoritative and relevant to a given set of circumstances. The application of the objects to novel circumstances involves not only the knowledge of the established interpretations but the capacity to adapt them to changing circumstances. What is canonical for one client is not the same as for another, just as one diviner's basket of objects and the interpretations he tends to give those objects differ from another diviner's objects and interpretations.[25] Two different diviners might give the same client different answers, but both answers are equally authoritative as long as the answers are arrived at through the medium of precedent. The conclusions of later diviners become authoritative when they are shown, through the use of inductive and deductive reasoning on the basis of the established interpretations of the objects, to be applicable to the specific status of the diviner vis-à-vis the client. Ndembu divination illustrates that canonical authority is not found in a given "text" but it is the demonstration of one's ability to show that one's conclusions are derived from a given text, through the medium of the traditional interpretation that designates that text as authoritative. In this sense, the Ndembu preoccupation with canon is not "about" the canon but about establishing and maintaining certain forms of interpretive authority.

II

The use of canonical authority in Ndembu divination highlights several important aspects of how a conception of canon is used in Ḥanafī scholarship.[26] On a basic level, the Ndembu notion of canon is analogous with the Ḥanafī conception that the Qurʾān's authority is dependent on the application of it to changing circumstances through the medium of the sunnah and subsequent generations of scholarship. Ḥanafī scholarship requires that an interpretation of the Qurʾān's practical significance be consistent with the established precedents of traditional interpretations in order to be authoritative.

As is the case for the individual Ndembu diviner, the Ḥanafī scholar must be able to demonstrate, using inductive reasoning, a link between his definition of practice and the Qurʾān through the medium of certain precedents considered to have canonical authority by the Ḥanafī school. The Ndembu diviner and Ḥanafī scholar have access to the canon only through the interpretations of earlier generations, which are recognized as conveying the authority of the canon. In the Ndembu case, this access is restricted by the initiation process an apprentice diviner must undergo to learn the traditional method of interpretation and acquire his own basket from the previous generation of diviners. The Ḥanafī student must likewise undergo a sort of initiation in which the school's authority is shown to be based upon previous generations of scholarship going back to the authority of the prophet as the model interpreter of the Qurʾān. The construction of this epistemology and the method it requires for the practice of Ḥanafī scholarship is sketched in the following chapters. These chapters describe how a particular concept of canon was developed and used to authorize and perpetuate a particular type of interpretive reasoning.

In Ḥanafī scholarship, the practical significance of the Qurʾān is determined by how it is applied in the recorded practice of the prophet. This practice of the prophet, or his sunnah, like the established interpretation of the objects in Ndembu divination, mediates between the revelation contained in the text of the Qurʾān and the definition of practice or sharīʿah derived from the revelation. By using the sunnah of the prophet as the medium through which to derive the definition of practice from the revelation, Ḥanafī scholarship delimits the canonical authority of the Qurʾān. Like the use of the range of objects in Ndembu divination, the different parts of the Qurʾān are not equally integral to the Ḥanafī definition of practice nor is the whole of the revelation used to define practice limited to the text of the Qurʾān. Only certain verses are considered to contain the general principles necessary to determine the practical significance of the revelation.[27] In some cases, parts of the revelation pertinent to the definition of practice are not found in the text of the Qurʾān.[28] Of the pertinent parts of the revelation found in the Qurʾān, most if not all require the amplification of the sunnah to be understood as applicable to the definition of practice. The relevance of the revelation, including that contained in the text of the Qurʾān, depends on its application to specific circumstances by the prophet, recorded in his sunnah. Without the application contained in the sunnah, the contents of the Qurʾān might still be considered to be revelation, but the "communication" of the revelation would be limited to the circumstances of its textual setting. The sunnah, like the established interpretation of the objects in Ndembu divination, serves to "close" the text of the revelation by making it pertinent to the definition of certain practices.

Chapter 1 describes the establishment of the epistemology introduced in the third and fourth centuries that defined the revelation and its authoritative interpretation in terms of texts. The recorded opinions of selected second century local authorities such as Mālik b. Anas and Abū Yūsuf illustrate how an earlier conception of the revelation and the sunnah was developed into a text-based epistemology that authorized the later interpretive reasoning of the Ḥanafī school. This text-based epistemology fixed the textual record of the sunnah of the prophet as the required interpretation of the revelation. By canonizing the sunnah, this epistemology, in effect, made meaning and the authority of the Qurʾān dependent upon how the prophet was reported to have understood and applied certain portions of the text of the Qurʾān as revelation. The theoretical works associated with al-Shāfiʿī show, in detail, how the canonization of the sunnah shifted the older guarantee of authority away from the clout of local definitions of practice and toward a notion of authority based on the transmission and interpretation of texts describing how the prophet applied the revelation to his circumstances. This development led to an increasing focus upon the sunnah and the different transmissions and interpretations of the sunnah, rather than upon the revelation itself, as the locus of authority.

Although the practical significance and thus the authority of the revelation was made to depend upon the sunnah, the significance of the sunnah itself was fixed only by subsequent scholarship's interpretation of the sunnah's contents. Chapter 2 shows how the emergence of Ḥanafī scholarship in the late third and fourth centuries was tied to the notion that the sunnah represented an epitome of how to interpret the revelation and that the opinions of certain Kūfan authorities of the second century were based on this epitome. The interpretation of the sunnah was thus fixed by the historical precedent of the opinions of certain second century local authorities concerning how the reported practice of the prophet is to be understood as an application of the revelation. This is evident from the scholarship that argues that knowledge of the specific circumstances to which the prophet applied the revelation was necessary to determine in general terms the sorts of reasoning he used. The fourth century Ḥanafī scholarship of al-Ṭaḥāwī and al-Jaṣṣāṣ demonstrates, through the analysis of selected opinions of certain Kūfan authorities, that the authority of its definition of practice is guaranteed by the consistency of these opinions with the prophet's interpretation in his sunnah. Thus, the significance of the sunnah as an interpretation of the revelation was established through the medium of certain second century opinions. This meant that later Ḥanafī scholarship was able to claim that the particular corpus of opinions on which their scholarship was based was itself an epitome of the interpretive reasoning used by the prophet to derive his sunnah from the revelation.

Yet, as is the case among the different Ndembu diviners, the opinions of the authorities acknowledged by later Ḥanafī scholarship are not necessarily in agreement with the opinions of authorities acknowledged by other classical sunnī schools. In the fourth century, the different classical schools were distinguished from one another by the different corpora of second century opinions each utilized to establish how the sunnah interpreted the revelation. In effect, neither the text of the Qurʾān nor the sunnah determined what would constitute an authoritative application of the revelation for the different schools; rather the different schools' use of particular sets of second century opinions delimited the practical authority of the revelation. The applicability and thus authority of the Qurʾān is fixed by the sunnah, the sunnah by the opinions, and the opinions by subsequent scholarship. The use of different second century opinions was of particular significance to Ḥanafī scholarship because opinions included in the corpus used by the Ḥanafī school were often in conflict with one another over how to understand the precedent of the sunnah. For the Ḥanafī scholarship of the fifth and sixth centuries, this meant that an authoritative definition of practice was not necessarily determined by agreement with a given opinion, but rather with the textual and logical considerations epitomized by certain groups of opinions considered to have canonical authority.

Chapter 3 examines the arguments of the classical Ḥanafī scholarship of the fifth and sixth centuries and, in particular, the distinction it makes between the textual basis of authority and the logical basis of the reasoning required to interpret the revelation. Earlier classical scholarship, such as that of al-Qudūrī, shows how the comparison of conflicting opinions from the corpus considered canonical by Ḥanafī scholarship indicate certain logical considerations that must be taken into account by later generations when applying the revelation to their own circumstances. The work of al-Dabūsī further consolidates this concept by organizing the selected second century opinions according to the different sorts of logical considerations that distinguish Ḥanafī from non-Ḥanafī reasoning. Later classical scholarship, like that of al-Sarakhsī, formalizes the distinction between the text-based epistemology and the logic-based methodology used in Ḥanafī scholarship. This distinction makes it necessary for subsequent scholarship to be consistent not only with the text of the revelation, but also with the logical considerations represented in the Ḥanafī opinions.

Similar to how the individual Ndembu diviner is constrained to understand the circumstances to which earlier diviners applied a given object in order to determine which meaning best applies to his client's circumstances, classical Ḥanafī scholarship stipulates that the Ḥanafī scholar must understand the context in which the opinions were formulated. Like the Ndembu diviner, the Ḥanafī scholar does not interpret the revelation alone or even directly, but instead interprets how the generations previous to him interpreted the revelation, as represented in the opinions and the interpretation of those opinions by subsequent scholarship. Using previous scholarship as examples of how to apply the revelation, the Ḥanafī scholar must compare the context in which the revelation was interpreted in precedented cases to distinguish what is specific to each of the cases from what the cases have in common. Through this type of reasoning, the Ḥanafī scholar induces a general principle of the revelation from the different precedented cases. This is not unlike how the Ndembu diviner induces a chidimbu by comparing the circumstances of precedented cases to the circumstances of his client. In both the Ndembu and Ḥanafī cases, a conclusion is deduced from this general principle and the objects or the revelation authoritatively applied to an unprecedented case.

Chapter 4 demonstrates how the postclassical Ḥanafī scholarship of the late sixth and subsequent centuries requires future Ḥanafī scholars to read "backward" through the scholarship of previous generations. In this sense, postclassical scholarship is primarily a pedagogic enterprise, teaching future Ḥanafī scholars the epistemological and methodological bases of the Ḥanafī school through a step-by-step commentary on how previous scholarship interpreted the opinions. Using previous scholarship as a heuristic device, postclassical scholarship, like that of al-Marghīnānī and the later commentaries on his work, maintains the interpretive tradition of the school by teaching that Ḥanafī scholarship is built upon the accretion of interpretations regarding the opinions of certain second century authorities. Postclassical scholarship, especially the shurūḥ scholarship of al-Ḥaddād and al-Maydānī, shows how the piecemeal analysis of earlier scholarship highlights the inductive and deductive reasoning required to determine the revelatory principles upon which the school is based. This scholarship focuses upon the notion that the authority of a given definition of practice is less about the interpretation of the revelation than about being able to demonstrate that a given definition is justified in light of earlier tradition.

III

This conception of canonical authority is used in Ḥanafī scholarship to maintain a certain tradition of interpretation. Ḥanafī scholarship makes authority dependent not on access to the revelation but on knowledge of how to manipulate the traditional interpretation of the revelation. Like the need for the Ndembu diviner to use the corpus of established interpretations to have his conclusions recognized as authoritative, Ḥanafī scholarship requires that an authoritative definition of practice be derived from the opinions of certain second century authorities, as interpreted by subsequent generations of Ḥanafī scholarship. The individual Ḥanafī scholar does not inherit the authority of the revelation by claiming to know how to interpret the Qurʾān. Rather, the authority of a given scholar's definition of practice is predicated on demonstrating the claim that this definition of practice is a continuation of earlier generations' definition of practice, originating with the prophet's definition of practice. To retain the authority of the prophet, subsequent generations of scholarship must not overcome a relatively limited canon of precedents but rather master the ability to reason on the basis of an accreting mass of traditional interpretations.

In both the Ndembu and Ḥanafī cases, no operative distinction is made separating the "original text" and "later interpretation" or between canon and application. The contents of the canon are not limited to the basket of objects or to the text of the Qurʾān, but include subsequent interpretations of the objects and Qurʾān. Canonical authority, in the Ḥanafī case, extends to the sunnah, the opinions of second century authorities, and subsequent generations of scholarship. In the Ndembu case, the contents of the basket are used as props to support the authority of diviners' claims. A diviner who was to analyze his client's situation without throwing and reading the basket of objects would lose his status as a diviner. There would be no reason for his client to attribute spirit possession or attach authority to the diviner's otherwise strategic questions and guesses. Use of the basket is a physical sign of the diviner's authority. Likewise, the contents of the extended Ḥanafī canon are appropriated to further the epistemological and methodological claims of the school. The exegesis of a particular passage from the sunnah or the opinion of a particular second century authority is a sign of the exegete's link with precedent and authority. By using a certain notion of canon to authorize its pedagogic agenda, Ḥanafī scholarship is able to perpetuate its own authority.

The Ḥanafī canon and the authority associated with it were developed and used as a pedagogic device for teaching future generations of Ḥanafī scholars a certain tradition of interpretive reasoning. By making the authority of the "canon" dependent on its traditional application, Ḥanafī scholarship focuses not upon the extension of the significance of a fixed set of words but rather upon the reasoning required to select which precedented interpretation of those words is most appropriate for the current circumstances. Interpretation, in the Ndembu case, is not about extending the canon but rather about limiting the conclusions made possible by the objects, range of established interpretations, and circumstances of the client. Likewise, the practice of interpretation in Ḥanafī scholarship does not concern exclusively nor even primarily the presumed inherent semantic value of a given text's contents. Rather, canonical authority is attributed to those scholars capable of imputing a semantic value to those contents in a manner shown to be both consistent with the interpretations of earlier generations and applicable to a present set of circumstances. The canon is used to authorize the person or institution that functions as a "broker" between the established authority of the past and the changing circumstances of the present.[29] In this sense, Ḥanafī scholarship's preoccupation with the notion of canon is less about a given text than about being able to preserve, through the appropriation of earlier tradition, a certain conception of authority.

Chapter **1**

The Authorization of Exegesis

Ḥanafī scholarship developed from debates among early Islamic groups concerning the legitimacy of the opinions of conflicting local authorities who lived at the end of the second century.[1] In the late fourth and fifth centuries, selected opinions of these authorities, associated with Madīnah and Kūfah among other locations, were used by the emerging classical schools of fiqh as the basis for the sharīʿah, the authoritative definition of practice. These selected opinions, however, were not only distinct but often in conflict with one another. The classical schools of fiqh that traced the authority of their definition of practice back to the revelation used these conflicting opinions to demonstrate that their definitions of practice were based on the prophet's interpretation of the revelation contained in the Qurʾān. To justify the equivalent authority of these conflicting opinions the classical schools adopted a text-based epistemology, associated with the theories of Muḥammad b. Idrīs al-Shāfiʿī [150–204], which provides that the later classical schools are equally authoritative even though they are based upon distinct and often conflicting local opinions.

The text-based epistemology that guarantees the equal authority of the classical schools is predicated on a twofold conception of the canon. This twofold conception of the canon defines the Qurʾān as the written source and the sunnah, being the practice of the prophet, as originally, the oral source for knowledge of the revelation.[2] By including the sunnah in the canon, classical fiqh scholarship provided both for the priority of the sunnah in determining the revelation's significance and for the later use of reasoned interpretation in that determination. Similar to how the Ndembu use an established interpretation to provide an authoritative model for the interpretation of the basket of objects, the classical schools used the sunnah as a model for how to interpret the revelation contained in the Qur᾿ān. This conception of canon, at the root of classical fiqh scholarship's epistemology, is what authorizes the opinions of the local authorities and subsequent exegetical activities of the schools.

By giving the basic outlines of this conception, the following pages show how a text-based epistemology legitimates the later interpretive reasoning required to derive a definition of practice from the revelation. The canonization of the sunnah is significant for how it ties the conception of authority to the revelation and how it leads to the definition of the revelation in terms of texts and their interpretation. The text-based epistemology of the classical schools defines the sunnah in a fashion that allows later scholarship to make exegetical claims equivalent in authority but not identical in content to the revelation.

Section I uses the opinions of Mālik b. Anas [90–179] and Abū Yūsuf Yaᶜqūb b. Ibrāhīm [113–182] to illustrate how the local authorities of Madīnah and Kūfah in the second century justified their opinions and the sort of epistemologies on which they relied.[3] This section shows that among these second century local authorities the concept and content of the "sunnah" was malleable because it was yet to be limited to a textual corpus. Section II introduces the notion of the canonized sunnah as a relatively fixed textual corpus. By defining the revelation as a text that requires interpretation as epitomized by prophetic practice contained in the textual corpus of the sunnah, the theories associated with al-Shāfiᶜī shifted the guarantee of the local authorities' opinions away from the local definitions of traditional practice and toward a notion of authority based on the transmission and interpretation of texts. Section III indicates the implications this epistemology had for the development of the classical schools' equal authority. It shows how the scholarship devoted to tracing the transmission of prophetic practice through successive generations of scholarship developed out of the idea of a canonized sunnah to authorize the classical schools by linking the opinions of select local authorities to the example of prophetic practice.

I

Sunnah as Local Practice

The classical notion of the sunnah as prophetic practice and its equation with the authority of the revelation contained in the Qurʾān was the result of a series of theoretical developments during the late second and early third centuries.[4] Before this time, the concept of the "sunnah," from which different local authorities claimed to derive their definitions of practice, referred to those actual practices supposed to be based upon the imitation of prophetic practices that often included practices later deduced from what was thought to be implicit in the prophetic model.[5] That this traditional practice was prophetic practice was based on the claim that this generation, received it from the previous generation who in turn received it from the generation previous to them, who received it from the prophet himself. The actual content of this traditional practice, then, was determined by the agreement of current authorities upon the agreement of the previous generation's authorities upon the agreement of the generation previous to that. The later logical differences separating the classical schools' positions on the definition of practice were originally local differences. The opinions of the second century authorities on which the classical schools built their scholarship were themselves based upon different local traditions of practice. The sunnah was thus defined as that on which there was consensus [al-ʿaml al-mujtamaʿ alay-hi] as opposed to that which was considered to be an innovation [bidʿah].[6]

The content of this traditional practice, informed not only by prophetic precedent but also by the agreed upon practices of later generations, took form at the end of the first and beginning of the second centuries.[7] In the sphere of ritual, for example, the rudimentary cultic practices of the Umayyad period were influenced by local customs.[8] Under the influence of local judges and governors, a more definitive traditional ritual practice was instituted.[9] There is also evidence of political influence in fiscal, penal, and international practices as well as in the sphere of family practice, especially marriage and divorce.[10] Moreover, this later, local influence is evident from the incorporation of foreign elements into the traditional practice of early Muslim societies.[11] This local character of the traditional practice is perhaps most obvious from the distance that separated the definitions of practice espoused by the different local authorities of the second century. The formation of a traditional practice on the basis of consensus in different locations led to the conception of differing definitions of what constituted the sunnah and authoritative practice.

This is exemplified in the conflict between the opinions of Mālik, Abū Ḥanīfah, and al-Shāfiᶜī over what constitutes usurious practice in exchanges by dry measure or weight.

> Mālik says: the practice according to us concerning items sold by dry measure or by weight which are not eaten or drunk, like safflower, date-stones, fodder-leaves, indigo dye, and like things is that there is no harm in taking from any of the things of these categories two for one, hand to hand. Two for one of the things from a single category are not taken at a later time [an exchange of one thing now for two things delivered at a later date]. If the two things are clearly of different categories then there is no harm in taking two for one at a later time. There is no harm in selling items from these categories which are already purchased but not yet received when the price is obtained from someone other than the original owner from whom they were purchased. Everything from all of these categories in which there is profit for people, if it is gravel and gypsum, one amount of them for two amounts of the same thing at a later time is usury. One amount for the same amount plus something extra at a later time is usury.[12]

> [Abū Ḥanīfah says]: usury is forbidden for things of the same species sold by dry measure and by weight at an unequal rate of exchange. The principle is dry measure accompanied by species or weight accompanied by species. When a person sells an item by dry measure or weight for the item of the same species at an equal rate, the sale is permitted. If it is at an unequal rate, it is not permitted.[13]

> al-Shāfiʿī says: it is not permitted to exchange in advance [such an exchange being at an unequal rate] things eaten or drunk of the same type which are sold by dry measure or weight. If the species of the two things differ then it is permitted to exchange them at an unequal rate, hand to hand. This is analogous to gold which is not permitted to be exchanged in advance for silver and silver which is not permitted to be exchanged in advance for gold. For everything which is eaten and drunk, and gold and silver, there is no harm in selling one of them for another [species] of them at an unequal rate at a later time.[14]

Summarizing the traditional practice of Madīnah, Mālik holds that food and nonfood items that are of benefit to people cannot be exchanged at an unequal rate if they are of the same species. Abū Ḥanīfah, representing the customary practice of Kūfah, forbids the exchange of any items of the same species which are sold by weight or dry measure. The opinion of al-Shāfiʿī, based on what he considered to be prophetic practice, is that items of food, gold, and silver cannot be exchanged at an unequal rate if they are of the same species. So, for example, cat litter sold by dry measure or weight could be exchanged for a larger amount of cat litter according to al-Shāfiʿī and Mālik because it is not food nor is it of benefit to people, but Abū Ḥanīfah would not permit the exchange. Both Abū Ḥanīfah and Mālik would forbid the exchange of cement mix by dry measure or weight at an unequal amount, but al-Shāfiʿī would permit it. Abū Ḥanīfah would allow the exchange of one pumpkin for two pumpkins as long as they were not sold by weight but neither Mālik nor al-Shāfiʿī would. Thus, different local traditions resulted in markedly distinct definitions of practice.

These local differences in the conception of what constituted the sunnah or traditional practice caused local authorities to use different approaches in justifying their definitions of practice as more authoritative than others. Although in theory all of the local authorities refer to the precedent of prophetic practice, because the content of that practice consisted of local practice considered to be traditional, definitions of practice differed. Because this conflict of opinions about the definition of practice then calls into question the universal nature of the local tradition upon which the opinions are based, authorities in different locations emphasized different sorts of epistemologies. In an attempt to support the authority of their own local tradition, these authorities had to base the authority of their opinions upon the relative legitimacy of their local conception of the sunnah. That is, local authorities authorized their opinions by claiming them to be based on a sunnah upon which the conflicting opinions of other local authorities were not based. The conflicting opinions of other local authorities were not authoritative because they were not based on the right sunnah. In effect, no established interpretation was recognized by the different groups even though the groups agreed in theory that their authority was based on the "sunnah."[15] Arguments for the authority of a particular opinion were thus cast in terms of what constituted the sunnah, which, in theory, all of the other authorities should follow in defining practice.

Madīnah

The late second and third century scholars associated with the fiqh "school" of Madīnah predicate the authority of their definition of practice upon the opinions of Mālik, which are supposed to represent the second century consensus concerning the traditional practice of Madīnah.[16] Mālik's opinions and the support for them are collected in the *Muwaṭṭāʾ* extant in two major redactions.[17] The basic format of the *Muwaṭṭāʾ* is that the text reports examples of practice and then gives Mālik's definition of a particular practice in the form of an interpretation or summary of the preceding examples. The authority of Mālik's opinion is predicated upon the authority of the information, taken as a precedent, reported in the examples of practice to which Mālik's opinion refers. In most cases,[18] Mālik's opinion refers to the practice of certain people associated with the early community in Madīnah, either as "companions" [ṣaḥābah] of the prophet or "followers" [tābiᶜūn] of the companions. For example, in the discussion concerning the prey that pilgrims are permitted to eat when in the sacred area [ḥaram] around Makkah,[19] Mālik's definition of practice refers to the practice of tābiᶜūn and ṣaḥābah:

> Mālik was asked what about meat of prey which is found on the road: can the sacralized person buy it? He said: as for that prey which is hunted in order to be offered to the pilgrim, I find it reprehensible and forbid it. As for that prey which a man has which is not intended for pilgrims but is found by a sacralized person who buys it, there is no harm in it.[20]

One of the precedents to which Mālik is referring is that set by Abū Hurayrah when he permits a group of pilgrims to eat the meat of prey that they got from people who were not pilgrims. The report is given in two versions.

> Yaḥyāʾ reported to me, on the authority of Mālik, on the authority of Yaḥyāʾ b. Saᶜīd who heard Saᶜīd b. al-Musayyib reporting on the authority of Abū Hurayrah: that he [Abū Hurayrah] was returning from Baḥrain, and when he reached Rabadhah he found a caravan of sacralized people from ᶜIrāq. They asked him about the meat of prey which they got from the people of Rabadhah. He commanded them to eat it. He [Abū Hurayrah] said: then I was doubtful about what I commanded them to do. So, when I returned to Madīnah I mentioned this to ᶜUmar b. al-Khaṭṭāb. ᶜUmar said: what did you command them to do? He [Abū Hurayrah] said: I commanded them to eat it. ᶜUmar b. al-Khaṭṭāb said: if you had commanded them otherwise I would have caused threats to be carried out on you.[21]

> Yaḥyāʾ reported to me, on the authority of Mālik, on the authority of Ibn Shihāb, on the authority of Sālim b.

> ᶜAbdallāh who heard Abū Hurayrah reporting to ᶜAbdallāh b. ᶜUmar that he passed by a group of sacralized people in Rabadhah. They asked him to issue a decision [fatwah] concerning the meat of prey they had gotten from people who were not sacralized and were eating it. He issued a decision to eat it. He [Abū Hurayrah] said: then I returned to Madīnah, to ᶜUmar b. al-Khaṭṭāb and I asked him about this. He said: what decision did you issue to them. He [Abū Hurayrah] said: I issued a decision to them to eat it. ᶜUmar said: if you had issued to them any other decision, I would have hurt you.[22]

Mālik's opinion is based on his interpretation of this practice, in particular that the pilgrims were permitted to eat the meat of prey because the prey was not killed with the intention of feeding it to pilgrims. Also, notice that although the authority of this practice is linked to ᶜUmar b. al-Khaṭṭāb, a prominent companion of the prophet, ᶜUmar only affirms the legitimacy of Abū Hurayrah's practice. By referring to the opinion of ᶜUmar, however, the *Muwaṭṭāʾ* is able to extend the authority of Abū Hurayrah's practice back to a previous generation of Medinese practice.[23] This is similar to how the *Muwaṭṭāʾ* uses the opinion of the prophet to ratify the report of the practice of a companion.

Another of the precedents on which Mālik bases the authority of his opinion concerning pilgrims' eating of prey is the report of some pilgrims who eat part of a wild ass killed by Abū Qatādah, who was not sacralized as a pilgrim at the time he killed the ass. There are two versions of this report also.

> Yaḥyāʾ reported to me, on the authority of Mālik, on the authority of Abū al-Naḍr, the client of ᶜUmar b. ᶜUbaydallāh al-Taymī, on the authority of Nāfiᶜ, the client of Abū Qatādah al-Anṣārī, on the authority of Abū Qatādah that he [Abū Qatādah] was once with the messenger of God. When they were at one of the roads to Makkah he fell behind along with his [the prophet's] companions who were sacralized; but he [Abū Qatādah] was not sacralized. Then he saw a wild ass, so he mounted his horse and asked his companions to give him his whip. They refused. So, he asked them for his spear, but they refused. So, he took his spear, attacked the ass, and killed it. Some of the compan-

> ions of the messenger of God ate from it, but some of them refused. When they caught up to the messenger of God they asked him about this. He said: this is food which God fed to you.[24]
>
> Yaḥyāʾ reported to me, on the authority of Mālik, on the authority of Zayd b. Aslam, that ʿAṭāʾ b. Yasār told him that Abū Qatādah the same report as Abū al-Naḍr about the wild ass except that in the report of Zayd b. Aslam the messenger of God says: do you have any of its meat with you?[25]

These two reports present an example of practice analogous to that given in the report of Abū Hurayrah. The permission for the pilgrims to eat the meat of prey that Abū Qatādah killed for himself supports Mālik's opinion. As in the example of Abū Hurayrah, here the practice of Abū Qatādah is ratified by an earlier opinion, that of the prophet. Although the reports link the practice to an earlier generation of Medinese practice, the practice of the companions sets the precedent for Mālik's opinion.[26] The role of the prophet in the reports is inconsequential without the rest of the story. In neither case are the prophet's words, "this is food which God fed to you" and "do you have any of its meat with you," unequivocal statements concerning the evaluation of the companions' practice.

In some cases, the *Muwaṭṭāʾ* does cite reports of the prophet's direct definition of practice as a precedent for the opinion of Mālik. For example, before giving Mālik's opinion about which animals pilgrims are permitted to kill, the *Muwaṭṭāʾ* lists four precedents.

> Yaḥyāʾ reported to me, on the authority of Mālik, on the authority of Nāfiʿ, on the authority of ʿAbdallāh b. ʿUmar that the messenger of God said: there are five animals, the killing of which is not held against a sacralized person: crow, kite, scorpion, mouse, and wild dog.[27]
>
> Yaḥyāʾ reported to me, on the authority of Mālik, on the authority of ʿAbdallāh b. Dīnār, on the authority of ʿAbdallāh b. ʿUmar that the messenger of God said: there are five animals. If a sacralized person kills them there is nothing

> held against him: scorpion, mouse, crow, kite, and wild dog.[28]
>
> Yaḥyā᾽ reported to me, on the authority of Mālik, on the authority of Hishām b. ᶜUrwah, on the authority of his father that the messenger of God said: there are five vicious things which are killed in the sacred area: mouse, scorpion, crow, kite, and wild dog.[29]
>
> Yaḥyā᾽ reported to me, on the authority of Mālik, on the authority of Ibn Shihāb that ᶜUmar b. al-Khaṭṭāb commanded the killing of snakes in the sacred area.[30]

The first three reports are different versions of essentially the same statement of the prophet, and the third report is a statement of the companion ᶜUmar b. al-Khaṭṭāb. Here, the precedent set by ᶜUmar's statement does not necessarily coincide with the prophet's statement. The practice of killing snakes in the sacred area is prescribed in addition to the practice of killing the five animals indicated by the prophet. The definition of practice by ᶜUmar, as presented here, is not a practice affirmed by a report of the prophet.[31] Yet, it appears that ᶜUmar's definition of practice is equivalent in authority with the definition of the prophet. It is evident from Mālik's opinion made on the basis of these precedents that his own elaboration of the definition of practice does not rely on reports of prophetic precedent. Rather, Mālik's definition of practice is derived from examples of practice from previous generations of Medinese, which include examples of prophetic practice.

The report of the prophet's definition of practice concerning the five animals is not simply repeated by Mālik as the last word on the definition of this particular practice. Mālik's opinion is an interpretation of the cited precedents.

> Mālik said: concerning the wild dog which was ordered to be killed in the sacred area, all animals that wound, attack, or scare people, like the lion, tiger, cheetah [fihd], and wolf are considered as wild dogs. As for those predatory animals which do not attack people, like the hyena, fox, cat, and other predatory animals that resemble them, the

> sacralized person does not kill them. If he kills them, then he pays a fine. As for harmful birds, the sacralized person does not kill them, except those the prophet specified: the crow and kite. If the sacralized person kills a predatory bird other than those two, then he pays a fine.[32]

On the one hand, Mālik extends, by analogy, the prophet's mention of the wild dog to include other predatory animals not explicitly mentioned by the prophet. With his restriction on the killing of predatory animals that do not attack people, Mālik indicates that the killing of other predatory animals is allowed because they pose a possible danger to pilgrims. On the other hand, Mālik limits the killing of harmful birds to those specified by the prophet although it might seem that other carrion-eating or predatory birds could be killed by pilgrims. This example shows how, in the *Muwaṭṭāʾ*, Mālik's opinion does not prescribe the practice of earlier generations but interprets this practice as a precedent to authorize a later definition of practice. It also shows that despite the privileged position given to prophetic practice in the *Muwaṭṭāʾ*, the authority of reported prophetic practice is relative to practice of the later generations of companions and followers.[33] That is, even though or because of the fact that reported prophetic practice is likely to represent the oldest precedent for the definition of practice, it is to be interpreted in light of the continuous practice of later generations.

This same use of later practice to interpret or supplement earlier precedents is evinced in how the *Muwaṭṭāʾ* relates Mālik's opinion to statements from the Qurʾān. Although the citation of the Qurʾān as support for Mālik's definition of practice is rare, like reports of prophetic practice, it is apparently not treated as a privileged source of precedented practice.[34]

> Mālik said: God the blessed and exalted said: You who believe, do not kill prey while you are sacralized. If a person from among you kills game intentionally, then there is a penalty like that which was killed in terms of pasturing animals. Two just people from among you decide whether a sacrificial animal is brought to the Kaʿbah, or an expiation of food for the poor, or the equivalent of that in fasting,

> so that he might taste the consequences of what he did. [sūrat al-māʾidah, 5:95]
>
> Mālik said: those who hunt prey while not sacralized and then kill the prey while sacralized are in the same position as those who buy prey while sacralized and then kill it. God has forbidden the killing of it and a penalty is incumbent for it.
>
> The matter according to us is that if a person gets prey while sacralized, a decision is made against him.
>
> Yaḥyāʾ said: Mālik said: the best I have heard concerning he who kills prey is that a decision is made against him: that it is established what prey he gets, its price in food is determined, and he feeds each poor person a *mudd,* or he fasts a day for every *mudd.* The number of poor people is determined: if there are ten then he fasts for ten days. If there are twenty then he fasts for twenty days. The number of poor people is what he does even if there are more than sixty poor people.
>
> Mālik said: I heard that a decision is made against a person who kills prey in the sacred area while he is not sacralized just like what is decided against a sacralized person who kills prey in the sacred area while he is sacralized.[35]

The only opinion of Mālik here given on the authority of Yaḥyāʾ, concerning the amount of food given to the poor and the length of the fasting, is a specification of the statement of penalty in the Qurʾān. Mālik supplies practical details absent from the Qurʾānic precedent. In the last opinion cited, Mālik goes beyond providing additional details to the Qurʾānic precedent. Mālik's opinion simply adds that the killing of prey in the sacred area by unsacralized people requires the same penalty required by the Qurʾān for killing by sacralized people.[36]

More significant, however, is the first opinion cited by Mālik, in which he equates a sacralized person's buying prey with a sacralized person's killing prey that was hunted while the person was not sacralized. This opinion is an attempt to harmonize the Qur᾽ānic precedent with the precedents of companions cited earlier. On the basis of the practice of al-Zubayr b. al-ᶜAwwām, Mālik concludes that it is permitted for a sacralized person to eat prey that was hunted and killed by that person prior to becoming sacralized.

> Yaḥyā᾽ reported, on the authority of Mālik, on the authority of Hishām b. ᶜUrwah, on the authority of his father that al-Zubayr b. al-ᶜAwwām used to take as provisions dried gazelle meat while he was sacralized.[37]

By emphasizing that the penalty assessed for killing wild animals is predicated on the killing being done while sacralized, Mālik's interpretation of the Qur᾽ānic precedent allows for the authority of the precedent set by the practice of the companion al-Zubayr b. al-ᶜAwwām. Mālik's interpretation also reconciles the Qur᾽ānic precedent with the practice ascribed to Abū Hurayrah and affirmed by ᶜUmar b. al-Khaṭṭāb of permitting pilgrims to eat the meat of prey others had hunted for themselves. The Qur᾽ānic statement is interpreted to mean that if a sacralized person purchased the meat of prey then that meat would have been hunted with the intention of having a sacralized person eat it, which Mālik contends is not permitted on the basis of companion and prophetic practice.[38] This example illustrates how the scholars associated with the late second and third century "school" of Madīnah consistently interpreted earlier textual precedents in light of later practice regarded as exemplifying a continuous tradition of Medinese practice that originates with the prophet.[39]

The early Medinese tradition, represented by Mālik's opinions in the *Muwaṭṭā᾽*, privileges the authority of a continuing tradition of practice over textual reports of prophetic practice. Mālik is quoted by Muḥammad b. ᶜAbd al-Bāqī al-Zurqānī [d. 1122] as saying that "not everything which occurs in a report of practice [ḥadīth] is to be taken literally."[40] This reflects the Medinese position that the text-reported prophetic practice is not to be taken as authoritative in and of itself but to be interpreted to support what is known of prophetic practice from later practices. The later practices of the companions and followers are thought to be better indications of prophetic practice than textual reports of what the prophet said or did. This is because the prophet's companions, their followers, and their followers' followers are thought to know prophetic practice through experience rather than through textual transmission. Although the arrangement of the *Muwaṭṭā*ʾ seems to privilege reports of prophetic practice, the ultimate authority of Mālik's conclusions demonstrate that the hierarchy of authority runs from local authority to followers to companions to prophet to Qurʾān (as shown in Figure 1.1). The later precedents are more authoritative than earlier ones because the earlier precedents are supported by textual reports alone whereas later precedents are supported by the fact that they represent the continuous practice of the community from prophetic times.

Hierarchy in *Muwaṭṭā*ʾ	**Hierarchy of Authority**
Qurʾān	Mālik
Prophet	Followers
Companions	Companions
Followers	Prophet
Mālik	Qurʾān

Figure 1.1. How the early Medinese conception of authority reflects a hierarchy of authority that is the inverse of the order of the precedents listed in the *Muwaṭṭā*ʾ.

This conception of authority is based on the consensus of later practices and ultimately on the authority of Mālik's interpretation of these practices as precedents. In the *Mudawwana al-kubrā* of ʿAbd al-Salām b. Saʿīd Saḥnūn [d. 240], Ibn Qāsim [d. 191] explains the basis of authority according to the Medinese.

> We [Medinese/Mālikīs] received this report [of prophetic practice], and if it had been supported by a practice passed down to those from whom we have taken it, which was taken by them from their predecessors, then we would fol-

> low the report. But, this transmission is like those which are not accompanied by a practice. . . . These sorts of reports were not repeated and established, the traditional practice was different, the whole community including the companions themselves acted according to a different practice. Therefore, these reports are neither impugned nor adopted in practice, but our practice is based on other reports which are supported by practice. These latter reports were passed on from the companions to the followers and the followers of the followers without rejecting or impugning other transmissions. These other transmissions which were eliminated from practice are not followed nor considered authoritative. Only what is corroborated by practice is followed and considered authoritative.[41]

This passage epitomizes the view of the "sunnah" in second century Madīnah, equating it with the traditional practice of the earliest community in imitation of the prophet that was passed on to successive generations.[42] It is evident from such explanations that the relative authority of earlier precedents is based on a suspicion of textual reports. The Medinese claim that their definition of practice is based on prophetic practice, but that transmitted through practice not through texts. As a necessary correlate to the Medinese claim is the assertion that consensus exists not only among the contemporary authorities of Madīnah but also within the opinions of the preceding generations.[43] Otherwise, the Medinese could not claim a majority tradition of continuous practice as the basis for knowing prophetic practice. Where disagreement does exist, however, the Medinese claim that the continuous local practice of Madīnah among a selected number of authorities is the most authoritative position. It is this view that, as late as the sixth century, allows al-Qāḍī ᶜIyāḍ to claim the specific authority of the Mālikī school, because of its basis in the traditional, local practice of Madīnah.[44]

Kūfah

The local authorities associated with the second century fiqh "school" of Kūfah recognized the existence of disagreement within both contemporary traditional practice and among the practices of the previous generations. The "sunnah" or traditional practice of the Kūfan authorities was not identified with a local practice considered to represent a continuous tradition from the time of the prophet. Because of their geographical location and historical circumstances, the Medinese could base their authority on the claim of such a continuous tradition. To their own advantage, the Kūfans stressed the lack of consensus both among the practices of previous generations and within the reports of prophetic practice. On the one hand, this lack of consensus undermined the geographical authority of Madīnah by indicating that taking the location of practice as a guarantee of its authority is tantamount to equating actual, contemporary practice with prophetic practice. On the other hand, the recognition of conflicting precedents allowed the Kūfans to accommodate a variety of conflicting opinions among themselves. Unlike the classical Mālikī school which could base the authority of its scholarship on the opinions of Mālik, the classical Ḥanafī school is based on the conflicting opinions of several local authorities loosely associated with Kūfah. By emphasizing the divergences within the corpus of authoritative precedents, the Kūfans could maintain the equivalent authority of conflicting opinions. The Kūfans focused their epistemological claims on the expertise of different local authorities in determining which precedents were most authoritative or suitable for defining contemporary practice.

Thus, the definition of practice given by later, classical Ḥanafī fiqh scholarship consists more often than not of the conflicting positions taken by the second century Kūfan authorities Abū Ḥanīfah [80–150], Abū Yūsuf, Muḥammad al-Shaybānī [132–189], and to a lesser extent Zufar b. al-Hudhail b. Qays al-ᶜAnbarī [110–158].

> [Abū Ḥanīfah says]: the endowment [waqf] of immovable property is sound, but the endowment of movable property and property which changes over time is not permitted.
>
> Abū Yūsuf says: when a person endows a landed estate with its cattle and its fieldworkers who are slaves, it is permitted.

> Muḥammad [al-Shaybānī] says: the endowment of war horses and weapons [used for waging war] in the path of God is permitted.[45]

Here, the general statement of Abū Ḥanīfah is contradicted by the exceptions stated by Abū Yūsuf and al-Shaybānī. Although later Ḥanafī scholarship argues that Abū Yūsuf considers the cattle and the enslaved fieldworkers as part of the immovable property of the estate,[46] the number and quality of both cattle and slaves changes over time in ways that a piece of land or a mosque would not. The opinion of al-Shaybānī, as is evident from another of his opinions that "all movable property the endowment of which is commonly practiced is permitted to be endowed,"[47] is based on accepting traditional or common practice as precedent. From this conflict of opinions, it is evident that the second century Kūfan authorities had different conceptions of what constituted the "sunnah" or traditional practice. Rather than reducing these different conceptions to a single opinion, the Kūfans allowed for different notions of "sunnah" to result in conflicting definitions of practice.

The authority of the different individual Kūfan opinions is justified in relation to what the particular authority in a given case chooses to represent as authoritative precedent. This is evident in the account, attributed to Abū Yūsuf, of the conflict of opinions between Abū Ḥanīfah and Muḥammad b. ᶜAbd al-Raḥmān b. Abī Laylā [74–148].[48] In some cases, the conflict of opinions between Abū Ḥanīfah and Ibn Abī Laylā rests upon differing interpretations of a precedent on which both agree. For example, both agree that it is permitted for a sacralized person to kill prey of the sea.

> [Abū Yūsuf] said: what about the case of a man who gets something equivalent to a fish from the prey of the sea? Abū Ḥanīfah used to say: there is nothing better from the prey of the sea than that which is like a fish. This we accept. Ibn Abī Laylā used to say: there is no harm in any of the prey of the sea.[49]

Presumably, both opinions are based upon interpretations of the same verse from sūrat al-māᵓidah [5:96], which states "permitted for you is the prey of the sea." Abū Yūsuf accepts the opinion of Abū Ḥanīfah, which restricts the application of the Qurʾānic precedent to "fish" alone, rejecting the broader conclusion of Ibn Abī Laylā. Later Ḥanafī scholarship sees in this disagreement the distinction between what properly constitutes prey of the sea: fish, sea birds, amphibians, crustaceans, water mammals?[50] In this context, Abū Yūsuf's choice of Abū Ḥanīfah's opinion over that of Ibn Abī Laylā is a matter of deciding that Abū Ḥanīfah's opinion represents a better interpretation of the Qurʾānic precedent.

In another case, Abū Yūsuf rejects Abū Ḥanīfah's opinion on the basis of how Abū Ḥanīfah interprets a precedent on which both he and Abū Yūsuf agree.

> Abū Yūsuf said: I asked Abū Ḥanīfah about the grass of the sacred area. He said: it is reprehensible to graze something upon the grass of the sacred area or to cut it. Abū Yūsuf said: I asked Ibn Abī Laylā about this. He said: there is no harm in cutting the grass of the sacred area or in grazing upon it. Abū Yūsuf said: I asked al-Ḥajjāj b. Arṭāḥ who related to me that he asked ʿAṭāʾ b. Abī Rabāḥ who said: there is no harm in grazing but it is reprehensible to cut it. This we accept.[51]

The opinion of Ibn Abī Laylā is rejected out of hand. It is apparently based upon a precedent, that the injunction against killing prey in the sacred area does not also apply to noncultivated plants, with which neither Abū Yūsuf nor Abū Ḥanīfah agree. Although Abū Yūsuf rejects Abū Ḥanīfah's opinion, he agrees with Abū Ḥanīfah on the principle that it is not permitted to cut the grass of the sacred area. Abū Yūsuf rejects Abū Ḥanīfah's forbidding of grazing because it is concluded on the basis of an analogy that equates cutting and grazing. The opinion of ʿAṭāʾ b. Abī Rabāḥ [d. 114] is based on a distinction between cutting and grazing that Abū Yūsuf accepts for the sake of convenience [istiḥsān], being that it is not possible for pilgrims to keep their mounts from grazing on the grass.[52]

In other cases, Abū Yūsuf accepts Abū Ḥanīfah's opinion over that of Ibn Abī Laylā because Abū Ḥanīfah's opinion is based on a more authoritative precedent. The determination of relative authority in these cases is predicated on the assumption that Abū Ḥanīfah is a better judge of which precedents are to be taken as authoritative.

> Abū Yūsuf said: I asked Abū Ḥanīfah and he said: there is no harm in removing dust and rocks from the sacred area. This we accept. Abū Yūsuf said: I heard Ibn Abī Laylā report, on the authority of ʿAṭāʾ b. Abī Rabāḥ, on the authority of Ibn ʿAbbās, on the authority of ʿUmar that it is reprehensible to remove dust and rocks from the sacred area. We received from Razīn, the client of ʿAlī b. ʿAbdallāh b. ʿAbbās that ʿAlī b. ʿAbdallāh wrote to him to send him a piece of *marwah* [type of white rock] which he took from the place where he prostrated himself to pray.[53]

The support given for Ibn Abī Laylā's opinion is parallel to the sort of support cited by the *Muwaṭṭāʾ* for Mālik's opinions. It is evident from Abū Yūsuf's rejection of Ibn Abī Laylā's opinion that his criteria for evaluating the authority of opinions does not rely on evidence of a continuous tradition of practice. Abū Yūsuf's citation of the highly unusual chain of transmission and the reference to the ambiguous practice of ʿAlī b. ʿAbdallāh [40–117] does not account for the justification of Abū Ḥanīfah's opinion over that of Ibn Abī Laylā. There appears to be no mention of a Razīn in the later, standard reference works, and it is not at all clear from the practice of ʿAlī b. ʿAbdallāh described what relation it has to removing dust and rocks from the sacred area.[54] Rather, the report of ʿAlī b. ʿAbdallāh's practice serves to reinforce the assumed authority of Abū Ḥanīfah's position. It is not the report that is determinate of authority but the presumed reputation of Abū Ḥanīfah for basing his opinions on authoritative precedents that distinguishes one local authority's opinion over that of another.

The assumed authority of Abū Ḥanīfah's opinions over Ibn Abī Laylā's transmission of a continuous tradition of practice is further evident from those cases where Abū Yūsuf rejects reports of precedented practice in favor of Abū Ḥanīfah's opinion even when it is unsupported by any reported precedent.

> Abū Yūsuf said: what about when a man shoots one of the pigeons from the sacred area? Abū Ḥanīfah said: incumbent upon him is its value. This we accept. Ibn Abī Laylā said: incumbent upon him is a sheep. I heard Ibn Abī Laylā, on the authority of ᶜAṭāᵓ b. Abī Rabāḥ [say] a sheep.[55]

The distinction between giving the value of a pigeon and giving a sheep in this context is not a matter of interpretation, but a difference of principle. Although later classical sources regard ᶜAtā b. Abī Rabāḥ as a trustworthy [thiqah] transmitter of prophetic practice from prominent companions, Abū Yūsuf here does not consider his report to establish an authoritative precedent on which Ibn Abī Laylā could base his opinion. The fact that Abū Yūsuf himself relies upon the precedents reported by ᶜAṭāᵓ b. Abī Rabāḥ at times indicates that the determination of authority among the Kūfans is not simply a matter of identifying reports of continuous traditional practice, but involves adjudicating among different versions of reported traditional practice. Abū Yūsuf accepts the practice of giving the value of a pigeon because Abū Ḥanīfah's opinion is derived from a different and presumably a more authoritative precedent. By recognizing the existence of contradictions among reports of traditional practice, Abū Yūsuf is able to base the relative authority of Abū Ḥanīfah's opinion upon the claim that his opinion represents a more authoritative tradition of practice.

In his *al-Radd ᶜalā siyar al-Awzāᶜī,* Abū Yūsuf critiques al-Awzāᶜī for following a continuous tradition of "common practice" rather than a tradition of practice that agrees with the practice of the prophet, his companions, and later scholars.

> One does not decide what is allowed and what is forbidden by reference to this, that one says 'people continue to practice this.' Much of what people continue to do is not allowed and should not be done even if I had explained a practice to you so that you knew it and you observed it in common practice because the prophet had already prohibited the practice. One only takes in this case [of common practice being against prophetic precedent] from the sunnah, on the authority of the prophet, and on the authority of the preceding generations of his companions, and scholars of fiqh.[56]

Note that Abū Yūsuf does not dismiss the possibility of common practice being considered as a continuation of prophetic practice. He does object, however, that not all common practice, by virtue of being continuous from the time of the prophet, is necessarily based on prophetic precedent. The notion that the existence of a continuous tradition of practice was evidence of its prophetic origins and thus authoritative was the mainstay of the Medinese. It is, therefore, important to note that, for Abū Yūsuf, the "sunnah" as traditional practice was not automatically equated with prophetic practice. The distinction Abū Yūsuf makes that one takes from the sunnah "on the authority of the prophet" indicates that the concept of the "sunnah" as an authoritative source for the definition of practice was not limited to the practice of the prophet. Yet, it is evident that, for the Kūfans, of the practices considered traditional, those of prophetic origin are the most authoritative. Abū Yūsuf is not promoting the idea that one must rely on reports of prophetic practice alone. His reasoning shows that the use of traditional practice as a source for an authoritative definition of practice in the second century is predicated on the claim that a particular traditional practice is consonant with prophetic precedent.

Abū Yūsuf is able to exploit the conflicting traditional practices to support his own opinions or those of other Kūfan authorities with whom he agrees. His claim is that in cases of contradiction, his opinions are based on the more authoritative practice, that originating with the prophet. The opinions of his opponents are based on local consensus alone.

> Abū Yūsuf said: the authorities from the Ḥijāz [ahl al-Ḥijāz] pronounce judgments so it is asked of them: on whose authority? They reply: this is the way things are done according to the sunnah. Perhaps, though, that it is only the judgment of the market inspector or of the administrator of one of the provinces. The statement of al-Awzāʿī that according to this [the opinions of local authorities] was the practice of apportionment [muqāsim] in the time of ʿUmar, ʿUthmān and so on is not accepted by us.[57]

Here, the claim that al-Awzāʿī's opinions or those of other Ḥijāzī authorities are based upon the general practice of companions, and ultimately the practice of the prophet, is challenged by Abū Yūsuf. The implication of Abū Yūsuf's remarks is that al-Awzāʿī and others pass off their own opinions or the opinions of local authorities with which they agree as being of earlier origin. Abū Yūsuf distinguishes between local consensus that is not necessarily of prophetic origin and the more authoritative traditional practice that does not reflect local but rather universal concerns. The opinions Abū Yūsuf accepts are considered authoritative, not because they reflect common practice but because they can be shown reasonably to be of traditional authority. This distinction emphasizes the necessity of the use for logic in determining a given opinion's authority. The question of authority is a matter of being able to choose on logical grounds, as opposed to on the basis of continuity of practice, which traditions are most likely to be of prophetic origin.

For Abū Yūsuf, what distinguishes Kūfan authorities' opinions is their reliance on logic to determine the authority of a particular precedent in formulating a definition of practice. Abū Yūsuf refers to the logic of an opinion either in defense of the opinion or to show its lack of authority.

> Abū Ḥanīfah said: horsemen get two portions [of booty]: one for himself and one for his horse. Infantry get one portion. al-Awzāʿī said: the prophet of God apportioned two portions to each horse and one to its owner. Muslims follow this practice today and there is no conflict concerning it.
>
> Abū Ḥanīfah said: a horse [faris] and a work horse [baradhūn] are equal. al-Awzāʿī said: the leaders of the Muslims [aʿimmah] who came before the fitnah after the killing of al-Walīd b. Yazīd did not apportion [booty] to work horses.
>
> Abū Yūsuf said: for Abū Ḥanīfah it is reprehensible to give precedence to a beast over a Muslim man by making the beast's share more than the man's share. As for work horses, one [share] is figured for them irrespective of that [their

> being work horses] for there is no distinction between a horse and a work horse. It is known from the Arabic expression, that there is no difference between these [two types of horses]: 'these horses [khayl]' meaning perhaps all of them or the bulk of them are work horses, and that there might be *muqārīf* [a kind of half-breed] among them. We know that, in war, work horses are more numerous of the two types of horses. . . . As for the statement of al-Awzāʿī: 'this being on the authority of the leaders of the Muslims from before . . . " this is like what is described of the Ḥijāzīs [ahl al-Ḥijāz], or someone's seeing some of the great men [mashāʾikh] of Syria who did not perform ablution well, or the witness [shahādah], or the bases [usūl] of fiqh. al-Awzāʿī collects this and says: this was the traditional practice [sunnah].[58]

In this passage Abū Yūsuf reports the conflict of opinions between Abū Ḥanīfah and al-Awzāʿī on two related issues and then resolves the conflict by reference to the logic of Abū Ḥanīfah's opinions. In the case of the number of portions given for horses, it seems that Abū Yūsuf accepts the opinion of al-Awzāʿī because it is supported by the existence of a continuous tradition of practice within which there are no conflicting precedents. Because there are no conflicting precedents for this practice, there is no need to adjudicate among different practices. This, combined with the claim that al-Awzāʿī's opinion is consonant with prophetic practice, makes the position more authoritative than that of Abū Ḥanīfah. Abū Yūsuf does resolve the conflict between the opinions of Abū Ḥanīfah and al-Awzāʿī by explaining the reasoning behind Abū Ḥanīfah's position. Although the opinion of Abū Ḥanīfah is not as authoritative as that of al-Awzāʿī because it contradicts prophetic practice, it is nevertheless a logically supported conclusion.

To resolve the conflict over the practice of apportioning booty to work horses, Abū Yūsuf takes a twofold approach. First, he reasons that a distinction should not be made between horses and work horses. His reasoning consists of a linguistic argument, that in Arabic the term "khayl" means horses of any type. Abū Yūsuf also argues that in war work horses are more common than non-work horses and that therefore should also receive a portion of the booty. Not unlike how he explains Abū Ḥanīfah's earlier opinion, Abū Yūsuf justifies Abū Ḥanīfah's opinion here by demonstrating that it is unreasonable to make a distinction between types of horses for the purpose of apportioning booty. Second, Abū Yūsuf critiques what al-Awzāʿī claims as the support for his opinion. As was shown in an earlier passage, here Abū Yūsuf equates the "sunnah" on which al-Awzāʿī bases his opinion with common as opposed to prophetic practice. Abū Yūsuf contends that a tradition of incorrect or nonprophetic practice, even when it is practiced by the local authorities of Syria with whom al-Awzāʿī had contact, is not to be considered authoritative. This lack of a reliable prophetic precedent along with the reasons not to distinguish among types of horses for the purpose of apportioning booty makes Abū Ḥanīfah's opinion the more authoritative one.

The notion of the sunnah as an authoritative source for the definition of practice current in second century Kūfah, represented in the work of Abū Yūsuf, reveals an epistemology more complicated than that used in Madīnah. Fundamentally, the Kūfans and the Medinese agree that the ultimate source of authority is the practice of the prophet, but the Kūfans emphasize the relative authority of the extant examples of prophetic practice. In some cases, the Kūfans use the criterion employed by the Medinese and accept a continuous tradition of practice, guaranteed by consensus, as evidence of prophetic practice. In most cases, however, where there is evidence of conflicting practices, the Kūfans contend that one must determine which practices are most authoritative. For the Kūfans, authority is established by distinguishing between common practice and the "sunnah," which is traditional practice originating with the prophet. In these cases, the weight of authority rests upon the capacities of the person defining practice to determine traditional practice from conflicting accounts of it. The Kūfans judge the authority of opinions on their logic. Abū Ḥanīfah's authority is based upon how well he determines which precedents are most consistent with what is known of the more general outlines of prophetic practice and the circumstances surrounding its implementation. Whereas the Medinese position can be reduced to the claim that later generations would not act against prophetic precedent, the Kūfan position is predicated on the assumption that the prophet would not contradict himself. Therefore, knowing the general logic of prophetic practice allows one to distinguish the more authoritative precedents from conflicting indications of prophetic practice on specific points.

Justifications for Conflicting Opinions

Both of the second century Medinese and the Kūfan conceptions of the sunnah anticipate the features of the epistemological claims of the classical schools. The relative inability of these different conceptions to account for more than limited contradiction within traditional local practice or to provide real consensus among a broad range of conflicting opinions, however, is what precipitated the need for an epistemology based upon the granted authority of a common corpus of practice.

On the one hand, the Medinese and Kūfans anticipate the structure of authority later standardized by the classical schools. In the *Muwaṭṭāʾ* and Abū Yūsuf's *Ikhtilāf* and *Radd,* the practice of later generations, especially that of the companions and their followers, is given authority equivalent with the authority of prophetic practice. The existence of a continuous tradition of practice guaranteed by consensus is taken to mean that the practice of later generations represents prophetic practice. In addition, the Medinese contend that because the companions and their followers experienced prophetic practice and would not act contrary to it, innovative practices or those aberrant from the prophetic example would not be supported by consensus.[59] This makes the practice of later generations more reliable as a source for prophetic precedent than isolated reports of prophetic practice unsupported by the practice of later generations. The Kūfans, likewise, reject the precedent of isolated reports of prophetic practice when the reports differ from the practice of later generations guaranteed by consensus.[60] Although the Kūfans do not privilege the traditional practice of Madīnah, their reliance upon later practice when it is guaranteed by consensus is predicated on the presumption that the companions and their followers maintain the practice established by the prophet and that therefore their practice is to be regarded as prophetic.[61]

On the other hand, the Medinese and Kūfans anticipate the method of reasoning later utilized by the classical schools. The opinions of the second century local authorities illustrate a method of interpreting prophetic or Qur᾿ānic precedents in light of the practice of later generations. In those cases where reports of prophetic practice are known alongside the practice of later generations, the Medinese and Kūfans see the later practice not as verifying the reports but rather as the reports supporting further the authority of the later practice. Both Mālik and Abū Ḥanīfah as reported by Abū Yūsuf regularly base their opinions upon interpretations of otherwise equivocal or vague references to a definition of practice reported from the prophet. Mālik's opinions in the *Muwaṭṭā᾿* are often portrayed as explaining the purpose or the main point of the examples of practice cited. Abū Yūsuf's works present Abū Ḥanīfah's opinions as the result of logical reasoning on the basis of past precedents. In either case, because of the structure of authority used by the Medinese and Kūfans and because of the nature of the information provided in reports of prophetic practice, these local authorities interpret reports of prophetic practice as further evidence of the authority of conclusions already drawn on the basis of later precedents.[62] This interpretive strategy is a rudimentary version of the later notion that within an example of prophetic practice is a certain "meaning" [maᶜnan] or "principle" [ᶜillah] that is amplified by later practices based on prophetic practice.

The ad hoc authorization of second century opinions provided only local or relative authority to the incipient Mālikī and Ḥanafī schools. The Mālikīs had to face the difficulties involved in recognizing the existence of contradictions and discontinuities within the received traditional practice of the Medinese, supposedly guaranteed by consensus. It is evident that, already in the second century, the Medinese were accused of defining the sunnah as common rather than traditional practice. The Ḥanafīs had to acknowledge that the authority of the opinions on which they relied was based on the presumption that select local authorities knew which precedents were logically consistent with prophetic practice. Because the authority of Abū Ḥanīfah, Abū Yūsuf, and later Muḥammad al-Shaybānī was largely inherent, it was difficult for later scholars to claim to continue that authority without some objective standard of logic against which to evaluate an ultimately relative authority. Using the epistemologies available to them, neither the Mālikīs nor Ḥanafīs could provide a means to reconcile the equal authority of several conflicting conceptions of the sunnah or definitions of practice based upon those different sunnahs. The local, ad hoc justifications needed to be converted into a more general standard of authority.

II

Text-Based Epistemology

The conception of the sunnah used by the second century Medinese and Kūfans was stood on its head sometime during the course of the third century.[63] The authority of the sunnah as prophetic practice, as conceived by the local second century authorities, was guaranteed by a continuous tradition of practice through generations going back to the prophet. It was defined as an interpretation having an authority that was conveyed by the link it represented with the prophetic past. Being regarded as either common practice or logically consistent practice, the content of the sunnah was considered prophetic on account of its receipt from these previous generations or derivation on the basis of these generations' practice. The theoretical works attributed to al-Shāfiʿī redefined the epistemological foundations of fiqh scholarship by attacking the Medinese and Kūfan conceptions of the sunnah.

First, al-Shāfiʿī critiques the way previous theories authorize certain opinions as being based on the sunnah. Previous theories of the sunnah were based on the notion that consensus guarantees the authority of traditional practice by protecting against innovation. This guarantee of consensus, however, works only when there is no significant disagreement or conflict of opinion among the available examples of practice, which is not often. In cases where there is no consensus, al-Shāfiʿī points out that the opinions of local authorities are based on the selection and interpretation of certain practices as authoritative from among a complicated transmission of reports and examples of prophetic practice.[64] This is evident from the presentation of Mālik's opinions in the *Muwaṭṭāʾ* and is acknowledged by Abū Yūsuf as the reason for the necessity of using logical reasoning. Thus, the authority of Medinese and Kūfan opinions is based on the presumption that the opinions and the sources of the opinions are consistent with prophetic practice although such consistency cannot be demonstrated. In light of this, al-Shāfiʿī contends that, because the content of the sunnah is determined from information not usually guaranteed by consensus, the authority of practices designated as having prophetic origins must come from the grounds on which local authorities reach opinions concerning those contents. This does not preclude consensus as a means for demonstrating the relationship between certain practices and prophetic practices as long as a real consensus exists. But, without being able to demonstrate the relationship between what is considered to be sunnah and prophetic practice, the authority of the "sunnah," according to al-Shāfiʿī, is based only on its status as actual contemporary practice. Therefore, al-Shāfiʿī argues that acceptance of the incipient Mālikī claim that the opinions of Mālik and what he regards as the sunnah are consistent with prophetic practice is tantamount to accepting de facto the local authority of Mālik.

This same sort of critique is leveled by al-Shāfiʿī against the justifications Abū Yūsuf gives for the authority of Kūfan opinions. Abū Yūsuf agrees with al-Shāfiʿī that, in the absence of a continuous tradition of practice guaranteed by consensus, the authority of a given definition of practice rests on the authority of the person giving the definition to logically determine what is the sunnah. Recognizing this, however, al-Shāfiʿī argues that Abū Yūsuf's solution to the lack of consensus is shortsighted. Abū Yūsuf's ad hoc justifications of Abū Ḥanīfah's opinions rely on what either Abū Ḥanīfah or Abū Yūsuf considers to be logically consistent with prophetic practice. Yet, just as with the Medinese claim, Abū Yūsuf's claim is predicated on the presumption that the opinions of Abū Ḥanīfah are consistent with prophetic practice because it is logical, not because he can demonstrate it to be consistent with a single acknowledged example of prophetic practice. In those cases where Abū Yūsuf does cite reports of prophetic practice, such as in explaining the support for al-Awzāʿī's opinions, he rejects them in favor of Abū Ḥanīfah's opinion. For al-Shāfiʿī, if the authority of local opinions is to be based on the authority of prophetic practice, then there must be an accepted means for demonstrating the link between the opinion and prophetic practice. Otherwise, both the contents and the authority of the sunnah would be equivalent to only the opinions of the local authorities.

By basing the authority of the sunnah not on consensus but on demonstrating a link between its content and prophetic practice, the work of al-Shāfiʿī shifts the focus of the local authorities away from the justification of opinions in terms of actual practice and toward a concept of authority based on the transmission and interpretation of texts.[65] This textual aspect is important because it is what allows the opinions of the present to be linked with the authority of the prophetic past. In the *Risālah,* al-Shāfiʿī systematically argues that the authority of the sunnah as prophetic practice cannot be established by devising means to decide ad hoc among which precedents are authoritative without first establishing criteria as to what constitutes prophetic practice. This sort of approach leads to a relative conception of authority, based on a conception of the sunnah that is relative to the individual purpose and authority for which it is conceived among different local authorities. Reliance on different local precedents (see Figure 1.2) leads to different opinions, the authority of which is relative to the local nature of the different precedents.

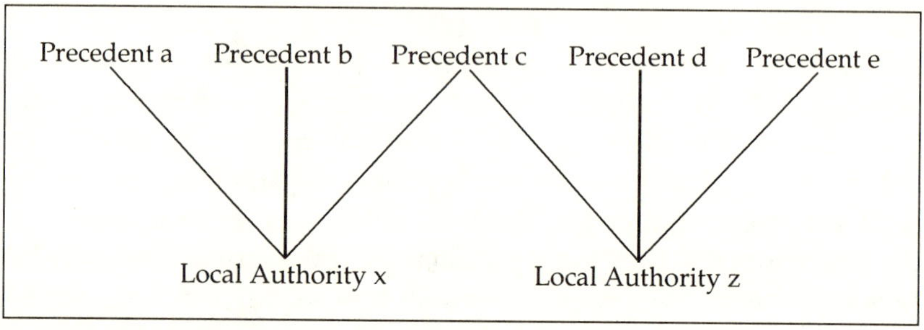

Figure 1.2. The relative bases of authority claimed by the Medinese and Kūfans for the opinions of their local authorities.

For al-Shāfiʿī, the identification of the sunnah with prophetic practice ultimately entails the delimitation of the sunnah to a textual corpus. By textualizing the sunnah (as shown in Figure 1.3), al-Shāfiʿī reduces the various bases of local authority to a single basis of authority. The Medinese and Kūfans still retain their local authority but it is no longer dependent on local claims but on claims to a common or universal standard.

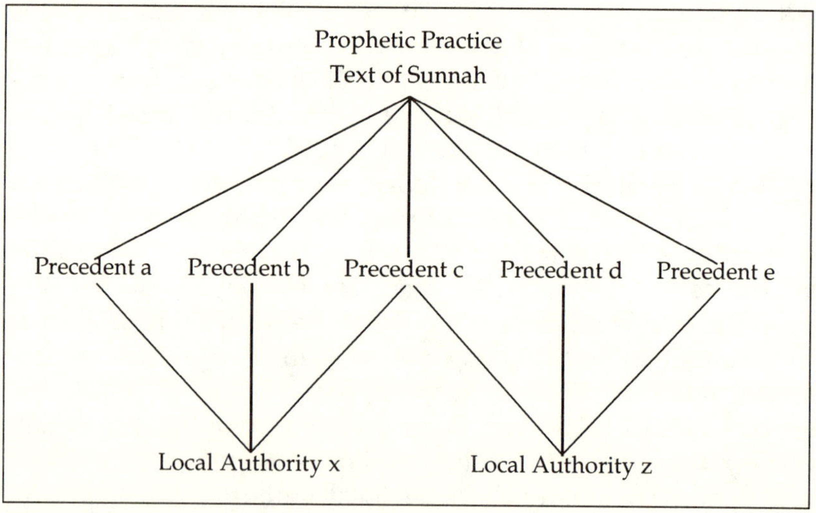

Figure 1.3. How the textualization of the sunnah results in a single basis of authority from which the Medinese and Kūfans can claim the authority of the different local precedents on which the opinions of their local authorities are based.

The Medinese and Kūfans retain their local precedents but insofar as the precedents can be demonstrated to be linked to prophetic practice, the local authority of the precedents is subsumed to their prophetic authority. This epistemological shift allows the conflicting opinions of the local authorities to be authorized as different interpretations of the same text.

Using this text-based epistemology, the claim that a given opinion was authoritative had to be demonstrated by establishing a transmission of information from the prophet to the local authority engaged in the definition of practice (see Figure 1.4). The knowledge of prophetic practice consists of the transmission of a text [matn], accompanied by a support [isnād] or a chain of transmission linking the text back to the prophet.[66]

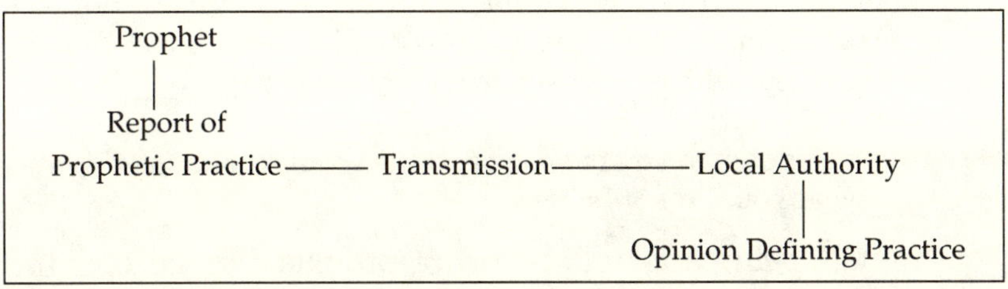

Figure 1.4. How the transmission of prophetic practice to a local authority links the authority of the prophet with the opinion of the local authority defining practice.

The text of each transmission refers to something the prophet said [qawlī] or did [fiʿlī] or to something someone else said or did with the tacit approval of the apostle being present or knowing about the saying or action and not condemning it [taqrīrī].[67]

By delimiting the sunnah to a textual record of prophetic practice, al-Shāfiʿī linked the authority of the sunnah to the authority of the revelation contained in the Qurʾān. He canonized the sunnah by claiming that it was a textual account of the prophetic practice required for understanding the text of the revelation contained in the Qurʾān. The "text" of the sunnah as a physical artifact of prophetic times became an established interpretation recognized by the different groups who hoped to authorize their opinions vis-à-vis some concept of "sunnah."

The requirement of using prophetic practice for interpreting the revelation is given in the revelation itself.

> Everything pertaining to conduct that the prophet allowed or forbade has, in fact, been allowed or forbidden by God because God ordered the prophet to allow or forbid it.[68]

Through the loose exegesis of several Qurʾānic verses, al-Shāfiʿī concludes that the sunnah of the prophet makes explicit that which God intended by his revelation contained in the text of the Qurʾān.[69] Moreover, the identification of "wisdom" [ḥikmah] with the sunnah, allows al-Shāfiʿī to attribute a particularly authoritative interpretive privilege to the sunnah.

> It is he [God] who has raised up a prophet from among the illiterate people to recite to them his signs [or verses], to sanctify them, to teach them the book and the wisdom even though they were previously in evident error.[70]

> God sent down to you the book and the wisdom, and taught you what you did not know.[71]

The sunnah, being a textual report of prophetic practice, is the epitome for the interpretation of the revelation. It is given by God as a necessary companion to the revelation contained in the Qurʾān.[72] According to al-Shāfiʿī, the prophet is a "sign" [ʿalam] and his practice is a "manifestation" [mubīn] of the revelation, in particular the practice depicted in the Qurʾān.[73] Because the prophet not only received and dispensed but also lived the revelation, knowledge of his practice is required to understand the revelation.

For al-Shāfiʿī, the proof or guarantee of the sunnah's authority vis-à-vis the revelation is the sunnah's capacity to confirm and expand upon the revelation contained in the Qurʾān.[74] As long as the contents of the sunnah do not contradict the contents of the Qurʾān, it can be demonstrated that the sunnah is a necessary and thus authoritative interpretation of the revelation. The sunnah is not only a reiteration but an extension of the revelation contained in the Qurʾān.

> God has given the proof of the [authority of] prophetic practice by providing that the sunnah of the prophet make

> clear the meanings of the duties laid down in his book, so that it might be known that the sunnah, whether that making explicit the meaning of God's commands as provided in the text of the book and read there, or that which the prophet establishes in the absence of such a text, represents God's command and is in agreement with the practice of the prophet.[75]

Thus, instead of insisting on the lack of contradictions among local authorities, characteristic of the claim that the continuous tradition of prophetic practice is guaranteed by consensus, al-Shāfiʿī contends that the authority of the sunnah is guaranteed by its fundamental agreement with the Qurʾān. The text-based epistemology replaces the second century use of reason to determine the relative authority of examples of traditional practice with the use of reasoning to demonstrate the absolute authority of the sunnah by harmonizing apparent textual inconsistencies.

The existence of apparent contradictions between the Qurʾān and the sunnah is to be resolved by interpreting the text of the sunnah as the specification [takhṣīṣ] of the text of the Qurʾān. In some cases, the sunnah specifies the Qurʾān by either particularizing the general or more commonly generalizing the particular. For example, the Qurʾān stipulates the performance of prayer, the paying of the offering [zakāt], and the pilgrimage to Makkah, but it does not provide the particulars of these obligations.[76] The sunnah, however, specifies the number of daily prayers, when they are to be performed, how to perform them, and distinctions between different types of prayers.[77] In this case, the sunnah makes explicit the particular requirements of the more general obligation stated in the Qurʾān. In another case, the Qurʾān stipulates that a widow is to wait four months and ten days before remarrying, and that a pregnant woman who is divorced must wait until her pregnancy comes to term before remarrying.[78] A literal interpretation might conclude that a pregnant woman whose husband dies must wait four months and ten days plus the duration of his pregnancy before remarrying.[79] The sunnah has a different precedent.

> The prophet said to Subayʿah, daughter of al-Ḥarīth, who gave birth to a child a few days after her husband's death: you are free and may get married.[80]

According to al-Shāfiʿī, the prophet's practice is based on the premise that the waiting period of four months and ten days stipulated by the Qurʾān is only intended for women who are not pregnant, the reasoning for the waiting period being to determine whether or not the woman is pregnant.[81] In this case, the sunnah generalizes the Qurʾānic definition of practice by identifying the reasoning behind its stipulation.

In other cases, the sunnah specifies the Qurʾān by defining practice that is not explicitly stated in the Qurʾān but is regarded by al-Shāfiʿī as having Qurʾānic precedent nonetheless. Most often, the sunnah contains definitions of practice that are made explicit from principles implicit in the Qurʾān. For example, the Qurʾān states that prohibited foods include carcasses, blood, pork, and animals during the slaughter of which God's name was not invoked.[82] In the sunnah, however, the prophet states that it is forbidden to eat animals that have fangs.[83] Here, the sunnah does not contradict the Qurʾān, but extends by analogy the basic principle of the revelation. The reason for the prohibition of carcasses, blood, and pork is that they are impure. The prophet's statement that fanged animals are not to be eaten is deduced from the principle that fanged animals are impure animals and are therefore of the same category as the impure animals mentioned by the Qurʾān as being forbidden to eat.[84] This line of reasoning allows al-Shāfiʿī to account for the bulk of the cases in which the sunnah seems to define practice independent of Qurʾānic precedent. Less common, but also used by al-Shāfiʿī to demonstrate the Qurʾānic basis of a practice defined in the sunnah that had no apparent Qurʾānic precedent, is the strategy of explaining the sunnah's definition of practice as being based on a Qurʾānic precedent that is no longer extant in the current text of the Qurʾān.[85]

By using interpretive reasoning to harmonize the sunnah with the Qurʾān, al-Shāfiʿī makes the authority of the sunnah and later conclusions drawn on the basis of the sunnah equivalent in authority with the revelation. The coherence of the text of the revelation contained in the Qurʾān is justified by reference to the sunnah. On the one hand, two types of statements in the Qurʾān do not require the sunnah to be interpreted.[86] Even in these two cases, although the sunnah does not supply the context, al-Shāfiʿī contends that the revelation must be understood within the larger context of the Qurʾān, in relation to referents outside of the text or through the medium of linguistic reasoning. For al-Shāfiʿī, the textual character of the revelation necessitates that the use of the Qurʾān to define practice entails determining the context of specific statements to assess their general or particular significance. On the other hand, some statements in the Qurʾān require the interpretation supplied by the sunnah. In those cases where it does not merely reiterate the Qurʾān, the sunnah extends the application of the revelation by identifying the underlying meaning or principle at work in the revelation. Thus, the sunnah specifies the revelation by contextualizing or providing the reasoning behind Qurʾānic statements. This same sort of interpretive reasoning is used by al-Shāfiʿī to demonstrate the coherence of the textual corpus of the sunnah. Just as the text of the revelation requires interpretation, so do the contents of the sunnah require interpretation to show that they are consistent with one another and thus consistent as a whole with the text of the revelation.

In some cases of apparent contradiction within the sunnah, among reports of prophetic practice, al-Shāfiʿī argues that a distinction must be made between statements of more general [ʿāmm] and more particular [khāṣṣ] significance. Some apparent contradictions are because certain reports either specify or expound on more general statements of practice mentioned in other reports.

> Sufyān reported to us, on the authority of al-Zuhrī, on the authority of Saʿīd b. al-Musayyib, on the authority of Abū Hurayrah that the prophet said: let no one sell to someone else what he has already agreed to sell to another person.[87]

> Mālik reported to us, on the authority of Nāfiʿ, on the authority of Ibn ʿUmar, that the prophet said: each one of

> the two parties to a sale is entitled to a choice [to cancel the sale] as long as they have not separated, unless the sale is [stipulated as] a sale in which the parties have the choice to cancel the sale [after having separated].[88]

Of these two reports, al-Shāfiᶜī explains that the first report is a more general statement of the principle that is likewise at work in the second report, although the second report provides additional specifics that delimit further the principle in the first report. Other apparent contradictions are explained by al-Shāfiᶜī as involving a statement of principle that applies to a specific case but is not to be generalized to other cases.

> Mālik reported to me, on the authority of Nāfiᶜ, on the authority of Ibn ᶜUmar, that the prophet prohibited *muzābanah.* Muzabānah is exchanging fresh dates for dried dates by dry measure, and exchanging grapes for raisins by dry measure.[89]

> Mālik reported to us, on the authority of Nāfiᶜ, on the authority of Ibn ᶜUmar, on the authority of Zayd b. Thābit, that the prophet permitted the owner of an *ᶜarīyah* [dates still on the palm] to exchange it for an amount of dried dates the palm is expected to produce.[90]

Here, the first report forbidding the exchange of fresh for dried dates by dry measure seems to contradict the second report which permits the exchange of fresh dates still on the palm for an estimated equal amount of dried dates.[91] The argument of al-Shāfiᶜī is that the second report is meant to be an exception to the general principle stated in the first report, that only in the case of dates still on the palm are non-dried dates to be exchanged for dried dates.[92]

In other cases of apparent contradiction, al-Shāfiᶜī demonstrates that the contents of earlier transmissions are abrogated by the contents of later transmissions. To illustrate this sort of apparent contradiction, al-Shāfiᶜī cites three reports in which the prophet leads the prayer sitting and instructs his followers to also perform the prayer sitting in imitation of him.[93] Then al-Shāfiᶜī cites another report in which the prophet performs his prayer sitting but Abū Bakr and his followers pray standing.[94] Following this, al-Shāfiʿī concludes that the authoritative practice is for people to pray standing even if the prayer leader prays sitting.

> The evidence of the sunnah and the consensus of the people indicate that prayers should be performed standing when men are able to stand but sitting when they are unable to stand. Those who can perform it standing by themselves are not to pray sitting.[95]

To account for this apparent inconsistency between the two reports of prophetic practice, al-Shāfiʿī explains that the second report in which the prophet's followers pray standing comes from the period when the prophet was about to die, and so it abrogates or supersedes the precedent previously established by the prophet's earlier practice. In the case of abrogated practices, as in the case practices the reports of which seem to contradict due to their differing general and specific significance, the context of the practice is integral not only to resolving apparent contradictions but to understanding the applicability of prophetic practice to the later definition of practice.

This attention to context is evident from how al-Shāfiʿī treats a rather convoluted series of reports concerning the direction the prophet faced when defecating. First, al-Shāfiʿī cites what he takes to be the prophet's most general statement.

> Sufyān reported to us, on the authority of al-Zuhrī, on the authority of ʿAṭāʾ b. Yazīd, on the authority of Abū Ayyūb al-Anṣārī that the prophet said: when a person defecates or urinates he does not face Makkah nor turn his back to it, but he turns either eastward or westward.[96]

This is then complicated by the citation of two more reports, concerning the actual practice of the companions and of the prophet. The first of these two was attached to the prophet's more general statement of practice.

> Abū Ayyūb said: when we entered Syria we found toilets already built facing Makkah. We therefore turned to face the other direction and asked God's forgiveness.[97]

> Some people said: when you defecate you do not face Makkah nor Jerusalem. But, ᶜAbdallāh [b. ᶜUmar] said: when I was on the roof of our house I saw the prophet defecating while sitting on two clay bricks facing Jerusalem.[98]

To explain this discrepancy, al-Shāfiᶜī refers to the context in which the prophet made the first most general statement. According to al-Shāfiᶜī, the prohibition against facing Makkah and Jerusalem while urinating or defecating is because, at the time the prophet made the statement, people were in the habit of relieving themselves in open country not in buildings. It is evident from his not mentioning other reports of prophetic practice making explicit the distinction between the two locations for defecation that al-Shāfiᶜī is supplying the context himself to make sense of the apparent contradiction. The mistake of Abū Ayyūb and Ibn ᶜUmar is in not making the distinction between the general and particular application of the prophet's general statement.[99] The general statement, according to al-Shāfiᶜī, applies to defecation only in the open country, which explains why Ibn ᶜUmar saw the prophet defecating while facing Jerusalem. By constructing a hypothetical context to explain the distinction between the two prophetic precedents reports, al-Shāfiᶜī demonstrates the interpretive liberties required by a text-based epistemology.

Thus, for al-Shāfiᶜī, the textual authority of the sunnah as prophetic practice is based on the premise that the fundamental consistency within and between the two canonical sources guarantees that the authority of the sunnah is equivalent to that of the revelation contained in the Qurʾān. The guarantee of this text-based epistemology also authorizes the interpretive reasoning of later scholarship responsible for deriving a definition of practice from the canonical sources. By equating the sunnah with the textual reports of prophetic practice and linking it with the text of the revelation contained in the Qurʾān, al-Shāfiᶜī distinguished between the sources [uṣūl] and the interpretive scholarship [fiqh] required to derive a definition of practice from those sources (see Figure 1.5).[100]

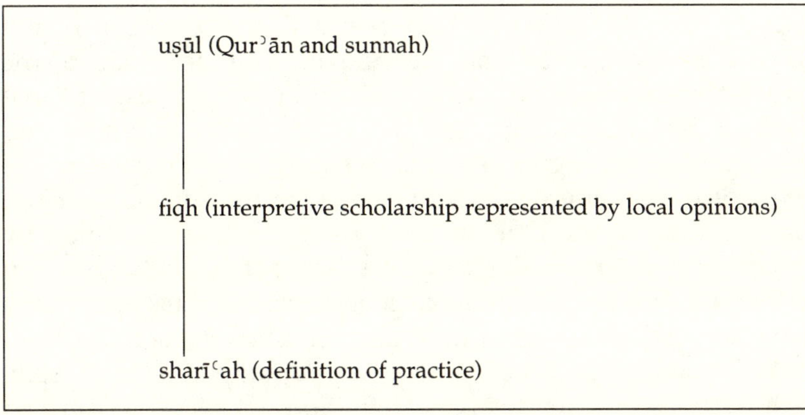

Figure 1.5. The distinction between the sources and definition of practice and the required mediating role of interpretive reasoning.

The relationship of the sunnah to the revelation and both to the interpretive reasoning of later fiqh scholarship is ultimately based on the pivotal distinction that the sources themselves are not the definition of practice [sharīʿah] but are dependent on interpretive reasoning to extract this definition from them.[101] The number of passages in the Qurʾān that define practice is limited,[102] and many of those need the specification of the sunnah for their interpretation. Moreover, the definition of the sunnah itself depends upon interpretive reasoning to resolve the apparent contradictions within and among reports of prophetic practice. Most significant to this distinction between the uṣūl and the sharīʿah, however, is the text of the revelation. The conception of the revelation as having stopped and being contained in the text of the Qurʾān and the integral role of the sunnah as the canonized interpretation of the Qurʾān is tied to the later use of interpretive reasoning to apply the revelation to novel circumstances.

By basing the proof of the authority of the sunnah on its fundamental agreement with the text of the revelation, al-Shāfiʿī provides for the use of interpretive reasoning in resolving apparent contradictions and extending the principles found in the revelation to the definition of practices unforeseen or not explicit in the Qurʾān and the sunnah. This definition of the proof of the authority of the sunnah authorizes the use of "analogical" reasoning [qiyās], specifically the use of inductive and deductive reasoning to generate a definition of practice on the basis of the canonical sources.[103] The way the sunnah specifies the meaning of the Qurʾān, contextualizing the revelation by uncovering the reasoning behind specific statements and then extending the specifics to make general conclusions, epitomizes how later scholars are to derive a definition of practice from both the sunnah and the Qurʾān. According to al-Shāfiʿī's epistemology, as long as this later definition of practice is derived from the revelation on the basis of the sunnah and does not contradict the sunnah, which also ensures that it does not contradict the revelation, it is considered authoritative. Just as the fact that the sunnah does not contradict the revelation contained in the Qurʾān proves its authority, so the fact that practices derived from it do not contradict the sunnah guarantees the authority of the later definition of practice.

It is important to emphasize that al-Shāfiʿī demonstrates the noncontradiction of the canonical sources, the different verses of the Qurʾān, the Qurʾān and the sunnah, and the different reports that make up the sunnah by supplying some sort of context for the textual precedents. This shows how al-Shāfiʿī conceives of the sort of interpretation required for the definition of practice on the basis of the canonical sources. His use of interpretive reasoning is similar to the Kūfans' technique for determining the relative authority of different precedents. Abū Ḥanīfah and Abū Yūsuf chose among examples of prophetic practice in light of their later conceptions of practice and the logical considerations that practice entailed. For al-Shāfiʿī, this sort of use of logic is tantamount to relying on an arbitrary criterion for what constitutes the standard against which reports of prophetic practice are to be evaluated.[104] By interpreting textual reports rather than choosing among examples of practice, al-Shāfiʿī privileges the textual corpus of the sunnah as a primary source of information on prophetic practice. As well, al-Shāfiʿī privileges the textual corpus of the sunnah by using reasoning not to discredit but to defend the integrity of reports of prophetic practice. This use of interpretive reasoning to harmonize the contents of the "sources" is significant because it provides authorization for later scholars to use interpretive reasoning to formulate their own definition of practice on the basis of these sources. Just as al-Shāfiʿī guarantees the authority of the sunnah by showing that it does not contradict the Qurʾān, so later scholars can claim the authority of their definition of practice as long as they can demonstrate that their opinions do not contradict the canonical sources.

For al-Shāfiʿī, the main issue involved in using the sunnah to authorize opinions is not deciding whose precedents are more authoritative, but determining how to control the derivation of a definition of practice from the sunnah, on the contents of which all parties can agree. It was not an issue of inventing ways to overcome the boundaries of the canon but of restricting the ways by which authoritative interpretations are allowed to be made. This equation of using the sunnah with having knowledge of prophetic practice did not dispense with the problem, recognized by the Medinese and Kūfans, of contradictions among and within the reports of prophetic practice. Instead of the corroboration of reports with practice, al-Shāfiʿī uses interpretive reasoning to resolve the contradictions in the reports. In making this change, al-Shāfiʿī's work introduces a conception of the sunnah dependent on the requirements of scholarship to interpret textual sources of authority. He allows for the equivalent authority of schools whose bases, although now supposed to be different interpretations of the same canonical sources, are the conflicting opinions of different local authorities.

The beauty of the text-based epistemology associated with al-Shāfiʿī is that it provides justification for conflicting local opinions while at the same time accommodating the specific local claims of the schools. By providing for the equal legitimacy of conflicting local opinions, this text-based epistemology authorized the schools' later independent development. Although built on the opinions of different local authorities, because of their reliance on a common epistemology, the schools are considered equally "sunnī" and their different definitions of practice equally "orthodox."[105] Using this epistemology, the schools were able to maintain the local bases of their authority. Each school could continue to rely on its local authorities' opinions and continue to claim the special merit or particular legitimacy on the basis of these authorities as "founders." Thus, the classical Mālikī school could continue to refer to Mālik as the summation of Medinese practice.[106] The Ḥanafī school could take from among the conflicting opinions of several different second century authorities loosely associated with Abū Ḥanīfah and Kūfah. Despite the claim that al-Shāfiʿī himself did not want others to imitate his definition of practice, his opinions were repeated and used as the basis for the Shāfiʿī school.[107] The text-based epistemology sanctioned and perhaps encouraged the notion that Abū Ḥanīfah, Mālik, and al-Shāfiʿī were responsible for the authority of their respective schools,[108] although not because of their knowledge of local practice but because of their knowledge of the "sunnah" as text. The opinions of the second century authorities, under the text-based epistemology, became examples of how to interpret the sunnah to define practice.

III

Bases and Extensions of Text-Based Authority

The introduction of this text-based epistemology led to a number of pervasive developments in the emerging fiqh scholarship of the third and later centuries. First, local authorities associated with the incipient fiqh schools of the third and fourth centuries utilized reports of prophetic practice to authorize the opinions of selected second century authorities.[109] The use of logical puzzles and maxims from local authorities was replaced by examples of prophetic practice as sources for the definition of practice.[110] Scholars juxtaposed reports of prophetic practice to one another to demonstrate their own local conception of the principles underlying the definition of practice.[111] Being unable to rely on the local authority of traditional practice alone, scholars sought to argue for traditional practice by finding and using precedents in reports of prophetic practice. Scholars both constructed lines of transmission back to the prophet from currently circulated local traditions[112] and, at the same time, collected reports of prophetic practice preserved by scholars in other locations.[113] This definition of certain local authorities' opinions in terms of prophetic practice led to the division of fiqh scholarship into the five classical sunnī schools. The opinions of different local authorities, authorized as different interpretations of the revelation contained in the canonical sources, became the independent focuses for different bodies of scholarship. Based on the interpretations of distinct and often conflicting local authorities, the schools were related by their interpretive links to a collection of common textual sources.

The weight given to the knowledge and interpretation of prophetic practice by the text-based epistemology also led to the systematic collection and organization of reports of prophetic practice.[114] Beginning in the third century, the reports of prophetic practice considered to be authoritative were compiled into six authoritative collections.[115] These collections, known as the "six books" [al-kutub al-sittah], do not contain all reports of prophetic practice but included those whose authority could be demonstrated by the verification of their transmission originating with the prophet.[116] It should be noted, however, that these "six books" are not identical with the canonical "text" of the sunnah. The six books are different attempts to delineate in "written" form what was, at that time, considered to be the "text" of the sunnah. The canonical text of the sunnah, as defined in the text-based epistemology, is not to be equated with a particular book or group of books, nor even necessarily with a written text.[117] When referring to the text of the sunnah, the classical schools do not limit themselves to the reports collected in the six books nor are all of the reports in the six books used as precedents by all or even any of the schools. The concept and production of a written sunnah is, rather, a result of the changing emphasis on the sunnah as consisting of textual reports of prophetic practice.

The verification of the transmissions themselves produced two related genres around the same time. In an attempt to check the authority of the reports and thus the claims of the burgeoning schools that the opinions on which they were based had prophetic precedent, a formal discipline [al-jarḥ wa al-taᶜdīl] was developed to examine critically the claims of various authorities that the reports of prophetic practice they cited were reliably transmitted to them from the prophet.[118] In addition to explaining the methodology involved in verifying the reports on the basis of the reliability of the people who transmitted them, this scholarship began to compile biographical lists of the companions of the prophet, their followers, and the followers of their followers who were said to have reported something concerning the practice of the prophet.[119] These lists (see Figure 1.6) included, on the one hand, the names and evaluations of the transmitters of the reports mentioned in the six books.[120] On the other hand, this scholarship compiled lists devoted exclusively to the names of either weak or trustworthy transmitters of prophetic reports.[121] In short, by verifying the contents of the sunnah and their oral transmission to the local authorities of the second century, this technical scholarship affirms the guarantee of noncontradiction required by al-Shāfiᶜī to authorize the opinions. This technical scholarship provides the theoretical framework for the claim of the classical schools that their scholarship was linked to the revelation and was thus equivalent to it in authority.

By the middle of the fifth century, the authority of the classical schools, based on the premises of the text-based epistemology, was guaranteed by the establishment that the opinions of the second century local authorities were consonant with the sunnah and, thus, with the revelation. The proof of the schools' authority was the demonstrated links between the practice of the prophet and the opinions of the local authorities. In his *Ṭabaqāt al-fuqahāʾ*, Abū Isḥāq al-Shīrāzī [393–476] traces the transmission of prophetic practice through the companions, their followers, and the followers of their followers, to the local authorities of the fourth generation whose opinions were the basis for the five classical schools.[122] This account of the opinions'

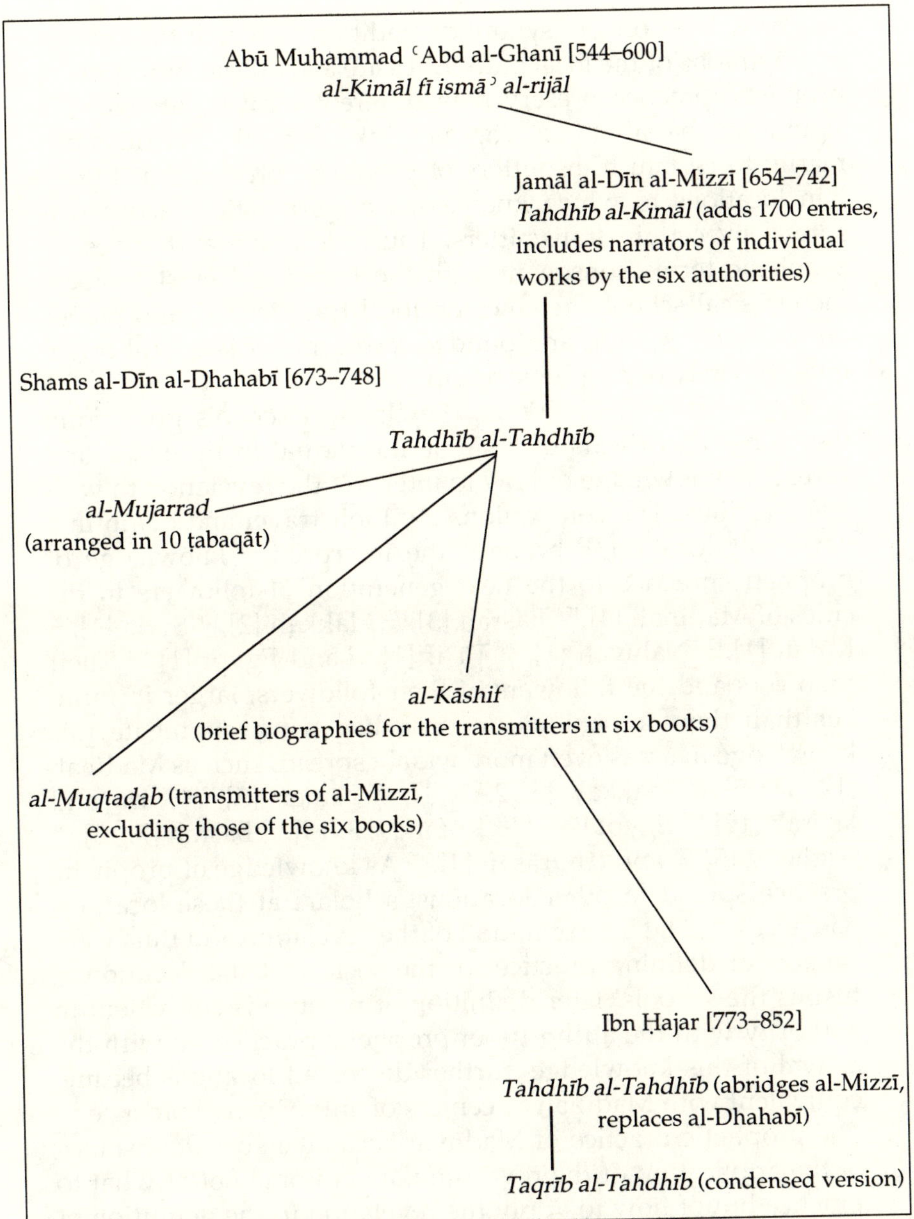

Figure 1.6. Biographical dictionaries devoted to the transmitters mentioned in the six authoritative collections of prophetic transmissions, showing the relation of the texts.

authority is a sort of "synoptic" tradition in which the sunnah and opinions of the local authorities are a synthesis of reports of prophetic practice preserved in different local traditions. It is significant that al-Shīrāzī does not link the local authorities primarily to certain transmitters of prophetic practice but to certain locations to which knowledge of prophetic practice was spread by certain transmitters. Thus, al-Shīrāzī authorizes, in prophetic terms consonant with the text-based epistemology, the classical schools' reliance on local traditions. The opinions on which the schools are founded are of immediate local origin but ultimately of prophetic origin.

According to al-Shīrāzī, the classical schools grew from the words and deeds of a single individual in the Ḥijāz and spread as knowledge of how to interpret the revelation to various locations. The companions, by their travel and death in a particular location,[123] brought the interpretive knowledge of prophetic practice to the next generation of followers in the cities of Madīnah [4],[124] Baṣrah [3],[125] Makkah [2],[126] Syria [1],[127] Kūfah [1],[128] Nāḥīyah [1],[129] Ṭāʾif [1],[130] and Egypt [1].[131] Their followers and the followers of their followers, larger in number than the companions, in turn, began to congregate this knowledge in areas even more widely spread, such as Madīnah [12, 11, 5],[132] Makkah [5, 2, 1, 1],[133] Yemen [5],[134] Syria and Jazīrah [12],[135] Egypt [2, 3],[136] Kūfah [7, 3, 15],[137] Baṣrah [7, 13],[138] Baghdād [5],[139] and Khurāsān [4].[140] As knowledge of prophetic practice spread to other locations, scholars at those locations had access to the interpretation of the revelation and thus were capable of defining practice for the society at that location.[141] Just as the schools' later definition of practice is equivalent in authority with the authority of prophetic practice, so with the arrival of this knowledge, further dispersed locations became equivalent with Madīnah as centers of authoritative practice.[142] The prophetic practice of Madīnah became a specific instance of the application of the revelation, an epitome not of what to practice but of how to apply the revelation to the definition of practice. In this way, schools in different locations could have different definitions of authoritative practice and still be equally orthodox. Thus, by verifying not only the generation of the founders of the schools on the basis of birth and death dates but also their locations when receiving and utilizing the interpretive knowledge of prophetic practice, al-Shīrāzī established the authority of certain local authorities as being equivalent with that of the prophet.

Utilizing this same model of authority, al-Shīrāzī and later scholars authorized the schools by constructing chains of transmission from the second century local authorities through the many generations of later scholarship.[143] Just as the opinions of the "founders" were authorized by establishing a connection between them and prophetic practice, so later scholars' definition of practice was authorized by its connection to the opinions of the founders. The first generation of scholarship after the founder is referred to as his companions [ṣaḥābah] just as their followers are referred to as the *tābiʿūn,* and the followers of their followers the *tābiʿī al-tābiʿīn,* paralleling the generations following the prophet (see Figure 1.7). Each subsequent generation of scholarship was authorized in terms of its historical relationship to the previous generation of scholarship, its authority going back to that of the founder which, in turn, rests upon that of the prophet.

This conception of the transmission of authority is predicated on the use by later scholarship of the opinions of certain local authorities as equivalent in authority with the practice of the prophet. Just as the authority of the opinions of the local authorities is based upon their use of prophetic practice as an epitome of how to interpret the revelation, so the authority of the definition of practice by later scholarship is based upon its use of the opinions of certain local authorities as epitomes of how to derive a definition of practice from the revelation. The authority of the definition of practice [sharīʿah] is thus dependent not on membership in a particular school or repeating the opinions of a particular founder but on the use of the opinions of certain authorities whose relationship to apostolic practice can be verified, as examples of how to use prophetic practice as an epitome of how to reason on the basis of the revelation.[144]

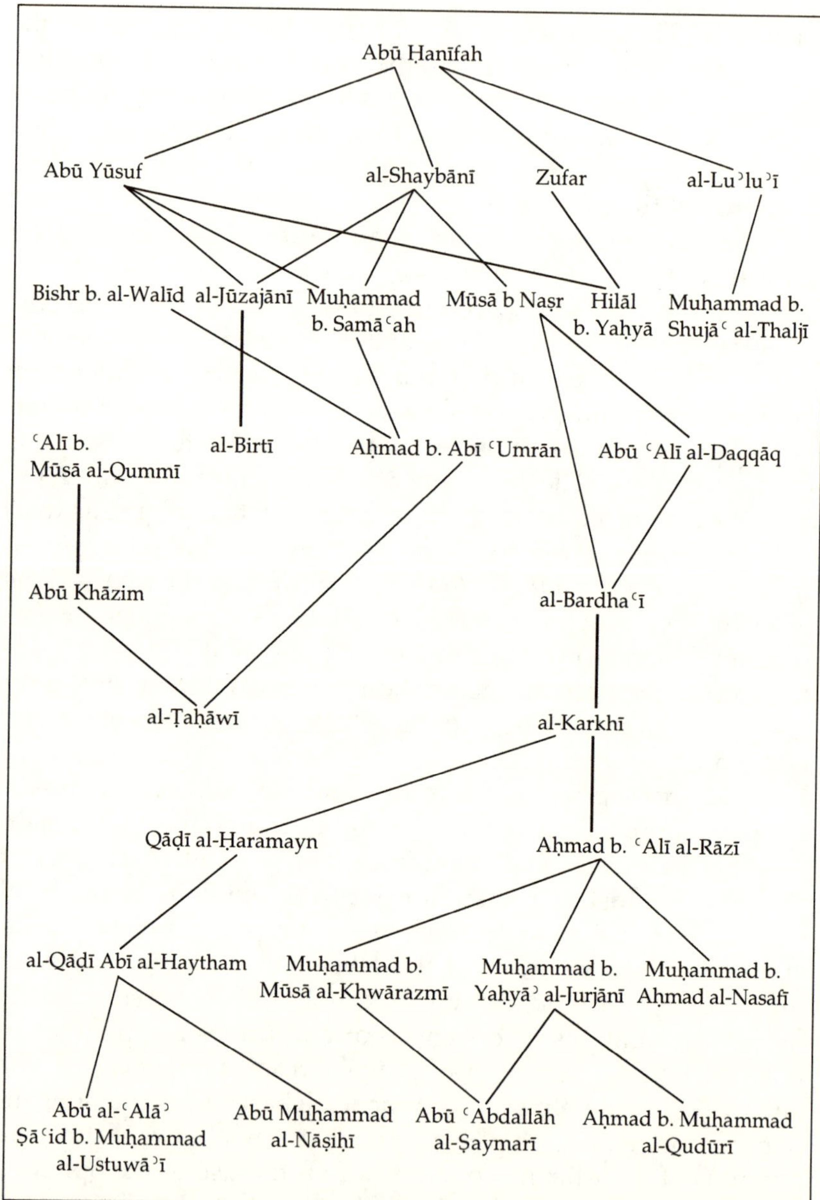

Figure 1.7. Transmission of authority from Abū Ḥanīfah, founder of the Ḥanafī school, through his ṣaḥābah, to scholars of the early classical period.

Conclusions

The conflict among the opinions of the local authorities could not be accommodated within the locally based epistemologies utilized in the second century. These epistemologies were not adequate to account for the continued authority of the "school" beyond the second century and the opinions of the local authorities themselves. By providing a common basis on which the opinions of different local authorities could be based equally, the text-based epistemology introduced in the third century allowed for the later development of the classical schools. Making the sunnah a "text" that represents or interprets the text of the revelation, al-Shāfiʿī's epistemology was able to provide for the authorities' conflicting local opinions. Subsequent scholarship based on a given local authority or group of authorities had general authority because it would be linked to the past on account of a continuous chain of texts and interpretation. This sort of "historical" authority did not tie subsequent scholarship to the opinions themselves nor to the contents of the sunnah, but allowed such subsequent scholarship to develop its own agenda using the opinions as tangible proof of its link to the prophetic past.

Under the terms of this text-based epistemology, the conflicting opinions on which the schools were to be based could be authorized as different interpretations of the same text. The requirement of using interpretive reasoning to demonstrate the consistency of the canonical sources resulted in the independent development of the different schools. Each school was ultimately based on the sunnah, but developed out of the definition of practice found in the opinions of a particular local authority, independent of other local authorities' opinions. Opinions could conflict as long as they were shown to be linked to and thus consistent with the sunnah. The practice defined by each school was authoritative as an interpretation of the revelation, but only through the medium of the local authorities' opinions, and the local authorities' opinions through the medium of the sunnah. This chain of authority or hierarchy of interpretation is the consequence of the classical fiqh notion that the sunnah epitomizes the sort of reasoning required to extract the sharīʿah from the canonical sources.

Chapter 2

Restricting Authority to the Classical Schools

Chapter 1 outlined the origins of the text-based epistemology that allowed for the equal authority of the classical schools, based on the conflicting opinions of different local authorities of the second century. By tying the opinions to the contents of a textualized sunnah, which was in turn tied to the text of the revelation contained in the Qurʾān, this text-based epistemology made the opinions equivalent in authority with the revelation. The local origins of the opinions, now regarded as different interpretations of the revelation through the medium of the sunnah, were superseded by the opinions' origins in prophetic practice. This link of the opinions to the past, however, required the scholars of the late third and fourth centuries to devise different methods for showing how the conflicting opinions of certain local authorities were derived from the revelation using the example of prophetic practice. The result was a more sophisticated account of the relationship of the sunnah to the revelation and the relationship of the opinions to the revelation through the medium of the sunnah.

Distinguishing this fourth century theory from the more rudimentary text-based epistemology associated with al-Shāfiʿī is the claim that the sunnah epitomized the sort of interpretive reasoning required to define the sharīʿah on the basis of the revelation. The contents of the sunnah were understood as having value insofar as they exemplified the sort of interpretive reasoning required to apply the revelation to changing circumstances. Like the range of meanings attributed to certain objects according to the established interpretation of the Ndembu diviners, the sunnah did not provide a single, definitive interpretation of the revelation. Rather, its contents, used as examples illustrating an interpretive method, represented a means to evince a link between the present and the past. The sunnah was used as palpable evidence of the continuity between the prophetic past and the classical schools. The authority of the classical schools, therefore, not only depended on the opinions being consistent with the contents of the sunnah but, moreover, on the reasoning used to reach those opinions being consistent with the epitome of reasoning reflected in the sunnah.

The following pages show how the authority of the classical schools depends on their definition of practice being tied to the text of the revelation via the interpretation contained in the sunnah. Section I outlines the formation of the classical schools in the context of the late third century disputes over the particular significance of equating prophetic practice with the authority of the revelation. The position of the classical Mālikī, Ḥanafī, and Shāfiʿī schools was the consequence of certain scholars utilizing the text-based epistemology associated with al-Shāfiʿī to maintain the sunnah's interpretive role in the definition of practice. Section II examines the development of a more elaborate theory of the sunnah's relationship to the revelation and the opinions. In particular, the works of ʿAbdallāh b. Muslim b. Qutaybah [d. 276] and ʿAbd al-Raḥmān b. Abī Ḥātim [240–327] illustrate a concept of authority focused on how the sunnah and thus later scholarship interprets the revelation. Section III demonstrates how the fourth century genres of ikhtilāf al-fuqahāʾ and aḥkām al-Qurʾān argue that expertise in the use of interpretive reasoning, more than knowledge of the revelation itself is integral to the definition of practice. The works of Muḥammad b. Jarīr al-Ṭabarī [225–310], Aḥmad b. Muḥammad al-Ṭaḥāwī [239–321], and Aḥmad b. ʿAlī al-Jaṣṣāṣ [305–370] show that knowledge of the sunnah meant knowing how to reason using the model provided in the sunnah by the prophet. In this context, the opinions of select second century figures are authoritative because they represent a definition of practice derived from the revelation in the same way that the sunnah was derived from the revelation.

I

Use of Interpretive Logic

The formulation of a more specific relationship between the revelation and the definition of practice represented in the opinions was developed during the late third and fourth centuries in response to the textual basis of authority introduced by the work associated with al-Shāfiʿī. The basic contention of the *Risālah* is that the sunnah of the prophet constitutes a sort of primitive sharīʿah.[1] That is, prophetic practice is, at the least, a specific case of the derivation of a definition of practice from the revelation. This implication of a text-based epistemology, making the sunnah a definition of practice equivalent in authority with the revelation, was accepted by sunnī scholarship on the whole. Whether this entailed that the sunnah was to be used exclusively as the only definition of practice or that, being the result of human reasoning, the sunnah authorizes the later definition of practice by the schools was still a matter of dispute at the end of the third century.

The dispute over what the authority of the sunnah entailed occurred because the text-based epistemology of the third century did not account adequately for the correspondence of the sunnah to the text of the revelation contained in the Qurʾān. This third century epistemology established that it was necessary to use the sunnah as a basis for the definition of practice and that interpretive reasoning was a necessary correlate to using the contents of the sunnah as precedent. Moreover, it established that the authority of the sunnah is guaranteed by its ability to provide a necessary interpretation of the Qurʾān, and that interpretive reasoning was required to determine how the sunnah does interpret the Qurʾān. As such, this epistemology provides a "negative" guarantee of the sunnah's authority. It makes the guarantee of the authority of the sunnah contingent on the contents of the sunnah not contradicting the contents of the Qurʾān. Besides disqualifying those second century opinions that could not be shown to be consistent with the canonical sources, this epistemology provided no means for prescribing the future definition of practice. There were no specific qualifications for what constituted apparent or justified contradictions. What allowed the classical schools to develop was a "positive" guarantee of the sunnah's authority, a modified text-based epistemology that accounted for how those contents of the sunnah that were authoritative specified the meaning of the revelation. The second century opinions on which the schools were founded could be regarded not as a limited range of examples that did not contradict the sources but as epitomes of how to interpret the sources.

This modified text-based epistemology emerged in the fourth century in the context of two major disputes over the implications of the equation of the sunnah with the authority of the revelation. First, there was a dispute over whether to use the privilege of the sunnah as proof that the sunnah is the final definition of practice or as proof that the use of interpretive logic is required in the definition of practice.[2] The scholars of the incipient Mālikī, Ḥanafī, and Shāfiʿī schools, called the *aṣḥāb al-raʾy,* were proponents of using the opinions of certain local authorities as indicative of a definition of practice beyond the sunnah. These scholars argued against the *aṣḥāb al-ḥadīth,* certain of whose opinions were used as the basis for the Ẓāhirī school, that the use of interpretive reasoning beyond the sunnah is necessary for extracting a definition of practice from the revelation.[3] Second, there was a dispute over whether or not the prophet's use of logic in the formulation of his sunnah required the later use of the sunnah as an example of how to derive a definition of practice from the revelation.[4] The aṣḥāb al-raʾy contended against the *ahl al-naẓar* that, although human reasoning is required for the interpretation of the revelation, it must be based on the example of the sunnah to retain its authority.[5] The result of the aṣḥāb al-raʾy scholars' response to both of these challenges was the fourth century consolidation of the classical schools on the basis of their different opinions as exemplifying how to define practice using the interpretive reasoning epitomized in the sunnah.

In response to the contentions of the aṣḥāb al-ḥadīth, the aṣḥāb al-raʾy argued that acceptance of the sunnah's authority entailed the use of later interpretive reasoning. Scholars following the opinions of other, rival local authorities of the second century such as al-Awzāʿī, Dāʾūd b. Khalaf, and Sufyān al-Thawrī, maintained a literalist position, that their opinions were not only consistent but of the same content as the contents of the canonical sources. This defense of certain opinions is evident from Abū Yūsuf's *Ikhtilāf,* discussed in Chapter 1, in which he critiques al-Awzāʿī for relying indiscriminately on reports of prophetic practice, without the support of logical reasoning. Some among the aṣḥāb al-ḥadīth, like Muḥammad b. Saʿd [168–230], held that the prophet both had divine inspiration in his normal sayings and actions[6] and received revelations not included in the Qurʾān.[7] This position gives the sunnah authority independent of its relationship to the revelation contained in the Qurʾān. Being a privileged instance of the application of the revelation, the sunnah was the final authoritative definition of practice according to the aṣḥāb al-ḥadīth. Although later proponents of this literalist position, the Ẓāhirīs, eschewed the rejection of logic per se by resorting to linguistic interpretation on the basis of textual indications [dalālāt],[8] the basic position of the aṣḥāb al-ḥadīth was that after the sunnah no further definition of practice was to be derived from the revelation.[9] This meant that the authority of the local opinions to which the aṣḥāb al-ḥadīth adhered was dependent upon establishing the identity of the opinions with the sunnah through chains of transmission.

This view was at odds with that being developed by aṣḥāb al-raʾy, who argued that the sunnah itself and the opinions of the different local authorities, including those used by the aṣḥāb al-ḥadīth, were more often than not in conflict with one another over the definition of practice. These differences in opinion were the result, at least in part, of the need to use logic to resolve apparent contradictions inherent in the canonical texts. Different local authorities, in an attempt to harmonize apparent contradictions within the sunnah or between the sunnah and the Qurʾān, could have produced varied results. By requiring interpretive reasoning, the textual character of the revelation and the sunnah encouraged the conflict of opinions. In the course of justifying the opinions of their own local authorities, the aṣḥāb al-raʾy acknowledged that the opinions of different local Medinese and Kūfan authorities were not identical with the contents of the sunnah but were consistent with it. The opinions represented different interpretations of how the sunnah specified the meaning of the revelation. The aṣḥāb al-raʾy recognized that intervening between the text of the revelation and the definition of practice was the use of interpretive reasoning, the result of which was the sunnah.[10] Establishing chains of transmission [asānīd] from the prophet to the later opinions, although necessary for demonstrating the local authorities knew the sunnah, does not explain how the local authorities derived their definition of practice from the revelation in specific cases.

The recognition of the interpretive distance between the revelation and the opinions is a necessary correlate of applying a relatively fixed text to changing circumstances. According to the aṣḥāb al-raʾy, the text-based epistemology, in defining the revelation as a corpus of texts, necessitates the use of reasoned opinion [raʾy] to determine the significance of the revelation for the definition of practice. The text-based epistemology demonstrates the necessity of logic both to demonstrate the consistency of the sources and to apply them to contemporary circumstances.[11] The aṣḥāb al-raʾy took the role of the sunnah as a specification of the revelation as proof of the necessity of the later use of logic designed to define practice.[12] The sunnah's authorization of a certain logic and the results of that authorization are what makes possible the application of the revelation to the later definition of practice.[13] In short, the emerging classical schools contended that the revelation itself was not the definition of practice, but rather that the revelation provided the source material on the basis of which scholarship could derive the definition of practice, just as the sunnah did.[14]

This position maintained by the aṣḥāb al-raʾy was challenged in the opposite direction by the *ahl al-naẓar,* who contended that logic was not only necessary for the definition of practice but sufficient in itself. According to the ahl al-naẓar, the logic used in the definition of practice did not have to be based upon the example of the sunnah.[15] For this reason, the ahl al-naẓar rejected the use of the sunnah altogether and argued for the definition of practice on the basis of reasoning [naẓar, kalām] alone.[16] The ahl al-naẓar claimed that the sunnah is one instance of the definition of practice, the result of the prophet's human reasoning to which all people have equal access. The authorization of the sunnah does not grant it a special status but ensures that all definition of practice is equivalent in authority with the revelation because the prophet is just as human as later scholars.[17] For the aṣḥāb al-raʾy, however, this relatively indiscriminate authorization of logic represents a return to the local epistemologies of the second century, basing the authority of the sunnah on the conflicting claims of the local authorities. It provides no means for authorizing the conflict of opinions other than consensus as the guarantee of the local authorities' reasoning. The conflict of opinions among the local authorities thus makes untenable the use of this epistemology for authorizing their definitions of practice.

The aṣḥāb al-raʾy, as well as Ibn Ḥanbāl and his followers, whose position in the debate with the ahl al-naẓar led to the formation of the classical Ḥanbalī school, maintained that the authority of interpretive reasoning and its results were tied to their association with the example of the sunnah.[18] These scholars argued that the textual definition of authority that allowed for the use of interpretive reasoning was based on the interpretive character of the sunnah, the authority of which was guaranteed by its agreement with the text of the revelation in the Qurʾān. The sunnah was seen as a necessary example of how to interpret the revelation, and therefore, the schools' later definition of practice must adhere to the definition of practice found in the sunnah.[19] Having accepted as the basis for the authority of their definition of practice the text of the revelation and the sunnah as the canonized interpretation of the revelation, the classical schools emerging from the position of the aṣḥāb al-raʾy, at least in theory, renounced the earlier second century practice of reasoning on the basis of local customs and precedents or convenience and public welfare.[20] Reasoning that took local considerations into account was allowed only when it could be demonstrated to be justified in the canonical sources and not on logical grounds alone. The maintenance of a distinction between the precedent of the sources and their application using interpretive reasoning was what allowed the classical schools to insist on a single basis of authority in light of multiple and conflicting definitions of practice.

By maintaining the necessity and integrity of both a set of textual sources and the use of interpretive reasoning, the scholars associated with the aṣḥāb al-raʾy laid the groundwork for a more elaborate theory of the sunnah as an interpretation of the revelation. This sort of relationship of the canonical sources to interpretive scholarship stressed the basic distinction between adherence [ittibāʿ] and inference [istinbāṭ].[21] The revelation and the sunnah are considered to be the origination [matbūʿ] of fiqh scholarship.[22] These two things are the sources for the later derivation of a definition of practice because of the divine origins of the former and the epistemological necessity of the latter. The specification of the meaning [maʿnan] of the contents of these sources, however, depends on human reasoning. Logic is required to disclose the sharīʿah from its sources. Not to recognize this distinction, the classical schools hold, is to confuse fiqh scholarship with its sources, the definition of practice with the revelation itself.[23] In making this crucial distinction, the classical schools justified the opinions of their local authorities as a result of the necessary interpretation of the canonical sources. The schools also restricted the free use of opinion, however, by requiring the demonstration of the agreement between the reasoning used to formulate a given opinion and the reasoning evidently used by the prophet to formulate the sunnah.

By working out the implications of equating the sunnah with the authority of the revelation, the aṣḥāb al-raʾy created a situation both more amenable to the development of classical fiqh scholarship and more complicated in its depiction of the relationship of that scholarship to its sources. Through the resolution of the disputes with the aṣḥāb al-ḥadīth and the ahl al-naẓar, the scholars of the emerging classical schools came to contend that the authorization of interpretive reasoning on the basis of the sunnah required the use of the sunnah as an epitome of how to reason with the text of the revelation to define practice. The justification of certain local authorities' opinions required not only a demonstration that they are based on precedents found in the text of the revelation, but also an account of how the reasoning used to derive the opinion from the revelation is epitomized in the way the prophet derived the sunnah from the revelation.

In subsequent centuries, this stance was developed into the conclusion that the prophet derived the sunnah less from the revelation itself than from principles he induced from the text of the revelation. During the late third and fourth centuries, clusters of selected local opinions were compiled and authorized in terms of their adherence to the example of the sunnah in their derivation of practice from the text of the revelation.[24] These different ways in which scholars of the classical schools chose to justify their own selection of local opinions in light of the epitome of the sunnah caused the differences both within and between the schools. Thus justifying the opinions of their own local authorities, the schools diverged not in their acceptance of a common set of canonical sources but in how they argued that the opinions of their authorities utilized those sources.

The schools were allowed to develop independent of one another as long as they drew on the same canonical sources for the defense of their different local bases. This is because their claim to rely on a shared text, albeit one whose contents were not definitely fixed, provided the physical evidence the schools needed to show their link to the authority of the prophetic past. As such, the attempt of the schools to argue within the parameters of the framework of prophetic precedent provided a minimum of standardization that fostered the independent development of conflicting but equally authoritative definitions of practice.

II

Stipulation of the Prophet's Reasoning

The use of prophetic practice as an epitome of how to reason on the basis of the revelation produced a situation in which the conflicting contents of the sunnah as well as the conflicting opinions of the local authorities concerning the definition of practice could be explained in terms of the use of different sorts of interpretive reasoning. That the conflicting contents of the sunnah were recognized as authoritative by the several schools meant that it was the concept of the sunnah as the representation of prophetic practice, rather than the contents of certain books, to which the schools imputed authority. The canonical status of the sunnah was due to how the text could be used to authorize conflicting opinions. The theoretical discussion of the different types of reasoning responsible for the opinions was made possible by a subtle shift in the text-based conception of authority, from one based on access to the revelation itself to one based on access to an authoritative interpretation of the revelation.

In the context of the third century text-based epistemology associated with al-Shāfiʿī, the opinions of certain local authorities are authoritative as long as they conform to the contents of the sunnah, which are considered to conform to the contents of the revelation contained in the text of the Qurʾān. This epistemology makes the authority of the opinions of a given local authority dependent on that authority having knowledge of the contents of the sunnah and thus of the revelation itself. In the course of the late third and fourth centuries, the focus of this text-based epistemology developed to emphasize the specific role the sunnah had in the definition of practice formulated by the opinions of certain local authorities. The fourth century version of the text-based epistemology stressed the reasons, beyond the fact that God ordered obedience to the sunnah, for the authority of the sunnah as a specification of the revelation. The distinction of this modified text-based epistemology is that an authoritative opinion is not that which reproduces the contents of the sunnah and the revelation but that which is in imitation [taqlīd] of the prophet's reasoning.

Ibn Qutaybah

This shift in focus is already evident in the theoretical framework surrounding the discussion of conflicting opinions against the backdrop of the text-based epistemology, in the earliest "classical" ikhtilāf works of the late third century.[25] Ibn Qutaybah's work, for example, shows how the sunnah is integral to understanding the revelation and is not in contradiction with the revelation contained in the Qurʾān nor resistant to the interpretive methods required for the definition of practice. These two points represent an important development in the text-based epistemology associated with the aṣḥāb al-raʾy scholars. On the one hand, Ibn Qutaybah contends that the sunnah does not contradict the received text of the revelation nor does any part of the sunnah contravene another part of the sunnah.

For example, Ibn Qutaybah shows, in a number of separate examples, how apparent contradictions between reports of prophetic practice are to be resolved.[26]

> People say that it is transmitted, on the authority of Mālik, on the authority of Ṣafwān b. Sulaym, on the authority of ʿAṭāʾ b. Yasār, on the authority of Abū Saʿīd al-Khudrī, that the prophet said: washing [ghusl] on the day of the congregational prayer is required for everyone capable of having a wet dream.
>
> People also say that it is transmitted, on the authority of Hammām, on the authority of Qatādah, on the authority of al-Ḥasan, that Samurah said the prophet said: those who perform ablutions [wuḍūʾ] on the day of the congregational prayer are considered to be good, but those who perform washing are better.[27]

According to Ibn Qutaybah, these two reports seem to contradict one another. In the first, washing is required and in the second either washing or ablutions suffices although washing is said to be preferable to ablution. The issue is whether washing [ghusl] is required, for the special circumstances of the congregation prayer that occurs once a week, instead of ablutions [wuḍūʿ]. Ibn Qutaybah explains how this is resolved by interpreting the two reports according to certain set standards of what is meant by "required."

> We say that the prophet's word that washing on the day of the congregational prayer is required for all those capable of having a wet dream is not intended to make the washing an obligation [farḍ] but to make it something that is required [wājib] for all Muslims like that which requires washing for the two festivals for the purpose of piety [faḍīlah].[28]

Here, Ibn Qutaybah makes a distinction between the washing being "required" and being "obligatory." This means that, in accordance with the more general stipulation known from other reports, only ablution is obligatory for a noon-time prayer. The prophet's requiring of washing is not intended to establish an obligation but to encourage mature Muslims to demonstrate their piety for the benefit of the congregation gathered for the special prayer.

Ibn Qutaybah's harmonizing of reports of prophetic practice and the Qurʾān with the sunnah as a whole is a demonstration of the principle established by al-Shāfiʿī, that authoritative (noncontradictory) prophetic practice interprets rather than contravenes the text of the revelation found in the Qurʾān. When the meaning of two texts appears to be a contradiction, one of the two texts is taken to be a specification [takhṣīṣ] of the other.[29] That this specification might sometimes entail the abrogation [naskh] of the explicit meaning of one of the two texts is justified by the nature of interpretive reasoning. Ibn Qutaybah recognizes that for one text to specify the meaning of another, the text doing the specification transfers its meaning to the text being specified. Abrogation is but an extreme illustration of this point. To argue that some reports of prophetic practice, at times, abrogate other reports or the Qur᾿ān, Ibn Qutaybah recognizes that, as an interpretation of the revelation, the sunnah contains a more explicit and systematic explication of the practical significance of the revelation than does the Qur᾿ān.[30] Once the intention of the two different texts is understood, their apparent contradiction is resolved. By allowing the sunnah to abrogate the Qur᾿ān, Ibn Qutaybah emphasizes that the interpretation of the prophet must be used as the primary source for the definition of practice. He recognizes that the necessity of having the sunnah interpret the revelation entails having the meaning of the Qur᾿ān originate in the sunnah.

The other major point stressed by Ibn Qutaybah is that later definitions of practice must be derived from the revelation using the same sorts of reasoning epitomized in the sunnah. This is an extension of the earlier feature of the text-based epistemology that the sunnah is not contrary to the methods and the bases of interpretation required to extract a definition of practice from the revelation. Ibn Qutaybah contends that the sunnah, as a device for specifying the meaning of the revelation, is on par with speculation [naẓar], rational proof [ḥujjat al-ᶜaql], and analogical reasoning [qiyās].[31] Although, in some cases, certain reports of prophetic practice seem to contradict reason, Ibn Qutaybah shows that, when interpreted as the prophet intended his practice to be interpreted, the sunnah does not contradict reason. For Ibn Qutaybah, this is because the prophet's practice is a reasonable interpretation of the revelation. To assume that a particular practice is unreasonable is not to understand the reasoning the prophet used in that particular case. Understanding the reasoning behind a particular practice, however, is tantamount to understanding the intention of the prophet in interpreting the revelation in the fashion he did. Therefore, the use of these different interpretive strategies to form the opinions of the second century local authorities is not only permitted but required because the prophet used these same methods when interpreting the revelation to form his sunnah.

In addition, Ibn Qutaybah argues that the different means by which knowledge of prophetic practice is known are of equivalent authority in specifying the revelation. Interpreting the revelation in light of the sunnah means interpreting in light of eyewitness reports of prophetic practice [ᶜuyūn], practice of the companions [akhbār],[32] and the continuous tradition of practice guaranteed by consensus [ijmāᶜ].[33] This broad definition of prophetic practice is not a reversion to the local epistemologies of the second century, but rather Ibn Qutaybah is making the case that interpretations of the revelation beyond the text of the sunnah are authoritative as long as they conform to prophetic practice. Insofar as the practice of companions and later traditional practices are not linked to an explicit prophetic precedent, they are interpretations of prophetic practice. The majority of reports of prophetic practice, those that do not give explicit statements defining practice but provide a narrative description of something someone saw the prophet do or say in relation to a specific context, by virtue of what is narrated along with the specific prophetic practice, are themselves interpretations of prophetic practice.[34] As long as later interpretations of the revelation can be shown to interpret the revelation as the prophet does in the sunnah, then they are authorized by the claim that the sunnah is a necessary interpretation of the revelation. This sort of epistemology allows for the later use of reports of companion practice [āthār] and traditional practice [ᶜamal] on grounds more explicit that those provided by the stipulation that later interpretations not contradict the sunnah. Ibn Qutaybah contends that the schools must demonstrate that their precedents and interpretations use the same reasoning as the prophet did to produce the sunnah, thus defining more narrowly the range of possible conclusions to be made on the basis of the sunnah. This stipulation provides the classical schools with a more nuanced defense of the authority of their localized opinions, yet it requires the schools to show how their definitions of practice conflict when they are derived from the same sources using the same sorts of interpretive reasoning.

Ibn Qutaybah's defense of the sunnah's authority establishes the rudimentary outlines of a methodology for interpreting the revelation with reasoning.[35] Written under the caliphate of al-Mutawakkil in the wake of the criticism against the ahl al-naẓar position,[36] Ibn Qutaybah's work insists that the normative value of the sharīʿah be tied to its derivation from a controlled interpretation of the revelation. It is established that the revelation requires interpretive reasoning, but also that this reasoning be restricted in such a way that its conclusions do not contravene the accepted contents of the revelation itself and the specification of the revelation contained in the sunnah (see Figure 2.1). This restriction of conclusions is not simply a matter of checking the contents of an opinion against the contents of the sunnah and the Qurʾān. Rather, Ibn Qutaybah argues that controlling for certain conclusions means ensuring that the authoritative conclusions be reached on the basis of the revelation, using the same methods as evinced in the sunnah.

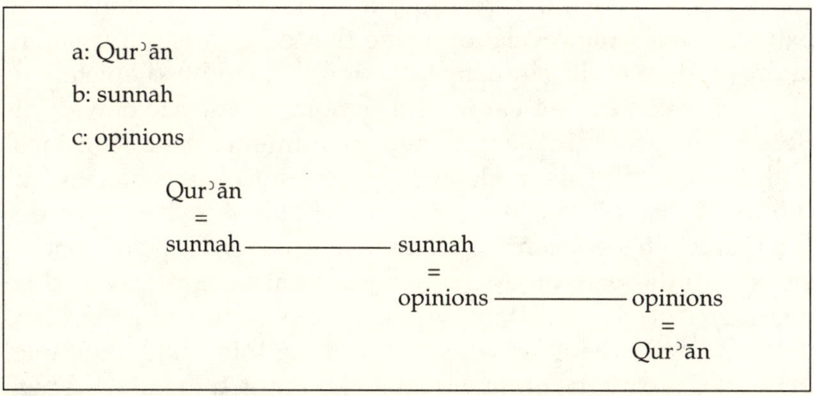

Figure 2.1. The syllogism by which Ibn Qutaybah claims that the opinions are equivalent in authority with the sunnah and the Qurʾān.

According to Ibn Qutaybah, if a = b and b = c, then c = a if one can control for the equivalencies by stipulating that the same methods of interpretation are used in each case. Thus, rather than expanding the possible significance of the revelation, the requirement of interpretation limits the revelation to how the sunnah interprets it. This scheme guarantees the authority of the scholarship extracting a definition of practice from the canonical sources only when the extraction agrees with the sources taken as a whole, the textual character of which requires interpretation. The position taken by Ibn Qutaybah entails that, to formulate an authoritative reasoned interpretation of the revelation, a scholar must take into account not only the text of the revelation but, more important, how that text was interpreted by local authorities and how the interpretation of the local authorities was based on the interpretation epitomized by the sunnah.

Ibn Abī Ḥātim

Ibn Qutaybah's work illustrates that, at the end of the third century, epistemological considerations focused on how the sunnah specified the revelation, and how the opinions were extracted from the revelation using the same sorts of reasoning as are evident in the sunnah. Although this modified epistemology improved on the earlier epistemology associated with al-Shāfiᶜī by providing a positive guarantee of the opinions' authority, it still was inadequate to account for the specific authority of the opinions on which the schools were based. Under Ibn Qutaybah's epistemology, a much broader range of conclusions than those given by the schools' local authorities could be considered to be consistent with the types of reasoning evident in the sunnah. Using analogical reasoning [qiyās], for example, one could justify the opinion that it is permitted to kill wild pigs in the sacred area, because, like the snakes that Mālik forbid on the authority of ᶜUmar,[37] pigs are impure animals. The types of reasoning identified by Ibn Qutaybah are ubiquitous enough to provide justification for a large range of opinions outside the purview of those selected and used by the classical schools as their bases. This meant there was a need to develop a theory that ensures that the general principles on the basis of which such analogies are made are shown to be consistent with the principles and the relative applicability of such principles known from other cases. Such a theory could disqualify the opinion concerning the pig on the grounds that ᶜUmar's permitting the killing of snakes is based on the fact that the prophet considered snakes to be predatory animals, the killing of which is permitted. By claiming access to the historical circumstance in which ᶜUmar, on the authority of prophetic practice, formulated his opinion, the schools could defend their more limited range of conclusions. To determine which principles are operative in a given precedent, one must understand the historical context in which the precedent is made.

In his seminal work *al-Jarḥ wa al-taᶜdīl,* Ibn Abī Ḥātim argues that the sort of methodology necessary to demonstrate the specific authority of selected opinions is based on a historicist conception of the relationship between the knowledge of the sunnah and the capacity to extract from it a definition of practice.[38] Ibn Abī Ḥātim maintains that authorizing the opinions in terms of the revelation is predicated on the local authorities having knowledge of how the prophet specified the revelation. The authority of the opinions is contingent on the results being consistent with the content of the canonical sources, but it is also dependent on the historical relationship of the local authority to the prophet. To be authoritative, an opinion must be based on knowledge of how the prophet enacted the revelation, not as a direct statement of the meaning of the revelation but as an example of how the prophet applied what he understood the revelation to mean in a particular case. By emphasizing knowledge of how the prophet applied the revelation, Ibn Abī Ḥātim defines the use of the sunnah not as a source for the content of the revelation but rather as a source for the methods the prophet used in extracting a definition of practice, his sunnah, from the revelation.

Like al-Shāfiᶜī and Ibn Qutaybah, Ibn Abī Ḥātim guarantees the authority of the sunnah by demonstrating its role as a specification of the revelation contained in the Qurʾān. Citing verses from the sūrat al-naḥl [16:44, 64], Ibn Abī Ḥātim states that God sent down to the prophet the book in which all things are made clear.

> Before you [Muḥammad], we [God] only sent men to whom we gave a revelation—ask the people who remind [Jews

> and Christians] if you do not know—with explications and scriptures. We revealed to you a reminder to make clear to people what was revealed to them so that they might think about it.

> We only revealed to you the book so that you can make clear to those among whom there is disagreement a guidance and a mercy for those who believe.

According to Ibn Abī Ḥātim, the prophet is to be the "explication" of the scripture for the Muslims. The book was revealed to the prophet so that he could make clear to people what practice God wanted them to follow. Ibn Abī Ḥātim's exegesis of this verse makes not only the significance but the purpose of the Qurʾān to be an authorization of the sunnah. God made the prophet to be the proper explication [mawḍaʿ al-ibānah] of that revelation.[39] Therefore, knowledge of prophetic practice is required to properly determine the significance of the revelation.

> The prophet is an explication [mubīn] of God and of his book: what is addressed to people and what God intended and meant by it. That practice which the book defines is illustrated by the meaning of the prophet's religion, his decisions, what he made to be obligatory, necessary, beneficial, and allowed.[40]

In effect, Ibn Abī Ḥātim follows the earlier versions of the text-based epistemology in defining textual interpretation as the guarantor of authority, meaning that the necessity of the sunnah for understanding the Qurʾān proves the authority of the sunnah. The earlier text-based epistemology associated with al-Shāfiʿī focused on the contents of the opinions and the canonical sources, holding that, as long as the opinions do not contradict the sunnah, just as the sunnah does not contradict the Qurʾān, then the opinions retain their authority. Ibn Abī Ḥātim, however, argues that the authority of the prophet specified in the Qurʾān is interpretive. As the explication of the Qurʾān, the prophet's practice illustrates by example what God intended by his revelation. Thus, to "not contradict" the sunnah, the opinions must not merely repeat prophetic practice but must explain how the sunnah exemplifies what is intended by the revelation.

According to Ibn Abī Ḥātim, the sunnah is like an historical record of how the prophet exemplified the revelation.

> The prophet stayed in Makkah and Madīnah for twenty-three years and established for the people the distinguishing characteristics [maᶜālim] of the religion. He made duties obligatory, established authoritative practice [sunnah], and made legal decisions. He forbade the forbidden and allowed the allowable. He established the people on the way of truth by both word and deed.[41]

Ibn Abī Ḥātim's stress on the historical context in which the sunnah was formulated shifts the epistemological foundations of the opinions from knowledge of the contents of the sunnah to knowledge of how, in particular circumstances, the prophet applied the revelation to create a specific definition of practice. An important heuristic dimension is present here between the particular and the general that the classical schools use to authorize their conflicting definitions of practice. Ibn Abī Ḥātim's contention is that the particular practices of the prophet are used to exemplify the general intentions of the revelation. The specific cases in which the prophet applies the revelation to define practice illustrate the more general principles of the revelation. Because it is a specific instance of the application of these principles, however, the particularized cases of the sunnah are not simply to be repeated. Through the media of specific cases, later generations are to extract the general and subsequently apply it by making it specific to their own historical circumstances.

Ibn Abī Ḥātim contends that this historically relative character of the sunnah has implications for the authority of later traditional practice. Just as the sunnah is a record of how the prophet applied the revelation to his specific circumstances, so the practice of his companions is an account of how the next generation applied the revelation to their specific circumstances on the model of prophetic practice. The particular cases of prophetic and companion practice are not necessarily consistent, but what is consistent is the companions' use of the principles on the more general basis of which the prophet defined practice specific to his circumstances. According to Ibn Abī Ḥātim, this interpretive consistency is because select people in later generations preserve the practice of the prophet.

> They [companions of the prophet] preserve from the prophet what he received from God, and what the prophet practiced, defined as practice, decided, judged, delegated, commanded, proscribed, forbade, and suggested they memorized and acquired.[42]

To be able to define practice consistent with how the prophet defined practice on the basis of the revelation, later generations must have a record of what the prophet said and did. The continuity of prophetic practice is guaranteed not only by the record of what the prophet said and did, however, but by later generations understanding the circumstances in and to which the prophet applied the revelation.

> They [companions] have understanding concerning the religion and learning concerning the command of God, his proscriptions and his intentions, through the manifestation [muʿāyinah] of the prophet, their witnessing of his interpretation of the book, and their taking and extracting of that from the prophet.[43]

Ibn Abī Ḥātim specifies that the companions' knowledge of what God intends practice to be comes from their witnessing of the prophet's practice, as an interpretation of the revelation. By understanding the circumstances of the prophet's practice, later generations can determine how and for what reasons the prophet defined specific practices in particular ways. This allows later generations to extend the example of prophetic practice to define their own practice, according to their own circumstances.

By describing the relationship of later generations to the prophet in this way, Ibn Abī Ḥātim makes the practice of later generations equivalent in authority with prophetic practice.

> The companions are those whom God chose for companionship [ṣuḥbah] of the prophet, for his assistance, the establishment of his religion, and the manifestation of his

> truth. Their obligation to him is as companions. God made them for us to be exemplars and the distinguishing characteristics [maᶜālim] of religion.[44]

Here, Ibn Abī Ḥātim compares the practice of the companions to prophetic practice. Like the prophet, the companions are chosen by God to exhibit the interpretation of the revelation in their practice. Ibn Abī Ḥātim refers to the practice of the companions, like that of the prophet, as displaying the "distinguishing characteristics" or "significance" [maᶜālim] of the revelation. This comparison is predicated upon the companions' relationship to the revelation through the medium of prophetic practice, as shown in Figure 2.2.

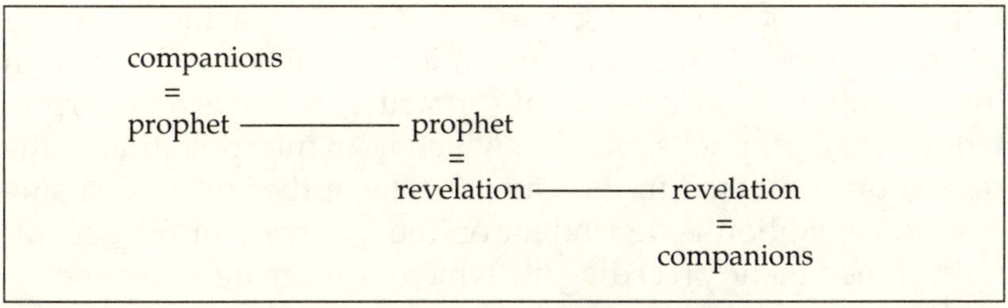

Figure 2.2. How Ibn Abī Hātim equates the authority of companion practice with the authority of the revelation through the medium of prophetic practice.

The practice of the companions, equivalent in authority to the practice of the prophet, becomes equivalent in authority to the revelation itself because it is already established that the practice of the prophet is equivalent in authority to the revelation. This formulation of the authority of later generations' practice is unlike that given by second century authorities like Muḥammad b. Saᶜd who claims that the practice of the companions was equivalent to the authority of prophetic practice because it was a model of the oldest prophetic community.[45] Ibn Abī Ḥātim's concept of authority, like that of Ibn Qutaybah, is based on the premise that the authority of later generations' definition of practice is due to their relation to the prophet whose practice is an interpretation of the revelation contained in the text of the Qurʾān. Because the companions had knowledge of how to interpret the revelation from observing the prophet, their definition of practice has the authority of the revelation.

Ibn Abī Ḥātim uses this same sort of reasoning to equate the authority of the practice defined by later generations of scholars with the authority of the revelation. Just as the authority of the companions was based on their relationship to the revelation through the medium of the prophet, so the authority of later generations is based on their relationship to the revelation through the media both of preceding generations and the prophet. The opinions of the second century authorities are interpretations of the third generation's practice, which is an interpretation of the second generation's practice, which is an interpretation of the companions' practice, which is an interpretation of the prophet's practice, which is an interpretation of the revelation contained in the Qurʾān. The authority of each successive generation is dependent on the authority of the generation immediately preceding it, which is ultimately dependent on the authority of the prophet to interpret the revelation. By inheriting knowledge of how to interpret the revelation from the preceding generation, select second century authorities [al-aʾimmah] have the authority to define practice.

> God does not single out the learned scholars so that they should articulate the traditional practice of other learned scholars, but God made certain learned scholars to be the distinguishing characteristics [maʿālim] of his religion in order to establish his way. He clothed them for the people in their good works.[46]

Here Ibn Abī Ḥātim equates the practice, or "good works" of select later scholars with both the practice of the companions and the prophet. All three groups' definitions of practice, based on knowledge of how to interpret the revelation, are defined as the "distinguishing characteristics" [maʿālim] of the religion.[47] The authority of the classical schools is guaranteed by the transmission of how the prophet interpreted the revelation, through the generations, to the local authorities of the second century on whose opinions the classical schools are based.

Ibn Abī Ḥātim replaces Ibn Qutaybah's basic account of the opinions' relationship to the revelation via the sunnah with a more complicated genealogy of how knowledge of the sunnah is transmitted to select second century authorities. Because it is imperative to know the context in and to which the prophet applied the revelation, the authority of later generations is dependent on their being able to understand the particular circumstances of the prophet's practice from the practice of earlier generations who knew the prophet's circumstances firsthand. Knowledge of the sunnah is knowing how the previous generation understood the prophet to be interpreting the revelation, on the basis of how the generation previous to it understood, on the basis of how the generation that witnessed the prophet do it understood (see Figure 2.3.). This historicist conception of the relationship of later opinions to prophetic practice laid the groundwork for a more formal rather than historicist model for the identification of how the prophet interpreted the revelation.

It is important to note that Ibn Abī Ḥātim's reason for the authority of the founders of the classical schools [al-aʾimmah] is not their knowledge of the contents of the sunnah but rather their knowledge of the interpretive reasoning responsible for those contents.

> [This is] the critical scholarship of those learned scholars possessed of acumen who are singled out by God with this virtue and provided this knowledge [of the sunnah] in each generation and epoch.[48]

Certain second century local authorities are considered *al-aʾimmah* because they have the virtue [faḍl] of acumen, meaning they are skilled in interpretive reasoning, and have knowledge of the sunnah, meaning how the prophet applied the revelation. Ibn Abī Ḥātim contends that knowledge of the sunnah is more than simply memorizing the different reports of prophetic practice. It includes being able to figure out how those contents have been understood by previous generations to

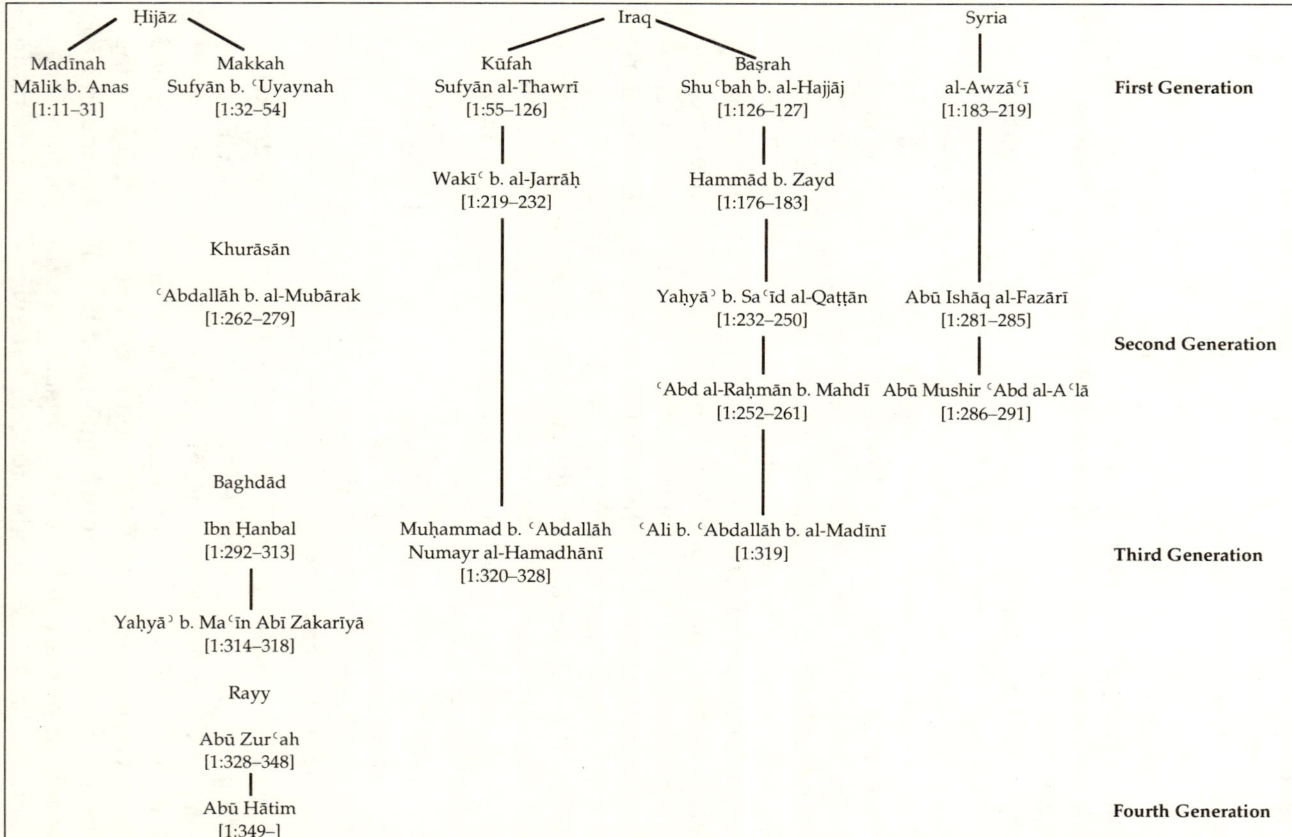

Figure 2.3. The four generations of scholarship following the companions of the prophet and the scholars by whom knowledge of the sunnah was transmitted to different locations.

represent the prophet's interpretive strategies. In particular, knowledge of the sunnah means knowing what later generations took to be what the prophet interpreted as being the general principles of the revelation that, although responsible for his adjudication of specific cases, are to be applied in any historical context. For Ibn Abī Ḥātim, being an authority of fiqh scholarship means being able to demonstrate God's intentions in his revelation by reference to how earlier generations understood the prophet to have illustrated these intentions in his practice.

On the basis of Ibn Abī Ḥātim's epistemology, the later generations' practice, including the opinions of select second century authorities, could be taken to be an extension of the sunnah. The practice and the opinions of the generations following the prophet were that many more examples of the same set of general principles found in the revelation by the prophet and applied by the prophet and these later generations to various circumstances. This conception of authority lays the epistemological foundations for the development of a general hermeneutics associated with the classical uṣūl al-fiqh scholarship of the fifth and sixth centuries. The implication of Ibn Abī Ḥātim's epistemology, taken by classical uṣūl al-fiqh scholarship, is that what ensures the specific authority of the schools' opinions is that they can be shown to have been deduced from the same principles, using the same methodology, on the basis of which the prophet deduced the sunnah. This implication allows the schools to contend that what distinguishes among their opinions and between their opinions and the opinions not considered authoritative is different interpretations of what later generations took to be the principles on the basis of which the prophet deduced the sunnah.

III

Interpretive Expertise of the Opinions

There are significant continuities between the second century Kūfan use of logical reasoning and this fourth century emphasis upon the authority and use of interpretive reasoning to define practice. The works associated with Abū Yūsuf, discussed in

Chapter 1,[49] show how the opinions of Abū Ḥanīfah were considered to be authoritative in the second century on account of Abū Ḥanīfah's use of logic to decide the relative authority of different examples of prophetic practice or precedents. In the context of fourth century developments, Abū Ḥanīfah's use of logic to decide among precedents was construed as the use of logic to determine the most authoritative interpretation of the revelation among those provided by preceding generations, meaning that interpretation most consistent with already established or accepted interpretations of how prophetic practice specifies the interpretation in other cases. This was allowed because the scholarship of the fourth century did not regard the opinions of the local authorities as necessarily consistent with all of the reports of prophetic practice considered to be a part of the sunnah, nor were all of the reports on which the local authorities are thought to have relied necessarily accepted as being part of the sunnah by other local authorities or later scholarship.[50] This meant that the content of the "sunnah" was elastic to the extent that different scholars could utilize different textual precedents and still claim to be using a corpus common to all the schools.

Related to this conception of the sunnah is the notion that, to be authoritative, an opinion needs to be derived from principles that are logically consistent with those known principles from which derived opinions already are established as authoritative. In the second century, this meant that the relative authority of examples of "sunnah" were judged in terms of what the individual local authority considered to be a general principle. Thus, Abū Ḥanīfah argues that two shares of booty are not given to every horse when only one share is given to the horse's rider because this elevates the horse above the person and contradicts the general principle that humans are more important than animals.[51] By the fourth century, for the classical schools emerging from the aṣḥāb al-raʾy, the principles from which the authoritative opinions were derived were those principles consistent with what is known of the principles from which the prophet derived the sunnah. The point is that the general principles the prophet used to derive the specific cases of the sunnah are considered to be the general principles or intentions behind the revelation contained in the Qurʾān. So, although it could be argued that Abū Ḥanīfah determined from the Qurʾān that, because human beings have more religious obligations than animals, human beings are more important than animals, this principle is not authoritative unless it can be shown to be a principle the prophet used in his derivation of the sunnah. The text-based epistemology of the fourth century restricts the interpretive privilege of the generations following the prophet to that which can be demonstrated to be consistent with reasoning behind the sunnah. To retain the authority of the revelation, the opinions of second century authorities must be shown to interpret the revelation through the medium of the established text of the sunnah.

Ibn Qutaybah and Ibn Abī Ḥātim contend that, to make their opinions consistent with the principles of the sunnah, later authorities must be familiar with the particular circumstances in which the prophet applied a general principle to the definition of a specific practice. To claim that their opinions from the second century are authoritative, the classical schools must demonstrate that their local authorities knew how the prophet interpreted the revelation because the previous generation knew the historical circumstances of the generation previous to it, which knew the historical circumstances of the companions, who knew the circumstances of prophetic practice. The al-aʾimmah are able to discern the general principles from the sunnah on the basis of the various definitions of practice derived from a relatively small set of principles by the prophet and by later generations who knew the principles the prophet used. This entails that, although further removed from the prophet, later generations have more examples, due to the proliferation of specific cases with each successive generation, from which to induce the principles used by the prophet, taken from the revelation. The opinions of the al-aʾimmah are the bases on which the classical schools are built because they thus represent the most immediate and informed examples from which the schools can themselves discern the principles of the revelation.

al-Ṭabarī

Classical ikhtilāf al-fuqahā᾽ scholarship attempts to account for how the opinions used by the classical schools, if in theory derived from the same principles as is the sunnah, are often in conflict with one another. Contemporaneous with the work of Ibn Abī Ḥātim, this ikhtilāf scholarship explains ad hoc how different opinions interpret the sunnah as an epitome of the reasoning required to understand the revelation. In his *Ikhtilāf al-fuqahā᾽*, al-Ṭabarī ratifies the opinions of certain local authorities by detailing their relationship to the revelation through the medium of the sunnah and the practice of later generations. On a given point of conflict, al-Ṭabarī lists the opinions of several local authorities, including those on which the classical schools are based (Mālik, al-Shāfiᶜī, Abū Ḥanīfah, Abū Yūsuf, al-Shaybānī) and those associated with "schools" that did not materialize in the classical period (al-Awzāᶜī, Ibn Abī Laylā, al-Thawrī, Abū Thawr, and others). After recounting these divergent opinions, al-Ṭabarī identifies the basis for the authority of each opinion. He shows, on the one hand, that the opinion is based on the text [khabar] of the sunnah or the consensus of earlier generations [ijmāᶜ]. On the other hand, al-Ṭabarī shows, in selected cases, how the local authority arrived at his opinion using interpretive reasoning.

For example, al-Ṭabarī lists the opinions of six local authorities concerning the right of canceling a sale, based on the differing interpretations of the prophet's statement that a sale can be canceled as long as the two parties have not separated.

> The two parties to a sale have the option of canceling the sale as long as they have not separated, except in an optional sale [bayᶜ al-khiyār].[52]

The six authorities' interpretations of this passage fall roughly into three groups. According to al-Ṭabarī, Mālik, Abū Ḥanīfah and his followers interpret "separation" [furqah] as a reference to the verbal conclusion of an exchange.

> Mālik says, on the authority of the statement of the prophet, that the purchasing parties have the option of canceling the sale as long as they have not separated. This is not dependent upon a fixed amount nor a fixed time.[53]

> Abū Ḥanīfah and his companions say: the separation is dependent upon a conversation.[54]

Both of these opinions agree that the prophet's statement means that a sale can be canceled even after the exchange of items is completed and that this option of cancellation continues until the parties agree they have "separated" or concluded the exchange.[55]

> The principle [ᶜillah] behind the opinion of Mālik is that the term 'separation' permits separation by statement [alone] because, interpreted linguistically, this does not prevent from being concluded that one says 'we separate from that in which we were.' When this takes place thus, and the exchange is simply the transfer of property from its owner to someone else by a fixed rate of exchange, and the exchange is contracted by speech between the two parties, then there is no separation from the place of their exchange that occurs by reason of this action.[56]

According to al-Ṭabarī, Mālik and Abū Ḥanīfah hold that the exchange itself is not enough to end the option of canceling the sale. The statement of the prophet means that the two parties must stipulate their separation to discontinue their option of cancellation.

Two other opinions cited by al-Ṭabarī state exceptions to the prophet's statement that the parties have the option of canceling the sale.

> al-Awzāᶜī says: the purchasing parties have the option of canceling the sale as long as they have not separated except in the sale of a third at the public auction of small livestock, partnership in cultivation, and partnership in commerce when it is transacted with the stipulation that there is no choice [in canceling the sale].[57]

Here, al-Awzā^cī simply lists three cases in which the parties do not have the option of canceling the sale, even before they have not separated. By excepting these three cases on account of the specific circumstances of exchange they involve, al-Awzāʿī limits the application of the prophet's general statement. The opinion of Sufyān al-Thawrī further limits the general applicability of the prophet's statement.

> al-Thawrī says: I received a report that the prophet said: the purchasing parties have the option of canceling the sale as long as they have not separated except in an optional sale and when the right to an option is reserved. If the seller and the buyer choose to do so, then the sale is concluded even if they have not [physically] separated. When the two parties agree on the terms of the sale [not having an option] then the sale is permitted even if they have not yet separated.[58]

According to al-Thawrī, the explicit statement of the prophet providing for the parties' option can be removed as long as the two parties agree upon forfeiting their right to the option. The interpretations of both al-Awzāʿī and al-Thawrī restrict the significance of the sunnah to allow for the authority of their own exceptional cases. This is opposed to the interpretations of Mālik and Abū Ḥanīfah, which extend the sunnah's applicability to authorize the practice of having the general option of canceling the sale.

The opinions of al-Shāfiʿī and Abū Thawr are distinct from both of these previous positions. According to al-Ṭabarī, al-Shāfiʿī and Abū Thawr interpret "separation" as being the physical separation of the two parties and that the parties do not have the right to forfeit the option of canceling the sale before that time nor the right to extend the option after that time.

> al-Shāfiʿī [and Abū Thawr] say: all purchasing parties, in the cases of advance payment, debt, nonmovable property, delayed delivery, or otherwise with agreed terms of sale or mutual consent, the parties not having separated from their place of meeting at which they agreed on the terms of the sale, have the right to cancel their sale. Likewise, the sale is

> incumbent upon each party as long as they do not have the right to rescind it unless by option, stipulation of option, or otherwise that which is described with agreement in the terms of the sale and by mutual consent, and the two parties separate after the sale from their place of meeting at which they agreed on the terms of the sale . . .[59]

The first half of this opinion makes clear that the two parties have the option to cancel the sale as long as they have not separated from the location at which they contracted the sale. Also, al-Shāfiᶜī and Abū Thawr take the prophet's statement to be applicable in all cases.

> The proof [of this interpretation] is established on the fact that the prophet did not permit his community to make speech concerning that which did not profit them. He said: the purchasing parties have the option to cancel the sale as long as they have not separated. That separation is [therefore] not exempted either by statement or anything else.[60]

According to al-Ṭabarī, because of the general prophetic principle that people are not bound by speech that does not benefit them, and the observation that forfeiting one's option of canceling a sale is not of benefit to the parties in an exchange, the option has to be tied to a physical rather than a verbal separation. This same principle is evident from the second half of al-Shāfiᶜī and Abū Thawr's opinion that, on the basis of the second half of the prophet's statement, states that the option to cancel the sale can be continued after the physical separation as long as they two parties stipulate such an option as part of the contract. For al-Shāfiᶜī and Abū Thawr, the intention of the prophet in allowing the option to continue after separation when stipulated is that these are cases where the extension of the option is of benefit to both parties and is therefore permitted.

By presenting the opinions of the local authorities in this way, al-Ṭabarī demonstrates that their different interpretations are derived on the basis of a principle [ᶜillah] extracted from the sources. These principles, supposed to be the ones the prophet extracted from the revelation, are evident from the context of the sunnah. This concept of "principles" operative in al-Ṭabarī is still rudimentary compared to the more developed concept used in the classical uṣūl al-fiqh scholarship of the fifth and sixth centuries. In al-Ṭabarī, *ʿillah* refers to the "reasoning" behind a text, or sometimes the "intention" of the prophet or God in speaking the text. A given opinion is the result of a local authority decontextualizing a principle from the prophet's application of that principle to a specific case, then recontextualizing that principle in a set of novel circumstances. Principles more or less explicit from the prophet's context, as is evident from the opinions based on the prophet's statement concerning the option of canceling a sale, are still subject to interpretation. The contention in al-Ṭabarī's work is that a relatively explicit statement of a principle can produce a wide range of opinions concerning that principle's applicability. Two local authorities might base their opinions on principles taken from two different examples of practice given in the sunnah. But, even when two local authorities agree on the same principle, taken from the same text, the two authorities can disagree concerning the significance of that principle to the definition of practice in a given case. In order to be authoritative, opinions must be shown to have been derived from principles, whether the same or conflicting with the principles used by other local authorities, and as such extrapolated from the different examples of the prophet's decisions found in the sunnah.

This notion that different principles, derived from different examples given in the sunnah, can be responsible for conflicting opinions is evident from al-Ṭabarī's analysis of the opinions concerning the irrigation of uncultivated land. In this case, al-Ṭabarī lists the opinions of different local authorities that fall roughly into two groups. On the one hand is the position agreed upon by Mālik and Abū Ḥanīfah, based on the prophet's prohibition of cultivating land in return for a fourth or a third of what is produced.[61]

> Mālik says: it is not appropriate to irrigate uncultivated land. The leasing of land for dinars, dirhems and other fixed prices is allowed for its owner. If a person gives his uncultivated land for a third or a fourth of that which is

> produced from the land, then his return is a risk because the crops can be plentiful one time and sparse another time, or perhaps destroyed. Had the owner of the land not taken a fixed rent which was of benefit to him, but took a risk, not knowing whether or not the produce would be plentiful or sparse, it is reprehensible.[62]

> Abū Ḥanīfah says: the cultivation of uncultivated land is not permitted as a mutual contract based upon a portion of the seedlings or part of that which is produced from the land.[63]

In both cases, the prohibition against leasing land for an uncertain amount of return is based on the conclusion that such an arrangement is likely to result in an inequitable exchange that leaves one of the two parties at an unfair advantage. This result would contradict the principle that usury [ribāʾ], in the sense of an exchange not being made for things of equivalent value, is forbidden, and thus the practice of transferring possession of land without a fixed rate of exchange is to be forbidden. On the other hand, al-Shāfiʿī, Abū Yūsuf, and al-Shaybānī permit the cultivation of uncultivated land in return for an uncertain amount of produce.

> al-Shāfiʿī says: the sunnah of the prophet is to permit a mutual contract based upon a date palm for something that is produced from the date palm. This follows the sunnah that the basis is found that the owner pays the other person for his work in terms of the produce.[64]

> Abū Yūsuf and al-Shaybānī say: cultivation of land for a third or a fourth [of its produce] is permitted just as is a mutual contract for palm dates.[65]

The opinion of Abū Yūsuf and al-Shaybānī directly contradicts the prophetic precedent on which Mālik and Abū Ḥanīfah's opinion is based forbidding the same practice. The opinions permitting the cultivation in return for produce, however, are based on the prophet's practice of permitting a hireling to receive wages in terms of the produce of the land he cultivates.

For al-Ṭabarī, these latter opinions allow the cultivation in return for an uncertain amount of produce when one considers the person cultivating to be working the land for the original owner, receiving the produce as wages. This is what distinguishes their opinions from those of Mālik and Abū Ḥanīfah who prohibit the cultivation for an uncertain amount of produce, considering the person cultivating to have leased the land from the original owner, in which case the uncertain amount of produce is in exchange for the transfer of possession and is thus usurious.

The work of al-Ṭabarī develops the contention that the authority of the opinions is predicated on their being derived from the same principles that the prophet used. According to al-Ṭabarī, the principle that is extracted determines the significance of the text in question. The principle becomes the specification or the definitive characteristic [maᶜālim] of the revelation.[66] In this sense, al-Ṭabarī's work provides an etiology of the local authorities' opinions as a theoretical exposition of how the definition of practice is derived on the basis of the interpretive reasoning epitomized in the sunnah. For al-Ṭabarī, fiqh scholarship is both a body of knowledge and a discipline. It comprises both certain facts (the principles contained in the sunnah) and certain methods (reasoning required to apply the principles to a definition of practice). Knowledge of the contents of the sunnah is essential, but it is not the defining characteristic of fiqh scholarship. The authority of the classical schools' scholarship is contingent on knowing how to apply the revelation, and more important, the interpretation of the revelation contained in the sunnah, to the definition of practice. Fiqh scholarship is about the reasoned determination of which principles are inherent in the revelation and how those principles should be understood to be relevant to contemporary circumstances. The opinions of the local authorities are foundational for the classical schools because they epitomize the knowledge and the process of reasoning required to specify the revelation's practical significance.

al-Ṭaḥāwī

In his work, al-Ṭaḥāwī develops the notion used by al-Ṭabarī that the authority of the sunnah's interpretation of the revelation depends upon the expertise to determine the revelatory principles from which the prophet deduced his sunnah. Written about the same time as al-Ṭabarī's work, although perhaps redacted at the end of the fourth century,[67] al-Ṭaḥāwī's ikhtilāf work develops a more nuanced explanation for the shared authority of conflicting opinions. This work presents an explanation of the Ḥanafī definition of practice, in terms of how the Ḥanafī authorities use the interpretive reasoning epitomized in the sunnah. By focusing on the reasoning used by the Ḥanafī authorities, al-Ṭaḥāwī emphasizes that the basis of the opinions is textual interpretation. This approach to the opinions' authority is a development of the approach used by al-Ṭabarī and Ibn Abī Ḥātim, in which the opinions are explained as the result of the local authorities extracting a revelatory principle from the context of prophetic practice and then applying the principle in a novel context. This basic approach explains how the opinions of different local authorities can be in conflict with one another, while at the same time it maintains that these opinions are derived from the same revelatory principles from which the prophet derived his sunnah. According to al-Ṭaḥāwī the conflict of opinions is due either to authorities extracting different principles from different texts or differently applying the same principle to new circumstances.[68] In either case, al-Ṭaḥāwī maintains that the sunnah, the medium through which the local authorities interpret the revelation, does not contradict itself nor the Qur'ān.

According to al-Ṭaḥāwī, the first major cause of conflicting opinions is the different application of the same principle.[69] Explaining the conflict of opinions as the result of local authorities differently interpreting the same principle is exemplified in al-Ṭaḥāwī's discussion of the Ḥanafī opinion that it is not forbidden to hunt the prey of Madīnah nor to cut down the trees there as it is in the sacred area around Makkah.[70] According to both Mālik and al-Shāfiʿī, to do these things is reprehensible [makrūh] but there is no penalty for doing them.[71] Citing a report of prophetic practice on the authority of Saʿd b. Waqqāṣ stating that if people find someone hunting or cutting down trees in the confines of the sacred area of Madīnah then they should take from that person anything he acquired there, al-Ṭaḥāwī raises the issue of interpretation.

> Saᶜd [b. Waqqāṣ] reported from the prophet that if people find someone hunting in the confines of the sacred area of Madīnah or cutting down trees there, they should take from that person what he acquired there.[72]

Although this report would seem to argue against the Ḥanafī opinion, al-Ṭaḥāwī explains that the conflict between the opinions is not due to the use of conflicting prophetic precedents. Indeed, this report would also argue against Mālik and al-Shāfiᶜī, because although their opinion makes hunting and cutting trees in Madīnah to be reprehensible, it does not require the penalty that the example of the prophet does. This point is significant for al-Ṭaḥāwī, who goes on to argue that the precedent of this prophetic practice has been abrogated by a later report of prophetic practice.

> The scholars of fiqh [Ḥanafīs, Mālik, and al-Shāfiᶜī] agree, however, that the things a person acquires there [in Madīnah] should not be taken. This proves that the report of prophetic practice has been abrogated. For the prophet [later] said: oh Abū ᶜUmayr, what of the little sparrow. But he did not disapprove of the prey nor take it from him.[73]

The agreement of the other local authorities concerning not requiring people to take the prey or foliage that a person took from Madīnah as a penalty proves that the other local authorities also agree that the earlier report of prophetic practice, given on the authority of Saᶜd b. Waqqāṣ, was abrogated. If the practice was prohibited, then a penalty would be required of the offender like the penalty for hunting in the sacred area of Makkah. This is followed by the citation of two more reports of prophetic practice that allude to the allowance of hunting and cutting down trees in Madīnah.

> Abū Nuᶜaym reported, on the authority of Yūnis b. Abī Isḥāq, on the authority of Mujāhid, on the authority of ᶜĀʾishah, that the camel of the prophet was wild. When the prophet went out it would play, become violent, run toward him, and run away from him. When the prophet sensed that it had gone in to lie down, he did not find it reprehensible to slaughter it.[74]

> Mūsā b. Muḥammad reported, on the authority of his father, on the authority of Salamah b. al-Akwaᶜ that the prophet said to him: if you were to hunt prey in the canyon for your group when you go out and I meet you, I love [to hunt in] the canyon.[75]

According to al-Ṭaḥāwī, these reports give support to the contention that the report given on the authority of Saᶜd b. Waqqāṣ was abrogated. The difference of opinion is thus not the result of conflicting reports of prophetic practice, but the result of the authorities differently interpreting the same report. The Ḥanafīs allow the killing and cutting in Madīnah outright, whereas Mālik and al-Shāfiᶜī allow it but find it reprehensible.

Continuing on this point, al-Ṭaḥāwī further explains that the opinion of al-Shāfiᶜī is based on a conflicting report of prophetic practice. He mentions that al-Shāfiᶜī considers hunting and cutting down trees in al-Ṭāʾif as being reprehensible because of a report that the prophet forbade these things.

> al-Shāfiᶜī says: it is reprehensible to hunt in al-Ṭāʾif and to cut its trees because the prophet forbade it.[76]

> Abū Jaᶜfar [al-Ṭaḥāwī] repeats what was heard in this report, but it is not the opinion of a single one of the learned scholars.[77]

Note here that, although al-Ṭaḥāwī claims that al-Shāfiᶜī's opinion is based upon a report of prophetic practice, he indicates that other scholars do not know of this report. No chain of transmission is given for this report, linking it from al-Shāfiᶜī to the prophet. This indicates that the report, like the one given on the authority of Saᶜd b. Waqqāṣ, is not to be regarded as authoritative. The mention of the claim that al-Shāfiᶜī's opinion is based on this report is meant to reiterate that conflicting opinions are not the result of conflicting reports of prophetic practice, for this would entail acknowledging that the sunnah does contradict itself. In this particular case, it is clear that, although the local authorities evaluate the importance of Madīnah differently, they agree that the prophet did not forbid hunting and cutting trees there.

Often the disagreement among the opinions is due to different interpretations of the specific implications of a principle, on the general nature of which the local authorities agree.[78] In his discussion of the unmixed sale [ṣarf], for example, al-Ṭaḥāwī compares the opinion of Abū Ḥanīfah to the opinions of al-Shāfiʿī and Mālik to show how the same principle is interpreted differently. The discussion begins with a disagreement over the meaning of "separation" similar to that discussed in al-Ṭabarī's ikhtilāf work.

> Our companions say: the mutual taking of possession in an unmixed sale, as long as the two parties have not separated, even if the period is extended, and the separation occurs in another place, is permitted. This is the opinion of al-Shāfiʿī.[79]
>
> Ibn al-Qāsim says, on the authority of Mālik: unmixed sale is not sound unless it is hand to hand. If a person does not pay in cash but remains with the other party, sitting until the break of morning the next day, and the two conclude the unmixed sale the next day, each taking possession on the morning of the next day, it is not sound. It is not an unmixed sale unless it is in the context of the conversation. If the two had moved from that [original] location to another location, their mutual taking of possession is not sound.[80]

The two definitions of what constitutes a sound unmixed sale are in conflict with one another, but it is evident from the opinions selected by al-Ṭaḥāwī that the disagreement concerns what constitutes the "separation" of the two parties from their contractual relationship. Both definitions agree that the mutual taking of possession, or a "hand-to-hand" exchange is a basic element of an unmixed sale. The authorities agree in principle but disagree as to how that principle is to be related to the specific case. This same point is illustrated by al-Ṭaḥāwī in relation to the issue of agency [wakālah].

> Our companions say: it is permitted to contract an unmixed sale and then appoint as an agent a man to take possession

> of the item of exchange as long as the two contracting parties have not yet separated. This is the opinion of al-Shāfiʿī.[81]
>
> Mālik says: the contracting party needs to take possession of the item. If two men had made an unmixed sale of dinars and one of the two took possession by the order of the owner [seller of the dinars], and he is present, then this is permitted.[82]

Again, both definitions agree on the principle that the taking of possession in an unmixed sale is to be mutual, but they disagree as to its specific application. Mālik insists that the original parties take mutual possession at the original time and location of the contract, whereas the Ḥanafīs and al-Shāfiʿī allow another person to make the actual exchange at a later time, as long as the two parties have not technically separated.

This same sort of disagreement over the application of an agreed upon principle in the context of a specific case is illustrated by al-Ṭaḥāwī in his discussion of the different interpretations of the meaning and implications of exchanging a "certain amount" [juzāf] of silver for gold.[83]

> Our companions say: there is no harm in this [selling gold for a certain amount of silver]. This is the opinion of al-Shāfiʿī.[84]
>
> Mālik says: there is no harm is selling this [certain amount of gold or silver] when it is ore or crafted jewelry. As for dirhems and dinars, it is not appropriate for one to be sold for another at a certain amount [juzāf], unless the coins are numbered and their number is known. Otherwise, this is a risk and a gamble. Ibn al-Qāsim mentioned this on the authority of Mālik.[85]

It is evident from the information al-Ṭaḥāwī includes in citing Mālik's opinion that Mālik considers the designation "certain amount" not to determine adequately that the exchange between the two parties is equitable. The specification of "this" amount of silver, as an item of exchange, is allowed only when the item is a certain amount of ore or a certain piece of jewelry. A certain amount of coins, however, must be further specified by number for the amount to be evaluated. For the Ḥanafīs and al-Shāfiʿī, a certain amount specified is an item of exchange assuming the "certain amount" is designated and set aside as such.[86] Through this comparison, al-Ṭaḥāwī shows that the authorities agree on a principle fundamental to the definition of all exchanges. They agree on the principle that the items exchanged must be of equivalent value and therefore that the extent of the items must be subject to evaluation. The disagreement of the authorities over the definition of this particular case allows al-Ṭaḥāwī to demonstrate how the opinions can be used to determine principles fundamental to the revelation.

By introducing further cases of conflict, al-Ṭaḥāwī demonstrates that the conflict between the authorities over the application of the same principle to different specific cases is often predicated on the certain interpretations of an earlier agreed on principle. The interpretation of the following opinions is based on the distinction already established that the Ḥanafīs and al-Shāfiʿī do not take "separation" to be determined by physically leaving the place where the contract was exchanged.

> Our companions and al-Shāfiʿī say: it is permitted to sell a dinar for ten dirhems that are not in the possession of one of the two parties, then to pay the other before separating.[87]

> al-Ḥasan [b. Ziyād al-Luʾluʾī] reports that he does not permit unmixed sale when one of the two items is not specified, but unmixed sale is permitted if a person says: "I purchase from you a thousand dirhems for a hundred dinars," whether one of the two parties has the coins on hand or not. If one of the two items of exchange is specified, and it is on hand, it is permitted for a person to say: "I purchase from you a thousand dirhems for those dinars," as long as he pays the dinars before the two separate.[88]

> [Ibn al-Qāsim] reports, on the authority of Mālik, similar to the opinion of Zufar, that a person needs to take possession of whatever is not specified at that location [of the contract].[89]

The Ḥanafīs and al-Shāfiʿī hold that one amount of coins are to be exchanged for another amount of coins even if one of the amounts of coins is not paid until a later time or at another location. This is because the two parties have not yet separated, and so the exchange of items is still considered to be mutual. For this same reason, Mālik forbids such an exchange, but only because he interprets "separation" differently. The opinion of al-Luʾluʾī [116–204] is included to emphasize that the principle at stake in these opinions is not only that the items of exchange be known but also that, in the case of an unmixed sale, the exchange of items must be mutual. The disagreement over the definition of an unmixed sale is thus due to the different authorities' criteria for establishing that an exchange be mutual.

The second major explanation for conflicting opinions is the use of different principles.[90] According to al-Ṭaḥāwī, although the local authorities use the same principles as did the prophet in deriving his sunnah, and these principles are consistent with one another, the local authorities often apply different principles to define the same practice. This is illustrated in the discussion of the eating of predatory animals. The opinion of Mālik makes a distinction between predatory land animals and predatory birds.

> Mālik says: there is no eating of lions, nor cats whether wild or domestic, nor fox, nor hyena, nor anything that is predatory. There is no harm in eating predatory birds: Egyptian vultures, eagles, other vultures, and other birds that do not eat carrion. These are not eaten.[91]

Mālik takes the principle in this case to forbid those predatory animals that have fangs.[92] His opinion is based on the fact that the prophet forbade the eating of predatory animals with fangs, which birds do not have, and are thus not forbidden although they might be predatory. This position is modified slightly by the opinions of al-Awzāʿī and al-Layth.

> al-Awzāʿī says: all birds are allowed except vultures are reprehensible.
>
> al-Layth says there is no harm in eating a cat but a hyena is reprehensible.[93]

The exception of vultures means that al-Awzāʿī considers them to be carrion eaters, like al-Layth who forbids the eating of animals that are carrion eaters but not necessarily those that have fangs like the cat. It is evident from their opinions, that for al-Awzāʿī and al-Layth, the principle behind forbidding predatory animals is that animals that eat carrion are not to be eaten. The opinion of al-Shāfiʿī is based on yet a third principle.

> al-Shāfiʿī says: there is no eating of predatory animals with claws which feed on people: lion, tiger, and wolf. There is eating of the hyena and the fox but not the vulture, falcon and birds like them because they are birds that feed on people.[94]

Here, al-Shāfiʿī restricts the forbidding of eating predatory animals to only those that feed on people. Although al-Shāfiʿī mentions clawed animals, it is clear from his allowance of eating the hyena and fox that for al-Shāfiʿī the principle in this case is that animals that feed on people are forbidden to be eaten.

According to al-Ṭaḥāwī, the Ḥanafī position on the eating of predatory animals is more complicated than the positions of the other authorities. On the one hand, the Ḥanafīs forbid the eating of predatory land animals and birds on account of the reports of prophetic practice that indicate this. Mālik contravenes this general injunction by limiting the principle to include animals with fangs only and therefore not predatory birds. On the other hand, al-Ṭaḥāwī states that the Ḥanafīs also forbid the eating of animals that eat carrion. This opinion is formed on the basis of an independent prophetic precedent indicating the reprehensible nature of carrion-eating animals.

> The prophet said there are five vicious animals that people kill whether they are sacralized or not. One of them is the spotted crow because the spotted crow eats carrion. Therefore, this [the fact that the spotted crow eats carrion] becomes the basis [aṣl] in the reprehensibility of animals which eat carrion.[95]

Thus, of all the animals that are forbidden to be eaten, some are forbidden because they are predatory and some are forbidden because they eat carrion. The opinion of al-Awzāʿī confuses these separate principles by applying the prohibition against carrion eaters alone to the prohibition against predatory birds and thus allows the eating of all predatory birds except vultures. Similarly, the opinion of al-Shāfiʿī, although it does forbid the vulture, does so not because it is a carrion eater but because it is a predatory bird. In this way, al-Ṭaḥāwī demonstrates that the Ḥanafī position is sound, and more nuanced in its extraction and use of principles from the sunnah than the opinions of the other authorities.

al-Jaṣṣāṣ

By focusing on the opinions as the authoritative interpretation of the revelation, al-Ṭaḥāwī emphasizes how the local authorities reason differently on the basis of the same principles. He also shifts the focus away from the sunnah and to the interpretive problems associated with applying the sunnah to specific cases. This etiology of the opinions demonstrates how the Ḥanafī opinions are derived from the same principles as those from which other opinions were derived and from which the prophet derived the sunnah. In his *Aḥkām al-Qurʾān,* al-Jaṣṣāṣ demonstrates, through a systematic exegesis of each chapter of the Qurʾān, that these same Ḥanafī opinions are integral to the interpretation of the text of the revelation. He shows that certain Ḥanafī opinions are necessary for understanding the principles the prophet induced from the revelation. By listing the verse, the opinion based upon it, and reports of prophetic practice relevant to the interpretation of that verse, al-Jaṣṣāṣ makes the opinions out to be an epitome of how to interpret the revelation through the medium of the sunnah. The opinions epitomize how scholars are to interpret the sunnah so that it correlates to the Qurʾān, disclosing what and how the prophet extracted as principles from the revelation.

For example, al-Jaṣṣāṣ shows that the Ḥanafī position that it is forbidden to eat prey killed in the sacred area is derived from a principle implicit in the text of the Qurʾān. Part of verse

95 of sūrat al-māʾidah states that pilgrims are forbidden to kill prey while they are sacralized. According to al-Jaṣṣāṣ, the general principle behind forbidding the killing of the prey is that it is forbidden to eat it.[96] That this is the principle is evident, first, from the mention in the next verse that the prey of the sea is allowed to be eaten.

> Allowed for you is the prey of the sea and its food as provisions for you and for travelers [on the sea].[97]

Second, the Ḥanafī interpretation of the verse is evident from the fact that the verse forbids prey being "killed" [qatal] and verse 3 of the same sūrah states that an animal must by "slaughtered" [dhabaḥ] according to certain stipulations to be eaten.

> Forbidden to you is that which is dead, blood, the meat of pigs, that over which other than the name of God has been invoked, that which is strangled, beaten to death, that killed by a fall, that killed by being gored, and that which predatory animals eat unless you slaughter it.[98]

Both of these indications are supported further by the reports that the prophet allowed the sacralized person to kill five animals, the killing of which would otherwise be prohibited according to the word of God, but that those animals, are not to be eaten.[99] According to al-Jaṣṣāṣ, the prophet forbade the eating of these five animals because as predatory animals they would not have been slaughtered as food according to the stipulations given in the Qurʾān. Therefore, as a specific exception to the general killing of wild animals forbidden in the Qurʾān, this prophetic practice indicates that the principle behind the verse in question is what the Ḥanafīs interpret it to be. The authority of this interpretation is finally demonstrated by the agreement of other reports of prophetic practice and the opinions of other local authorities that it is forbidden to eat already dead prey, meaning prey that is not necessarily properly slaughtered.[100]

Going beyond the claim of the third and early fourth centuries, associated with al-Shāfiʿī, Ibn Qutaybah, and Ibn Abī Ḥātim, that the Qurʾān was to be interpreted in light of the sunnah, al-Jaṣṣāṣ contends that the Qurʾān is to be interpreted in light of the opinions of the local authorities, in particular those on which the Ḥanafī school is based.[101] For this reason, the opinions effectively replace the need to return to the sunnah or the Qurʾān to define practice. The applicability of the revelation is contained in the principles the prophet extracted from the Qurʾān. These principles are the same as the principles used by the local authorities and are thus evident from the opinions. In effect, by the end of the fourth century, the opinions themselves became canonized. Because of the way their authority was guaranteed by their acknowledged basis in the sunnah, the opinions became the necessary basis for the later definition of practice. For the scholars of the classical schools, the revelation is to be interpreted through the medium of the opinions to the extent that the opinions are to be interpreted in lieu of the revelation itself. The opinions illustrate what the principles are by extending them to analogous cases. For the classical schools associated with the aṣḥāb al-raʾy, these opinions of certain authorities, in effect, replace the collection of reports of prophetic practice like those found in the six books of the aṣḥāb al-ḥadīth. Having already ratified these opinions as being interpretations of the revelation derived through the medium of, and thus not in contradiction with, the sunnah, the classical schools could dispense with the contents of the sunnah and the Qurʾān except to illustrate for pedagogical reasons the acknowledged basis of these opinions' authority.

The work of al-Jaṣṣāṣ complements the work of al-Ṭaḥāwī in its contention that understanding how to define practice entails interpreting the opinions of the local authorities as different examples of how to interpret the sunnah. By showing that the text of the revelation contained in the Qurʾān is to be understood through the medium of the opinions, al-Jaṣṣāṣ's work, in effect, ratifies the authority of the opinions used by al-Ṭaḥāwī. The opinions result from the extension of principles used by the prophet to derive the contents of the sunnah to novel and often incongruous cases. That Abū Ḥanīfah mentions it is allowable for pilgrims to kill wolves and foxes can be taken to mean that it is also allowable to kill coyotes and dingoes, just as the prophet's statement that it is allowable to kill wild dogs is not meant to limit the license of pilgrims' killing predatory animals to wild dogs alone. Just as the practice of the prophet applies the principles of the revelation to cases unforeseen or not mentioned in the Qur᾿ān, so the opinions of the local authorities apply the same principles to cases unforeseen or not mentioned by the prophet. From the end of the fourth century onward, the focus of the emerging classical schools was on how the opinions interpret the sunnah as a guide to how the sunnah interprets the revelation.[102] The focus of classical fiqh scholarship is on the logic of the opinions.

Conclusions

The modified text-based epistemology, developed at the end of the third and throughout the fourth century, evolved from the idea that the sunnah epitomized the interpretive reasoning required to understand the revelation contained in the Qur᾿ān. As a canonical text, the sunnah could be used as tangible proof of the link between the schools and the prophet. In particular, the scholars associated with the aṣḥāb al-ra᾿y contended that the sunnah represented the definition of practice that the prophet derived from principles he extracted from the Qur᾿ān.

This conception of the sunnah guaranteed the authority of the opinions as had the third century theory of the consistency among the contents of the sources and the opinions. In addition, this conception provided the means for the classical schools to claim the specific authority of the opinions on which they were based. In the context of this epistemology, the Mālikīs could interpret the opinions of Mālik in relation to the canonical sources in such a way as to justify their reliance on the continuous tradition of Medinese practice, as could the Ḥanafīs use interpretive reasoning to justify the logical bases of the opinions of certain Kūfan authorities. The notion that the sunnah and the opinions were deduced from the same principles, which were induced from the revelation, allows for a variety of authoritative definitions of practice. In this sense, authority depends on a scholar or school not just asserting that its definition of practice is contiguous with that of the prophet, but demonstrating the reasons why it is contiguous.

The focus upon demonstrating continuity between present scholarship and the prophetic past is predicated on the modified text-based epistemology of the fourth century. This epistemology allowed the classical schools to restrict the authority of the revelation to the opinions used by the classical "sunnī" schools.[103] Developed from this modified epistemology was the outline of a methodology that controls for deviation from the opinions of the classical schools by providing for the institutionalization of fiqh scholarship. The full institutionalization of the classical schools, however, was not made possible until the development in the fifth and sixth centuries of a formal exegetical methodology associated with classical uṣūl al-fiqh scholarship.

Chapter **3**

The Logic of the Opinions

The institutionalization of the classical schools in the fifth century was made possible by the epistemological developments of the fourth century that resulted in the canonization of the opinions of certain second century authorities. In Chapter 2, the ikhtilāf scholarship showed how the scholars associated with the aṣḥāb al-raʾy based the authority of certain opinions on the claim that the sunnah epitomized the sort of interpretive reasoning required to apply the revelation to a definition of practice. This claim allowed the burgeoning classical schools to claim further that the opinions on which their scholarship was based were themselves an epitome of the interpretive reasoning used by the prophet to derive his sunnah from the revelation.

By the end of the fourth century, the use of selected opinions as an epitome of the prophet's interpretive reasoning replaced the need for later scholars to use the sunnah as a guide for how to interpret the revelation. The canonical authority previously attached to the Qurʾān and sunnah was extended to include a corpus of opinions selected from certain second century local authorities. The opinions had been in wide circulation since at least the middle of the third century, the object of scholarship designed to demonstrate that the opinions were consistent with the sunnah.[1] In the fifth century, however, the opinions were "canonized" in the sense that they, rather than the sunnah or the Qurʾān, became the primary focus of classical fiqh scholarship. Like the revelation and the sunnah before, the opinions were conceived of as a textual corpus. This textual corpus represented a link between classical scholarship and the past generations of the schools' founders. The scholarship of the classical schools in the fifth century is designed to analyze the theoretical implications entailed in assigning canonical authority to a textual corpus of selected second century opinions.

The following pages examine how the classical Ḥanafī scholarship of the fifth century appropriated selected opinions of certain second century Kūfan authorities. Section I examines the scholarship associated with the late fourth and early fifth century compendia or *ikhtiṣār* literature. This section shows how the *Mukhtaṣar* of Aḥmad b. Muḥammad al-Qudūrī [362–428], in particular, delimits the corpus of opinions representative of Ḥanafī fiqh. Section II illustrates how the *Taʾsīs al-naẓar* of ʿUbaydallāh b. ʿUmar al-Dabūsī [d. 430] further condenses the corpus of Ḥanafī opinions according to the sorts of reasoning responsible for the conflicts among the opinions. The work of al-Dabūsī develops a rudimentary outline of the interpretive methods characteristic of the Ḥanafī opinions. Section III shows how the corpus of Ḥanafī opinions was used by Muḥammad b. Aḥmad al-Sarakhsī [d. 483] to illustrate the epistemological basis of the Ḥanafī school. By abstracting a formal methodology from the opinions in the Ḥanafī canon, al-Sarakhsī distinguishes between the textual basis of the school's epistemology and the logical basis of the interpretive reasoning required to define practice. The development of Ḥanafī scholarship in the fifth century demonstrates how a certain corpus of opinions was defined and utilized as epitomizing the interpretive reasoning required to apply the revelation to the definition of practice.

I

Delimiting the Canon of Opinions

The canonization of the opinions on which the classical schools were based was accomplished separately in the context of the different schools' establishment as independent institutions. In the case of the Mālikī school, the institutional authority of the opinions associated with the local authorities of second century Madīnah was defined in the second half of the fourth century by the work of ʿAbdallāh b. Muḥammad al-Abharī [287–375][2] and Ibn Abī Zayd al-Qayrawānī [310–386].[3] The theoretical implications of this work was developed in the late fifth century works of Ibn ʿAbd al-Barr [d. 463][4] and Sulaymān b. Khalaf al-Bājī [d. 474],[5] which grounded classical Mālikī scholarship on the *Muwaṭṭāʾ* redacted by al-Maṣmūdī.[6] The fifth century commentaries on al-Muzanī's condensation of the opinions of al-Shāfiʿī by Muḥammad b. Aḥmad al-Azharī [d. 370][7] and Abū al-Ṭayyib al-Ṭabarī [348–450],[8] as well as the work of Ibn al-Maḥāmilī [368–415],[9] in particular, focused subsequent Shāfiʿī scholarship on the *Kitāb al-umm.* For the Ḥanbalī school, the commentary of Abū Yaʿlā al-Farrāʾ [d. 458][10] on al-Khiraqī's [d. 334][11] compendium also helped to establish the canonical authority of the opinions attributed to Ibn Ḥanbal in the *masāʾil* works of the third and fourth centuries.[12] Selections from the corpus of opinions associated with certain Kūfan authorities were compiled and used in the fourth century works of al-Ṭaḥāwī, ʿUbaydallāh b. al-Ḥusayn al-Karkhī [260-340],[13] and al-Jaṣṣāṣ among others. In the fifth century, certain opinions from these earlier compilations were redacted in the work of al-Qudūrī, which became, at the end of the sixth century, the basis for the subsequent development of Ḥanafī scholarship.

It is important to stress that a particular redaction of a corpus of opinions should not be confused with what a school uses as its "canon" of opinions. The opinions redacted in the late fourth and fifth centuries, with few possible exceptions, were regarded as selections from the larger corpus of opinions considered to be canonical. Just as the canonical "text" of the sunnah was not necessarily fixed in writing, nor limited to what was contained in a certain book, so the canonical corpus of a school's opinions was not identified solely with a particular redaction of opinions in the fourth and fifth centuries.[14] In the late sixth and seventh centuries, the claim that the corpus of opinions is contained in a certain collection of books is not the cause but the result of the canonical status of the opinions.[15]

Many of the opinions eventually collected and authorized as "Ḥanafī" were presumably in circulation as early as the end of the second century. The oral and especially written transmission of some of these opinions in the third and fourth centuries is evident from the works of Hilāl al-Raʾy [d. 245],[16] al-Khaṣṣāf [d. 261],[17] but especially the fourth century works of al-Ṭaḥāwī, al-Marwazī, al-Karkhī, al-Jaṣṣāṣ, and Abū al-Layth al-Samarqandī [d. 373].[18] It is this corpus of opinions, developing over two centuries and not necessarily limited to those written down in these texts, that assumed canonical status at the beginning of the fifth century.

What distinguishes the fifth century conception of this corpus of opinions from that of earlier centuries is the ends for which the opinions are appropriated. Earlier scholarship focused on illustrating the authority of the opinions. In the works of al-Ṭaḥāwī and al-Jaṣṣāṣ, for example, the Ḥanafī opinions are compared with the opinions of other local authorities to demonstrate how the opinions were linked to the revelation through the medium of the sunnah. The opinions were considered authoritative because these scholars showed the opinions to be interpretations of the revelation that conformed to the interpretations of the prophet. This sort of scholarship laid the epistemological foundations that allowed the scholarship of the fifth century to use the corpus of Ḥanafī opinions as a canon. Because the scholars of the previous century had already established the opinions' link to the revelation, the scholars of the fifth century were able to use the corpus of Ḥanafī opinions in place of the sunnah as the guide for how to define practice.

This focus on the opinions as exhibiting a certain logic characteristic of the sorts of interpretive reasoning used by the Ḥanafī authorities is evident in the compendium of Ḥanafī opinions compiled by al-Qudūrī at the beginning of the fifth century. In his *Mukhtaṣar,* al-Qudūrī uses selected Ḥanafī opinions to illustrate how the Ḥanafī opinions epitomize the sorts of reasoning required to define practice. The *Mukhtaṣar* is a condensation of the corpus of Ḥanafī opinions compiled and discussed in the ikhtiṣār and ikhtilāf works of the fourth century.[19] For example, in the *Mukhtaṣar* of al-Ṭaḥāwī, the discussion of delayed delivery [salam] consists of over fifty separate statements, covering eleven different aspects of the practice, occupying about four pages in the published edition.[20] In the *Mukhtaṣar* of al-Qudūrī, the discussion of delayed delivery is reduced to seven main points, all of which illustrate the general principle operative in the Ḥanafī opinions concerning this practice.

> Delayed delivery is permissible for items sold by dry measure, weight, and number, the individual items of which do not differ such as the walnut and egg, and those sold by dhirāʾ. The delayed delivery of animals, parts of animals, skins by number, firewood by faggots, and trefoil by bales is not permitted.
>
> Delayed delivery is not permitted unless the item to be delivered be in existence from the time of the contract to the time of the delivery date. Delayed delivery is not sound unless it is delayed. It is only permitted with a fixed deadline.
>
> Delayed delivery is not permitted by the dry measure or dhirāʾ of a particular man, nor with respect to the food of a particular village, nor the fruit of a particular group of palm trees.
>
> According to Abū Ḥanīfah, delayed delivery is only sound in accordance with seven stipulations being mentioned in the contract: fixed species, fixed type, fixed deadline, knowledge of the amount of capital insofar as the contract depends on its sum such as items sold by dry measure, weight, and number, and the specification of the place in which the contract will be fulfilled when the bearing of it and provisions for the bearing are involved. Abū Yūsuf and Muḥammad al-Shaybānī say the specification of the capital is not needed when it has been particularized, nor is the specification of the place of delivery needed, the item being delivered at the location of the contract. The delayed delivery is only sound if the purchaser takes possession of the capital before separating from the buyer.
>
> Usufruct is not permitted concerning the capital nor the item to be delivered before the purchaser's taking possession

> of it. Neither partnership nor favorable resale is permitted concerning the item to be delivered before the purchaser's taking possession of it.
>
> Delayed delivery of clothing is permitted when the clothing is specified according to length, width, and piece. Delayed delivery of gems and pearls is not permitted. Delayed delivery of adobe and baked brick does no harm when it is specified according to a fixed brick mold.
>
> Of all that of which the apprehension of its property and the knowledge of its amount is possible, delayed delivery is permitted. Delayed delivery of that the apprehension of whose property is not possible and whose amount is not known is not permitted.[21]

This discussion of delayed delivery brings the logic of the opinions to the forefront. Statements one, two, three, and six illustrate, through the use of specific examples, that delayed delivery depends on the use of fixed standards of weight, size, and quality. Items that vary in quality or whose standard measurements are not sufficiently equivalent from one portion to the next are not allowed to be used for delayed delivery. Statement four lists the fixed provisions and statement seven makes explicit the general principle underlying all of the statements. According to al-Qudūrī, the general principle behind the Ḥanafī opinions is that an item of a delayed exchange must be able to be evaluated in generic terms as equivalent in value to other like items of the same measurement. This guarantees that the equity of the exchange contracted, although not concluded until a later date, is not subject to the contingent fluctuation of price.

The *Mukhtaṣar* of al-Qudūrī also uses selections from the conflict of Ḥanafī opinions to illustrate the sorts of interpretive decisions made by the Ḥanafī authorities. Unlike the ikhtilāf works of the fourth century, al-Qudūrī's work focuses only on the conflict among the opinions of the Ḥanafī authorities. He mentions the opinions of Abū Ḥanīfah, Abū Yūsuf, Muḥammad al-Shaybānī, and Zufar as a means of highlighting the reasoning characteristic of Ḥanafī fiqh.[22] In many cases, al-Qudūrī contrasts the opinions of Abū Yūsuf and Muḥammad to those of Abū Ḥanīfah to indicate a general principle on which all three authorities agree.

> When a mouse or something similar is found in a well, and it is not known at what time it fell in, and it is not bloated nor decomposing, then repeat the prayers of a day and a night if ablution was performed in it [water of that well] and wash everything with which the water came into contact. If the mouse has become bloated or decomposed, then repeat the prayers of three days and nights, according to the opinion of Abū Ḥanīfah. Abū Yūsuf and Muḥammad say it is not incumbent upon those who find a mouse or something similar which has become bloated or decomposed in the well to repeat anything until they ascertain the time at which what they found fell in.[23]

It is clear from the opinion of Abū Yūsuf and Muḥammad that the point of repeating prayers is to make up for the fact that the ablutions performed before those prayers were performed with tainted water. Therefore, the number of prayers required to be repeated depends upon how long the water has been tainted with a bloated or decomposing mouse. The opinion of Abū Ḥanīfah is based on the same principle, but rather than determining how long the mouse has been in the well, Abū Ḥanīfah arbitrarily assigns the repeating of three days' worth of prayers.

In other cases, al-Qudūrī uses the juxtaposition of the different opinions to circumscribe the general principle upon which all three authorities agree.

> According to Abū Ḥanīfah and Muḥammad, purification without water [tayammum] is permitted with every type of earth, like dust, sand, rock, gypsum, lime, kohl, and arsenic. Abū Yūsuf says that purification without water is only permitted with dust and fine sand alone.[24]

Here, the more restrictive opinion of Abū Yūsuf evinces the general principle behind the opinion of Abū Ḥanīfah and Muḥammad. Although al-Qudūrī does not make it explicit, both opinions are based on the verses in the Qurʾān, especially that found in sūrat al-māʾidah 5:6, which says purification without water is to be performed with "good earth" [ṣaʿīd ṭayyib].[25] The comparison of the two opinions, however, indicates that the principle on which both are based is that found in the Qurʾān, that purification without water is to be performed with dirt of some type. Abū Ḥanīfah and Muḥammad take this to include several different kinds of earth, whereas Abū Yūsuf restricts the practice to only dust and fine sand. The juxtaposition of these two opinions show that the conflict of opinion here is the result of the authorities applying the same principle differently.

Often, al-Qudūrī uses the outright disagreement of the opinions concerning the definition of a particular practice to demonstrate that the authorities agree of a single general principle.

> Abū Ḥanīfah says that for the small and the large things that the earth sprouts there is a tithe, regardless of whether it is irrigated or watered by the sky, excepting firewood, reed stalks, and grass. Abū Yūsuf and Muḥammad say that the tithe is only required for perennial fruit [meaning produce that retains its character all year long and is not dependent on the sun for ripening, such as wheat, beans, dried dates, spices], when it amounts to five loads, a load being sixty ṣāʿs according to a ṣāʿ of the prophet. According to Abū Yūsuf and Muḥammad there is no tithe for vegetables [meaning nonperennial fruits such as greens like herbs and succulents like cucumbers, and apples]. For all that which is watered by bucket, waterwheel, or waterscoop there is half a tithe according to the opinions of Abū Yūsuf and Muḥammad.[26]

In this case, the practices defined by Abū Ḥanīfah are in direct contradiction to the practices defined by Abū Yūsuf and Muḥammad. Yet, the particular details al-Qudūrī mentions in connection with the different opinions point to a more general principle from which all of the opinions are deduced. Abū Ḥanīfah's excepting of firewood, reed stalks, and grass indicates that items normally not cultivated but picked from the earth growing naturally are not subject to tithe. This means that, according to Abū Ḥanīfah, the produce subject to tithing is that which is cultivated, regardless of whether it is irrigated artificially or naturally. Abū Yūsuf and Muḥammad's juxtaposition of perennial fruit and vegetables, along with their restricting of the tithe to perennial fruits grown in bulk, indicates that the tithe is due only on commercial produce. This distinction is further reinforced by al-Qudūrī's mentioning of the opinion that, regardless of whether it is perennial or not, all produce irrigated by artificial means is subject to half a tithe. The principle in this case is that produce grown for sale, as opposed to that grown for personal consumption, is subject to a tithe.

Although al-Qudūrī's text is dominated by the conflict of Ḥanafī opinions, another technique that al-Qudūrī uses frequently is to present a single Ḥanafī opinion in terms of a conditional statement. Often, al-Qudūrī gives the definition of practice itself as examples of how specific cases are to be evaluated.

> If a person combines [in a sale] a freeperson and a slave or a live and a dead sheep, the sale of both items is invalidated. If a person combines a slave and a slave to be emancipated at its master's death, or his own slave and the slave of another person, the contract concerning the slave that he owns is valid.[27]

Here, the validity of two different types of exchange is defined in terms of specific details having certain results. The details mentioned in the protasis of the first statement, combined with the evaluation mentioned in the apodosis indicate that the exchange of certain items that cannot be sold like a freeperson or are not of any benefit like a dead sheep invalidates the sale. This is emphasized by juxtaposing the first to the second statement, the details of which do not involve unmarketable items but items not owned by the person making the exchange. By stating that the exchange of that item owned by the person making the exchange is valid, al-Qudūrī contrasts the reasoning behind the two statements. The principles behind the two opinions become evident because, although the details in the protases seem similar, the evaluation stated in the apodoses are distinct.

In some cases, al-Qudūrī uses a long string of conditional statements to illustrate the general principle behind the Ḥanafī position.

> If a person buys a heap [of something], on the condition that it is one hundred qafīzes [unit of dry measurement], for one hundred dirhems and then finds the heap to be less, the purchaser has a choice: if he wants he takes the part found missing from his portion from the price, and if he wants he dissolves the sale. If he finds the heap to be more than one hundred qafīzes, then the surplus belongs to the seller.
>
> If a person purchases cloth on the condition that it is ten dhirā's [measurement of length] for ten dirhems, or land on the condition that is one hundred dhirā's for one hundred dirhems, then he finds the cloth or the land to be less, the purchaser has a choice: if he wants he takes it at full price, and if he wants he returns the item [dissolving the sale]. If he finds the cloth or the land to be more than the dhirā's which were specified, then the surplus belongs to the purchaser, the seller having no choice.
>
> If the seller says "I sell you this on the condition that it is one hundred dhirā's for one hundred dirhems, each dhirāʾ for a dirhem," and the purchaser finds it to be less, then he has a choice: if he wants he takes the part found missing from his portion from the price, and if he wants he returns his portion. If he finds it to be in excess, then the purchaser has a choice: if he wants he takes the whole amount, and if he wants he dissolves the sale.[28]

Here, al-Qudūrī juxtaposes three cases with different details. In the first case, the sale of a heap designated to be of a certain amount puts the seller and the purchaser at equal risk. If the heap is not actually the amount designated, the party not receiving an equitable exchange is compensated, or the sale is dissolved and recontracted for a different amount. This is because, without measuring out the exact amount contained in the heap, it is not possible to know, before the exchange, if the heap actually consists of the amount designated. In the second case, each of the parties to the exchange of an item by its length, which can be estimated differently than can the amount of a heap, has no recourse to the other party if the item is not of the specified length. If the item is actually longer, the purchaser gets the extra amount, but if the item is actually shorter, then the seller keeps what amounts to extra compensation, unless the whole sale is dissolved and recontracted. The difference between the two cases is highlighted by the third case, which allows the purchaser recourse if the seller designated the item to be of a certain length without the purchaser being able to verify the claim before the exchange. The reason that neither party has recourse in the second case is that the equivalence of the exchange is established by the contracted item seen by both parties, not its description which is incidental to the exchange. All three cases are based on and thus illustrate the same principle, that to be sound an exchange must be contracted for equivalent values.

In some cases, al-Qudūrī states the general principle outright and then lists a number of conditional statements that demonstrate the practical implications of the principle.

> The fast is the abstinence from eating, drinking, and sex during the day, with intention. If the faster eats, drinks, or has sex out of forgetfulness, he has not broken the fast.
>
> If he sleeps and he has a nocturnal emission, looks at a woman and ejaculates, or anoints himself with oil, cups himself, applies kohl, or kisses, he has not broken the fast. If, by a kiss or a touch, he ejaculates, then making up the fast is incumbent upon him without expiation [for breaking the fast]. There is no harm in the kiss when he is in control of himself, but it is reprehensible if he is not in control of himself.
>
> If he involuntarily vomits, he has not broken the fast. If he vomits on purpose, filling his mouth, then making up the fast is incumbent upon him without expiation. If a person swallows a pebble or a piece of metal, he breaks the fast.

> If a person has sex purposefully in one of the two openings, or eats or drinks that which is nourishing to or therapeutic for him, then making up the fast is incumbent upon him and incumbent is an expiation just like the expiatory fast for making a statement of consanguinity [ẓihār].
>
> If a person has sex with that which has no pudendum, and he ejaculates, making up the fast is incumbent upon him, but no expiation is necessary.
>
> There is expiation for spoiling a fast only during [the month of] Ramaḍān.
>
> If a person injects himself, snuffs, puts drops in his ears, takes internal medicine, or uses cerebral medicine and the medicine reaches his insides or his brain, he has broken the fast.
>
> If he drips from his urethra, he has not broken the fast according to Abū Ḥanīfah, but Abū Yūsuf says that he has broken the fast. If a person tastes something with his mouth, he has not broken the fast, but this is reprehensible for him. It is reprehensible for a woman to chew food for her child when she can avoid it. The chewing of mastic does not break the fast, but it is reprehensible.[29]

As this long list of conditional statements evinces, the general principle that the fast means intentional abstinence from eating, drinking, and sex is subject to interpretation in any number of different situations. For example, what if a person does not intend to have sex, but kisses someone, and on account of that kiss ejaculates? Is it permitted for people to eat nonfood items or to take medicine during the fast? By juxtaposing these different conditions to one another, al-Qudūrī demonstrates the parameters involved in the application of the principle behind the practice of fasting. This range of information provides the reader with examples of how the Ḥanafī authorities go about determining the practical significance of a given principle.

This use of conditional statements to illustrate the practical parameters of a given principle is also operative in al-Qudūrī's description of improbable circumstances.

> If a person who is purified by purification without water sees water during his prayer, his prayer is void. If he sees it after he sits at the point of the testimony [shahādah], or he had wiped his slippers and then the period of his wiping elapses, or he doffs his shoes with a slight action, or he was illiterate and then he knows a verse, or was naked and then finds clothes, or was only able to motion and then is able to perform the bowing and prostration, or he remembers that there is a prayer incumbent upon him before this one, or the prayer leader while reciting becomes impure and appoints an illiterate person as successor, or the sun rises during the dawn prayer, or the time of the afternoon prayer arrives during the congregational prayer, or he was one who wiped his splint and then it fell off on account of the leg being healthy, or he had an excuse and then he lost his excuse, his prayer is invalid according to the opinion of Abū Ḥanīfah. Abū Yūsuf and Muḥammad say his prayer is finished [at that point].[30]

This string of improbable circumstances exemplifies how the Ḥanafī authorities differently apply the same principle. The basic principle is that certain actions invalidate the performance of the prayer, and thus require that the prayer be performed again. For Abū Ḥanīfah, the circumstances listed here constitute a breach of the obligation to pray. Abū Yūsuf and Muḥammad do not want the prayer in which these things occur to continue, but contend that these circumstances do not affect the performance of the actions fundamental to the obligation of prayer, such as the bowing and prostrations.[31] In this case, al-Qudūrī uses a particular collection of conditions to explain how the conflict of opinions is the result of the authorities' different application of the same principle, based on different interpretations of what constitutes the obligation of performing the prayer and what invalidates it.

The *Mukhtaṣar* contains few references to the links between the Ḥanafī opinions cited and the earlier canonical sources. There are two references to the Qurʾān and four references to the sunnah, only two of which include the identity of the person reporting the practice, in the entire text of the *Mukhtaṣar*. The links al-Qudūrī does mention are not used to show the authority of the opinions but to illustrate the sorts of reasoning behind the opinions. At the beginning of the *Mukhtaṣar,* al-Qudūrī mentions both the Qur᾿ān and prophetic practice as the textual bases for the Ḥanafī opinions concerning purity [ṭahārah].

> God the exalted said: "oh you who believe, when you prepare to pray wash your faces and your hands up to the elbows, and wipe your heads and your feet up to the ankles." The obligatory duty [farḍ] of purity is the washing of the three limbs [face, hands, and feet], and the wiping of the head, the elbows and the ankles entering into the wash.[32]

The Ḥanafī opinion concerning the obligatory practice of purification is here shown to be a reiteration of the definition of the practice given in the revelation. This construing of the opinions as a reiteration of the revelation is similar to one of the ways the scholarship of the previous century showed the sunnah to be an interpretation of the Qur᾿ān.[33] A similar technique is used to show that Ḥanafī opinion is based on textual reports of prophetic practice.

> The obligatory duty for wiping the head is to the extent of the forelock because al-Mughīrah b. Shuᶜbah reported that the prophet came to a trash dump, urinated, and performed the ablution [wuḍūᶜ], wiping his forelock and his slippers.[34]

Here, al-Qudūrī indicates that the practice of purification, made obligatory by the revelation, is specified by the practice of the prophet. The sunnah defines further the details of the practice described in the revelation. By mentioning the precedent of both the Qur᾿ān and prophetic practice, al-Qudūrī demonstrates how Ḥanafī opinion interprets the revelation through the medium of the sunnah.

In another case, al-Qudūrī explains how the Ḥanafī opinion, in conflict with the opinions of the other schools' authorities, is based on an interpretation of a particular prophetic precedent. Here, al-Qudūrī explains why the Ḥanafīs permit the exchange at an equal rate, regardless of quality, of certain items sold by dry measure or by weight.

> Everything which the prophet of God fixed as forbidden to be sold at an unequal rate on account of it involving sale by dry measure is always considered forbidden as being sold by dry measure, even if people relinquish selling it by dry measure, such as wheat, barley, dried dates, and salt. All that which he fixed as forbidden to be sold at an unequal rate on account of its involving sale by weight is always considered as being sold by weight, such as gold and silver.[35]

Note that, unlike the references to prophetic practice in al-Ṭaḥāwī's work, al-Qudūrī's reference does not involve a chain of transmission nor does it quote the report of what the prophet said or did. Here, al-Qudūrī states the gist of the various reports of prophetic practice, which al-Ṭaḥāwī lists,[36] as a means to explain the Ḥanafī opinion that, although not made explicit here, is known from other contexts to be in conflict with the opinions of the other schools' authorities, who allow the exchange at an equal rate of different sorts of items.[37] The Ḥanafī opinion, based on the principle that it is dry measure or weight among items of the same species that permits exchange at an equal rate, as opposed to food or nonfood items which benefit people, is explained by al-Qudūrī as a particular interpretation of prophetic practice.

In another case, al-Qudūrī uses a reference to the sunnah to explain the conflict of opinions among the three main Ḥanafī authorities. The opinions are given in the context of al-Qudūrī's discussion of the hermaphrodite.

> When a father dies, leaving a son and a hermaphrodite as descendants, then the assets are divided between them, according to Abū Ḥanīfah, into three portions: two portions to the son and one portion to the hermaphrodite, the hermaphrodite being considered a female according to Abū Ḥanīfah concerning the estate unless it is proven otherwise. Abū Yūsuf and Muḥammad say the hermaphrodite is entitled to half of a male's estate and half of a female's estate. This is the statement of al-Shaᶜbī. Abū Yūsuf and Muḥammad disagree concerning the analogy with al-Shaᶜbī's statement. Abū Yūsuf says the assets are divided between them [two heirs] into seven portions: four to the

> son and three to the hermaphrodite. Muḥammad says the assets are divided between them into twelve portions: seven to the son and five to the hermaphrodite.[38]

In this case, all three Ḥanafī authorities disagree concerning the percentage of an estate given to a hermaphrodite. The opinion of Abū Ḥanīfah, as al-Qudūrī indicates, is based on the assumption that the hermaphrodite is considered a female heir, in which case the hermaphrodite receives one third of the estate. Both the opinions of Abū Yūsuf and al-Shaybānī are based on the statement of the first century authority ᶜAmir b. Sharāḥīl al-Shaᶜbī [d. 103 or 110] that the hermaphrodite is to receive half of what a male heir and half of what a female heir would normally receive. The conflict between Abū Yūsuf and al-Shaybānī's opinions is due to their different application of the same principle mentioned by al-Shaᶜbī. To understand the definition of this single practice, however, one must recognize the different interpretive strategies of the authorities and the different principles from which they deduce their opinions. By making the source of the opinions explicit, al-Qudūrī highlights how the logical decisions of the authorities rather than the "sources" determine the specific definition of practice.

The recognition that the logic of the specific Ḥanafī interpretations define the practical significance of the "sources" is made explicit by al-Qudūrī in two cases. In the first case, al-Qudūrī cites a verse from the Qurʾān as the basis for the stipulation of those people that are to receive the alms collected from the community.

> God the exalted said: "the alms are only for the poor and the destitute . . . [the worker, those whose hearts are reconciled, slaves, debtors, those in the way of God, and the wayfarer—it is an obligatory duty from God]." From these eight types, "those whose hearts are reconciled" is dropped because God empowered Islam and dispensed with needing these people.[39]

Although the Qurʾān clearly states that alms are to be given to these eight types of people, al-Qudūrī claims that only to seven of these types of people are alms to be given. The reasoning given by al-Qudūrī is that God's statement applied to a particular set of historical circumstances that were no longer relevant by the fifth century. The category of "those whose hearts are reconciled," referring to specific groups of people to whom the prophet gave alms for specific reasons, is no longer applicable to the definition of practice.[40] A similar case is made for a statement of the prophet.

> The prophet of God prohibited false bidding, bidding on something already bid for by someone else, preempting imports, a city-dweller selling for a desert-dweller, and selling after the call to prayer of the congregational prayer. All of this is reprehensible, but by it the contract is not spoiled.[41]

Although the prophet prohibited these practices, al-Qudūrī states that they are reprehensible but permitted, the exchange of items in these circumstances being valid.[42] Whereas in the case of the Qur᾿ān, the statement defining practice is simply null, in the case of this report of prophetic practice, the statement of the prophet is still taken to be an indication that certain practices are not encouraged although legitimate. In both cases, the precedent given in the sources is abrogated [mansūkh] by the interpretive decision of later scholarship.[43] With these cases, al-Qudūrī shows how the interpretive reasoning of the opinions is integral to understanding how to apply the revelation.

The work of al-Qudūrī shows that the opinions' definition of practice is not a simple matter of interpreting the revelation. By juxtaposing the opinions to one another in certain ways, al-Qudūrī demonstrates that the Ḥanafī definition of practice is deduced from a set of principles induced from the information in the revelation and the sunnah. The opinions epitomize both what principles are to be induced from the canon, and how to deduce a definition of practice from those principles. Disagreement concerning the application of a given principle is common, and al-Qudūrī uses the disagreement to illustrate the principle on which the authorities agree. The agreement of the authorities on a given principle, however, is on only the most general level. For example, al-Qudūrī shows that although the Ḥanafī authorities agree that prayer is obligatory and that certain things are required for its performance, the authorities disagree over what things are required to satisfy this obligation. The authorities agree that a hermaphrodite is to be treated differently than a male heir, but they disagree whether to treat it as a female heir or a half-male and half-female heir. In this way, al-Qudūrī's work proves the significance of the Ḥanafī opinions as an epitome of how to derive a definition of practice from the canon. By construing the opinions as different examples of "acceptable" interpretations, al-Qudūrī makes the opinions to provide a rudimentary methodological framework for explaining how the opinions apply the canon. In the course of the fifth and sixth centuries, this framework is developed to theorize about the sorts of interpretive reasoning characteristic of the Ḥanafī opinions.

II

Logical Structure of the Opinions

Contemporaneous with the work of al-Qudūrī, the work of al-Dabūsī also emphasizes the logical basis of the corpus of Ḥanafī opinions. In his *Taʾsīs al-naẓar,* al-Dabūsī develops the rudimentary methodological framework employed by al-Qudūrī to distinguish the sorts of reasoning used by the Ḥanafī authorities. He illustrates the logical basis of the opinions by focusing exclusively upon the conflict both between the Ḥanafī authorities and those of other local authorities, and among the three main Ḥanafī authorities themselves. Like the *Mukhtaṣar* of al-Qudūrī, the *Taʾsīs* illustrates the logic peculiar to the different authorities' opinions by giving a series of conditional statements that delimit the parameters of the conflict. The *Taʾsīs,* however, organized according to the general explanations of the reasoning responsible for the conflict of opinions, goes beyond the *Muktaṣar* in providing an overview of the different logical assumptions that distinguish the opinions of the different authorities. The claim of al-Dabūsī is that the Ḥanafī opinions exhibit the sort of logic required to determine the practical significance of the canon. To understand the practical significance of the revelation, one must understand from the corpus of opinions how the different authorities take certain logical considerations into account when defining practice.

Building upon the ikhtilāf works of al-Ṭaḥāwī, al-Jaṣṣāṣ, and al-Qudūrī, al-Dabūsī demonstrates that, although the different schools' authorities agree on the use of the Qur$^{\supset}$ān and the sunnah as canon and agree on the sorts of methods used to interpret this canon, they disagree over how the canon is to be applied to different cases. According to al-Dabūsī, the opinions of the different authorities are, in theory, deduced from the same principles the prophet induced from the revelation, but the authorities disagree over which principles to use in a given case and how a given principle is to be understood in light of the particulars of specific cases. On the most general level, the authorities of the different schools disagree over which principles to apply to similar cases. The opinions of Mālik and al-Shāfi^{c}ī are shown to be in conflict with the opinions of the Ḥanafī authorities because they are deduced from different principles. On a more specific level, al-Dabūsī shows the opinions of Zufar and Ibn Abī Laylā to conflict with the opinions of the three main Ḥanafī authorities not in principles but in the application of the principles. These opinions more closely connected to the Ḥanafī school because of their association with the Kūfan tradition of fiqh scholarship, are the result of different deductions from the same principles from which the three main Ḥanafī authorities' opinions are deduced. On the most specific level, the opinions of Abū Ḥanīfah, Abū Yūsuf, and Muḥammad al-Shaybānī agree both in principle and in deduction. The conflict among the Ḥanafī opinions is due, according to al-Dabūsī, to the authorities' different interpretations of the specific circumstances to which the practice deduced from a given principle is applied (see Figure 3.1).

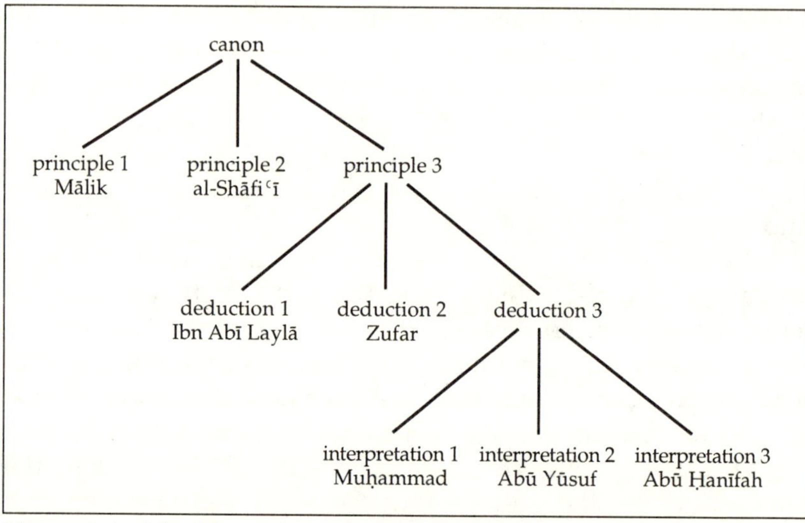

Figure 3.1. The hierarchy indicated by the reasons for the conflict of opinions between the authorities of the different schools, the Kūfan authorities, and the Ḥanafī authorities.

In this way, al-Dabūsī uses the conflict among the opinions to outline a hierarchy of the reasoning responsible for the different definitions of practice. This scheme also provides a means for determining the epistemological basis of a given opinion, relative to the sort of reasoning used by a given authority to interpret the principles induced from the revelation.

On the most general level, al-Dabūsī shows that the opinions of the different schools' authorities conflict over which principles are to be applied to given cases. For example, al-Dabūsī contends that the conflict of opinion between the Ḥanafī authorities and Mālik is due, in part, to the difference between how the Ḥanafīs and Mālik establish the principle relevant to the same cases.

> According to our three scholars a report transmitted on the authority of the prophet by means of a single transmission [khabr al-āḥād] is established in the place of sound analogy [qiyās ṣaḥīḥ]. According to Mālik sound analogy is established in the place of a report by means of a single transmission.[44]

This general statement explaining one of the reasons for the conflict of opinions is followed by conditional statements exemplifying how the authorities' use of different principles affects their definitions of practice.

> Our companions say that semen is a physical impurity which must be purified by rubbing the [effected] cloth when it [semen] is dry. We take this from a report. According to Mālik, it is not purified except by washing with water, like [is the case with] urine.[45]

> Our companions say that it is not permitted for a slave to marry more than two wives. We take this from a report. Mālik says he is permitted to marry four like a freeman. He takes this from analogy.[46]

In these two examples, al-Dabūsī demonstrates how the Ḥanafī opinion, deduced from a principle taken from a report of prophetic practice, conflicts with the opinion of Mālik, deduced from a principle taken from an analogous case. Mālik requires washing dried semen out of clothes with water because urine is to be washed out of clothes with water, just as he allows a slave to marry four wives because a freeman is allowed to marry four wives. In both cases, the Ḥanafīs differ because of a prophetic precedent that was reported to them.

The conflict between the Ḥanafīs and Mālik, in this case, is explained in terms of a disagreement over the evaluation of the relative authority of different sources. Mālik considers a report of prophetic practice preserved by a single transmission to be less reliable than using analogy to determine the revelatory principle relevant to defining the particular practices. Despite his reference to the evaluation of the sources, al-Dabūsī's emphasis is not on the opinion's relation to the sources, but on the logical considerations of the different authorities that are authoritative because they are derived from the sources. Note that al-Dabūsī does not give the text of the report on which the Ḥanafī authorities' opinion is based. Throughout his work, al-Dabūsī assumes the interpretation of the particular report to yield the principle used by the Ḥanafī authorities. In some cases, though, al-Dabūsī does mention the companion of the prophet on whose authority the practice is reported.

> Our companions say that a group of people kill as a single person. We take this from the report of ᶜUmar b. al-Khaṭṭāb. According to Mālik [a group] does not kill as one. He takes this by analogy and disregards the report.[47]

In cases like this, perhaps cases in which the transmission of the report is questionable,[48] al-Dabūsī cites the transmitter to reiterate the Ḥanafī claim that although these reports are supported by only a single transmission, they are considered to go back to the prophet and are thus better indicators than is analogy of what principle is to be applied in a given case. Here, al-Dabūsī remarks that although Mālik normally relies on reports of prophetic practice given on the authority of ᶜUmar b. al-Khaṭṭāb, because of his practice of using analogy rather than reports supported by a single transmission he differs in principle from the Ḥanafīs.

This same sort of distinction between principles is used by al-Dabūsī to explain the conflict of opinion between the Ḥanafīs and al-Shāfiᶜī. In one case, al-Dabūsī shows that the conflict of opinions is the result of the Ḥanafīs and al-Shāfiᶜī using principles derived from different sources.

> According to our companions, the opinion of a companion is used instead of analogy when it does not conflict with the opinion of [another companion] of the same rank. This is when it cannot be said that his opinion is by means of analogy because analogy [would yield] a conflicting opinion, and it cannot be said that his opinion is haphazard. Therefore, it is evident that his opinion was heard from the prophet of God. According to Abū ᶜAbdallāh al-Shāfiᶜī analogy is used instead [of the companion's opinion] because he does not regard the imitation of a companion [as authoritative] and thus does not accept his opinion.[49]

The conflict here is again cast in terms of a disagreement over the authoritative status of different sources. In this case, the different logical considerations of the two sides are justified by conflicting claims about the authority of different sources of prophetic precedent. The different logical considerations are evident from the example of several specific cases.

> A sheep is required for a person who requires of himself to slaughter his son. We take this from the opinion of Ibn ᶜAbbās. According to Abū Yūsuf and al-Shāfiᶜī, nothing is incumbent upon the person. This is taken from an analogy.[50]

In this example, al-Dabūsī explains the logical considerations of the different opinions in terms of the authorities' appeal to different principles. The Ḥanafī authorities, minus Abū Yūsuf, appeal to the practice of the companion Ibn ᶜAbbās to keep from concluding that the person is required to sacrifice his son. Abū Yūsuf and al-Shāfiᶜī argue that a person requiring himself to sacrifice his son is invalid and thus, like other oaths invalidated by the specifics of what is promised, requires nothing of the person making the oath. This example shows that, for al-Shāfiᶜī, it is better to deduce an opinion from a principle taken from an unrelated but analogous case of prophetic practice than to deduce an opinion from a principle taken from the practice of a companion. The Ḥanafī authorities would rather base their opinion on the practice of a companion than use analogy, in the case that it is evident that the practice of a companion itself is based directly on the practice of the prophet. Thus, although the Ḥanafīs and al-Shāfiᶜī agree that a person who obligates himself to sacrifice his son should not carry out the obligation, because they appeal to different sources and thus different principles, their definitions of this practice are in conflict.

In another case, al-Dabūsī shows that the conflict of opinion due to the use of different principles is often particular to defining a specific practice. This is evident from al-Dabūsī's discussion of the conflict over the principle operative in the determination of kinship.

> According to us, the consideration in establishing kinship is the soundness of the bed, establishing the husband's relationship to his house. It is not based on sex. According to al-Shāfiᶜī, the consideration in kinship is actual sex.

> If a person marries a woman, and he is gone from her for two years and [during that time] she bears a child, the kinship is established with her husband because it is his bed and he is [the husband] of the house establishing kinship. According to al-Shāfi^{c}ī, the kinship is not established with the husband when it is not possible for him to have had the sex [which produced the child].[51]

In this case, because the conflict is limited to the definition of establishing kinship, al-Dabūsī does not characterize the disagreement in the general terms of the two sides appealing to the authority of different sources. Here, as in the previous cases, al-Dabūsī's main focus is on the logical basis of the opinions. Although al-Dabūsī does not mention the sources from which the different positions were derived,[52] he clearly states the different principles used by the different authorities in this particular case. It is also evident from the example that the Ḥanafīs determine kinship on the basis of the relationship of the man to the woman who bore the child, not on the basis of whether that man is the biological father of the child as is the basis for al-Shāfi^{c}ī's opinion.

On a less general level than the conflict between the authorities of the different schools, al-Dabūsī discusses the conflict between the different local authorities associated with second century Kūfah. Unlike the conflict between the different schools' authorities, which is a conflict over principles and sources, the conflict between the Kūfan authorities is due to the deduction of different conclusions from the same principles (see Figure 3.2).

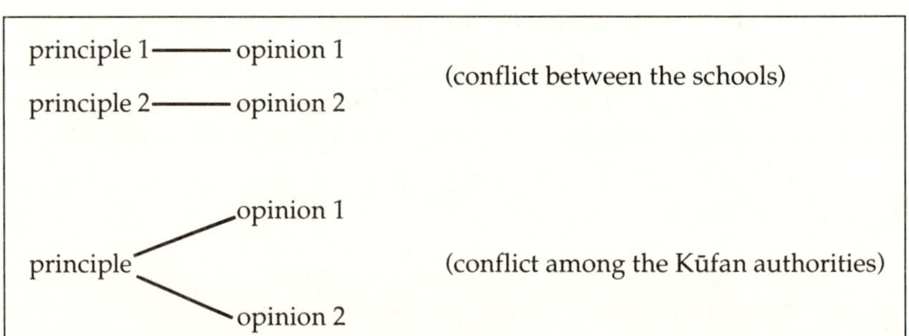

Figure 3.2. How al-Dabūsī distinguishes the conflict of opinion between the schools and the conflict among the Kūfan authorities.

According to al-Dabūsī, the difference between the deductions of the main three Ḥanafī authorities and those of Ibn Abī Laylā and Zufar is one of degree. As a general rule, Ibn Abī Laylā and Zufar apply the principles directly to the specific cases of practice. In those cases where there is disagreement with Ibn Abī Laylā and Zufar, the main three Ḥanafī authorities make exceptions or take "local" details into account in specific cases (see Figure 3.3).

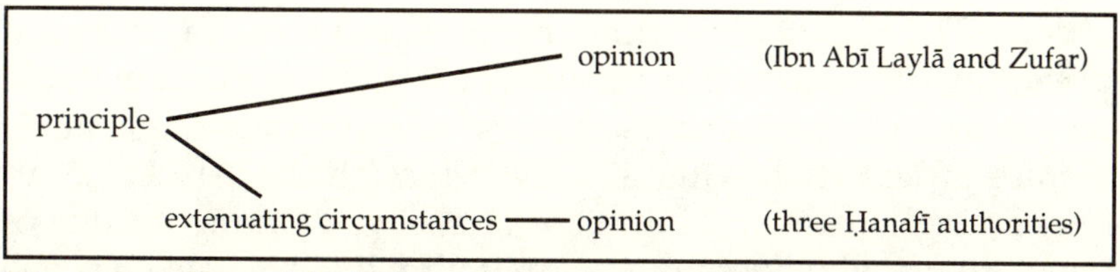

Figure 3.3. How al-Dabūsī explains that the conflicting opinions of the Kūfan authorities are deduced from the same principles.

Because of this agreement on a general level, the conflict of opinions among the Kūfan authorities is limited to the disagreement over the details of specific cases. The general reasons given by al-Dabūsī for the conflict of opinions is followed by only a few examples relating to a limited range of cases.

Ibn Abī Laylā's application of principles in a manner more direct than that of the three Ḥanafī authorities is evident from al-Dabūsī's discussion of the disagreement over the significance of personal legal responsibility.

> According to Ibn Abī Laylā, if a person has authority over something in himself, the authority of its proxy is to no one else. According to us, it is permitted to be authorized in some situations and not in others.
>
> Our companions say that testimony is not permitted to be the testimony of one man but only of two men. According to Ibn Abī Laylā, it is permitted because the authority to establish testimony is to him alone. He has the authority to establish it on his own account.

> Our companions say that when a slave works for a partner who does not manumit slaves, he does not claim restitution from the manumitter [be manumitted by the other partner]. According to Ibn Abī Laylā, the slave claims restitution from the manumitter because the nonmanumitter has charge of the joint responsibility and thus the authority of the proxy [of the slave] is to no one else, but is established on his account alone.[53]

Here, the disagreement is a matter of a general versus a more limited application of the same principle. Ibn Abī Laylā holds that, in general, a single person is legally responsible for his actions. The Ḥanafī authorities, claim that in some cases, exemplified by the cased cited by al-Dabūsī, the actions of a single person are not sufficient. In the case of testimony, the Ḥanafīs require at least two witnesses, even though Ibn Abī Laylā allows a single witness. In the case of a slave working for one of two partners who does not manumit him, Ibn Abī Laylā has one partner manumit the slave, but the Ḥanafīs do not allow the unilateral manumission because that would put the financial responsibility of the slave upon only one of the slave's two owners. The Ḥanafīs make a distinction between a person's legal responsibility to his slave and a person's financial responsibility to his partner, whereas Ibn Abī Laylā insists that the practice in this case must reflect the general principle without allowing for other variables.

This same insistence on individual cases directly conforming to the relevant principle is illustrated by al-Dabūsī in his discussion of the conflict over what dissolves a contracted exchange. Unlike the principle of a person's legal responsibility, which cuts across any number of practices, in some cases the conflict over the different application of the same principle is limited to the definition of a specific type of practice.

> According to Ibn Abī Laylā, in the context of defining social practice [bāb muʿāmalāt], when part of something is dissolved, the whole thing is dissolved.

> According to Ibn Abī Laylā, in the case of an item of delayed delivery, when part of the capital is left and a person

> takes only part of the item of delayed delivery, it is not permitted and the delayed delivery is dissolved because it was dissolved for the part he took, and therefore it is dissolved concerning the part that remained. According to us, it is not dissolved concerning the part that remains.[54]

Again, al-Dabūsī shows that Ibn Abī Laylā's opinions result from a somewhat indiscriminate application of the principle that certain actions taken in the course of an exchange cause the exchange to be invalid and thus dissolved. The Ḥanafī opinions likewise take this principle to be operative, but allow that those parts of the exchange that have not been effected by the invalidating actions are still subject to a valid exchange, and thus the exchange as a whole is not dissolved by its partial dissolution. Ibn Abī Laylā's opinions reflect more directly the principle used, whereas the Ḥanafī opinions reflect a more complicated set of logical considerations beyond the general level of the principle.

In the conflict between the opinions of Zufar and the main three Ḥanafī authorities, al-Dabūsī displays a similar distinction between the more and less discriminate application of principles. According to al-Dabūsī, the opinions of Zufar are often in conflict with those of the other Ḥanafī authorities because Zufar does not allow for other considerations specific to the circumstances to affect the application of principles. The conflict of Zufar's opinions are divided into five sections by al-Dabūsī, the first two of which discuss Zufar's not allowing exceptions that are allowed by the other Ḥanafī authorities. In some cases, this means that Zufar's opinions are more lenient than those of the other Ḥanafī authorities.

> According to our three companions, when something is established in the place of something else in the performance [of a particular practice], it is not established in its place in all performances [of that practice]. According to Zufar, it is established in its place in all performances.[55]

> When a man, performing the bowing and prostration, imitates someone performing them with [just] his head, it is not permitted according to us because the motions for the

> one [using just his head] is the performance established as permitted for him [alone] and not established for the performance of anyone else. According to Zufar, when this is established as permitted in one person's prayer, it is established as permitted in the prayer of others.[56]

Because Zufar insists on the strict application of the principle, he does not distinguish between the principle and the circumstances peculiar to the specific case. Zufar allows people to perform the prayer, imitating someone motioning just with his head, on the principle that such prayer is allowed. The other Ḥanafī authorities do not allow people to forgo the bowing and prostration unless they must because of a physical disability. According to the opinion of the three main Ḥanafī authorities, performing the prayer with head motions is permitted in the place of the bowing and prostration as an exception, not as a general rule. So, even though Zufar's opinion clearly demonstrates that it is permitted to perform the prayer with head motions instead of the bowing and prostration, his opinion allows in general a practice that should be permitted only in exceptional cases.

In other cases, the fact that Zufar does not recognize exceptions made for extenuating circumstances makes his definition of practice to be stricter than that of the other Ḥanafī authorities.

> According to our three companions, it is permitted to suspend a stipulated practice in cases of things contracted and other cases in which the intention does occur by the things being done. According to Zufar, when something is set as permitted or spoiled, it is not to be transferred from that state when the intention occurs by the things being done unless it is renewed or performed over again.
>
> When a person sells a slave with the stipulation of choice [sharṭ al-khiyār], and subsequently the day of breaking the fast comes, the person suspends giving the alms for breaking the fast until he clears up this matter of the slave with the owner. According to Zufar, he does not suspend the giving of alms, but he is required to make the choice [about who owns the slave], because incumbent upon the owner of the slave are alms for the slave.

> When a person sells a reprehensible thing, the sale is suspended until the item becomes satisfactory. If the exchange is made satisfactory, it is permitted. If it is not satisfactory, it is not permitted. According to Zufar, the sale is spoiled even if the reprehensible exchange is later made satisfactory because once established as spoiled the sale does not return to being permitted, unless it is recontracted.[57]

The main three Ḥanafī authorities allow a person to put off giving alms for the breaking of the Ramaḍān fast when the extent of that person's possessions is unclear, in this case because the sale of the slave is still pending. This is because, if the person owned the slave, he would be responsible for fulfilling the slave's obligation to pay alms, paying alms on behalf of that slave. Zufar insists that the almsgiving must be performed, but he also recognizes the problem inherent in a person assessing the amount of alms due when the extent of his possessions is not established. Rather than allowing the suspension of the almsgiving, Zufar requires the choice stipulated in the sale to be made at that time and the exchange concluded. The same reasoning is evident from the second example in which Zufar insists that an unequitable exchange is to be recontracted even if the exchange can be made equitable. Zufar demands a stricter application of the principle, whereas the other three Ḥanafī authorities allow certain practices as long as they eventually result in people fulfilling what the principle obligates.

In the last three sections describing the conflict of Zufar's opinions, al-Dabūsī illustrates how Zufar's insistence on the strict application of principles results in the impractical definition of practice.

> According to our companions, that which is not specifically stated for the different parts but is required for part of something, is like that which is required for all of it. According to Zufar, that required for part of something is not like that which is required for all of it.

> If a person gives his slave permission in one type of commerce, he becomes authorized in all types. According to Zufar, he does not become authorized except in that one type in which his owner authorized him.[58]

Here, Zufar insists on the strict application of the principle that a slave can act as the agent of his master in those cases the master has specified. The other three Ḥanafī authorities consider the authorization of a specific type of activity to satisfy this principle and thus allow activity of that type in general.

> According to our companions, conflict in a description is not taken into consideration. According to Zufar, it is taken into consideration.
>
> Our companions say that when one of two witnesses testifies that he divorced his wife by an unconditional divorce, and the other testifies that he divorced her by a revocable divorce, the testimony that he divorced her by a revocable divorce is accepted. Zufar does not accept [either of] the two testimonies.[59]

In this case, because Zufar insists that the two witnesses must agree in their description of the type of divorce made, the general testimony on which the two witnesses do agree, that the man divorced his wife, is not to be accepted. The other three Ḥanafī authorities accept the least harsh of the two types of divorce to which was testified.

> According to our three companions, if there is a little of some things, the person is excused from them. According to Zufar, there is no excuse from them.
>
> If a person had prayed on the ground and there was in the ground wine, vomit, urine, or some excuseable thing, it being dry and all traces of it being gone, his prayer is permitted according to us because the ground has dried up the physical impurity and none remained except as an insignificant amount. There is excuse from an insignificant amount. According to Zufar, his prayer is ruined because what remains of the physical impurity is incumbent upon the person [who prayed on the effected ground]. Even if it is a little, there is no excuse from it.[60]

Again, Zufar's insistence upon the principle that certain things are physical impurities keeps him from permitting the carrying out of an obligated practice even if there is no longer any trace of the physical impurities. Because they focus on certain principles, without regard for the local details that affect the practical significance of those principles, Zufar's opinions are untenable in relation to the opinions of the other three Ḥanafī authorities. Although both Ibn Abī Laylā and Zufar agree with the three main Ḥanafī authorities in principle, al-Dabūsī shows that their definition of practice is not as nuanced, and therefore less appropriate to the circumstances than that of the three main Ḥanafī authorities.

On the most specific level, al-Dabūsī demonstrates that the conflict of opinion among the three main Ḥanafī authorities is the result of their differing interpretations of the particular details involved in the circumstances to which a given principle is applied. All three of the authorities agree both on which principles are to be used in the definition of a given practice and that the application of these principles is to be mediated by the extenuating circumstances of specific cases. The cases in which they disagree are due to the authorities' different evaluation of the relevant extenuating circumstances. In various cases, the authorities interpret differently the relative weight of certain variables in limiting or extending the application of a given principle. Ultimately, though, al-Dabūsī shows that conflict among the three Ḥanafī authorities over circumstantial details is less significant than their agreement on the sort of logical equilibrium that results from the "just" application of the principles to specific circumstances.

This characterization of the Ḥanafī opinions is illustrated by al-Dabūsī in a case similar to the one in which Ibn Abī Laylā claims that the partial dissolution of an exchange results in the dissolution of the whole exchange. The Ḥanafīs disagree with Ibn Abī Laylā, claiming that only the portion of the exchange that is spoiled is to be dissolved. In the case here, al-Dabūsī further qualifies the Ḥanafī position.

> According to Abū Ḥanīfah, when a contract includes something that spoils most of the exchange, it is required to be considered spoiled in all of it. This is just like if a man had sold two slaves in one deal for a thousand dirhems, then it

> became apparent that one of the two was free, the contract is spoiled. According to Abū Ḥanīfah's companions, the exchange is permitted for the portion of the [one person that is a] slave.[61]

Unlike the example of delayed delivery given in the context of the conflict with Ibn Abī Laylā's opinion, here one half of the items being purchased, the free person, is not a valid item of sale. Abū Ḥanīfah and his companions agree that a partially spoiled sale should not invalidate the whole sale, but they disagree over what constitutes "partial," for the sake of allowing the otherwise strict application of the principle that the exchange of certain items spoils the sale. The same disagreement is illustrated by al-Dabūsī in the case of an exchange involving delayed delivery.

> When a man makes a delayed delivery of wheat for barley and oil, it is not permitted according to Abū Ḥanīfah and Abū ᶜAbdallāh [al-Shāfiᶜī] because the delayed delivery of wheat for barley [which is not permitted] is more prevalent than the rest [of the exchange] and therefore pervades the whole sale. According to the other two authorities, the exchange for the portion of the oil is permitted.[62]

The Ḥanafīs agree that the delayed delivery of wheat for barley is not permitted, because to avoid usury, items exchanged at a delayed time must be of the same species. Moreover, the Ḥanafīs agree that the principle of certain items spoiling a sale should not be strictly applied to require the spoiling of the whole sale when only part of the items are invalid. As in the previous one, here Abū Ḥanīfah contends that because the exchange of wheat for barley with a delayed delivery is invalid, so the exchange for the oil is also invalid. Abū Yūsuf and Muḥammad allow the exchange of the wheat for the oil, disregarding the barley as the invalid portion of the exchange. In both cases, al-Dabūsī indicates that Abū Ḥanīfah stresses the prohibition required by the principle, whereas Abū Yūsuf and Muḥammad stress the specific aspect of the exchange that is allowed.

This same sort of disagreement over the relative emphasis of the details of a specific case is evident from another group of examples given by al-Dabūsī.

> According to Abū Ḥanīfah, that which includes language by means of general things is not like that which includes language by means of a statement with specific things. This is like when a person has three slaves and he says you [plural] are free except for Sālim, the freedom of the two is sound. If he had said Sālim is free, Bazīᶜ is free, and Mubārak is free, except for Sālim, then it is not sound. This is likewise the case [if he says] those [plural but not dual] are free except for Bazīᶜ, it is not sound. According to the other two authorities, that which includes language by means of general things is like that which includes language by means of a statement with specific things.[63]

Here, the general explanation given by al-Dabūsī is illustrated by an example involving the specificities of Arabic grammar. Both Abū Yūsuf and Muḥammad do not allow a general statement to be excepted by a more specific statement. Abū Ḥanīfah, however, allows a person to make an exception to a general statement, but he does not allow a specific statement to be excepted by another specific statement, such as "you are free, except for you." The same evaluation of general and specific statements works the other way around as well.

> When a man requires of himself to walk to the sacred area or to the mosque of the sacred area, according to Abū Ḥanīfah, it is not incumbent upon him because that which includes general things does not make it like a specific case. . . . According to the other two authorities, it is incumbent upon the man, whether it is the pilgrimage or the lesser pilgrimage, because it is made like a specific obligation for him . . .[64]

From this example, it is clear that Abū Ḥanīfah does not consider the specific wording of a person's obligation to require other than the general obligation required of all people. This is because the specific statement, although allowed to make an exception to a general rule, is not equivalent with the general rule and therefore does not require more than what is required by the general rule. Abū Yūsuf and Muḥammad regard both the general and the specific obligation to be of equal weight and thus require the pilgrim to walk if he specifies walking as his obligation. As al-Dabūsī shows from these cases, the conflict among the Ḥanafī opinions is a consequence of their differing local interpretations of language usage in specific cases.

Often, al-Dabūsī shows, the authorities' divergent evaluations of specific circumstances is a result of the authorities different local experiences. Although the authorities may agree, in principle and in application, on the definition of a particular practice, they disagree simply because they regard certain details to refer to different things.

> When something predominates in the existence of things, it becomes the precedent even if it is not found [there in all cases] like regarding the sleeper as having become impure from having sexual intercourse [during the night] because it [having sex] is predominate for people in this state and thus the sleeper is considered to have been effected even if he was not [in actuality].[65]

> If a person prays on a boat, is afraid for himself [that he might fall off], and so motions with his head [instead of bowing and prostrating], his prayer is permitted according to Abū Ḥanīfah because the motioning of the head predominates on boats and so this becomes his legal state even if it was not the case [that he was afraid of falling off]. According to the other two authorities, his prayer is not permitted.[66]

In these two cases, the experience of Abū Ḥanīfah causes him, for the purpose of defining practice, to consider all sleeping people as having had sex, and all people on boats to be afraid of falling off. Abū Yūsuf and Muḥammad do not necessarily regard sleep as indicating sex and a boat ride as indicating fear, but make a distinction among the different experiences of the different people who sleep and ride on boats. A similar divergence in how the authorities understand specific things is illustrated by al-Dabūsī in the discussion of intoxicating fruit juices.

> According to Abū Ḥanīfah and Abū Yūsuf, all juice extracted with water and then cooked or used in cooking, in a small amount, is not an intoxicating liquor, and is permitted, like treacle and pulp.

> Abū Ḥanīfah and Abū Yūsuf say that the infusion of dried grapes and dates, when it is cooked, is permitted to be drunk for medical purposes and for spicing food. According to Muḥammad and al-Shāfiʿī, it is not allowed to be drunk, when it is strong, for medical purposes and for spicing food.
>
> Abū Ḥanīfah and Abū Yūsuf say that grape juice, when it is cooked so that two thirds evaporate but a third remains, or a third evaporates then water is added to it and it is boiled on the fire, or it does not boil but the fire is hot enough for it to boil, and it is then strong, it is permitted to be drunk for medical purposes and for spicing food because the remaining is that to which water was added until the mixture became under the regimen of dried grapes and dried dates. This is specified by Abū Yūsuf. According to Muḥammad and al-Shāfiʿī it is not allowed to be drunk.
>
> Abū Ḥanīfah and Abū Yūsuf say that the skin of grapes, after the juice has been drained, when water squirts from them after the juice has been extracted with water, and they are cooked over a fire, and are left until the mixture becomes strong and boils, if it boils a little it is not considered to be an intoxicating liquor. According to Muḥammad, in either case it is forbidden.[67]

Here, the authorities disagree because of their different assumptions regarding what constitutes an intoxicating liquor made from fruit juice, when it is used for medical or cooking purposes. Apparently, Abū Ḥanīfah and Abū Yūsuf allow certain concoctions not considered to be sufficiently intoxicating, which Muḥammad does not allow, on the basis of their particular experiences.

The work of al-Dabūsī demonstrates how certain logical considerations, working on different levels depending upon the authorities being discussed, result in the conflicting definitions of practice. Although the different authorities share an adherence to a common epistemological basis that guarantees their opinions to be interpretations of the same canon, they take different principles to apply to a given set of circumstances, the details of which themselves are taken to be of different significance. By distinguishing three levels of conflict among the authorities, al-Dabūsī is able to isolate the logic characteristic of the Ḥanafī opinions. The focus on the corpus of Ḥanafī opinions as an epitome of how to interpret the revelation required fifth century scholarship to explain how the conflict between Abū Ḥanīfah and Abū Yūsuf is different from the conflict between Abū Ḥanīfah and Ibn Abī Laylā or al-Shāfiʿī. To explain these differences, al-Dabūsī shows that the specific logical considerations of particular cases indicate the more general bases for the conflicting opinions. To understand how the opinions epitomize the interpretation of the revelation, one must understand what is peculiar to the reasoning of the different authorities in different cases. By understanding the differences in detail, one can determine whether the opinions are based on different principles from different sources, or just different interpretations of the details specific to one case. This more theoretical analysis of the Ḥanafī corpus of opinions focused subsequent scholarship not upon the opinions themselves, but upon the types of interpretive logic they represented.

III

Inductive Logic of the Opinions

The monumental work of al-Sarakhsī, written at the end of the fifth century, formalized the distinction between the textual basis of authority and the logical basis of the reasoning required to interpret the revelation. Building on the theoretical advances of al-Dabūsī and al-Qudūrī, al-Sarakhsī contends that the significance of the Ḥanafī opinions as a canon is to be found in how they epitomize the different logical considerations affecting the induction of principles from the revelation. The principles from which a definition of practice is to be deduced are only rarely explicit from the text of the revelation or even from the application of them in the sunnah. To disclose the principles and define practice requires interpretive reasoning that, although authorized by the revelation through the medium of the sunnah, is of a logical rather than textual character. For al-Sarakhsī, this means that, to understand the practical significance of the revelation, one must first understand the logical considerations behind the opinions of certain local authorities. Ḥanafī scholars must read backward from the logic of the corpus of Ḥanafī opinions to the text of the revelation.

According to al-Sarakhsī, the corpus of Ḥanafī opinions is deduced from a set of principles induced from the revelation through the medium of the sunnah (see Figure 3.4).[68] Through the medium of the sunnah means that the Ḥanafī authorities interpret the revelation using the same methods that the prophet did and thus deduce practice from the same principles from which the prophet deduced his sunnah.

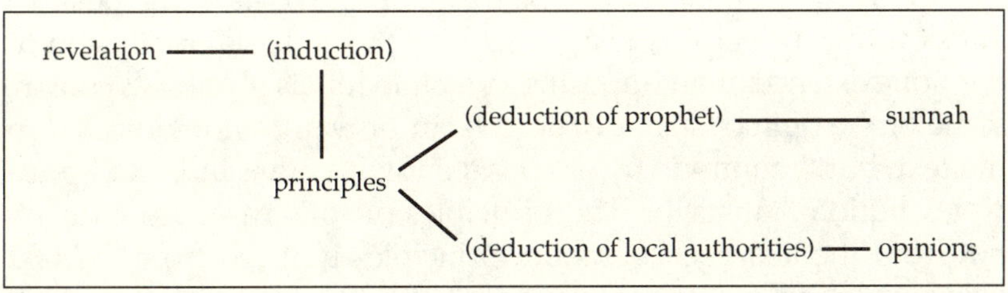

Figure 3.4. How the opinions are deduced from the principles the prophet induced from the revelation and from which the prophet deduced his sunnah.

This claim is a continuation of the theories developed in the third and fourth centuries that claimed that because the sunnah did not contradict the revelation, the reasoning used to resolve apparent contradictions was the sort of reasoning the prophet used to interpret the revelation. The contents of the sunnah were explained as having been deduced from principles induced from the revelation. The interpretive reasoning used to show that the opinions of the local authorities do not contradict the sunnah and thus the revelation indicates the methods used by the authorities in deducing a definition of practice from the principles the prophet induced from the revelation.

According to al-Sarakhsī, the interpretive reasoning epitomized by the Ḥanafī opinions shows that the principles from which the definition of practice is deduced are induced from the revelation using four main methods.[69] The first three of these methods are similar to the ways al-Shāfiʿī claimed that the sunnah interpreted the revelation. First, some of the opinions are deduced from principles that are explicit in the text of the revelation [ʿibārat al-naṣṣ].[70] Second, some of the opinions are deduced from principles that are only indicated in the language of the text [ishārat al-naṣṣ].[71] These principles are disclosed from the text by analyzing the language used in particular verses. Third, some of the opinions are deduced from principles to which the text alludes by mentioning specific examples based on a nonexplicit principle [dalālat al-naṣṣ].[72] In this case, the principle is induced from the text using analogical reasoning [qiyās].[73] The analogy can be made on the basis of the positive allusion to a principle [qiyās al-jalī] or on the basis of allusion to the nonexistence of an opposing principle [qiyās al-ʿaks].[74] Fourth, some of the opinions are deduced from principles not indicated in the text, but "required" by or consistent with other indicated principles [iqtiḍāʾ al-naṣṣ].[75] The principles, in this case, are induced not from the text itself but from principles induced from the text using analogical reasoning [qiyās al-khafī]. This final method, which generally means extending the sunnah to include the practice of the companions, allows the authorities to reason on the basis of what they consider to be proper [istiḥsān], or in the interest of public welfare [istiṣlāḥ], from the most general of principles behind the normal principles.[76]

It is important to stress that al-Sarakhsī outlines this methodology not primarily as a prescription, but as an ex post facto explanation of how the logical considerations of the Ḥanafī authorities are linked to the revelation.[77] The *Mabsūṭ* of al-Sarakhsī is a sustained attempt (thirty volumes) to show how certain logical considerations, characteristic of the Ḥanafī opinions, determine the interpretation of the revelation. In this work, al-Sarakhsī shows that, although the epistemology of the opinions originates with the revelation, understanding the significance of the revelation originates with the opinions (see Figure 3.5).

Epistemology	Methodology
revelation	logic
principle	deduction
opinion	induction

Figure 3.5. How the methodology of the opinions is the inverse of their epistemological status.

The authority of the opinions is their link to the revelation, but the significance of the revelation is how it is used by the opinions. References to the textual indication of a principle do not explain how a particular opinion is reached but only that it is ultimately derived from the text of the revelation. Only indirectly, through the medium of a principle that must be induced from the revelation and through the medium of the particular interpretation of that principle's range of practical application, are the opinions tied to the text of the revelation.

This distinction between the textual basis of the epistemology and the logical basis of the methodology is exemplified in how al-Sarakhsī explains individual cases of the Ḥanafī definition of practice. In his discussion of hunting in the sacred area, al-Sarakhsī shows that the determination of what occasions blame for killing prey is predicated on the logical considerations involved in assessing "agency" or who and what actions led to the killing of the prey. Although the prohibition against killing prey in the sacred area is supposed to originate with the text of the revelation, the reasoning necessary to understand why the killing is prohibited and therefore what particular actions require a penalty is to be found in the logic of the opinions rather than the text. To distinguish this logic, al-Sarakhsī compares the Ḥanafī opinions on specific "test cases" to the opinions of al-Shāfiᶜī.

> If a sacralized person points to prey, whether inside or outside of the sacred area, and the prey to which he pointed is killed, then incumbent upon the person who pointed is a penalty, according to us, according to what is considered proper [istiḥsān].

> According to analogy [qiyās] there is no penalty incumbent upon the person who pointed. This is accepted by al-Shāfiʿī, because the penalty is required for the killing of the prey in the text. God says: "if one of you kill it intentionally . . ." Pointing is not in the meaning of killing because killing is an action tied to the killer and the thing killed.
>
> As for the pointing, its indication is not tied to the cause [of the killing] but to the prey [itself]. An indication of this is that a penalty for the prey of the sacred area is incumbent upon a nonsacralized killer . . .
>
> This indicates that the sanctity of the prey in relation to the rights of the sacralized person is not stronger than the sanctity of a Muslim and his assets, and therefore the pointer is not responsible for the Muslim nor his assets by reason of this indication.[78]

Neither al-Shāfiʿī nor the Ḥanafīs regard the principle in the verse as being explicit from the text [ʿibārat al-naṣṣ] nor indicated in the language of the text [ishārat al-naṣṣ]. According to al-Shāfiʿī, however, the specific logical equation provided by sūrat al-māʾidah [5:95], that killing prey requires a grazing herd animal as a compensatory substitute, suggests that the factor occasioning the penalty is the death of the prey as the loss of property. This means that the principle behind the text is analogous to the principle found in cases where a Muslim person is killed or assets are destroyed. Because, in this latter case, the person who points to a Muslim, who is then killed, or to assets, which are destroyed, is not liable for the death or destruction; therefore, in the case of the prey of the sacred area, the person who points is not responsible.

This same reasoning is attributed to al-Shāfiʿī by al-Sarakhsī in the context of determining the penalty for a group of sacralized people killing a single prey.

> When a group of sacralized people participate in killing a prey, then incumbent upon each one of them is a whole penalty. According to al-Shāfiʿī, incumbent upon all of them is a single penalty.

> This is because it is founded upon the consideration of the object [maḥall]. For this reason he says the pointer who is not tied to the action by the object is not liable for anything, and the object in this case is a single object. Therefore, only a single penalty is incumbent upon the group.
>
> He makes an analogy on the basis of the prey of the sacred area, that if a group of nonsacralized people participated in killing a prey of the sacred area, there would be a single penalty incumbent upon them.
>
> He also makes an analogy on the basis of commercial practice. If a prey is owned, there is nothing incumbent upon those who kill it except a single value to its owner.[79]

The logic used by al-Shāfiᶜī is the same in this case as in the case of the person pointing at prey. A single penalty is required for the group's killing of the prey in analogy with the single compensation required for the destruction of regular property. The "object" of the killing is singular, even though other people were involved, whether by pointing or by participating in the act of killing, a single penalty is required for the destroyed property of the sacred area.

In the case of the group killing and the person pointing, al-Sarakhsī shows that the Ḥanafī opinion is deduced from different principles than are al-Shāfiᶜī's opinions. The Ḥanafī opinions are based on the principle of the "agency" of the people involved, requiring a penalty for pointing at prey that is killed and for participating in the killing of prey. As long as an action results in the killing of prey, it is considered to be hunting, which is prohibited in the sacred area not because it destroys property but for one of two other reasons, because it violates the sanctity of the sacred area or the sacralized state of the pilgrim in the sacred area. According to al-Sarakhsī, the Ḥanafīs claim that these two principles are not to be found in the specific logic of the text to which al-Shāfiᶜī refers but are to be determined by analogy [qiyās al-khafī] with the more general logic behind both this verse and restrictions relating to other practices in the sacred area. The use of istiḥsān rather than qiyās, in the case of the penalty required for the person pointing at prey, is justified by al-Sarakhsī with references to the practice of companions.

> We disregard qiyās in agreement with the companions of the prophet. A man said to ᶜUmar: "I pointed to a gazelle while sacralized, and one of my companions killed it." ᶜUmar said to ᶜAbd al-Raḥmān b. ᶜAwf: "what do you think about this?" He said: "I think that incumbent upon him is a sheep." So ᶜUmar said: "I think this is incumbent upon you."
>
> ᶜAlī and Ibn ᶜAbbās were asked concerning a sacralized person who pointed to the egg of an ostrich which was subsequently taken and cooked. They both said incumbent upon the person who pointed is a penalty for the egg.[80]

In the case of the penalties required for the group killing a prey, al-Sarakhsī explains the general logic behind the Ḥanafī opinions.

> What we require being linked to [the authority of] God and our proof is what we explained, that the requirement incumbent upon the sacralized person is a penalty for his action. The penalty for each one of the people acting is a whole penalty for the crime each committed against his sacralized state. Therefore, a complete penalty is made incumbent upon each one of the people as if they were not participating with anyone else, as that which is an expiation [kifārah] for killing.[81]

This reasoning explains the logic behind the Ḥanafī opinions in both cases. The penalty is incumbent upon sacralized people who participate in the killing of prey, whether by pointing or by helping with the killing itself, because their intention to kill the prey violates their sacralized state. According to al-Sarakhsī, the violation of God's command to be sacralized when performing the pilgrimage requires a blood sacrifice as an expiation for a sin rather than a substitute animal as a compensation for destroyed property.

Several cases are presented by al-Sarakhsī in which the Ḥanafī definition of practice coincides with that of al-Shāfiᶜī, but in each case the conclusions were deduced from different principles. In the first case, both the Ḥanafīs and al-Shāfiʿī require a single penalty upon two nonsacralized people who kill a prey in the sacred area. For al-Shāfiʿī, a single penalty is due, regardless of the number or the sacralized nature of the killers, as compensation for destroyed property. The Ḥanafī reasoning is more complicated.

> If two nonsacralized people kill a prey in the sacred area by a single blow, then incumbent upon each one of them is half of a penalty. This is not the case when each one of the two people hit the prey with a different blow, in which case what is incumbent upon each of them is according to the damage they cause by their respective blows. Incumbent upon each person is half of the value based on the damage done by one of the two blows.[82]

By requiring half a penalty upon each killer, al-Sarakhsī distinguishes this case from the case of a group of sacralized people killing prey. Incumbent upon two sacralized people killing prey, whether the prey is within or outside of the sacred area, are two penalties, one for each of the killers. Incumbent upon two nonsacralized people killing prey within the sacred area is a single penalty. In the case of sacralized people killing prey, the penalty is required because each of the people violated his own sacralized state, regardless of whether the prey was protected or not. In the case of the nonsacralized people, the penalty is required because the people violated the sanctity of the sacred area. Whereas al-Shāfiʿī's opinions are based on the single principle that killed prey is to be treated as destroyed property, the Ḥanafī opinions are based on two different principles that entail two distinct reasons for forbidding the killing of prey in the sacred area. Therefore, the Ḥanafīs contend that actions that result in the killing of prey affect either the person killing the prey, the sacred area where the prey lives, or both. The assessment of penalties depends upon whether the action of the killer(s) violates his own sacralization, the sacrality of the sacred area, or both.

That the assessment of penalties for nonsacralized people killing prey of the sacred area depends not upon the destruction of property but upon the violation of the sacred area is emphasized by al-Sarakhsī in subsequent cases.

> If a nonsacralized person takes prey out of the sacred area but does not kill it, incumbent upon him is a penalty by means of istiḥsān. If he chases it out of the sacred area, not knowing when it will return to the sacred area, because when it is in the sacred area it is protected, this protection extends to it when it is chased out.[83]

On the one hand, al-Sarakhsī explains that this opinion is based on istiḥsān, not on qiyās as it would be were it to be deduced from the principle of property damage as al-Shāfiʿī does. On the other hand, by mentioning that the protection of the sacred area extends to the animal when it is chased out of the sacred area, as opposed to going out of its own accord, al-Sarakhsī stresses that the requirement of this penalty is like the requirement of a penalty for the sacralized person who points at prey. Even if the prey was killed outside of the sacred area by a nonsacralized person, because the person chased the prey out with the intention of killing it, a penalty is incumbent upon him. This point is made explicit in al-Sarakhsī's explanation of another case.

> When a nonsacralized person shoots prey from outside the sacred area [when it is] inside the sacred area, or from inside the sacred area [when it is] outside of the sacred area, encumbent upon him is a penalty for it. This is reported on the authority of Jābir and Ibn ʿUmar. This is because when prey is in the sacred area, it is protected by the sacred area. If the hunter is inside the sacred area, he is prohibited from shooting prey of the sacred area because God said do not kill prey while you are sacralized. When the hunter enters the sacred area, he becomes sacralized.[84]

In this case, al-Shāfiʿī would require a penalty only for the first of the two conditions described. The Ḥanafīs require a penalty for both cases, the assessment of which depends upon which of the two conditions described in the case apply. If the animal had been in the sacred area, then the penalty is assessed because the hunter violated the sacred area. If the animal had been outside of the sacred area and was shot by a nonsacralized person inside of the sacred area, then the penalty is due because the hunter, despite being nonsacralized, is considered to be sacralized because he is inside the sacred area, and thus his killing of prey violates his sacralized state.

Having distinguished how the Ḥanafī principles of violating a person's sacralization or the sacred area operate separately from al-Shāfiʿī's principle of "property," al-Sarakhsī demonstrates how the Ḥanafī opinions determine what actions qualify as implicating their agent in the crime of killing the prey. This determination is dependent on the authorities' understanding of what constitutes the "agency" involved in either of the violations. The Ḥanafī understanding of this agency is illustrated by al-Sarakhsī through a series of loosely related cases in which the details, varying slightly from case to case, indicate the more general logical considerations of the authorities. In his discussion of the agency involved in pointing to prey that is subsequently killed, al-Sarakhsī lists a number of different cases.

> If a sacralized person points out prey to another sacralized person commanding him to kill it, but the person commanded commands the other person to kill it, and he then kills it, then there is a whole penalty incumbent upon each one of them because each one of them committed a crime against the prey for what was engineered: the killer by way of the immediate cause [of the prey's death], the second commander for pointing out the prey to the killer, and the first commander for indicating to the second commander the location of the prey. In the case that the second commanded the first to kill the prey not indicating the location of the prey, then they are both liable for the prey together, because the action of the second person commanded is like the action of the person who commanded him. If the second commander had killed it, then a penalty would be required upon the first commander.[85]

Although the person first pointing is the one who eventually kills the prey, the second is liable as an accomplice in the pointing of the first and is therefore also liable for pointing. If the second person is not considered to be an accomplice in the pointing of the first, he is still liable because his commanding the killing of the prey is equivalent to pointing out the location of the prey that is subsequently killed. The reasoning behind this is illustrated in the following three examples.

> If a sacralized person had sent word to another sacralized person about prey, but the second had not seen the prey until he received the word of the first sacralized person, whether the first person is telling the truth or lying, and the second person searches for the prey and kills it, then incumbent upon each one of them is a penalty for the prey, because each one of them committed a crime in what was engineered.
>
> If a sacralized person sends a sacralized person to a third sacralized person and says that so and so says to you that in such and such a spot there is prey, and the second person goes and kills the prey, then incumbent upon each of the people, the sender, the one sent, and the killer, is a whole penalty.
>
> If a sacralized person points out prey to a man who had already learned of the prey by himself and then kills it, there is nothing incumbent upon the person who pointed out the prey because the killer was able to kill the prey without it being pointed out to him.[86]

In these three examples, al-Sarakhsī demonstrates that the penalty required for pointing out prey is tied to the knowledge of the prey's location, which ultimately leads to the killing of the prey. So, even if a person lies or is not even present, if the information that comes from that person leads to killing the prey, that person is liable for pointing out the prey's location to the killer.

> If a sacralized person gets a knife from another sacralized person to slaughter prey and he slaughters the prey with the knife, then there is no penalty incumbent upon the owner of the knife, but it is reprehensible for him to give the

> knife. . . . When a sacralized killer has a weapon and he kills prey with this weapon, then there is nothing incumbent upon the person who gave the knife to him because even if he did not give it to him he had the capacity to kill the prey. When the killer is not capacitated by what is given to him, there is nothing incumbent upon the giver just as there is nothing incumbent upon the pointer when the person to whom he is pointing out the prey already knows the location of the prey.[87]

In this final case, al-Sarakhsī shows that the penalty for pointing is not predicated on the pointer giving the killer the capacity to kill the prey. Unlike the case of the sacralized person sending a sacralized person to a third sacralized person with information about the location of prey, in this case neither the knife nor the sacralized owner is liable for the killing of the prey. This is because, in the latter case giving a person a knife is not necessarily done with the intention of killing a particular prey in the same way as pointing to prey that is subsequently killed does entail the pointer's intention. The sacralized state of a person is violated when that person acts as an accomplice to killing not only when that person's actions contribute to the killing, but when the actions that contribute to the killing were performed with the intention of them resulting in the killing of the prey.

Using other cases, al-Sarakhsī discusses the issue of agency in relation to what actions violate the sanctity of the sacred area. He uses the distinction between shooting an arrow and using a hunting dog to illustrate that violation of the sacred area, unlike violation of a person's sacralized state, is not necessarily tied to the hunter's intention to commit a violating act.

> If a man shoots at prey which is outside of the sacred area, the man being outside of the sacred area, and he hits the prey inside the sacred area, there is a penalty incumbent upon him because of his crime. This is the opinion of Abū Ḥanīfah. This is based on the fact that the going of the arrow until it reaches the prey is due to the strength of the bowman, so he is the immediate cause of this action which requires a requital.

> This is different from if he had sent his dog after the prey outside of the sacred area, and subsequently the dog tracked the prey until it killed it inside of the sacred area, in which case he is not liable because this is not a crime. The dog's tracking of the prey is an action caused by the dog and is not a crime against the prey of the sacred area by the person sending the dog.
>
> The difference [between the two cases] is that the bowman is the immediate cause of his arrow hitting the prey. In the case of an immediate cause there is no difference between whether it was intentional or not, with regards to whether a penalty is incumbent upon him. It is considered that if he shot an arrow under his own power and hit property or a person, he is liable for what he hit.[88]

In these two cases, al-Sarakhsī shows that the hunter's direct action, violating the territory of the sacred area, requires a penalty. This is unlike the actions that affect the person rather than territory, exemplified by the opinion that pointing to prey that is killed is an indication of the pointer's intention to violate the sanctity of his own personal state. If a hunter is hunting prey outside of the sacred area, but ends up killing prey inside the sacred area, he is liable for violating the sacred area. If, however, the hunter's dog chases prey into the sacred area and kills it there, the hunter is not liable because he did not intend for his dog to enter the sacred area. In the case of violating the sacred area, the intention of the hunter works in the defense only of the hunter because intention is irrelevant to the action that violates the territory, which, in the case of the dog, is not the action of the hunter. The hunter's lack of intention makes the killing of the prey the responsibility of the dog's actions.[89]

These examples show how al-Sarakhsī privileges the logical considerations of the opinions over the wording of the revealed text when attempting to understand the practical significance of the revelation. This is due to a recognition that, although the opinions are interpretations "of" or "based on" the text, neither the opinions themselves nor the specific logical considerations on which they are founded are to be found in the wording of the text. Of the four types of textual indications outlined by al-Sarakhsī, the first is by far the most infrequently used by the Ḥanafī authorities. The few cases in which the Ḥanafī authorities rely on a principle that is explicit from the text [ᶜibārat al-naṣṣ], the information explicit in the text must be supplemented by the specifications provided by the sunnah and the significance of those specifications interpreted by the authorities to arrive at a full definition of a particular practice.[90] When the principle is not explicit from the text, its induction is largely a matter of the authorities' choice as to which method they will use. For example, neither al-Shāfiᶜī nor the Ḥanafīs regard the principle relevant to hunting in the sacred area to be explicit from the text of the revelation. The opinions of both al-Shāfiᶜī and the Ḥanafīs are authoritative because they are based on the revelation, interpreted through the medium of the sunnah. According to al-Sarakhsī, the different logical choices these authorities make when determining the method by which to induce the principles applicable to a given case are responsible for the conflict among their opinions.

Although these logical choices are not determined by the text of the revelation, al-Sarakhsī shows that they are not arbitrary. The authorities induce principles on the basis of how the prophet induced principles as represented in his sunnah. That the different schools' authorities induce different principles, however, means that there is no agreement on what the principles are that the prophet used in defining his sunnah. Because the principles are not explicit from the text of the sunnah, as they are not explicit from the text of the revelation, al-Sarakhsī claims that the authorities must induce the principles from the cases the prophet deduced from the principles he induced from the revelation. The principles behind the prohibition of killing prey in the sacred area are derived indirectly from the revelation by the Ḥanafīs, from the practice of the prophet's companions. It is the claim of al-Sarakhsī that the corpus of the Ḥanafī opinions rather than the sunnah or the Qurʾān is the most accessible guide to the practical significance of the revelation. The scholarship of the fourth century established that the sunnah is to be used to understand the Qur᾿ān, and the scholarship of the fifth century showed that the opinions are to be used to understand how the sunnah understands the Qur᾿ān. The result of this development, illustrated by the work of al-Sarakhsī, is that the opinions themselves become the primary text on which subsequent scholarship is to focus. Classical Ḥanafī scholarship is able to claim the authority of the revelation for its definition of practice because it can demonstrate that its conclusions are deduced from the principles of the revelation, induced and used by the prophet and epitomized by the corpus of Ḥanafī opinions. To deduce practice without the canonical opinions as a guide would be equivalent to taking the place of the authorities directly vis-à-vis the sunnah, just as deducing practice without the sunnah would be equivalent to taking the place of the prophet vis-à-vis the revelation itself.

Conclusions

The Ḥanafī scholarship of the fifth century focuses on a certain corpus of opinions as evidence of the Ḥanafī school's epistemological and methodological bases. On the one hand, this corpus proves the authority of the school by demonstrating, through the interpretive reasoning of the authorities, the link between the opinions on which the school is based and the revelation. The corpus of opinions, or "body of texts," is tangible evidence of a contiguous chain of interpretation from the prophet to classical scholarship. Building on the theoretical advances of the fourth century, the scholarship of the fifth century shows how the opinions are deduced from principles induced from the revelation through the medium of the sunnah. This sort of formulation, developing from the notion of the opinions as a logical extension of the sunnah, stands in a direct relationship to the notion of the sunnah as an extension of the revelation in the Qur᾿ān.

On the other hand, this corpus evinces how the revelation is to be applied to define practice. With the opinions defined as a textual corpus, the Ḥanafī school has the physical resources to make the logical claim that its scholarship is equivalent in authority with the practice of the prophet. By focusing on the logic of the opinions, this sort of scholarship shows how the methodology of the authorities is dependent on the epistemological basis of the school's authority. If the opinions are deduced from principles induced from the revelation, as the work of al-Qudūrī, al-Dabūsī, and al-Sarakhsī shows, then the Ḥanafī school can claim that the principles used by its authorities are the same as the ones used by the prophet in his sunnah.

Because the opinions do not appear to be consistent with the Qurʾān, sunnah, the opinions of other authorities, or even among themselves, it is important to stress the logical rather than textual basis of the inductive and deductive reasoning used to formulate a definition of practice on the basis of the revelation. In the course of the sixth and later centuries, this emphasis on the logical basis of the reasoning required to interpret the revelation, epitomized in the opinions, entailed the use of the opinions as a means with which to illustrate the epistemological and methodological basis of Ḥanafī fiqh scholarship to future Ḥanafī scholars. By using the opinions to instruct future scholars on how to define practice, Ḥanafī scholarship was able to maintain the authority of its particular interpretation of the revelation.

Chapter 4

Maintenance of Authority

Chapter 3 showed how the classical Ḥanafī scholarship of the fifth century appropriated a select corpus of opinions to illustrate the sorts of logical considerations required to understand the practical significance of the revelation. In doing so, classical scholarship expanded the notion of "canon" to include the opinions on which it focused and the school was based. Selected opinions were shown to be, as was the sunnah a century earlier, an epitome of how to interpret the revelation in order to define practice. This corpus of opinions was established in fifth century texts as indicative of both the methodological and epistemological bases of Ḥanafī scholarship.

The "postclassical" Ḥanafī scholarship of the late sixth and subsequent centuries takes a step further than the claim of fifth century scholarship that the principles induced from the revelation by the prophet are to be found in the sunnah as it is interpreted by the local authorities of the second century.[1] Just as the classical scholarship of the fifth century built on the claim of fourth century scholarship that the sunnah epitomized the reasoning required to interpret the revelation, so postclassical scholarship assumes that the opinions epitomize the same reasoning because this had been established by classical scholarship. This meant that to understand the practical significance of the revelation required understanding how classical scholarship induced from the deductions of the opinions the principles that the opinions induced from the sunnah, which is itself deduced by the prophet from principles induced from the revelation. In this way, postclassical Ḥanafī scholarship extends canonical authority to the previous generation of scholarship, demonstrating that the continued authority of the school depends on later generations building on the scholarship of previous generations.

The following pages demonstrate how postclassical Ḥanafī scholarship is essentially commentarial in its insistence that future scholars read "backward" through the scholarship of previous generations, interpreting the revelation in light of how it was interpreted by the generation previous to them. Section I shows how postclassical scholarship teaches students the epistemological foundations of the school by delineating the interpretive link between Ḥanafī scholarship and the revelation. Postclassical scholarship illustrates how the opinions of later Ḥanafī scholars are authoritative because they build on and supersede the opinions of earlier generations. Section II examines how postclassical scholarship directs future generations' interpretations of the revelation through the medium of previous scholarship. By analyzing certain classical texts, sentence by sentence and word by word, in light of both previous and subsequent scholarship, postclassical scholarship shows in what ways the significance of the revelation is determined by the interpretations of later scholars. Postclassical scholarship uses classical scholarship as a heuristic device to teach students the mechanics of the inductive and deductive reasoning required to determine the revelatory principles on which the school is based. By privileging the role of the principles in authorizing the opinions, postclassical scholarship uses the arguments of earlier scholarship as a pedagogic tool to maintain a certain tradition of interpretation. Because claiming the authority of the revelation for a definition of practice is predicated on the use of certain principles, the scholarship of later generations must demonstrate through inductive reasoning that its own conclusions were deduced from the same principles as were the opinions and the sunnah.

I

Structure of Authority

Through a step-by-step analysis of the reasoning represented by the opinions, postclassical scholarship delineates how the authority of future scholarship is dependent on the authority of previous generations. It teaches that, to be authoritative, future scholars' interpretation of the revelation must be built on the interpretations of previous generations. On the one hand, this scholarship shows that the authority of the opinions is predicated on their link to the revelation through the medium of the sunnah. The opinions are authoritative because they are built on the practice of the companions, which is, in turn, built on prophetic practice, which is built on the revelation. On the other hand, postclassical scholarship demonstrates how the authority of future scholarship is linked to the revelation through the medium of the opinions and linked to the opinions through the medium of classical scholarship. Each subsequent generation of scholarship is to interpret the opinions as they were interpreted by the generation of scholarship previous to it.

Instead of explaining the opinions as deductions from the same principles from which the sunnah was deduced, this later scholarship shows how the principles from which the opinions are deduced have to be induced from the scholarship that compiled and interpreted the opinions. Unlike the classical scholarship, which sought to justify the opinions as epitomes of the reasoning required to interpret the revelation, this postclassical scholarship comments on previous scholarship to illustrate how the interpretive reasoning epitomized by the opinions is to be identified and learned. By appropriating the scholarship of the previous generation rather than interpreting the opinions directly, subsequent generations are grafted into the chain of authority reaching back to the opinions and thus inherit the authority of the revelation.

In the *Hidāyah* of ᶜAlī b. Abī Bakr al-Marghīnānī [d. 593],[2] the text of the *Mukhtaṣar* of al-Qudūrī is used to detail how

Ḥanafī scholarship is linked to the revelation through a continuous chain of tradition back to the prophet. By making explicit the connection between the opinions in the *Mukhtaṣar* and the revelation, al-Marghīnānī demonstrates that the authority of classical scholarship is dependent on its relationship to the revelation via the practice of previous generations. In its discussion of hunting in the sacred area, for example, the *Mukhtaṣar* simply states the Ḥanafī definition of the practice but does not mention the reasoning used to reach those opinions nor the textual indications from which they were derived.[3] Of the forty separate statements into which al-Marghīnānī divides the opinions in the *Mukhtaṣar*, ten are attributed to specific Ḥanafī authorities,[4] five are mentioned as being based on prophetic practice,[5] another four are shown to be based on passages from the Qurʾān,[6] and another two are supported by a report on the authority of a companion.[7] In nine places the Ḥanafī opinion is juxtaposed to the opinion of al-Shāfiʿī,[8] and it is juxtaposed to the opinion of Mālik in two places.[9] The use of istiḥsān is mentioned in connection with one statement,[10] but the specific reasons for particular conclusions are given for almost every opinion.

In those cases where al-Marghīnānī mentions a verse from the Qurʾān as the basis of the Ḥanafī opinions, he does so, as did al-Sarakhsī a century earlier, to illustrate the necessity of using the opinions to determine the practical significance of the revelation. The two discussions by al-Marghīnānī examined in what follows are comments on the following passage from the *Mukhtaṣar*.

> (The penalty according to Abū Ḥanīfah and Abū Yūsuf is that the person establish the value of the prey in the location it was killed or in a location near if it was killed in the open country. Two just people determine the value. Then, the killer has a choice in the redemption. If he wants he buys a sacrificial animal for that value and sacrifices it, or if he wants he buys food for it and gives the food as alms to each poor person half a sāʿ of wheat or a sāʿ or dried dates or barley, or if he wants he fasts.)[11]

The discussion of Abū Ḥanīfah and Abū Yūsuf's opinions cited here concerns their disagreement with Muḥammad and al-Shāfiʿī over the interpretation of the Qur'ānic verse from sūrat al-mā'idah [5:95], which is the basis for all the opinions. Part of the disagreement, al-Marghīnānī shows, is on linguistic grounds.

> Muḥammad and al-Shāfiʿī say it is the choice of the two judges in this matter [what the penalty is to be]. If they decide on a sacrificial animal, one resembling what was mentioned [earlier] is required. If they decide on food or fasting [as an expiation], then incumbent on the person [who killed the prey] is what Abū Ḥanīfah and Abū Yūsuf said [earlier].
>
> The reason for Muḥammad and al-Shāfiʿī's opinion is the word of God: two just people from among you determine a sacrificial animal for it [as substitute for the prey killed]. The word "sacrificial animal" is mentioned as assigned because of the interpretation of God's word "determine for it," the direct object of "determine" being the "determination." Then food and fasting is mentioned by word or there is a choice connected to them.
>
> We say: the expiation is connected with the penalty not with the sacrificial animal by the indication that it is in the nominative case. Likewise, the word of God "or the equivalent of it in fasting" is in the nominative case. Therefore it is not an indication of the choice of the two judges. It merely falls on them to determine the extent of the destruction [of the prey], and then, the choice, after that, is incumbent on the person [who killed the prey]. The two judges evaluate the destruction in the place where the prey was hit.[12]

According to al-Marghīnānī, the conflict of opinions stems from a disagreement over the grammar of the phrase "a penalty like what was killed [taken] from among grazing herd animals, determined by two just people from among you, a sacrificial animal brought to the Kaʿbah, an expiation of food to the poor, or the equivalent of it in fasting." Muḥammad and al-Shāfiʿī take it to mean that the two just people determine whether the penalty is to be a sacrificial animal, food to the poor, or fasting. Abū Ḥanīfah and Abū Yūsuf say the two just people determine only the value of the prey killed, and the person who killed the prey chooses which of the three penalties to take. This latter reading is supported by al-Marghīnānī's reference to the nominative case of the three choices, which, if the choices were to be the object of the two just persons' determination, would be in the accusative case. The Ḥanafī position here, represented by the opinions of Abū Ḥanīfah and Abū Yūsuf, is shown by al-Marghīnānī to be derived from the language of the Qurʾān [ishārat al-naṣṣ], disclosed by close linguistic reasoning.

Another part of the disagreement between the opinion of Abū Ḥanīfah and Abū Yūsuf and the opinion of Muḥammad and al-Shāfiʿī centers on what constitutes a "penalty like what was killed [taken] from among grazing herd animals." In this case, al-Marghīnānī illustrates how the Ḥanafī position is a continuation of the interpretation of the revelation used by the companions and the prophet.

> Muḥammad and al-Shāfiʿī say: required for the prey is that which resembles it: for a gazelle a sheep, for a hyena a sheep, for a rabbit a lynx, for a jerboa a fattened female kid, for an ostrich a fattened she-camel, for a wild donkey a cow, according to the word of God: a penalty like what was killed [taken] from among grazing herd animals. "Like it from among grazing herd animals" means what is similar to what was killed in appearance because value is not a grazing herd animal.
>
> The companions require a resembling animal by nature, and the resemblance for the ostrich, gazelle, wild donkey, and rabbit is what was explained. The prophet said: the hyena is prey for which is a sheep.
>
> That for which nothing resembling it can be found, according to Muḥammad, requires a value, like the sparrow, pigeon, and that which is similar to them. When a value is required, Muḥammad's opinion is like that of the other two authorities.
>
> al-Shāfiʿī requires a sheep for a pigeon and establishes a resemblance between them on the basis that both of them exist in groups and bleat or coo. According to Abū Ḥanīfah

> and Abū Yūsuf, unrestricted similarity is similarity in form and significance.[13]

Here, al-Marghīnānī delineates three different opinions. First, the opinion of Abū Ḥanīfah and Abū Yūsuf given earlier is that the value of the prey is to be determined by two just people. For the value thus determined, the person who killed the prey must purchase a sacrificial animal, feed the poor, or fast for a number of days equal to the amount of food he would have given the poor. Second, the opinion of al-Shāfiʿī is that the penalty for the killed prey, when the two just people determine a sacrificial animal is to be given, is selected from grazing herd animals that resemble the prey in appearance. Third, the opinion of Muḥammad is that, in the case of the grazing herd animals mentioned by the prophet and the companions as resembling certain prey, the specified animals are to be sacrificed. The distinction between Muḥammad and al-Shāfiʿī's opinions is illustrated by al-Shāfiʿī's opinion that a sheep is required for a pigeon, for which Muḥammad requires value.

In this case, the opinion of al-Shāfiʿī, although based on the practice of the companions and the prophet, does not take into account the principle from which the prophet and the companions' practice is deduced. This principle, according to al-Marghīnānī is the one used by the Ḥanafīs; namely that an animal equivalent in value to the prey is required as a penalty. This is evident from al-Marghīnānī's understanding of the prophet's requiring of a sheep for a hyena discussed below.[14] The prophet requires a sheep because it is equivalent to the value of the hyena assessed in terms of the value of the hyena's skin because the meat of the hyena is not eaten. It is also evident from al-Marghīnānī's statement that Abū Ḥanīfah and Abū Yūsuf regard "similarity" to be of both form and significance whereas al-Shāfiʿī regards similarity to refer to form alone. This means that the opinion of Muḥammad is deduced from the same principle as is the opinion of the other two Ḥanafī authorities. When a grazing herd animal is to be sacrificed as the penalty, the sacrificial animal is determined in accordance with the value of the prey. In the case of the hyena, ostrich, gazelle, wild donkey, and rabbit, Muḥammad disagrees with the other two authorities only because he interprets sūrat al-māʾidah 5:95 to mean that two just people determine which penalty is to be assessed not the value of the prey killed. Outside of the animals specified by the companions and the prophet, Muḥammad says that the value of the prey must be determined without the precedent of previous generations and a grazing herd animal of an equivalent value given. This case allows al-Marghīnānī to demonstrate that the Ḥanafī opinions are consistent not necessarily with the surface content of but with the reasoning behind the practice of previous generations.

In another case mentioning the Qurʾān, al-Marghīnānī shows how the Ḥanafī opinion, although in conflict with that of al-Shāfiʿī, which is based on his interpretation of the Qurʾān, is supported by the practice of a companion.

> (When a sacralized person kills prey or points out prey to someone who kills it, a penalty is incumbent on him.)
>
> As for the killing, the word of God is: do not kill prey while your are sacralized, those among you who kill it intentionally are penalized. The verse is the textual indication concerning the requirement of the penalty.
>
> As for the pointing, there is disagreement with al-Shāfiʿī who says: the penalty is dependent on the killing, and pointing is not killing, therefore because the pointing resembles an allowed act, it is allowed. According to us is what we transmit from the report of Abū Qatādah. ʿAṭāʾ says: the people concur [ijmāʿ] that there is a penalty incumbent for pointing, because pointing is one of the dangers to the sacralized state [of the pilgrim] and because it threatens the protection of the prey.[15]

This discussion is similar to the discussion found in al-Sarakhsī on the penalty required for pointing out prey which is subsequently killed.[16] That a penalty is incumbent on the sacralized person who kills prey is explicit in the Qurʾān [ʿibārat al-naṣṣ] and agreed on by al-Shāfiʿī and the Ḥanafīs. Concerning pointing, however, al-Marghīnānī states that al-Shāfiʿī allows it because the Qur᾿ān connects the penalty to the killing, and pointing is not killing.[17] The Ḥanafīs require a penalty for pointing, not because it is stipulated in this verse of the Qur᾿ān, but because pointing violates the sacralized state of the person pointing, and when it results in the death of the prey, pointing violates the sanctity of the sacred area. This reasoning is linked to the revelation by al-Marghīnānī's citing of ᶜAṭā᾿ b. Abī Rabāḥ's statement that the authority of requiring a penalty for pointing is guaranteed by consensus in the generations following the prophet. Unlike al-Shāfiᶜī who infers his opinions analogically from the absence of the "pointing" mentioned in the Qur᾿ān, the Ḥanafīs establish a continuity between their definition of practice and the prophet through the practice of the previous generations.

This same sort of continuity from the prophet to the Ḥanafī authorities is evinced by al-Marghīnānī in his discussion of the conflict of opinion between the Ḥanafīs and other local authorities. In this first case, the opinion of Zufar is juxtaposed to the Ḥanafī opinion.

> (If a person kills prey, the meat of which is not eaten, like predatory animals and animals like them, then a penalty is incumbent on him . . . but the penalty does not exceed the value of a sheep.)
>
> Zufar says the value of the penalty required is based on the value of an animal whose meat is eaten.
>
> We rely on the word of the prophet regarding the hyena as prey for which a sheep is given because the value of the hyena is dependent on the place where it is beneficial for its skin.[18]

Zufar assesses the penalty required for predatory animals like that required for nonpredatory animals, in terms of the value of the animal as food. The other Ḥanafīs take the penalty to be assessed in terms of the value of the predatory animal's skin because the prophet required a sheep as penalty for a hyena. By mentioning this prophetic practice, al-Marghīnānī shows that while Zufar's opinion might be based on a revelatory principle operative in other cases, the Ḥanafī opinion is more consistent with the prophet's particular interpretation of the revelation. A similar point is made in a different case involving the opinion of Mālik.

> (There is no harm if a sacralized person eats the meat of prey he hunted and slaughtered while not sacralized as long as a sacralized person did not point it out to him nor command him to take it as prey.)
>
> Mālik disagrees when a person hunts prey for the purpose of a sacralized person.
>
> The prophet says there is no harm in the sacralized person eating the meat of prey which he did not hunt. There is a report in which the companions mention the meat of prey being lawful for the sacralized person.[19]

Again, al-Marghīnānī shows the Ḥanafī opinion to be a continuation of the practice of the prophet and his companions. According to al-Marghīnānī, Mālik holds that it is the eating of prey while sacralized that is forbidden. The Ḥanafīs, on the authority of the companions and the prophet, forbid the killing of prey in the sacred area but not the eating of prey from outside of the sacred area while sacralized.

In some cases, al-Marghīnānī shows that the practice of the prophet, although agreed on by other local authorities as the basis for their interpretations of the revelation, requires the further interpretation of the Ḥanafī authorities. The statement of the prophet in this case, excludes certain animals from requiring a penalty when they are killed by a sacralized person.

> (There is no penalty for killing a crow, kite, wolf, snake, scorpion, mouse, and vicious dog.)
>
> This is based on the word of the prophet that there are five things which are killed, whether outside or inside of the sacred area: a kite, snake, scorpion, mouse, and vicious dog. The prophet also said that the sacralized person kills a

> mouse, crow, kite, scorpion, snake, and vicious dog. He mentions wolf in some of the transmissions.
>
> It is said that intended by "vicious dog" is wolf or that certainly it means wolf. The intention of mentioning crow is to refer to those things that eat carrion because they were created harmful. As for the magpie, it is not excluded because it is not named a crow and was not created to be harmful.
>
> According to Abū Ḥanīfah, the vicious dog and the nonvicious dog, whether domesticated or wild, are equal because this depends on a certain species. Likewise, the tent mouse and the wild mouse are equal. The lizard and the jerboa are not from the same species and are not excluded because they were not created harmful.[20]

This passage makes explicit a number of interpretive decisions in the formulation of the Ḥanafī opinions. First, al-Marghīnānī states that the Ḥanafī exclusion of seven different animals is based on two separate reports of prophetic practice. In the first report, five of the seven animals, omitting the crow and the wolf, are mentioned. The second report mentions six of the animals, including the crow but still omitting the wolf. The Ḥanafī exclusion of the wolf is explained by al-Marghīnānī by the fact that in some other reports the prophet mentions the wolf and that, in any case, the designation "vicious dog" is meant to refer to a wolf. Second, al-Marghīnānī uses the mention of crow to generalize the category of animals excluded to include all those that eat carrion. The magpie is used as an example of a false analogy with the crow to reinforce further that the principle of eating carrion is the criterion for inclusion into the category of excluded animals. Third, al-Marghīnānī argues that the criterion for determining excluded dogs and mice is species, so that all dogs and all mice are excluded from the prohibition on killing. This is reinforced with the example of the lizard and the jerboa as not being excluded as false analogies with the mouse because they are not of the same species as the mouse.

In several cases throughout his discussion of hunting in the sacred area, al-Marghīnānī explains the Ḥanafī opinions as being deduced analogically from principles established as having been induced from the revelation by the prophet and confirmed by the practice of the companions. The determination of whether it is permitted to kill certain animals, whose status as prohibited prey is not explicit from the practice of previous generations, evinces this sort of reasoning.

> (There is nothing incumbent for the killing of gnats, ants, fleas, and ticks) because these things are not prey, being born from a person's body. This applies both to black and red ants. Those [insects] which are not harmful are not allowed to be killed but there is no penalty required [for killing them].[21]

> (There is nothing incumbent on a person for slaughtering a tortoise) because it is a predator and a small reptile. Therefore, it resembles the black beetle.[22]

Certain insects, such as ants, are allowed to be killed because they are both not prey and predatory. This is reinforced by the statement that insects that are not harmful, although not prey, are not allowed to be killed. The tortoise is allowed to be killed because it is a predatory animal, and also because it is not considered to be prey. According to al-Marghīnānī, the tortoise resembles the black beetle, which is not prey to humans but only to other crawling animals, and therefore the killing of it is not prohibited.[23] The Ḥanafī opinion regarding ants and tortoises, although the status of these animals has no precedent, is shown to be consistent with the principles used by previous generations to determine the status of other animals. In other cases, al-Marghīnānī explains that the Ḥanafī opinion is deduced from even more general principles used by previous generations.

> (If a person had wounded prey, plucked its hair, or cut a limb from it, he is responsible for what he diminished), taking into consideration the part for the whole as in commercial practice. (If he had plucked the feathers of a bird or

> cut the legs of prey so that is prevented from leaving its domain, then the entire value of it is incumbent on him) because he caused the animal to be removed from its protected state so therefore a penalty is paid by him.
>
> (If he breaks the egg of an ostrich, then its value is incumbent on him.) This is reported on the authority of ᶜAlī and Ibn ᶜAbbās, the reason being that the egg is basically prey. It has the capacity to become prey, and prey deposited it in its place and protected it from spoiling. (If a dead chick comes out of the egg, then the value of a live one is incumbent on the person.) This is istiḥsān. Qiyās is that there is no penalty equivalent to the egg because the [value of the] live chick is not fixed. It is istiḥsān because the chick is ready to emerge from the egg alive, and a crack before that time or [a breaking of the egg] that is the cause of the chick's death takes the egg out of the protection of its mother. In this regard, when a person hits the stomach of a gazelle and causes its fetus to miscarry and the mother dies as well, the value of both is incumbent on the person.

Both of these cases are deduced from principles induced from other cases using analogical reasoning [qiyās al-khafī]. The first case is deduced from the principle of proportional responsibility applied in cases of commercial transactions. Although the revelation does not forbid the injuring of prey in the sacred area, commercial practice based on different principles from the revelation does hold people responsible for damage they do to another's property, which can be applied to damage done to the prey of the sacred area. The second case is based on qiyās al-khafī and istiḥsān rather than qiyās al-jalī. The value of a live chick is required for breaking an egg, out of which a dead chick emerges, because breaking the egg is considered to have been done with the intention of killing the chick that is regarded as prey. In all of these cases, al-Marghīnānī shows that the new rulings are authoritative not because they repeat the old practices, but because they are considered to represent what the companions and the prophet would have said had they applied the revelation to these particular cases.

In the generations of scholarship subsequent to al-Marghīnānī, this analysis of the links between the opinions and the revelation are expanded with more numerous and critical references to how the opinions are built on the practice of the companions and the prophet. Ibn al-Humām [d. 681], in his commentary on the *Hidāyah,* gives the reports of the companions' practice that al-Marghīnānī references as evidence for "resemblance" meaning something comparable in nature.

> (The value is not a grazing herd animal.)
>
> For this the companions agree in requiring something similar in form in the *Muwaṭṭāʾ* of Mālik.
>
> We received the report from Abū al-Zubayr, on the authority of Jābir: that ʿUmar determined a ram for a hyena, a goat for a gazelle, a she-kid for a rabbit, and a fattened she-kid for a jerboa.
>
> al-Shāfiʿī reported that: ʿUmar, ʿUthmān, ʿAlī, Zayd b. Thābit, Ibn ʿAbbās, and Muʿāwiyah said: for an ostrich that a sacralized person kills a fattened female camel is required. But this report is weak and does not have a continuous chain of transmission back to the prophet. Concerning this he said: If we said for an ostrich a fattened female camel, it is by analogy but not by this report because it is not established among scholars as a report of prophetic practice.[24]

Ibn al-Humām mentions three different sources for the practice of the companions on which al-Marghīnānī supposes Muḥammad's opinion to be based. Note, however, that only the fattened she-kid for a jerboa and fattened she-camel for an ostrich are supported by the companions' practice. This discrepancy between the companions' practice and Muḥammad's opinion, and the discrepancies among the companions themselves, shows that Muḥammad's opinion is not derived from the companions' practice but is consistent with it because he uses the same reasoning as they. Ibn al-Humām reinforces this use of the companions' practice by mentioning al-Shāfiʿī's objection to his own report of the six companions. The report is not claimed by al-Shāfiᶜī as the basis for his opinion because there is no evidence that the prophet required the same animals that these six companions did. For al-Shāfiᶜī, this means that one has to determine which animals are required in analogy with the prophet's requirement of a sheep for a hyena. Ibn al-Humām, following al-Marghīnānī, indicates that the report of the companions' practice is used not as the basis for Muḥammad's opinion, but to demonstrate that both the companions and Muḥammad are deducing a definition of practice from the same principles being those from which the prophet deduced that a sheep is required for a hyena.

This same issue of what is meant in sūrat al-māʾidah 5:95 by "like what was killed" is taken up in the several commentaries on the work of ᶜAbdallāh b. Aḥmad al-Nasafī [d. 710], itself based on the work of al-Marghīnānī. In his *Tabyīn al-ḥaqāʾiq,* ᶜUthmān b. ᶜAlī al-Zaylaᶜī [d. 743] cites an additional three reports on the authority of companions regarding how to determine which sacrificial animal to give as a penalty for certain prey.[25] Ibn Nujaym [d. 970], in his *Baḥr al-rāʾiq,* also cites Abū ᶜUbaydah and al-Aṣmaᶜī as support for the relationship between the designation in sūrat al-māʾidah 5:95 of grazing herd animals as substitutes for wild animals.

> This is just as Abū ᶜUbaydah and al-Aṣmaᶜī said: the intention behind [the stipulation of] the value of the prey is the value of its meat.[26]

These additional comments demonstrate in more detail the contention of al-Marghīnānī, that the interpretations of the Ḥanafī authorities are consistent with the interpretations of previous generations.

In other cases, the comments of later scholarship provide a more critical view than did al-Marghīnānī of the opinions' relation to previous generations' interpretations of the revelation. Concerning al-Marghīnānī's statement that Muḥammad's opinion is supported by prophetic practice, Ibn al-Humām provides two reports about the hyena from the prophet.

> (The prophet said: the hyena is prey, for it a sheep is required.)
>
> Abū Dāʾūd transmits that Jābir b. ʿAbdallāh said: "I asked the prophet about the hyena, whether it was prey. He said: yes. He required a ram to be given when a sacralized person hits it.
>
> al-Ḥākim also reports that Jābir said: the prophet said: "the hyena is prey, when a sacralized person hits it, a mature ram is given for it and eaten."[27]

As in the case of the reports of the companions' practice, here Ibn al-Humām shows that the opinion of Muḥammad is consistent with the prophet's practice. These two reports show that Muḥammad's opinion is authoritative because it is deduced from the same principle as was the prophet's practice. These same reports, used by al-Marghīnānī to support the opinion that the penalty for a predatory animal is not to exceed a sheep, are criticized by ʿAbd al-Ḥakīm al-Afghānī [d. 1326].

> (We rely on the word of the prophet regarding the hyena as prey for which a sheep is given because the value of the hyena is dependent on the place where it is beneficial for its skin.)
>
> This report is not known, but the known report is: Jābir asked the prophet whether the hyena was prey. The prophet said yes and required a ram for it when a sacralized person kills it. This is transmitted by Abū Dāʾūd. He alone adds the mention of the ram. Others transmit this report but do not mention the ram in it. al-Ḥākim transmits this report with the addition of the ram on the authority of Jābir. He says: the prophet said: the hyena is prey. When a sacralized person hits it, there is a mature ram given and eaten for it.[28]

Here, al-Afghānī points out that there is no known report of prophetic practice requiring a sheep for a hyena because of the value of the hyena's skin. He argues that the reports used to support Muḥammad's earlier opinion regarding the appropriate penalty for certain prey do not support the opinion regarding the penalty assessed for predatory animals. The transmission of the report by al-Ḥākim which includes the prophet's statement that "there is a mature ram given and eaten for it," indicates that the ram is given for the value of its meat as food not for the value of its skin.

A similar criticism is leveled by al-Afghānī against al-Marghīnānī's reference to the report concerning Ibn ᶜAbbās's practice of requiring a penalty for breaking an egg.

> (This is reported on the authority of ᶜAlī and Ibn ᶜAbbās, the reason being that the egg is basically prey. It has the capacity to become prey, and prey deposited it in its place and protected it from spoiling.)
>
> The responsibility of spoiling is not connected to the egg's capacity. The statement of this on the authority of ᶜAlī is obscure [gharīb] according to al-Zaylaᶜī. The report of ᶜAlī and Ibn ᶜAbbās's opinion by Ibn Abī Shaybah is considered to be weak [ḍaᶜif] by ᶜAbd al-Razzāq and al-Dāraquṭnī.[29]

Here, al-Afghānī's analysis of how the Ḥanafī opinion is linked to previous generations is more discerning than that of al-Marghīnānī. First, al-Afghānī adds that ᶜAlī is a relatively unauthoritative source for the precedent of requiring a penalty for breaking an egg. Second, he points out that Ḥanafī scholarship subsequent to al-Marghīnānī considers that the precedent of regarding an egg as prey concerns the potential of the egg to become a prey and not its protection from spoiling. The opinion that breaking an egg requires a penalty is still considered by al-Afghānī as sound and consistent with the practice of the companions, but not necessarily for the reasons given by al-Marghīnānī. By criticizing al-Marghīnānī's explanation of the opinions, al-Afghānī is able to demonstrate how the findings of later scholarship supersede the claims of earlier scholarship. He does not undermine the authority of the opinions originally given in the *Mukhtaṣar,* but rather demands a more explicit and accurate analysis of how the opinions are linked to the revelation.

This criticism of the opinions as explained by al-Marghīnānī is also carried out through the media of the generations of scholarship previous to al-Marghīnānī. For example, in his exposition of al-Marghīnānī's discussion of the specific grazing herd animals required by the companions for certain prey, Ibn al-Humām cites the different interpretations of Muḥammad's opinion concerning the choice that is up to the two just people in the determination of a penalty for killing prey.

> The majority of the schools' leaders [mashāʾikh] disagree concerning the stipulation of Muḥammad's opinion. al-Ṭaḥāwī decrees, on his authority, that the choice is up to the judges. If the two judges determine a sacrificial animal is incumbent on the person, then the killer is responsible to find one resembling a grazing herd animal by nature or determine its value if it is like a bird just as the two other authorities say. al-Karkhī decrees the opinion of Muḥammad to be that the choice up to the killer is not, if a sacrificial animal is chosen, to specify the animal resembling the prey. According to al-Shāfiʿī, the resemblance is required regardless of anyone's choice. He has the choice to feed the poor in which case the food is a substitute for the resemblance, but not for the fast as is stated in the *Badāʾiʿ*.[30]

The different interpretations of al-Ṭaḥāwī and al-Karkhī are used by Ibn al-Humām to show that it is not enough to know the content of the opinions to understand their practical significance. In the text of the *Mukhtaṣar,* Muḥammad's opinion is merely cited as the statement that he requires certain animals for that prey which has a stipulated equivalent. The *Hidāyah* shows how Muḥammad's opinion is related to the practice of earlier generations, but he does not indicate how the opinion is to be generalized in light of the other two authorities' opinions. Ibn al-Humām provides the information necessary for the reader to understand that Muḥammad's opinion entails at least two possible consequences for the Ḥanafī definition of practice. Assuming that the two judges make the decision that a sacrificial animal is required, then al-Ṭaḥāwī holds that the killer is responsible to find a sacrificial animal resembling the prey or determine its value when there is no comparable sacrificial animal. Another possibility, according to al-Karkhī, is to combine Muḥammad's opinion with that of the other two Ḥanafī authorities, in which case the judges determine that a sacrificial animal is required, and they also determine the animal or the value of the animal to be sacrificed. Without indicating which interpretation is more sound, Ibn al-Humām demonstrates how previous generations of scholarship serve to specify later scholarship's interpretation of the opinions.

On this same issue of Muḥammad's opinion, Ibn Nujaym cites Ibn al-Humām's discussion and supplements it with material from a number of additional sources.

> In his *Kitāb al-manāsik,* al-Kirmānī says the value of the prey is in terms of its meat according to us. Zufar says its value is required by the designation of what is killed. If a person had killed a trained falcon, we require the value of its meat. According to Zufar, the value of its training is required.
>
> In the *Ikhtiyār:* when the intention of the penalty is value, two just people determine it in terms of meat not animals. The intention is that it is determined in terms of essence and not in terms of description because description is non-essential. If description had been the issue it would be like when birds sing, then their value is extra on account of that, taking the singing into account for the penalty.
>
> In the *Badāʾiʿ,* consideration is given to the difference in property. When something owned is destroyed, then the value is determined in terms of essence and description, except when it is described to the sacralized person for irrelevant things like the value of a rooster for its ability to peck, and a ram for its ability to butt. It is not determined like a singing slave girl. The intention is not that the value is established in terms of the prey's meat after it is killed but while it is living, in consideration of its essence indicating that it is what is eaten for its meat. When its meat has no value, its value is determined in terms of its skin.[31]

By citing these additional interpretations of the opinions, Ibn Nujaym broadens the discussion to include the consideration of a more intricate understanding of the opinions. The earliest opinion that the penalty is determined in terms of the value of the prey's meat by Abū al-Faḍl al-Kirmānī [d. 543], juxtaposed to the opinion of Zufar, is developed in the later arguments of al-Kāsānī [d. 587] and ᶜAbdallāh b. Maḥmūd al-Mūṣulī [d. 683]. This increased sophistication and complexity of the issue turns the focus away from the reasoning of the opinions themselves and more toward the reasoning used to interpret the reasoning of the opinions. It demonstrates how later scholarship is not only based on previous scholarship, but how being based on previous scholarship is necessary for understanding the full practical import of the revelation.

Through the incorporation of previous scholarship into its own discussion of the opinions, postclassical scholarship complicates rather than simplifies the interpretation of the revelation. From the exposition of a single Ḥanafī opinion, postclassical scholarship constructs a discussion covering several pages of argument in which the opinion becomes a pretext for demonstrating the structure of the school's authority. This structure of generation built on generation instructs future scholars how the authority of their own interpretations depends on their reasoning being consistent with the reasoning of previous scholarship. To be authoritative, a definition of practice must be deduced from principles induced from the revelation. The logical considerations that guide these inductive and deductive decisions are not prescribed in the text of the revelation, however, but are to be learned through examples of how earlier scholars reasoned. The latest generation of scholarship learns to induce from the previous generation's deductions what that generation induced from the deductions of the generation previous to it.

To circumvent the scholarship of a previous generation is to break the chain of interpretation that links the authority of the revelation to postclassical scholarship. Each generation of furūᶜ scholarship makes its own arguments about how the opinions are linked to the revelation, but each generation's arguments must take into account the arguments of previous generations to be considered authoritative. Such a construct teaches that to be a Ḥanafī is to follow Ḥanafī precedent as a guide for the sort of reasoning required to determine the practical significance of the revelation.

II

Direction of Interpretation

Just as it uses the scholarship of previous generations to illustrate the epistemological foundations of the school, postclassical scholarship teaches students how to interpret the revelation through the medium of previous scholars' interpretations. This sort of postclassical scholarship utilizes a variety of pedagogic devices to limit students' interpretations to the way earlier scholarship interpreted the opinions to have interpreted the sunnah to have interpreted the revelation. To approach the opinions through subsequent scholarship, postclassical scholarship divides the *Mukhtaṣar* of al-Qudūrī,[32] among other compilations of Ḥanafī opinions, into individual statements, which are then explained one by one in light of subsequent scholarship. By taking these individual statements out of the *Mukhtaṣar* and putting them into the context of later scholarship, postclassical scholarship shows that the authority of future scholarship depends on that scholarship knowing how the logical decisions of Ḥanafī scholarship affect the interpretation of the opinions. The whole point of postclassical scholarship is to demonstrate that future scholarship will continue to be as authoritative as previous generations as long as it is deduced from the same principles that earlier generations of scholarship take to be the principles from which the original opinions are deduced.

On the most basic level, postclassical scholarship directs students' interpretations of the opinions in the *Mukhtaṣar* through simple explanatory devices. For example, certain words, the meaning of which is often obscured by centuries of changes in usage, are defined for the student. In some cases, the definition is as simple as giving the voweling of the otherwise unvoweled Arabic term and a more recent synonym.

> (Delayed delivery of clothing is permitted when the clothing is specified according to length, width, and piece [ruqᶜah]) with a qāf like a weighed lot. The meaning is given in the *Maghrīb:* it is said a piece [ruqᶜah] of this cloth is good, meaning its thickness and consistency speaking metaphorically.[33]

In this case, ʿAbd al-Ghanī al-Maydānī [d. 1298] explains the meaning of the term *ruqʿah* as something akin to "piece." By giving a gloss to this term, al-Maydānī makes clear what is not evident from the original text, that the stipulation concerning the delayed delivery of cloth is dependent on the quality of the cloth being specified. Often, a term is not obscure but knowledge of its morphology and its technical usage is pertinent to understanding the discussion in which it is used. This sort of instruction is particularly important in those cases where the morphology and syntax used are specific to the technical usage of the terminology.

> [iqrār] legally means the notification or avowal of the right of another on one's self.
>
> The person making the acknowledgment is termed *muqir.* The person in whose favor the acknowledgment is made is termed *muqir li-hu.* The thing that is the subject of the acknowledgment is termed *muqir bi-hi.*[34]

This particular case, taken from al-Marghīnānī, instructs the student about the technical usage of key words in the following discussion. By distinguishing the common usage of these terms from their technical meaning in fiqh scholarship, postclassical scholarship is able to state the gist of the definition given in what follows.

> (usury [ribāʾ]) with a kasra on the rāʾ, and an alif maqṣūrah. The dual is ribawān with a wāw in the root, but ribayān is said because of vowel reduction like in miṣbāḥ. The adjective is ribawī with a kasr. A fatḥah is a mistake.
>
> Linguistically it means unrestricted excess. Legally it means the unrestricted excess of an item of exchange over a legal standard of measurement stipulated by one of the two parties contracting the exchange of the item in question.[35]

Here, al-Maydānī provides an overview of the morphology of the term *ribāʾ*, indicating to the reader how to interpret, on a linguistic level, the significance of the various forms of this word used in the discussion that follows. Also, by giving the technical usage of the term *ribāʾ*, al-Maydānī summarizes the principle behind the opinions' definition of usury. This sort of glossing allows postclassical scholarship to prejudice the reader's interpretation of the subsequent discussion by indicating which issues are most pertinent and how they are to be understood in what follows.

In other cases, Abū Bakr b. ʿAlī al-Ḥaddād [d. 800] uses his explanation of two pre-Islamic practices prohibited in the *Mukhtaṣar* to indicate the general principle behind the determination of which types of exchanges are invalid.

> (Sale is not permitted by the casting of a stone [ilqāʾ al-ḥijr], and the touching of the goods [mulāmasah].) These were sales in pre-Islamic times which are now prohibited by the lawgiver.
>
> As for sale by the casting of a stone, also called sale of the pebble, it is when two men haggle over a commodity, the claimant being the one who puts down a stone or pebble and thus completes the sale, even if the owner of the sale item is not satisfied.
>
> As for the sale by touching the goods, it is when two people compete over a commodity, the purchaser being the one who touches the commodity at which point the commodity is sold whether its owner is satisfied or not.[36]

By adding that, in both cases, the sale is completed whether or not the owner of the item being sold is satisfied, al-Ḥaddād emphasizes the reason for the prohibition of these two practices. These practices are not allowed because, like the other types of exchanges prohibited in this same section of the *Mukhtaṣar,* they do not provide means for the two parties involved in the exchange to determine an equitable rate of exchange. If the sale is decided by the dispute among two possible purchasers alone, then there is no room for the seller to decide on the equity of the exchange. Thus, from the comparison of these unusual cases, as understood by later scholarship, with the other cases discussed in the rest of the section, readers are able to determine the general principle from which the various opinions are deduced.

This definition of certain key terms is also used by postclassical scholarship to indicate the reasoning behind a particular practice through the explanation of a single opinion. The comments of al-Ḥaddād allow readers to see in language of the *Mukhtaṣar* the logical distinctions made by later generations of scholarship.

> (The journey for which the ritual obligations are changed is that in which a person is headed for a destination, the distance between which and himself is a trip of three days by camel or by foot.)
>
> The intended destination is taken into account when the traveler makes his decision to travel. The stipulation of the intended destination is that the person says he is headed for such and such a place, but not that he is just going because he might go about the whole earth and not intend a particular place. Even though the distance between where he goes and where he started is a trip of three days, he does not qualify as a traveler. Likewise, the intention itself without the actual travel does not make him considered a traveler. The consideration depends on both of the two things.[37]

In his explanation of this statement, al-Ḥaddād focuses the readers' attention on the wording "headed for a destination." According to al-Ḥaddād, this is significant because it is meant to indicate that, to shorten their ritual obligations, travelers must intend to make a journey of at least three days. The importance of the intention, although not necessarily evident from the original statement, is explicit from the example given by al-Ḥaddād that a person could travel around the whole earth and still not be considered a traveler without intending a particular destination of three days' distance. In his explanation of the second statement, al-Ḥaddād focuses on the issue of distance.

> (This is not taken into account for travel by water.)
>
> That is, traveling in open country is not taken into account for traveling in the sea nor is traveling in the sea taken into account for traveling in open country. What is taken into account for both places is what is appropriate to the circumstances.

> If a place has two ways of getting there, one of them being in the water and it being reached in three days when there is steady wind, the second being in the open country, being reached in two days, when the person goes by way of water he shortens his ritual obligations but when he goes by way of open country he does not shorten them. If he had, when he went by way of open country, arrived in three days and, when he went by sea, arrived in two days, he would shorten his ritual obligations in the open country and not in the sea.
>
> The consideration concerning the sea is three days with steady wind.
>
> Abū Ḥanīfah says when a person in a civilizational center has two ways to go, one of which takes three days and the other two days, if he wants he goes the long way and shortens his ritual obligation, and if he wants he goes the short way and does not shorten his ritual obligation.[38]

The original statement is expanded by al-Ḥaddād into a discussion of the stipulation that the journey be a distance of three days. By supplying the example of the journey accomplished by either a sea route or a land route, and the opinion of Abū Ḥanīfah concerning the choice between two routes of different lengths, al-Ḥaddād shows that the original mention of "by camel or by foot" is meant to stress that the length of three days refers not to a distance but to the period of time the traveler is to spend traveling.

By showing how the opinions of previous scholarship are deduced from the same principles as are the original opinions, postclassical scholarship encourages readers to induce certain principles from the cases listed in the *Mukhtaṣar.* Postclassical scholarship also uses the conflict of opinions to direct readers' to interpret the cases in the *Mukhtaṣar* to have been deduced from specific principles, which postclassical scholarship identifies. In many cases, postclassical scholarship expands on a conflict of opinions mentioned in the *Mukhtaṣar.*

> (If a person [preparing to pray] says in place of the extolation: "God is most sublime [ajall]" or "most great [aᶜẓam]" or

> "the Merciful is great [al-Raḥmān al-akbar]," it is permitted according to Abū Ḥanīfah and Muḥammad. Abū Yūsuf says it is only permitted along with the pronouncement of the extolation [takbīr] itself.)
>
> According to Abū Ḥanīfah and Muḥammad it is reprehensible for people to enter prayer without saying the extolation itself. The opinion of Abū Ḥanīfah concerning the substitute for saying the extolation indicates that the basic principle here is that God is great and saying something else is a substitute for that. If the person praying says "God is most sublime" or "most great" inadvertently, the prostration of inadvertence is not required of him except when he does it at the opening of the prayer for the festival. When he says it inadvertently at that time the prostration of inadvertence is required of him.
>
> Abū Yūsuf says when the extolation is best it is only permitted to be of four phrases: Allāhu akbar, Allāhu al-akbar, Allāhu kabīr and Allāhu al-kabīr. . . . If the person praying had said "The Compassionate is great [al-Raḥīm akbar]," it is permitted according to Abū Ḥanīfah and Muḥammad. There is disagreement with Abū Yūsuf who says: if he had said "the Merciful is great [al-Raḥmān akbar]" it is not considered legally valid because it is from the joint names [al-ismāᶜ al-mushtarikah] of God. If he had said "in the name of God the Merciful, the Compassionate" it is not considered legally valid because it is used as a blessing as if he had said "Oh God bless me in this." But, if he had said "oh God [Allāhumma]" and nothing else, it is sound that it is not considered legally valid, as if he had said "oh God forgive me" or "I ask God's forgiveness" . . .
>
> If the person praying had opened his prayer in Persian and he is better at Arabic, it is permitted according to Abū Ḥanīfah but reprehensible. According to Abū Yūsuf and Muḥammad it is not permitted except when the person praying is not as good in Arabic as in Persian.[39]

Here, al-Ḥaddād provides the reader with the additional information necessary to determine the reason why the authorities disagree and the general principle on which they do agree. All three authorities agree that an extolation must be said before starting prayer, but Abū Yūsuf insists that the extolation [takbīr] must consist of some grammatically sound combination of the two words *Allāh* and *kabīr* but the other two authorities allow other words that have a similar meaning. That this disagreement has something to do with the intentions of the person saying the extolation is indicated by al-Ḥaddād's inclusion of the conflict over whether it is permitted to say the extolation in Persian if the person saying it is better in Arabic. Saying the extolation in Persian, when it would be easier in Arabic, is like saying something equivalent to "Allāhu akbar" but using different words. Only if this is done inadvertently, al-Ḥaddād claims, does Abū Ḥanīfah allow the practice. By making the comparison between the substitute words and saying the extolation in Persian, al-Ḥaddād explains that although Abū Ḥanīfah permits substitute words for the extolation, he finds the practice reprehensible. This means that the disagreement is not over whether or not the extolation is to be said, or what the person saying it must intend by it, but over whether or not a person's inadvertently saying the extolation incorrectly invalidates his prayer.[40] By providing these specific details, al-Ḥaddād circumscribes how readers are to interpret this particular conflict of opinions. Otherwise, the conflict of opinion could be interpreted as indicating a lack rather than the existence of coherency among the logic of the Ḥanafī authorities.

Frequently, postclassical scholarship cites additional cases of conflict among the Ḥanafī authorities, not mentioned in the *Mukhtaṣar* but taken from other classical and postclassical scholarship to emphasize the authorities' use of certain principles. This is evident from al-Ḥaddād's comparison of the statement in the *Mukhtaṣar* that the exchange of walnuts and eggs by a standard of measurement rather than by their relative values is permitted to Abū Ḥanīfah's opinion mentioned by al-Karkhī and al-Marghīnānī that the exchange of salted fish by a standard of measurement is not permitted.

> Delayed delivery is permitted with salted fish by a fixed weight and fixed variety because their measurement is fixed and the extent of their properties is determined by the item not being outside of the marketplace.
>
> Delayed delivery of salted fish is not permitted by number because of the disparity between them, and because salt is half of the item's intrinsic value because it is salted.
>
> There is no choice for the delivery of fresh fish except at the time of the delivery by a fixed weight and a fixed variety because there is a break in the time from when it was caught until it arrives in the city. If there were no break it would be permitted. Otherwise, it is permitted by weight but not by number.
>
> According to Abū Ḥanīfah, the delayed delivery of fish having large quantities of meat is not permitted because the exchange is dependent on the amount of meat. This is the basis for the statement in the *Hidāyah* and in al-Karkhī that the delayed delivery of fish is not permitted according to Abū Ḥanīfah, whether fresh or salted, because the fish vary according to fat and lean and are therefore to be exchanged like meat. Abū Yūsuf says that it is permitted with salted fish when it is specified by a fixed weight.[41]

The conflict of opinion here is between Abū Ḥanīfah, who does not allow the exchange of fish by a standard of measurement, and Abū Yūsuf, who allows the exchange of fish by a standard of measurement when they are salted. This conflict, not a part of the opinions in the *Mukhtaṣar,* is evident only from al-Karkhī and al-Marghīnānī's reports that Abū Ḥanīfah forbids the exchange of fish by a standard of measurement. According to al-Ḥaddād, the reasoning behind Abū Ḥanīfah's opinion is that different fish have different amounts of meat on them, and therefore that fish are to be exchanged like sheep, in terms of their value relative to their differing amounts of meat. In light of this, Abū Yūsuf's permission to exchange salted fish by a fixed weight but not by number is understandable and analogically related to the opinion concerning the exchange of walnuts and eggs. Salted fish cannot be sold by number because of their differing amounts of meat, but it can be exchanged by weight because then, regardless of the number of fish, the extent of the meat is equal to its weight. By detailing the reasons given by previous scholarship for the conflict over the exchange of fish, al-Ḥaddād indicates the reason for the permission to exchange walnuts and eggs by number. Walnuts and eggs are to be exchanged by number because their value is not, like fish whether salted or not, relative to the amount of their meat or their size.

In relation to this same issue, al-Ḥaddād illustrates the logic behind the prohibition of exchanging gems and pearls by a standard of measurement by reference to a conflict of opinions between Abū Ḥanīfah and Abū Yūsuf for reasons similar to why they disagreed about the exchange of fish.

> (Delayed delivery of gems and pearls is not permitted) because there is disparity among them.
>
> As for the delivery of bread, there is a conflict of opinions. In the *Hidāyah,* it is said that the delayed delivery of bread is permitted in the *Ṣaḥīḥ*. Beware, however, of the opinion in the *Ṣaḥīḥ* because of what was reported from Abū Ḥanīfah that is it not permitted, as mentioned in the *Mabsūṭ*. It says, as for the delayed delivery of bread, it is not permitted according to Abū Ḥanīfah because there is disparity in its being well-cooked or not.
>
> In the *Dhakhīrah,* on the authority of Imām Khwāharzādeh, the delayed delivery of bread is not permitted according to Abū Ḥanīfah by weight or number. According to Abū Yūsuf, it is permitted by weight. The choice of the leaders of the school is the opinion of Abū Yūsuf when it comes to the stipulations of delayed delivery which people actually use.
>
> This is likewise the case in the *Nihāyah* and the *Ṣighār* of al-Luʾluʾī, which permit the exchange [of bread] according to weight. Delayed delivery is permitted according to this scholarship because it is possible to know the weight of bread.

> The delayed delivery of pomegranates, watermelons, cucumbers, and thafrajal is not permitted because they differ according to whether they are big or small.[42]

With this case, al-Ḥaddād demonstrates how later scholarship's interpretations of conflicting opinions sometimes resort to ad hoc solutions. Aside from the example of bread, in this case al-Ḥaddād compares the exchange of gems and pearls to the exchange of fruit. The exchange of gems, pearls, or fruit by a fixed standard of measurement is not permitted because the individual items' values differ relative to the items' sizes. As the discussion over the exchange of fish showed, there is disagreement concerning whether certain items like bread are to be exchanged according to a fixed weight. In this case, Abū Ḥanīfah does not permit the exchange of bread by weight or number because the value of bread, like the value of gems and fruit, differs relative to the quality of the individual loaves. Abū Yūsuf permits the exchange of bread by weight, but his reasoning is not analogous with the reasoning behind the permission to exchange fish by weight. This is because, although the value of fish as meat can be equated with the weight of the fish, the value of bread relative to its being more or less well-cooked or the value of gems relative to their size and quality cannot be equated with these items' weight. According to al-Ḥaddād, Abū Yūsuf's opinion is based on practical considerations, meaning that it ignores the possibility that the value of bread might differ relative to its quality. It is only because it is possible to know the weight of bread that it is to be sold by a fixed weight.

By giving additional examples for the meaning of a given word or phrase, al-Ḥaddād is able move the focus of readers' attention away from the definition given in the *Mukhtaṣar* and toward later scholarship's definition of practice. Postclassical scholarship anticipates the interpretations of readers by listing additional cases supposed to be deduced from the same principle as the original case.

> (Abū Yūsuf and Muḥammad say that the tithe is required for only perennial produce, when it amounts to five loads, a load being sixty ṣāᶜs according to a ṣāᶜ of the prophet.)

> Perennial produce is that which retains its character all year long without turning brown and for which the sun is not needed for ripeness, like wheat, barley, pearl millet, rice, jāwars millet, lentils, Indian peas, beans—including dajar, ḥumus, and barʿī—endive, dried dates, raisins, and other food items that resemble these things. For those things that remain for a year or are generally beneficial after that time such as saffron, safflower, pepper, cumin, mustard, and coriander there is a tithe required. For sesame there is a tithe required. If a person extracts oil before taking a tithe from it, he takes the tithe from the oil but does not take anything from the dregs.[43]

> (According to Abū Yūsuf and Muḥammad there is no tithe for greens.) Greens are those things that are not perennial fruits such as leafy vegetables and succulents. Leafy vegetables include leeks, herbs, chard, and such things. Succulents include the cucumber, melon, eggplant, quince, pomegranate, apple, and such things. As for the onion, Muḥammad relates that for it there is a tithe required because it does not spoil in the hands of people and is of general benefit.[44]

The information provided by al-Qudūrī in the original opinions of Abū Yūsuf and Muḥammad is more explicit than the general principle that a tithe is required for cultivated food items, but it is still open to a range of interpretations. The possible significance of the terms "perennial produce" [thamarah bāqīyah] and "greens" [khaḍrāwāt] is narrowed by al-Ḥaddād's juxtaposition of the two things as dried and wet produce. By cataloging examples of what is meant by the original terms, al-Ḥaddād preempts the need for future scholars to deduce their interpretations from the original terms themselves. The examples replace the relative imprecision of the original terms with the detailed interpretation of later scholarship.

In the context of this same discussion, al-Ḥaddād uses the explanation of imprecise terms in Abū Ḥanīfah's opinion to give a definition of practice that conflicts with the plain meaning of the original opinion.

> (Abū Ḥanīfah says that for the small and the large things that the earth sprouts there is a tithe, regardless of whether it is irrigated or watered by the sky, excepting firewood, reed stalks, and grass.) Because these things are not customarily cultivated but are picked from the earth growing naturally. Likewise for palm leaves there is nothing required because they are from the branches of trees and there is no tithe for trees. Likewise for straw there is nothing required also because it is the stalk of grain like trees are to fruit, and because of the intention of its use. If a person intends a tree for use as a tree per se, then tithe is required for it. As for reed stalks, there are three types: sugar cane, fragrant cane, and Persian cane. For sugar cane and fragrant cane there is a tithe required. Fragrant cane is spikenard [sunbul]. As for Persian cane there is nothing required for it because it is not cultivated. This is when it is on the periphery of land. As for when these things are taken from the earth as cane, tree, or a crop of grass, are irrigated, and people are kept away from them, a tithe is required.[45]

Abū Ḥanīfah's opinion is interpreted as having been deduced from the more general principle that a tithe is required for cultivated produce. No tithe is required for palm leaves like firewood nor straw like grass because neither is cultivated. For some reed stalks, however, a tithe is required although Abū Ḥanīfah's opinion seems to exclude reed stalks from requiring a tithe. This conflict is a result of the more discerning interpretation of later scholarship, dividing "reed stalks" into three different types of cane, two of which require a tithe. What al-Ḥaddād shows by differentiating between types of reed stalks is that Abū Ḥanīfah's exclusion of reed stalks, deduced from the principle that only cultivated produce require a tithe, must refer only to Persian cane because of the three types it is not cultivated. Seen in this light, the distinction among the types of reed stalks, made by later scholarship, is necessary to show that Abū Ḥanīfah's opinion does not contradict the principle from which it is deduced.

In some cases, al-Ḥaddād shows that later scholarship's interpretation conflicts with the plain sense of the original opinion because of a logical rather than natural distinction made by later scholarship.

> (The pure person does not pray following a person who has incontinence of urine, nor a pure woman following a woman with an irregular discharge, nor a literate following an illiterate, nor a clothed following the naked.)
>
> If the illiterate leads illiterate people it is permitted, but if he leads literate people his prayer and their prayer is spoiled. al-Jūzajānī says that merely his prayer is spoiled when he knows that a literate person follows him. In the *Ẓāhir al-riwāyah* there is no difference. In al-Karkhī, the illiterate spoils his prayer only by the intention of leading a literate person in prayer. If he did not intend to lead a literate person in prayer, then it is not spoiled like with [leading] women.
>
> If the illiterate began to lead the prayer and then a literate person enters, his prayer is spoiled. al-Karkhī says his prayer is not spoiled because it [the part of the prayer that has been performed when the literate person enters] is only to the extent of his performing his prayer with the recitation before beginning. If the illiterate was present and the literate was already praying, he does not join in, but he prays by himself.[46]

By detailing the reasons for each of the conflicting opinions in these two passages, al-Ḥaddād indicates that although the opinions themselves differ, there is a single principle on which they agree and from which they are deduced. In the case of an illiterate person leading literate people in prayer, Mūsā b. Sulaymān al-Jūzajānī [d. 200] and al-Karkhī hold that only the illiterate's prayer is spoiled because he intends to lead literate people. The opinion stated by al-Ḥaddād differs in that in holds that the prayer of the literate followers is also spoiled. This same distinction holds for the second case in which the prayer of either the literate or the illiterate is already in progress. Yet, both opinions agree on the general principle that an illiterate is not to lead literate people.

The reason for this is given in the conflict of opinions between the three Ḥanafī authorities.

> If the illiterate leads both literate and illiterate people in prayer then the prayers of everyone are spoiled according to Abū Ḥanīfah because the illiterates were able to perform their prayers with a recitation had they joined together in prayer with the [rest of the] literate people. According to Abū Yūsuf and Muḥammad, the prayer of the illiterate leader and the prayer of those like him [illiterates following him] is permissible because if the illiterate had prayed by himself and the literate prayed by himself it is permitted.[47]

According to al-Ḥaddād's interpretation of Abū Ḥanīfah's opinion, the illiterate prayer leader ruins the prayer because the prayer could have been performed with a recitation if one of the literate people had led the prayer instead of the illiterate. The same reasoning is used by Abū Yūsuf and Muḥammad to come to a different conclusion, that only the prayer of the literate people is ruined. This is because the illiterates, had they been alone without any literate people, would have been permitted to perform the prayer without the recitation by a literate person. The conflict of opinion is not due to later scholarship deducing its interpretation from different principles but is the result of different logical distinctions being taken into consideration when deducing from the same principle. Similar to the case of the reed stalks, here al-Ḥaddād shows that Ḥanafī scholarship is consistent because it works off the basis of the same revelatory principles.

The inverse of this, that previous scholarship agrees on the original definition of practice but not on the particular reasons adduced to explain it, is demonstrated by al-Ḥaddād in his comments on the statement that it is reprehensible to put baked bricks on a grave site.

> (A baked brick and wood are reprehensible, but reeds are not harmful.)
>
> It is said that baked brick is reprehensible only because it is made with fire and is therefore not auspicious. Therefore,

> rock and wood is not reprehensible. In the *Hidāyah* it says that this determination of the principle is not sound. If fire is used in baking bricks, it is not the basis for the principle behind the reprehensibility because if it is customary to wash the corpse in hot water, fire was already used.
>
> al-Sarakhsī says the consideration in determining the principle is that it is said on account of the prohibition of building because that is what is in common between the baked brick and wood, for wood does not require the use of fire.
>
> The Bukhārīs say baked brick is not reprehensible in our cities [around Bukhārā] on account of it touching the corpse because of the ground's weakness so that Muḥammad b. al-Faḍl says if the coffin had been made of iron he sees no harm in it in this area. But is appropriate to place an adobe brick on that which is touching the corpse.
>
> Al-Timirtāshī says baked brick is reprehensible only when it is touching the corpse. When it is on top of an adobe brick, it is not reprehensible, because it preserves the corpse from predatory animals and protects it from excavation.[48]

This example is significant because it shows that al-Ḥaddād recognizes that previous scholarship does not always agree on the reasoning behind the opinions of the Ḥanafī authorities. The amount or quality of information from which later scholarship is to induce the principles used by the authorities is often not sufficient to restrict later interpretations to the same general conclusions. In this case, al-Ḥaddād points out how al-Sarakhsī's conclusion is based on the logical consideration of what both baked brick and wood have in common since both are prohibited together. The Bukhārīs and Muḥammad b. ᶜAlī al-Timirtāshī [d. 1004] interpret the reprehensibility of baked brick to be tied to its touching the corpse, meaning that to build using baked brick is allowed as long as it is laid on top of adobe brick. The interpretation of al-Timirtāshī reduces the prohibition of baked brick to a technicality by citing the need to protect corpses from animals and the elements. Appealing to the opinion of

Muḥammad b. al-Faḍl, the Bukhārīs allow baked brick altogether because of the burial conditions in their area. With the exception of recommending putting an adobe brick immediately adjacent to the corpse, this interpretation circumvents the original prohibition by limiting the principle so that it prohibits only the brick's touching the corpse. Although he gives no clear indication of which principle is behind the original prohibition, al-Ḥaddād does direct the interpretations of readers by limiting their options to the precedents listed here. Postclassical scholarship limits the conclusions of future scholarship by showing how logical considerations determine the induction of certain principles.

Conditional Cases

These few examples show how postclassical scholarship supports the traditional Ḥanafī interpretation of the revelation by demonstrating that it is deduced from what previous scholarship interprets to be the principles from which the opinions in the *Mukhtaṣar* are deduced. Postclassical scholarship takes advantage of the readers' unfamiliarity with the opinions to direct the readers' interpretations toward the logical considerations taken into account by previous scholarship. Another method commonly used by postclassical scholarship to direct readers' interpretation is to mention hypothetical cases supposed to be deduced by later scholarship from the same principles as the opinions in the *Mukhtaṣar*. By listing the selected opinions of later generations of scholarship, postclassical scholarship shows future scholars that the authority of their scholarship depends on them being able to determine from the deductions of previous scholarship what previous scholarship took to be the principles from which the opinions in the *Mukhtaṣar* were deduced. In this sense, the pedagogical approach of postclassical scholarship is to provide readers with the information necessary to induce from the opinions of later scholarship the specific logical considerations that must be taken into account to arrive at an authoritative interpretation of the *Mukhtaṣar*. This sort of approach to the analysis of the *Mukhtaṣar* is evident from al-

Ḥaddād's exposition of a single passage listing items which are not permitted to be sold.

> The sale of fish still in the water is not permitted, nor is the sale of birds in the air. The sale of an embryo and a litter is not permitted. There is no sale of milk in the udder, wool on the back of a sheep, a cubit of cloth taken from sewn cloth, of a tree trunk in a roof, or by the blow of a hunter.[49]

By illustrating each of these cases with additional opinions taken from later scholarship, al-Ḥaddād shows how the prohibition of these specific items is deduced from more general logical considerations relevant to the regulation of commercial practice at large.

According to al-Ḥaddād, the deduction of the first two examples of the fish still in the water and the birds in the air is based on the fact that the seller is not in possession of the item of exchange.

> (The sale of fish still in the water is not permitted, nor is the sale of birds in the air.)
>
> If a person sells fish in a basin, only if he cannot catch the fish, is the sale not permitted because he is selling that which he does not possess. If he catches it and then throws it back, the sale is permitted if he is able to catch it again without hunting for it because the purchaser has the option of viewing it. If the seller does not possess the fish, the catching is delayed, and the seller has to hunt for it, the sale is not permitted until he is able to deliver the fish. This is the opinion of the ʿIrāqīs. As for the Balkhīs, it is not permitted even if he is able to deliver it.[50]

Here, al-Ḥaddād uses the opinion of later scholarship, that selling fish in a basin is prohibited, to distinguish the original statement regarding selling fish in the water from the later statement concerning selling by the blow of the hunter. Otherwise, readers might assume that the statement here refers to the sale of fish in the open water, in which case the prohibition against it would be based on the uncertainty of the seller being able to catch a fish. In the case here, al-Ḥaddād makes explicit that the prohibition is based on the fact that the seller does not have possession of the fish and thus that the purchaser cannot determine its quality by viewing it. That the viewing is the crux of possession, al-Ḥaddād illustrates with the later disagreement of opinions between the ᶜIrāqī and Balkhī scholars. The ᶜIrāqīs allow the transaction assuming that the purchaser is able to determine the quality of the fish on its delivery. The Balkhīs require the viewing prior to the transaction itself, assuming either that the exchange of fish is according to a standard or measurement and as such provides for no choice of viewing after the conclusion of the contract, or that the water in the basin is opaque in which case the fish caught might not be the same one for which the exchange is contracted. In the opinion of the Balkhīs, the difference between the fish for which the sale was contracted and the fish delivered entails that the purchaser is ignorant of the quality of the item purchased which could lead to an exchange based on unequal values.

The prohibition against selling birds in the air is also shown by al-Ḥaddād to be based on the assumption that the seller does not have possession of the bird, although not for the purpose of viewing but to establish ownership.

> As for the sale of birds in the air, this is because they are not owned just because they are caught. If birds are sent from a person's hand, then there is no measurement for delivery. If a person had sold a bird on the go or flying, then it is obvious that it is not permitted.
>
> According to Qāḍī Khān, if a tame bird returns to his house and the person is able to catch it without artifice, then it is permitted [to be sold]. As for the sale of the escaped bird, if the purchaser is able to catch it or he has it in his house, then it is permitted.
>
> If he is not able to take the bird except by litigation with a judge, the sale is not permitted. According to al-Karkhī, the sale is spoiled because the seller is not able to deliver the bird at the close of the contract, just like the bird being in the air.

> According to al-Khujandī, the sale is not permitted at the present, but if the bird appears and is delivered, then the sale is permitted.[51]

The bird is distinguished from the fish by the inclusion of the case involving litigation taken from the scholarship of al-Karkhī. By comparing the prohibition of selling a bird whose ownership is not established to selling a bird in the air, al-Ḥaddād shows that the sale of a bird in the air is prohibited because the seller's ownership of the item being exchanged cannot be established. Qāḍī Khān's [d. 592] opinion establishes that fish cannot be sold even in a basin of water, but birds can be sold outside of a cage as long as the seller's ownership can be established by the fact that a tame bird is caught without artifice or the escaped bird being in the hands of the seller or in the seller's house along with the seller's other possessions. Otherwise, because of the difference in the living conditions of fish and birds, it is not possible for the purchaser to determine the value of the particular bird as an item of exchange. By giving examples of cases deduced by later scholars from the same principle as the original case with slightly different extenuating circumstances, al-Ḥaddād allows readers to see how previous scholarship takes into account the necessity of establishing ownership in establishing the validity of an exchange. These additional cases also exemplify the explanation al-Ḥaddād himself gives for the original case.

The reasoning behind the second case listed in the *Mukhtaṣar,* the prohibition against selling an embryo and a litter, is shown by al-Ḥaddād to be based on the fact that neither item is known to exist.

> (The sale of an embryo and a litter is not permitted.) A litter is that which is carried in an embryo. The sale of an embryo is not permitted without the mother nor the mother without the embryo because it is not known whether the animal in the embryo exists or not.

> If a person sold the animal's offspring before it was separated from its mother and then delivered it [after it was born], the exchange is not permitted.[52]

As in the previous cases of the fish and birds, al-Ḥaddād states what he takes to be the reasoning behind the opinion from the *Mukhtaṣar* and then gives another case to exemplify further this reasoning. In this case, the example illustrates the logic of the original case by clarifying that it is not the selling of offspring that is prohibited but the selling of that offspring before it is born. Unlike the fish and birds, the embryo and the litter are not able to be seen before they are delivered by the animal bearing them. Therefore, even if the purchaser is able to take possession of the offspring at the time of the exchange, if the exchange was contracted while the offspring was still inside of its mother, the exchange is not permitted. This is because, like the fish in the water and birds in the air, while the offspring is yet unborn, its value cannot be determined. The offspring could be stillborn in which case the contract, based on the ignorance of the item of exchange, for a live animal would be invalidated.

The third and fourth cases mentioned in the *Mukhtaṣar* are grouped together by al-Ḥaddād to illustrate the single point that either the measurement or the quality of the items of exchange must be known to avoid an exchange based on an inequality of value.

> (There is no sale of milk in the udder) because it is not known how much it is and is thus subject to usury, nor (wool on the back of a sheep) because it needs still to be cut from the sheep and its amount is not specified.
>
> Likewise, it is not permitted to sell pearls still in oysters. If a person purchased a chicken and found a pearl in its stomach, then he would own it. If a sheep had been slaughtered but not skinned and a person sold its intestines, it is permitted. The purchaser has a choice when he sees it.[53]

In this case, al-Ḥaddād adds three more contrasting cases himself to distinguish the cases of milk and wool. The selling of pearls still in oysters is just like selling milk in the udder because, although milk is sold by a standard of measurement and pearls according to their quality, in neither case is the measurement or quality able to be ascertained. The *Taysīr al-Qudūrī fī al-fiqh al-Ḥanafī* of Muḥammad Muṣṭafā Ṭabaᶜ and

Rajab al-ᶜĀyadī states that the exchange of neither is permitted because it leads to an inequality in value.[54] It is permitted to purchase a chicken and keep a pearl found it its stomach because the chicken, rather than the pearl, is being exchanged. Finally, al-Ḥaddād states that the sale of sheep intestines is permitted once the sheep has been slaughtered, indicating that the permission is based on the fact that the purchaser has the opportunity to view and assess the amount of the intestines. Thus, the intestines of a flayed sheep and pearls in chickens are allowed to be sold for the same reason that pearls in oysters and milk in udders are not allowed to be sold. Although the details of some of the cases are unlikely to occur, these contrasting cases allow readers to determine which variables in the original case are dependent on the circumstances particular to that case and which are independent of the particular case and generally applicable.

According to al-Ḥaddād, the exchange of the items in the fifth and sixth cases is prohibited because an item cannot be exchanged if its delivery is predicated on the impairment of some larger property to which the item is attached.

> (Or a cubit of cloth taken from sewn cloth, or a tree trunk in a roof) because the person is not able to deliver the items except by the impairment of the cloth and the roof.
>
> If the seller had cut a dhirāᶜ of cloth or pulled out the trunk before the purchaser dissolved the deal, the exchange becomes sound and ceases to be spoiled. When a person sells a pit for a dried date and a seed for a watermelon before they have been transformed [into the fruit from which they were taken], it is a sound exchange.[55]

By comparing the original case to the exchange of seeds for the produce of a plant into which the seeds will grow, al-Ḥaddād shows that the original exchange is not disallowed because of the unknown quality of the cubit of cloth or tree trunk. If the prohibition were based on the items' unknown quality, then the exchange of a seed for a watermelon, without knowing ahead of time the quality of the watermelon, which is sold by size and quality, would not be allowed. The reasoning for the prohibition of the cloth and the tree trunk is adduced by al-Ḥaddād in his exposition of the unmixed exchange of silver for silver.

> (If a person sells a sword ornamented with silver for one hundred dirhems, its ornamentation being worth fifty dirhems, and the purchaser turns over fifty dirhems of its price, the sale is permitted, the revenue considered to be for the silver portion, even if this is not made evident. . . . If the two parties do not reciprocally take possession until after they separate, the contract regarding the ornamentation is invalidated) because it is an unmixed sale. The sale of the sword itself is likewise invalidated if it cannot be separated from the ornamentation without damage, because its delivery is possible without damage. It is also not permitted to sell the sword without the ornamentation like a tree trunk in a roof.[56]

By making the connection between the sword and the tree trunk, al-Ḥaddād allows the reader to compare the examples to one another to discover the reasoning behind all three cases. Juxtaposed to the case of the seeds for fruit, these cases show that the exchange of the cloth, tree trunk, and sword is prohibited because of the damage needed to be done to the larger property of which the item is originally a part.

The final case listed in the *Mukhtaṣar* is used by al-Ḥaddād to illustrate the logic behind all of the previous cases and of commercial practice in general.

> (Or by the blow of a hunter.) This is when the prey results from the casting of a single snare. The reason is because the exchange is based on ignorance. The purchaser does not know whether the hunter will deliver something or what it will look like.[57]

First, al-Ḥaddād shows that the exchange is not permitted because the value of the item being exchanged is based on the chance of the blow. Similar to the case of the embryo and the litter, the item to be exchanged, although theoretically in existence, is not in the possession of the seller. This is also analogous to the sale of fish in water or birds in the air, which al-Ḥaddād stated is not permitted because the person is selling that which he does not yet possess.[58] Second, because it is not certain that the hunter will even deliver something, it is not possible to exchange the item before the two parties separate as is required for the exchange of items whose value depends on their quality. Nor is it possible to set a fixed deadline as is required for the exchange of items whose value depends on a standard of measurement. Third, because it is not possible to see the item of exchange until after it has been sold, the purchaser has no way of evaluating the item whether by its weight or by its quality. Under any of these circumstances, the exchange makes the purchaser ignorant of the value of the exchanged item, and, as such, leads to an exchange based on unequal values.

Logical Structure of Previous Scholarship

Postclassical scholarship limits readers' induction to certain principles by attaching logical significance, through the medium of previous scholarship, to the details of the Ḥanafī authorities' opinions. The specific details mentioned in the opinions are taken by postclassical scholarship as being indicative of the logical structure of the authorities' reasoning. In a given opinion certain details are specific to the particular circumstances of the case and other details are representative of more general logical considerations. By adducing further details with which to compare the original details, postclassical scholarship indicates to readers which variables are dependent on the specific circumstances and which are independent because they are tied to the general principle being applied. In light of the comments of postclassical scholarship, the *Mukhtaṣar* is read as a sort of workbook, providing examples as heuristic devices for readers to determine the reasoning behind the Ḥanafī opinions. Readers' decisions as to which details represent what principles are made in relation to the information provided by the selected precedents cited by postclassical scholarship. Therefore, postclassical scholarship not only allows but requires the interpretation of the Ḥanafī opinions to be consistent with the interpretations of previous scholarship.

This sort of determination of readers' interpretations is evident in how postclassical scholarship discloses the logic responsible for the Ḥanafī definition of commercial practice from the exposition of details in selected cases. Postclassical scholarship contends that the fundamental principle behind the definition of commercial practice is that ignorance concerning the value of items of exchange leads to an exchange based on the inequality of value, which is not permitted. From this basic principle is deduced that equivalence in value is to be established with two types of exchanges. Equivalence in value can be established by assessing the price [thaman] of the items of exchange in terms of their quality, or, in the case of certain items, equivalence in value can be determined by the measurement [qadar] of the items being exchanged. Postclassical scholarship demonstrates how the establishment of equivalence through these two types of exchanges informs the more specific cases mentioned by the opinions.

By interjecting short explanatory glosses into a passage taken from the *Mukhtaṣar,* al-Maydānī mentions the basic principle behind the practice of exchanging according to a standard of measurement.

> (and) the basic principle of this is that (of all that of which the apprehension of its property and the knowledge of its measurement is possible) by dry measure, weight, and number in a single species (delayed delivery is permitted) because it does not lead to inequality in value.
>
> (Of that which the apprehension of whose property and the knowledge of whose extent is not possible) because it is not by dry measure, weight, and there is disparity with one of the items measured by number (delayed delivery is not permitted) because ignorance of these things leads to inequality in value.[59]

The exchange of certain items is permissible when the value of those items is not contingent on the market but set according to conventional standards of measurement. A delay in the delivery of these items does not affect their value because their value is not dependent on their quality relative to price but on a standard of measurement which does not change. In his commentary on the *Kanz al-daqāʾiq* of al-Nasafī which comments on the *Hidāyah* which quotes an earlier passage from the *Mukhtaṣar,* al-Zaylaʿī states the same principle.

> (Delayed delivery of items sold by dry measure and weight [of the item of value] is sound) because of what we previously transmitted from the prophet and because of what is meant by the phrase. Beware of al-Nasafī's words "of the item of value" as referring to dirhems and dinars because these things are species of price but there is no item of value unless something is exchanged for them. Delayed delivery is not sound unless the value is present and the delivery of the item of exchange is delayed, in which case it is permitted, but not the opposite.[60]

In part, this is a reference to the mention of coins as not permitted to be exchanged by weight in Muḥammad b. Aḥmad al-Isbījābī's [fl. 500s] commentary on the *Mukhtaṣar,* and repeated by al-Ḥaddād. Also, al-Zaylaʿī asserts that the delayed delivery of items is dependent on the value of the items being present at the time of the contract, meaning that although the items themselves are not present, their value will be the same at the time of their later delivery as it is at the time of the contract. The basic contention of this postclassical scholarship is that the value of certain items of exchange does not change over time, and thus knowledge of the items' values can be determined by a standard of measurement even when the items are not present at the time of the contract.

The contention is illustrated by al-Ḥaddād in his exposition of the mention of the walnut and the egg in the *Mukhtaṣar* as items whose delayed delivery is permitted and thus whose exchange is based on their measurement according to a certain standard.

> (Delayed delivery is permissible for items sold by dry measure, weight, and number, the individual items of which do not differ such as the walnut and the egg.)
>
> The intention in mentioning items sold by weight is not two coins because their value is determined according to

> quality and the items of delayed delivery are those things which do not require an appraisal of quality. Items sold by dry measure like wheat, barley, pearl millet, milk, rice, and other such things, if their measure can be determined in weight, are permitted.
>
> The egg is permitted to be an item of delayed delivery according to us. Both small and large eggs are equal in the conventional practice of people concerning their disparity, as opposed to the watermelon, cucumber, and pomegranate, for the disparity among these things is in their appearance. It is not said that the egg is such and such quality. This is likewise the case for the walnut.
>
> Zufar said delayed delivery is not permissible for the egg and the walnut. As for the egg, he reports, on the authority of Abū Ḥanīfah, that he did not allow the delayed delivery of ostrich eggs because among the eggs there is a disparity.[61]

First, al-Ḥaddād uses the example of the egg as an epitome of those items whose value does not change over time, being dependent not on the quality but on the unit measurement. Just as certain items are to be exchanged by weight or dry measure, so the egg is to be exchanged by number because different eggs are not considered to be of disparate qualities when sold. Second, al-Ḥaddād contrasts eggs to both coins whose value is determined according to their content of precious metal and certain fruits whose value is determined according to their weight. Eggs and fruit are both unlike coins in that the value of neither is dependent on quality. Eggs are not like fruit whose value is dependent on the different sizes of the individual fruits, and thus knowledge of the eggs' value can be determined from their number whereas the weight of the fruit must be determined.[62] Third, Zufar's report of Abū Ḥanīfah's opinions concerning ostrich eggs is mentioned by al-Ḥaddād to reiterate the reasoning for the exchange of regular eggs by number. Ostrich eggs are not to be exchanged by number because of a disparity in quality among the individual eggs, a disparity Zufar takes to apply to all eggs. Postclassical scholarship takes Abū Ḥanīfah's opinion as an exception to the general rule, to indicate that all eggs but ostrich eggs are to be exchanged by number because individual non-ostrich eggs are not considered to differ in quality.

Having shown how the egg epitomizes the sort of item whose value is known by its measurement according to number, al-Ḥaddād uses the mention of exchanging skins, paper, bricks, and animals by number in the *Mukhtaṣar* as opposing examples.

> (nor skins by number) because possession of them is not taken by their appearances alone, nor are they customarily sold by weight but by number. For skins to be sold by number would be a form of disparity because they are evaluated according to their size. If someone specified the measurement of something with a fixed amount, mentioning its length, width, and type, then its exchange is permitted.
>
> Likewise, the delayed delivery of paper is not permitted unless the paper is stipulated according to fixed length, width, and type. Then, its delayed delivery is permitted.[63]

Although skins are sold by number but are not exchanged on the basis of them being per se skins but according to their size, it is not possible to determine their value according to their number. Likewise, even though the value of skins is determined by their size, like the value of watermelons, it is not permitted to exchange skins by weight like watermelons because their size cannot be determined by their weight but is dependent on the quality of the individual skins. In this sense, the exchange of paper is like the exchange of skins, sold by the number of pages like eggs but also by the size of the page like watermelons.

This same point is made by al-Ḥaddād in relation to the statement concerning the exchange of bricks.

> (Delayed delivery of adobe and baked brick does no harm when it is specified according to a fixed brick mold). Because, although the possession of bricks is taken by number, it is taken according to a fixed standard when length, width, and thickness is mentioned.[64]

When the disparity among the size of bricks can be controlled, then the exchange of bricks is like the exchange of eggs. The example of bricks is used by al-Ḥaddād to reiterate the reasons epitomized by the example of eggs in contrast to the example of skins. The prohibition of exchanging animals and animal parts by number is in contrast to both eggs and skins.

> (The delayed delivery of animals and parts of animals.) Because possession of them is not taken according to their appearance alone. There is also a disparity of fatness and leanness, year, type, and the intensity of the animal's running and ambling, this having to do with the weakness of the legs. There could exist two horses equal in years and appearance and then one of them could be sold at double what is paid for the other. The disparity between them is not an external attribute.[65]

The value of animals, like the value of skins, cannot be established by number because they vary in size, nor by weight because the disparities in value among animals cannot be determined by weight. Unlike the value of skins, though, the value of animals cannot be determined by their external attributes. Animals are exchanged according to qualities that are known only from a negotiated exchange.

By commenting on the details mentioned in the *Mukhtaṣar* in relation to the different standards of measurement, al-Maydānī illustrates the same sorts of reasoning evinced by al-Ḥaddād's comments on the items of exchange.

> (Delayed delivery is not permitted with the dry measure of a particular man nor by the dhirāᶜ of a particular man) when its measurement is not known because its delivery is being delayed and perhaps there will be a decrease in value which will lead to an inequality in value.[66]

As the explanation of this particular statement, al-Maydānī states the general consideration that the determination of which items are exchanged according to their measurement is based not on the items themselves but on their being exchanged according to a standard of measurement. When the measurement of an item is not known, regardless of whether it is capable of being exchanged according to its measurement, its exchange cannot be predicated on its value as determined by its measurement. This conclusions is illustrated by al-Maydānī using several specific examples.

> There is no harm if it is a dry measure that is not subject to a decrease or change such as a large bowl or the like. If it is something made into a bag by weaving, such as a basket made of palm leaves or stockings, then it is not permitted because of the inequality in value. According to Abū Yūsuf, this is excepting waterskins because of their use.[67]

By juxtaposing the bowl and the waterskin to woven containers, al-Maydānī illustrates that knowing the value of items by their measurement is not dependent on using certain standards of measurement but on the standard of measurement used not changing. In practice, it is permitted to use the dry measure of a particular man, as long as it is measured in a bowl and not a basket out of which some of the amount of the item being exchanged could fall. Value determined by baskets and stockings varies from measurement to measurement and thus leads to ignorance regarding the amount of the items being exchanged.

> (Nor with respect to the food of a particular district, nor the fruit of a particular group of palm trees) because it might be denuded by a plague and then be lessened from the measurement agreed to be delivered. This does not apply, however, if there is a place name [nisbah] to differentiate the description of the item but not to particularize a particular crop.[68]

Like the prohibition against exchanging items measured by woven containers, the prohibition against exchanging the food and fruit in this case is due not to the possibility that the specified items might be of a different quality than most food and fruit but because the measurement of the original amount might change over time.

These examples show how postclassical scholarship uses the details from the *Mukhtaṣar* to show that, in some cases, the value of items is to be established by the measurement of the items rather than by their quality. On the one hand, al-Ḥaddād interprets the examples listed in the *Mukhtaṣar* to epitomize the categories of which items are to be exchanged by measurement and which by quality. On the other hand, al-Maydānī illustrates through the medium of similar examples what constitutes a legitimate standard of measurement. In both cases, the examples act as variables whose significance depends on the basic distinction between the two ways of establishing knowledge of value, which in turn depends on the general principle that ignorance of items' values leads to inequality in an exchange. Postclassical scholarship shows how the examples mentioned in the opinions are deduced from this general principle and basic distinction, and also how to induce the distinction and the principle from the deduced examples. This same sort of reasoning is exhibited by postclassical scholarship in its commentary on the exchange of items according to their species, directing readers to induce more general predicates from specific details. Postclassical scholarship shows that the exchange of items by a standard of measurement must be between items of the same species.

The establishment of equivalence between items of exchange, al-Ḥaddād contends, must take into consideration a rate of exchange determined in accordance with the species of the items and their respective values. Items of the same species are not to be exchanged at an equal rate if they are of unequal value.

> (The sale of wheat for flour or oatmeal is not permitted.) There is no comparison of measurement and no equality between the two items because the wheat, its flour, and its oatmeal are one species. When wheat is sold for flour, it becomes as though flour is sold for flour plus extra because there is flour in all wheat when it is separated into pieces by grinding, which is the extra [i.e., the grinding].
>
> On account of this, the exchange of cooked wheat for uncooked wheat is not permitted. . . . The exchange of flour for flour is permitted when the two are equal in quality.[69]

Both wheat and flour are exchanged by the same standard of dry measurement and are of the same species but are of unequal value. The quality of the flour is different from the quality of the wheat because the flour consists of wheat plus grinding. Exchanging wheat for flour or oatmeal at an equal rate of exchange would produce a lopsided exchange. An equal rate of exchange is to be used when the items are of the same species and of the same quality. Wheat and flour are of the same species but the flour requires extra production to be ground from the wheat just as cooked wheat requires extra production not required for uncooked wheat. By adding the grinding and the cooking, al-Ḥaddād indicates the reason why wheat is not exchanged for flour or oatmeal at an equal rate although all three are of the same species.

This general consideration of the extra production required for certain items of the same species is made more explicit in al-Ḥaddād's comments on the examples of olives and sesame seeds.

> (The sale of olives for olive oil and sesame seeds for sesame oil is not permitted unless the olive oil and the sesame oil is greater than that which is in the olives and the sesame seeds, so that the oil is of an amount similar to the olives and the seeds, the surplus being in the dregs.)
>
> If the measurement of that which is in the oil and the olives or the sesame seeds is not known, it would not be permitted. Under these same circumstances, it is permitted to exchange grease and milk for butter, grapes for grape juice, and dried dates for molasses.[70]

The exchange of olives for olive oil and sesame seeds for sesame oil is parallel to the exchange of wheat for flour, as are the cases of grease and milk for butter, grapes for grape juice, and dried dates for molasses. In each case, the exchange is between two items of the same species but of unequal quality. The difference in the examples mentioned here is that it is possible to measure the amount of the original item and compare it to the amount of the item produced from the same species as the original item. This allows the exchange of the oil to be at an unequal rate, there being less oil in the olives than in the olive oil, but the exchange of the olives to be at an equal rate, there being the same amount of olive oil as there is olives in terms of amount. Like the exchange of wheat for flour being like the exchange of flour for flour plus extra, the exchange here is considered to be of olive oil for olive oil plus the dregs. That the knowledge of the relative amounts is what permits this practice is evident from al-Ḥaddād's comment that if the measurement of the relative amounts is not known, the exchange is not permitted.

When both of the items are of the same species and the quality of both has been altered by the requirement of extra work for their production, then the exchange of the items at an equal rate is permitted. This is illustrated by al-Ḥaddād through the interpretations of previous scholarship concerning a hypothetical case analogous to the wheat for flour exchange.

> There is disagreement concerning exchanging cotton for spun yarn. It is mentioned in the *Dhakhīrah* that the selling of spun cotton for unspun cotton, at an equal rate of exchange, is not permitted because the cotton is diminished by the spinning. This is the case with wheat for flour.
>
> In the *Fatāwah* of Qāḍī Khān, the sale of spun yarn for cotton, at an equal rate of exchange, is not permitted because they are of the same species and are both sold by weight.
>
> In the *Nihāyah,* the sale of spun cotton for cloth is permitted.[71]

Here, al-Ḥaddād compares the definition of analogous cases from the *Dhakīrah* and the *Fatāwah* to the case mentioned in the *Nihāyah.* The result is that the distinctions made in the previous cases are reiterated by these cases. The prohibition of exchanging spun cotton for unspun cotton at an equal rate is because both items are of the same species and their values are determined by weight, yet they are of unequal quality because of the spinning required to produce one of the items. The exchange of spun cotton for cloth is permitted, however, because both of the items, being of the same species and evaluated in terms of a standard of measurement, require production. These examples illustrate that production required for only one of the items leads to an inequality in value in which case items of the same species cannot be exchanged at an equal rate.

If, however, the items of exchange are of different species, then it is permitted to exchange them at an unequal rate because it is assumed that they are of unequal value.

> (The sale of meat for animals is permitted according to Abū Ḥanīfah and Abū Yūsuf. Muḥammad says it is not permitted unless the meat which is on the animal be less than that for which the meat is contracted.)
>
> Muḥammad's opinion is when the meat and the animal are of the same species, like when a person sells mutton for a sheep. As for when the two are of different species, if a person sells beef for a sheep or a similar animal, it is permitted with the price determined according to the different amounts of meat. The meaning of "according to" is that the beef is more than the meat on the sheep considering the meat of its species, the remainder being an equivalent for the head, skin, and trotters.
>
> This exchange is like when a person sells what is sold by weight for what is not sold by weight because animals are not customarily sold by weight.[72]

The conflict of opinions from the *Mukhtaṣar* is used by al-Ḥaddād to indicate the significance of species to the establishment of equivalence. Because of the difference in size between a bovine and a sheep, it is argued that the amounts of meat will be unequal and thus the two are to be exchanged at an unequal rate, unless the head, skin, and trotters of the sheep are exchanged for the extra meat of the bovine. Muḥammad allows the exchange of two items of the same species at an equal rate on the consideration that the amount of the meat on the animal can be ascertained to be less than the amount of meat for which it is being exchanged. This interpretation of Muḥammad's opinion given by al-Ḥaddād makes the exchange of meat for animals like the exchange of olives for olive oil, which is regarded as the exchange of olive oil for olive oil with the extra olives for the dregs. Otherwise, if the animals and the meat are of different species, as in the opinion of Abū Ḥanīfah and Abū Yūsuf, the exchange is permitted at an unequal rate because the relative values of the items are being evaluated by their different qualities not by a standard of measurement.

That the determination of equivalence in the former case is dependent on the species and not the size of the animal is made explicit by al-Ḥaddād.

> As for bovine and buffalo meat, it is of a single species. This is likewise the case for goats and sheep, and Bactrian and Arabian camels. The exchange of an unequal amount of their meat is not permitted because they are a single species even if they seem to differ.[73]

Despite the disparity in appearance, meat of the same species is considered to be of equal value and thus cannot be exchanged at an unequal rate. This same contention is made through the exposition of just the opposite case.

> (The milk of a cow for that of a goat) because although they are both types of milk which is a single species, the meat is of different species.
>
> (And fine date vinegar for grape vinegar is permitted to be sold at an unequal rate) because there is a difference between the two types of vinegar, therefore the sale of one of them for the other at an unequal rate is permitted.
>
> (The sale of bread for wheat and flour at an unequal rate is permitted) because the bread, on account of its being produced, is removed from the species of its ingredients and is sold by number and weight whereas wheat is reckoned by dry measure.[74]

According to al-Ḥaddād, all three examples are determined on the basis of whether the items being exchanged are of the same species. The permission to exchange these items at an unequal rate is explained by al-Ḥaddād as due to a distinction between the means used to produce the items. In the first two cases, species is determined not by the product but by the producer, whereas in the third case in which the bread is not a natural product of wheat or flour, species is determined by the product. By making this distinction between natural and artificial production, al-Ḥaddād is able to emphasize how the consideration of species is tied to evaluating items by their measurement, and the consideration of artificial production is tied to evaluating items by their relative quality.

This distinction is made by al-Maydānī in the case of exchanging items at an equal rate because they are of the same species although their appearance suggests that they are of unequal value.

> (The sale of ripe dates for dried dates is permitted) and ripe dates (like for like) by dry measure according to Abū Ḥanīfah because the ripe date is a date and the sale of a date for its like is permissible.
>
> (The sale of grapes for raisins is permitted) just as is the exchange of all dried fruit.[75]

Although wheat cannot be exchanged for flour because both are of the same species and the flour requires artificial production, which affects its value, ripe dates can be exchanged for dried dates. This is because dried dates are a natural product of ripe dates. The distinction is reduced to a simple explanation by al-Bābartī, as reported by al-Maydānī.

> In the *ᶜInāyah,* it is said that everything which changes naturally, such as fresh and dried dates or good and bad, is not considered to be of unequal value. Everything which changes by artificial means such as wheat to flour or cooked wheat and uncooked wheat spoils the exchange.[76]

The general consideration of production affecting the equal values of same species items is clearly stated in this passage. Artificial production removes an item from its original species, meaning the item's value is not determined by a standard of measurement equal to the same standard of measurement of an unproduced item from the same species. Natural production allows the item to remain in its original species, and as such dried fruit is to be exchanged at an equal rate for ripe fruit despite the apparent difference in quality because the natural change in the fruit does not affect its value.

These examples show how readers of postclassical scholarship are instructed to reason inductively by reversing the deductive reasoning of previous scholarship's interpretations of the opinions. The logic of the opinions is disclosed by readers' interpretations of the interpretations of the opinions.

If *a*, then *d*.	*a* = species/species: flour/flour, spun cotton/cloth.
If *b*, then *e*.	*b* = species/nonspecies: date vinegar/grape vinegar.
But, if natural production, then *d*.	
If *c*, then either *d* or *e*.	*c* = species/species + production.
But, if artificial production, then *e*.	
Where	*d* = equal rate of exchange (measurement) and *e* = unequal rate of exchange (quality).

On the one hand, the exchange of items of the same species (*a*), such as flour for flour or spun cotton for cloth, is to be at an equal rate of exchange (*d*), because the equal values of the items is determined by the measure of each item being equal. On the other hand, the exchange of items of different species (*b*), such as date vinegar for grape vinegar, is to be at an unequal rate of exchange (*e*), because the inequality between the items' values due to differing qualities is equalized by an unequal rate of exchange. To reiterate this basic division between types of exchanges, postclassical scholarship shows that the exchange of items of the same species when one of the two item's value has been affected by production (*c*) is exchanged at an unequal rate of exchange (*e*) if the item's quality is altered by artificial means.

Through its exposition of these logical considerations, postclassical scholarship teaches that the Ḥanafī authorities reason by making logical distinctions among the implications of a given fundamental principle induced from the revelation. From these logical distinctions, then, are deduced more specific opinions taking into consideration the details of particular cases.

Principle:	ignorance of value of items leads to unequitable exchange.
(deduction)	
Logical distinctions:	knowledge of value is established by measurement or quality.
(deduction)	
Opinions:	wheat for wheat, ripe dates for dried dates, but not wheat for barley or for flour at an equal rate.

By construing the opinions to be deduced from more general logical distinctions, which are deduced from more general principles, postclassical scholarship directs readers to induce back-

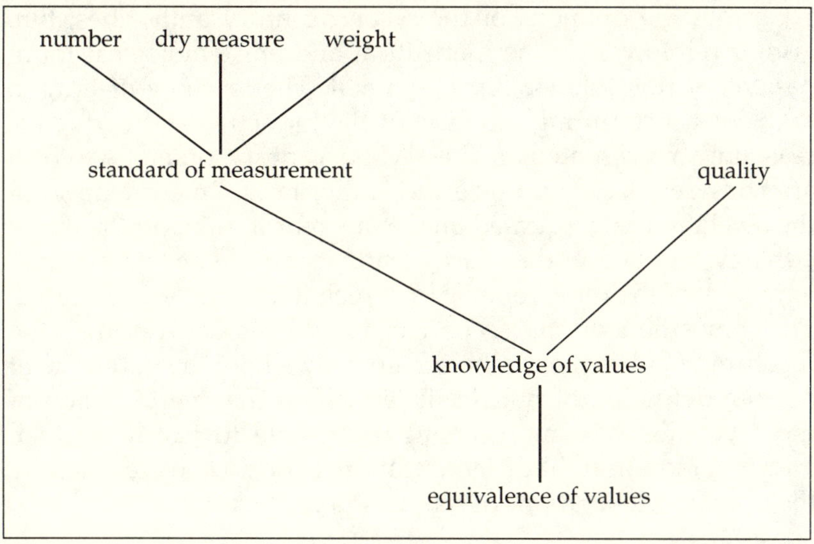

Figure 4.1. How readers induce the general principle behind the definition of commercial practice through the details mentioned in specific cases.

ward from the details of particular cases the principle originally induced from the revelation by the prophet (see Figure 4.1). Postclassical scholarship circumscribes the principles future scholars can claim are to be induced from the revelation. To be authoritative, future scholarship's conclusions must be deduced from the principles induced from the revelation. This induction, though, must be consistent with the conclusions of previous generations of scholarship. Otherwise, future scholarship cannot demonstrate, using the methodology and epistemology developed by the classical schools, that its conclusions are consistent with the revelation itself.

Conclusions

The continuity of Ḥanafī fiqh scholarship is maintained by teaching future scholars how to reason through the medium of previous scholarship. This pedagogic approach not only perpetuates the interpretive tradition of the school by demonstrating that Ḥanafī scholarship is built on the accretion of interpretations regarding the opinions of the second century authorities, but, also, it reinforces the hermeneutical and epistemological foundations of fiqh scholarship in general. The teaching of how to define practice through the use of the inductive and deductive reasoning represented in the second century opinions, which are considered to epitomize the authoritative interpretation of the revelation, is predicated on the theoretical claims of the methodology outlined in the fourth century and the text-based epistemology of the third century on which it, in turn, is predicated. The exposition of the second century opinions through the medium of subsequent scholarship shows how the authority of a given definition of practice is less about the interpretation of the revelation and more about being able to justify a given interpretation in light of the traditional conclusions reached by the previous generations of scholarship.

Conclusions

In the first volume of his work *Human Understanding,* Stephen Toulmin contends that continuity rather than change deserves explanation.[1] That ideas should be constantly changing, along with changes in society and technology, is expected. That ideas do not change, especially over a 1,200 year period, is surprising. What is relevant to understanding how ideas form and affect life is not how paradigms are overthrown in moments of revolutionary change,[2] but how paradigms are instituted and maintained by the culture that uses them. That aspect of culture called "religious," in its occupation with perpetuating certain interpretations of given "texts," exemplifies how traditional paradigms are established and continued as sources of authority.

The preceding pages have shown how a certain conception of canonical authority, especially one requiring the induction of certain principles and the deduction of opinions from those principles, is authorized and used to maintain a certain tradition of interpretation within Ḥanafī scholarship. In the third century, a text-based epistemology was constructed, canonizing the sunnah by requiring the use of interpretive reasoning to extract a definition of practice from the revelation. The opinions of selected second century local authorities were canonized in the fourth and fifth centuries as being the result of the inductive reasoning epitomized by the sunnah. As epitomes of how to interpret the revelation through the medium of the sunnah, the opinions authorized the conclusions of later scholarship. In the sixth and later centuries, the scholarship of previous generations, epitomizing the interpretive reasoning of the opinions, was used to direct future scholarship backward through the precedents of the opinions and the sunnah to the revelation. By showing that future scholarship's conclusions must be deduced from principles that are to be induced from the deductions of previous generations, Ḥanafī scholarship creates and maintains a paradigm that authorizes its own interpretive privilege.

I

The maintenance of a certain epistemological and methodological paradigm in Ḥanafī scholarship is accomplished by the manipulation of authority through the medium of certain texts. This manipulation is predicated on a particular conception of canonical authority. For Ḥanafī scholarship, the canon is not necessarily a fixed set of things, but rather the agreement that a set of things is authoritative. The contents of this set are neither the purview of a particular school nor are they to be identified with a single or several written versions of them. Different collections of Ḥanafī opinions, for example, were considered authoritative and used for centuries before they were reduced to a written text. The opinions listed in fifth century texts like the *Mukhtaṣar* of al-Qudūrī are supplemented by opinions mentioned in the postclassical scholarship of the sixth and later centuries. Ḥanafī scholars did not "copy" collections of opinions but wrote commentaries on previous scholarship that included certain opinions. Later attempts to delimit a body of writings as a canonical "text" of the opinions are based on extractions from the opinions earlier scholarship used. The authority of the opinions was already assumed by the scholarship from which the written canon is compiled. This is similar to the later attempts to reduce the contents of the sunnah, already in use by different local authorities, to a written text in the six books. The partisan nature of the six books is evident because the opinions of the local authorities later considered authoritative are not all based on reports found in the six books nor are all the six books' contents necessarily considered authoritative by all of the different local authorities or the later schools. Attempts to put the contents of the sunnah or the corpus of opinions into writing are not the cause but the result of a certain set of things being considered canonical. This relationship between the authority of a canon and its contents suggests that the existence of a canonical "text" is most important insofar as its contents can be used to authorize a certain definition of practice.

For Ḥanafī scholarship, that which is canonical in the sense of what is used to demonstrate and perpetuate a certain interpretive authority, is not the contents of the canon but rather the interpretation of those contents. The significance of the revelation itself, for example, is not contained in the plain text of the Qurʾān. What is canonical about the Qurʾān are the principles to be induced from its text, although not always on the basis of clear indications. Often a principle is to be induced not from a statement in the text but on the basis of logical reasoning from an analogous statement or from a statement no longer extant in the text. To know which principles to induce from which statements using which sorts of reasoning, Ḥanafī scholarship contends that one must understand how the sunnah interprets the Qurʾān. The sunnah specifies the authority of the revelation found in the Qurʾān, just as the opinions specify the revelation through the sunnah, and later scholarship through the opinions. The revelation does not pass an inherent authority onto those who decide to interpret it, but rather the contents of the Qurʾān are canonical because they are integral to the definition of practice as the medium through which the prophet induced the principles of the revelation, which are, in turn, understood through later scholarship's interpretation of the opinions' interpretation of the sunnah. By stipulating certain later interpretations as required for understanding the practical significance of the revelation, Ḥanafī scholarship effectively eliminates the authority of interpretations outside of the precedents it acknowledges. To read the contents of the Qurʾān, ignoring how later tradition interprets those contents, is not to interpret the canonical significance of those contents because it is the traditional interpretation based upon the prophet's interpretation that guarantees the revelatory status of the Qurʾān.

It is this conception of canonical authority that Ḥanafī scholarship teaches future scholars, through the medium of previous scholarship, to continue a certain tradition of interpretation. Ḥanafī scholarship does not stipulate what the definition of practice is to be, but rather stipulates how one can arrive at an authoritative definition of practice. By stipulating a method rather than certain conclusions, Ḥanafī scholarship teaches future scholars the reasons why certain conclusions are authoritative. Precedents are not meant to be repeated but rather used as heuristic examples indicating how previous scholarship arrived at its conclusions, and what made those conclusions authoritative. Using the methodological considerations that go into the opinions of previous scholarship, postclassical scholarship illustrates the epistemological foundations necessary for the continued authority of future scholarship. Future scholarship is authoritative only insofar as it can demonstrate that its conclusions are consistent with the conclusions of previous generations of scholarship. To be consistent, a conclusion must be deduced from the principles the prophet induced from the revelation. Rather than just stating these principles, Ḥanafī scholarship requires future scholars to induce these principles from the deductions of previous scholarship. This pedagogical approach controls for innovation by showing the necessity of building on traditional interpretations. Without previous scholarship, including the sunnah, there are no authoritative means for applying the revelation because later tradition established the epistemological paradigm that makes the Qur᾿ān interpretable as canon. Future scholarship is authoritative not because it does not deviate from the conclusions of previous generations, but because it accepts and puts to its own uses what previous scholarship established as authoritative.

Ḥanafī scholarship's use of canonical authority provides a more complicated and more nuanced model of the relationship between "canon" and its "application." In this case, the canon is not regarded as a particular "text" fixed in writing, to which later scholarship has continual direct reference; rather, canonical authority is a concept developed to authorize and maintain a particular tradition of interpretation. Ḥanafī scholarship is less about overcoming the limitations of a "closed" text and more about using certain texts with canonical authority as pedagogic devices to further the school's interpretive agenda. The conferring of canonical authority on a given text is not a cause but a result of the next generation using that text to authorize its own purposes. Canonical authority depends on the continued use of a text to epitomize a certain tradition of interpretation. The authority of the revelation contained in the Qurʾān is dependent on its application by the prophet in his sunnah. The authority of the sunnah is dependent on its use by the local authorities as an epitome of how to interpret the revelation. The authority of the local authorities' opinions is dependent on their use by classical scholarship, the authority of which is itself dependent on its use for pedagogical purposes by postclassical scholarship. Ḥanafī scholarship locates canonical authority in these texts to use them to illustrate the epistemology and methodology involved in doing fiqh scholarship.

II

The notion of canonical authority developed from the case of Ḥanafī scholarship is analogous to the sort of authority said to be associated with certain "sacred" objects. A privileged example of this are the *churinga,* pieces of wood or stone used by the tribes of northern Australia to represent the bodies of their ancestors.[3] The churinga is particularly apropos to the canon because the authority of both is contingent on their use, in highly controlled settings, to perpetuate certain social orders.

Similar to how texts are collected together in a "canon," the churinga of a given clan are tied into bundles and stored in a place, usually a cave or crevice, designated as the receptacle or storehouse of the churinga.[4] The contents of this storehouse are not fixed by type or number of churinga. On the one hand, the churinga in a given location can be of various sizes and shapes, of wood or stone,[5] and can be associated with the totems of a number of different clans.[6] Some churinga are only a few inches long but others can be over five feet in length.[7] On the other hand, the number of churinga kept by a given clan in its storehouse is not fixed. Other clans might borrow or lend churinga to the clan,[8] or a clan might inherit the churinga of another extinct clan.[9] In addition, when new children are born new churinga are often made by relatives or clan elders from some wood at the spot where the mother is supposed to have been impregnated by the totem.[10] The contents of the clan's churinga storehouse, despite their flux and variegation, are acknowledged by the clan as a whole as having sacred authority.[11] Indeed, the exact contents of the churinga storehouse are not supposed to be known to anyone but the initiated men of the clan. Rather, that certain objects of wood and stone are said to be kept in the churinga storehouse gives these objects their authority as churinga.

Just as a text is basically a collection of symbols or sounds, the churinga in themselves are merely pieces of wood or stone. Some of the churinga are drawn or engraved with nonrepresentational marks. Yet, the presence of these marks on some churinga is not what distinguishes them from other pieces of wood and stone.[12] The fact that a particular text is labeled "holy" is not the cause of it being canonical, nor does the fact that a bundle of sticks or pile of rocks is found in a crevice mean that they are churinga.[13] Churinga being stored in a crevice is the result of those objects being identified (on account of their use) as churinga rather than ordinary pieces of wood and stone. A given stick or rock is considered to be a churinga, having sacred authority, when it is used as an implement of authority in certain contexts, just as a given text is considered to be canonical when it is applied through its interpretation to a particular context. The appropriation of a given text or piece of wood to promote the authority of the person or institution doing the appropriation is what distinguishes a canon or churinga.

Access to churinga and the bearing of them in certain contexts authorizes clan members in different social circumstances. In political contexts, churinga are used to authorize the clan members that bear them. The lending of churinga to a neighboring clan, for example, creates a sort of reciprocal authority between the borrowing and lending clans.[14] At other times, churinga are carried by a messenger to another clan, authorizing the bearer as an official representative of his clan.[15] This use of the churinga to represent the clan's authority vis-à-vis other clans is based on the use of the churinga in ritual contexts within a given clan to authorize the standing of certain members relative to other members. Spencer and Gillen begin their description of the churinga with the insight that the sacred authority of these objects functions to perpetuate the social structure of the clans.

> Amongst the aborigines of the Centre, as indeed everywhere else where they are found, considerable mystery is attached to their [churinga's] use—a mystery which has probably had a large part of its origin in the desire of the men to impress the women of the tribe with the idea of the supremacy and superior power of the male sex.[16]

An example of this is that, among the Arunta, each clan member has a "secret" or churinga name that is not to be spoken aloud.[17] These names, which are given to both male and female children at birth by the elders of the clan, are only known to the initiated men of the clan. Women and children are not allowed to know these names. When handling the churinga in a ritual setting, however, the initiated men of the clan speak these churinga names among themselves. This structure of initiated and uninitiated within the clan, accomplished through the medium of the churinga, is extended by analogy to a dichotomy between members and nonmembers of the clan with the churinga playing the same intermediary role.

The relative authority of clan members is established by restricting access to the churinga as the medium of sacred authority. On the one hand, there are clan members who are not allowed to have contact or even see the churinga. Women and children, and by extension men from other clans, are not allowed to see the churinga on punishment of death.[18] Storing the churinga in a secret place and attaching various restrictions to the area surrounding the churinga storehouse physically separates the initiated men from the rest of the clan and from the men of other clans.[19] The only access afforded uninitiated clan members to the churinga is through the medium of the initiated clan members. Upon his return from initiation and his initial viewing of the churinga, the new initiate is painted with marks representing the location of the storehouse he visited and the churinga he viewed.[20] Thus, the initiated members of the clan represent to the noninitiated members the sacred authority which the churinga themselves represent to the initiated members when they are among themselves.

On the other hand, the clan members who are allowed to have contact with the churinga must first undergo the ritual initiation of circumcision and subincision.[21] Within the group of initiated clan members, access to the churinga is still restricted according to age:

> It is only the old men who continually see and examine the Churinga of the group, which are very rarely indeed seen by anyone who does not belong to the latter. Time after time, when the *Ertnatulunga* [churinga storehouse] is visited, the Churinga are rubbed over and carefully explained by the old men to the younger ones, who in course of time come to know all about them that the old men can impart, and so the knowledge of whom the Churinga have belonged to, and what the design on each one means, is handed on from generation to generation.[22]

Over time, the young initiates gradually learn the churinga names of other clan members and are instructed in the significance of the churinga by the elders of the clan.[23] The younger initiates' access to the churinga, and through it sacred authority, is made only through the medium of the elders and the elders' access through the medium of previous generations.[24] Thus, the uninitiated and non-clan members are restricted relative to the initiated members, and the younger initiated members are restricted relative to the older initiated members (as illustrated in Figure C.1).

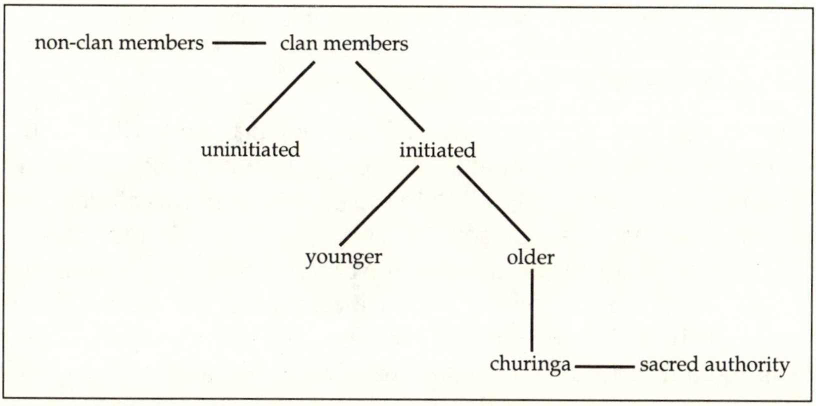

Figure C.1. The hierarchy of social standing relative to the groups' access to the churinga and through the churinga to sacred authority.

These sorts of restrictions create a hierarchy of social standing not based on the groups' position vis-à-vis other groups, but the groups' access to the churinga relative to other groups' access to the churinga.[25] Because the churinga represent sacred authority, they can be used to structure social order.

The restrictions associated with the churinga set the stage for its use as a prop to extend the authority of previous generations to certain groups within the present generation. The authority of the churinga is based on the notion that the churinga represent a palpable link between the ancestors of the mythical past and the clan leaders of the present.[26] This notion is evinced by how the significance of the churinga is passed down to future generations. In the cases where markings are present on the churinga, the nonrepresentational and polysemeous character of these markings make their interpretation dependent upon the explanation of the older, more experienced initiates.

> In one Churinga each [marking] will represent a tree, on another a frog, on another a kangaroo and so on, so that it will easily be realized that to obtain a true interpretation of any one Churinga, it is absolutely essential to obtain the

> information from some one to whom it is personally known, and such a one can only be an old man of the particular local totemic group to which it belongs.[27]

The significance of the churinga is, in practice, embodied in the elders, who alone are capable of explaining why a given piece of wood or stone represents a link to the ancestors. In this context, the churinga themselves represent the bodies of the clan's ancestors.[28]

Likewise, for the uninitiated, the representation of the churinga by markings painted on the new initiates' bodies is palpable evidence of the link between the ancestors and the new initiate and thus the authority of the initiate relative to the uninitiated members of the clan.[29] Bearing these markings, the initiates' bodies take on the same identity and authority relative to the uninitiated members of the clan that the elders are given relative to young initiates and the churinga relative to the elders (as shown in Figure C.2).

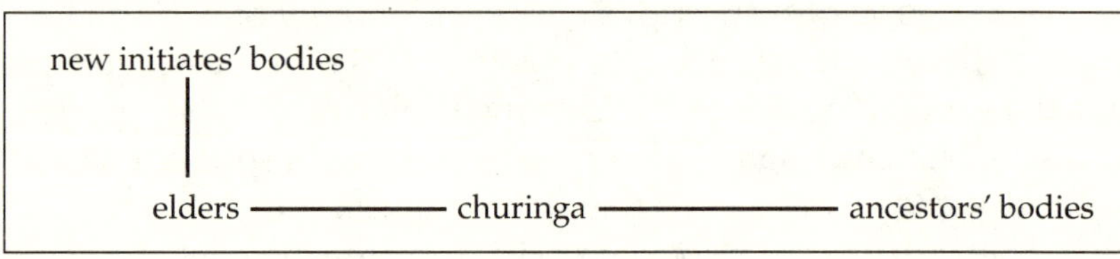

Figure C.2. How the new initiates' bodies represent the authority of the past through the medium of the elders' interpretation of the churinga as the ancestors' bodies.

In each of these cases, the new initiates, elders, and the churinga are physical representations of the ancestors' bodies and thus carry the authority of the ancestors. This access to the ancestors through the medium of the churinga has the effect of granting the standing of the past to the clan members of the present.[30]

III

The analogy of the churinga and the sacred authority associated with them emphasizes some general features of canonical authority that arose in the course of explaining the specific case of Ḥanafī scholarship. Fundamental to this analogy is the stress put on the significance of the churinga as an object rather than as a container of semantic value. This suggests that the authority of a canon is not derived from the semantic value of its contents, but rather from its value as a tangible link to the past.

The linguistic contents of a canon are analogous to the nonrepresentational marks exhibited on some of the churinga. On the one hand, it is important to recognize that the semantic value of a canon's contents and churinga's marks are not inherent in the signs themselves, whether the signs are abstract drawings or groups of letters. The value or meaning attached to a particular sign or collection of signs comes from the interpreter. Although most words have a wider conventional usage than the churinga's markings, the contents of a canon must be understood in light of an interpretation established by previous generations of scholars, just as the churinga's markings must be explained by the elders familiar with the markings' traditional interpretation. On the other hand, the authority of the churinga is not dependent on its markings, nor is the authority of the canon predicated upon its contents. Those churinga that do not have markings are still considered authoritative. In several of the Ḥanafī cases, canonical texts are referenced to support the authority of a given assertion without mention of the particular contents of the text or an explanation of the reason for the reference. Often, in those cases where a particular passage is cited from a canonical text to support an assertion, the assertion being made is explained to be in direct contradiction to the cited passage.

Both the churinga's markings and the canon's contents are used as a means to emphasize the interpretive expertise of the speaker using the churinga or canon vis-à-vis the audience's relative lack of expertise. The markings of the churinga are used in the initiation process to authorize the elders by providing an opportunity for the elders to display their knowledge as superior to that of the new and younger initiates. In Ḥanafī scholarship, especially that of the postclassical period, the contents of canons like the *Mukhtaṣar* of al-Qudūrī were used to further the pedagogic agenda of present scholarship. Postclassical Ḥanafī scholarship used the contents of classical texts to teach students how to practice interpretive reasoning. In both cases, the churinga's markings and canon's contents function as an implement to the authority of the initiation or teaching, capitalizing on the initiates or students' ignorance relative to the elder or teacher's knowledge of the markings or contents. The authority of both the elder and teacher is based on their access to the source of authority through the medium of the churinga's markings and the canon's contents. The semantic value of the markings and contents, imputed by the elder or teacher in a display of their authority, is a pedagogic device. The selection of a given churinga because of its markings or canon because of its contents for instruction shows that the choice of a particular churinga or canon is motivated, at least in part, by the consideration of how that churinga or canon can be profitably appropriated in the service of authorizing its user's agenda.[31]

The shift away from the notion that canonical authority is attached to the semantic value of the canon's contents further mitigates the assertion that a requirement of a text being canonical is its being "closed." Using a canon to authorize its user's agenda does not necessitate that the contents of that canon be fixed.[32] The collective "canon" of churinga kept in the churinga storehouse is not closed. New churinga are sometimes made at the supposed site of a child's conception; other churinga are borrowed from or loaned to other clans. Likewise, Ḥanafī scholarship does not limit the contents of its canon to a single, fixed set of written texts. The canonical corpus of the revelation is not fixed in the Qurʾān, nor are all the contents of the Qurʾān of equal canonical status. The sunnah is not delimited to a given written or unwritten text, nor is the corpus of opinions attributed to the Ḥanafī authorities. In the case of the churinga and the Ḥanafī canon, each generation adds a new layer to the set of contents considered authoritative. The inclusion of new texts and the exclusion of old texts as what is considered canonical is, in part, according to what an audience is willing to accept as authoritative. But, the relative lack of the audience's knowledge of the canon's contents or criteria for determining what does or does not belong allows the canon to be defined according to its application in specific circumstances and toward specific ends.

Canonical authority is not limited to some "original" text but rather is used as a concept to extend authority from a posited source to the present users of the canon. The sacred authority of the churinga is not limited to the original churinga of the ancestors in mythical times. New churinga carry the same authority, just as the bodies of new initiates do as representations of the ancestors' churinga. The link between the representation and the original is established because the present generation's representation or interpretation of the churinga is derived from the representations of previous generations. Knowledge of the churinga, given by the elders to the inititates, makes the initiates take on the authority of the ancestors because the ancestors' authority is based upon their knowledge of the churinga which the initiates now possess relative to the generations that precede them.

Likewise, the link of the present generation of Ḥanafī scholarship to the revelation is established through the medium of previous generations. The present generation acquires the authority of the revelation when its interpretations or representations of the revelation are consistent with those of the prophet, second century authorities, and subsequent scholarship (see Figure C.3).

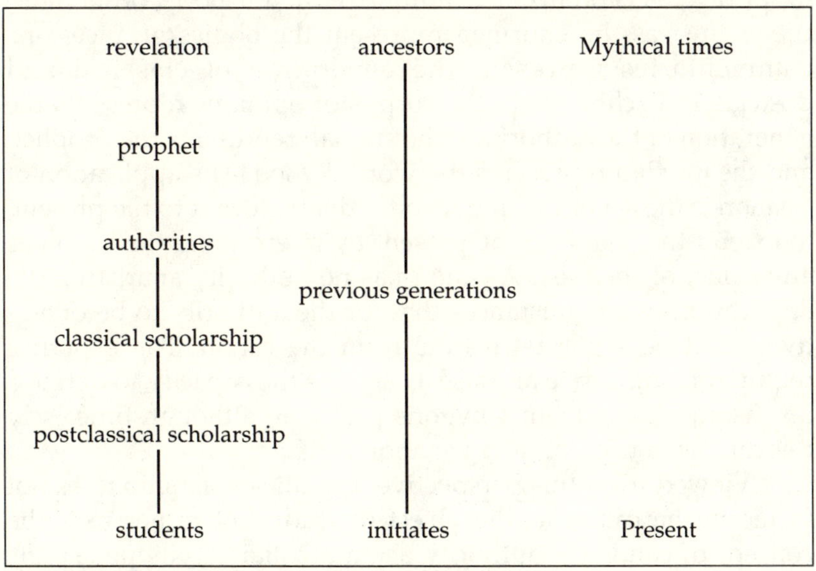

Figure C.3. The chain of transmission that extends the authority of the original source to the present generation.

This chain of authority establishes a hierarchy in which the authority of a given generation is relative to the authority of the generation previous to it, and the previous generation's authority relative to the generation previous to it. The reliance on the authority of a previous generation by a subsequent generation is what makes the previous generation authoritative. The present generation has the authority of the revelation or the ancestors because is succeeds and thus inherits the authority of the first generation from successive generations. Canonical authority originates with a given source, but it is operative to the same degree in the texts that succeed and inherit that source on account of their appropriation of previous generations' use of that authority.

Canonical authority is effective only when a "canon" is applied. Canonical authority is always applied authority. This is because the authority of a canon, like the authority of the churinga, is due to the link that a given piece of wood or group of words represent between the mythical past and the present.[33] A canon is a symbol or representation of the past whose temporal priority is capitalized to authorize the purposes of its interpreter. Just as the churinga represent the bodies of ancestors, commentaries represent the generation of classical and postclassical scholarship, the corpus of opinions represents the generation of the authorities, the sunnah represents the prophet, and the Qurʾān represents the word of God. The application of a canon is the act of making its precedent relevant to the present, to extend the past into the present by interpreting the canon as an artifact of the past. A canon has no authority apart from its application to circumstances that for the authority to be operative, must be separate in time from the canon. The expertise required to authorize and use a canon is the capacity to define a text as an artifact from a bygone past that, although timelessly relevant, is in need of interpretation.

Viewed from this perspective, Ḥanafī scholarship does not focus on the canon as the object of study but rather uses the concept of canonical authority as an auxiliary to its pedagogic focus. Ḥanafī scholarship is about constructing an epistemology and methodology that allows its canon to retain the status as applicable and thus the basis of authority, yet requiring application and thus not adequate in and of itself. In this sense, canonical authority is less about the canon itself than it is about the process surrounding the institutionalization of the canon's authority and the method allowing the use of the canon to perpetuate the present aims of those responsible for institutionalizing its authority. It is about constructing a continuity with the past to provide for innovation. The notion of canon is used in Ḥanafī scholarship to maintain a set of relationships that uphold the role of traditional precedent in defining what is unprecedented and novel.

Ḥanafī scholarship is not about learning the canon but rather learning from the canon how to make arguments consistent both with the revelation and with human reason. Students use authoritative texts to learn how to argue that their definitions of practice are authoritative. Although the canon epitomizes how to argue it does not stipulate what to conclude. Ḥanafī scholarship fixes the epistemology and methodology to be used but leaves the practical significance of the revelation open to its continuing application to novel circumstances. This means that each generation of scholarship must be prepared not to imitate the past but to demonstrate that the application of the revelation, although its own, has the authority of previous generations going back to the prophet. The continued authority of the revelation and its interpretation is thus dependent on future generations making the revelation relevant to their own circumstances in a manner consistent with how previous generations made it relevant to their circumstances.

Notes

Foreword

1. See Jonathan Z. Smith, *Map Is Not Territory* (Leiden: E. J. Brill, 1978), pp. 299–300; idem., *Imagining Religion* (Chicago: University of Chicago Press, 1982), p. 43. More recently, John B. Henderson, *Scripture, Canon, and Commentary: A Comparison of Confucian and Western Exegesis* (Princeton, N.J.: Princeton University Press, 1991): Jeffrey Timm, ed., *Text in Context: Traditional Hermeneutics in South Asia* (Albany: SUNY Press, 1991); Laurie L. Patton, ed., *Authority, Anxiety, and Canon: Essays in Vedic Interpretation* (Albany: SUNY Press, 1994).

Introduction

1. Among the recent studies that have most informed my own thoughts, see Miriam Levering, ed., *Rethinking Scripture: Essays from a Comparative Perspective* (Albany: SUNY Press, 1989); Douglas Renfrew Brooks, *The Secret of the Three Cities: An Introduction to Hindu Śākta Tantrism* (Chicago: University of Chicago Press, 1990); John B. Henderson, *Scripture, Canon, and Commentary: A Comparison of Confucian and Western Exegesis* (Princeton, N.J.: Princeton University Press, 1991); Steven D. Fraade, *From Tradition to Commentary: Torah and Its Interpretation in the Midrash Sifre to Deuteronomy* (Albany: SUNY Press, 1991); Laurie L. Patton, ed., *Authority, Anxiety, and Canon: Essays in Vedic Interpretation* (Albany: SUNY Press, 1994).

2. Jonathan Z. Smith, "Sacred Persistence: Toward a Redescription of Canon," in his *Imagining Religion* (Chicago: University of Chicago Press, 1982), p. 43. This article was previously published in *Approaches to Ancient Judaism,* ed. W. S. Green (Missoula, Mont.: Scholars Press, 1978), vol. 1, pp. 11–28. This

approach to the study of religion is exemplified in J. Z. Smith "A Pearl of Great Price and a Cargo of Yams: A Study in Situational Incongruity," *History of Religions* 16 (1976): 1–19, reprinted in *Imagining Religion,* pp. 90–101.

3. For an overview of this "older" view of religion, see Wilfred Cantwell Smith, "The Study of Religion and the Study of the Bible," *Journal of the American Academy of Religion* 39 (1971): 131–140. On the effect of this view in Islamic studies, see Willem A. Bijlefeld, "Islamic Studies Within the Perspective of the History of Religions," *Muslim World* 62 (1972): 1–11.

4. The term *practice* is more accurate than *law* or *orthodoxy.* The term *law* is misleading insofar as it suggests the range of practices regulated in more modern or Western contexts. The term *orthodoxy* suggests a focus on "belief" rather than "practice," which is not characteristic of the sharīᶜah. On the use of *practice* and the range of activities it encompasses, see Pierre Bourdieu, *Outline of a Theory of Practice,* trans. Richard Nice (Cambridge: Cambridge University Press, 1977). Originally published as *Esquisse d'une theorie de la pratique, précédé de trois études d'ethnologie kabyle* (Geneve: Librairie Droz, 1972).

5. This account is taken from Smith, "Sacred Persistence," p. 43.

6. See Smith, ibid., pp. 50–51. Smith states that his account is based on Victor Turner, *Ndembu Divination,* Rhodes-Livingstone papers 31 (Manchester: Manchester University Press, 1961).

7. Smith, ibid., p. 49. In general terms, the linguistic distinctions being applied can be found discussed in Jakobson's critique of Saussure in Roman Jakobson, "Langue and Parole: Code and Message," in his *On Language,* ed. Linda R. Waugh and Monique Monville-Burston (Cambridge, Mass.: Harvard University Press, 1990), pp. 80–109.

8. This use of *local* is meant to replace terms like *indigenous* and *native,* which are problematic in that they suggest that a certain text "belongs" to a certain group rather than being appropriated and applied to specific circumstances of a particular place and time. See the usage in Clifford Geertz, "Local Knowledge: Fact and Law in Comparative Perspective," in his *Local Knowledge* (New York: Basic Books, 1983), pp. 167–234.

9. Turner, "A Preliminary Analysis of Ndembu Divinatory Symbolism," in his *Revelation and Divination in Ndembu Ritual* (Ithaca, N.Y.: Cornell University Press, 1975), pp. 213–214. This paper was originally read to the Intercollegiate Seminar of Departments of Anthropology at London University in February 1958.

10. Turner gives information on twenty-eight different objects, called *tuponya.* Some of the tuponya are figurines, called *ankishi,* resembling humans in various positions. Others, called *yipwepu,* consist of three or four oblong fragments of calabash strung together. The mwaka is the nut of a mucha tree. The ng'oma is a drum carved out of wood. See Turner, ibid., pp. 215–229.

It is also important to note that the divination being described here is only one of more than ten recorded types of divination practiced among the Ndembu. For further information, see Turner, ibid., p. 213, and C. M. N. White, *Witchcraft, Divination and Magic* (Northern Rhodesia: Lusaka Government Printer, 1947).

11. This is an inversion of H. A. Junod's statement, cited by Turner, that "The Diviner's basket is a resumé of their whole social order, of all their institutions." See H. A. Junod, *Life of a South African Tribe* (London: Macmillan, 1927), p. 571, quoted in Turner, "A Preliminary Analysis" p. 216. The basket becomes such a resumé only when it is applied by a skilled Ndembu diviner.

12. See Turner's remark that the objects "are mnemonics, shorthands, cyphers; and each one refers to a whole series of stereotyped ways of thinking about and evaluating Ndembu society and culture. They serve as general reminders to the diviner of certain general rubrics of Ndembu culture." Turner, "A Preliminary analysis," p. 239.

13. See Turner, ibid., p. 216. This point is recognized by Smith, "Sacred Persistence," p. 50. That this knowledge is not entirely "public" but rather "professional" is evident from how it is guarded from the general public. See Turner, ibid., p. 215.

14. Turner, ibid., pp. 214–215.

15. See ibid., p. 216.

16. See ibid., p. 215. Also, see the account given in Turner, "Some Kinds and Methods of Ndembu Divination," in his *Revelation and Divination in Ndembu Ritual,* pp. 289–291.

17. See Turner, "A Preliminary Analysis," p. 215.

18. See Turner, "Some Kinds and Methods," pp. 247–292.

19. This is a loose inversion of Jack Goody's idea that changes in thought are extensions of an original idea. See Jack Goody, *Domestication of the Savage Mind* (Cambridge: Cambridge University Press, 1977). The Ndembu case suggests that later changes are construed as extensions of earlier ideas to appropriate the authority of the earlier ideas. This point is discussed briefly in

Marilyn R. Waldman, "Primitive Mind/Modern Mind: New Apporaches to an Old Problem Applied to Islam," in *Approaches to Islam in Religious Studies,* ed. Richard C. Martin (Tucson: University of Arizona Press, 1985), pp. 91–105, esp. 98–99.

20. Turner uses the example of how interpretations change according to changing circumstances to support his, perhaps dubious, claim that the anthropologist is able to interpret a society's symbols better than the society itself. In part, this seems to be based on the assumption that the symbols have a definition apart from their application to particular circumstances. See Turner, "A Ndembu Doctor in Practice," in his *The Forest of Symbols* (Ithaca: Cornell University Press, 1967), pp. 359–393.

21. Turner, "A Preliminary Analysis," p. 240.

22. See the discussion of this term in ibid., p. 240.

23. This sort of reasoning is exemplified in the few cases Turner cites in "Some Kinds and Methods," especially from the explanations Muchona gives for how he arrived at his conclusions.

24. See Smith, "Sacred Persistence," esp. pp. 49–50.

25. For an example of how the interpretation of a single "symbol" is affected by the different contexts to which it is applied, see the telling analysis in V. Turner, "Symbols in Ndembu Ritual," in his *Forest of Symbols* (Ithaca, N.Y.: Cornell University Press, 1967) esp. pp. 22–47. This article was originally published in *Closed Systems and Open Minds: The Limits of Naivety in Social Science,* ed. M. Gluckman (Edinburgh: Oliver and Boyd, 1964). In the case of divination, however, the symbols used as well as the interpretation given are dependent upon the context.

26. It is important to recognize that the Ndembu notion of canon has heuristic value vis-à-vis the conception of canon in Ḥanafī scholarship. The comparison of these cases, however, is not intended to explain Ḥanafī scholarship in light of Ndembu divination nor to suggest that the two disparate cases have a homological relationship. Rather, as a privileged example in the current academic conception of canon, the Ndembu case suggests a number of analogies with prominent features of Ḥanafī scholarship's use of canon. These analogies are useful only insofar as they lead to a more nuanced explanation of the particulars of Ḥanafī scholarship. Only after having examined the Ḥanafī case more fully is it possible to determine the generic value of the features common to both the Ḥanafī and Ndembu notions of canon.

27. For an early example of the systematic Ḥanafī use of the Qurʾān as the basis for the definition of practice, see Aḥmad b. ʿAlī al-Jaṣṣāṣ [305–370], Aḥkām al-Qurʾān, ed. Kilsisli Rifʿat (Istanbul, 1335–1338; reprint, Cairo, 1347; reprint, Beirut: Dār al-Kitāb al-ʿArabī, 1978).

28. On the use of revelatory principles contained in verses that have been "abrogated" or removed from the current text of the Qurʾān [naskh al-tilāwah dūna al-ḥukm] and the implications of not identifying the revelation solely with the text of the Qurʾān, see the discussion in John Burton, *The Collection of the Qurʾān* (Cambridge: Cambridge University Press, 1977).

Of less relevance to the Ḥanafī case is the important sunnī tradition of the sayings of the prophet that are considered to be part of the revelation although not contained in the text of the Qurʾān. On this tradition, see William A. Graham, *Divine Word and Prophetic Word in Early Islam: A Reconsideration of the Sources, with Special Reference to the Divine Saying or Ḥadīth Qudsī,* Religion and Society 7 (The Hague: Mouton, 1977). Also see J. Robson, "Ḥadīth ḳudsī," in *Encyclopaedia of Islam,* ed. B. Lewis and others, 2d ed. (Leiden: E. J. Brill, 1965), vol. 3, pp. 28–29

29. This idea of a "culture broker," is taken, in part, from Richard T. Antoun, *Muslim Preacher in the Modern World: A Jordanian Case Study in Comparative Perspective* (Princeton, N.J.: Princeton University Press, 1989); and Robert Hefner, *Hindu Javanese: Tengger Tradition and Islam* (Princeton, N.J.: Princeton University Press, 1985).

Chapter 1. The Authorization of Exegesis

1. Note that, throughout, the characterization of the "classical schools" is most pertinent to only three of the five sunnī schools: Ḥanafī, Mālikī, and Shāfiʿī. The character and development of the Ẓāhirī school is relatively unusual in sunnī fiqh scholarship, largely on account of its emphasis on a so-called literalist tradition of interpretation. The relatively late third century career of Ibn Ḥanbal [d. 241] likewise makes the origins and early development of the Ḥanbalī school distinct from those classical schools that evolved out of the "ancient schools" of the second century. On the Ẓāhirī school, see Ignaz Goldziher, *Die Ẓâhiriten: Ihr Lehrsystem und ihre Geschichte. Beitrag zur Geschichte der Muhammedanischen Theologie* (Lepizig, 1884), trans. Wolfgang Behn, *The Ẓāhirīs: Their Doctrine and their History: A Contribution to the History of Islamic Theology* (Leiden: E. J. Brill, 1971). On Ibn Ḥanbal [d. 241] and the somewhat different development of the Ḥanbalī school, see W. M. Patton, *Aḥmed ibn Ḥanbal and the Miḥna: A Biography of the Imām*

Including an Account of the Mohammedan Inquisition Called the Miḥna 218–234 A.H. (Leiden: E. J. Brill, 1897); Goldziher, "Zur Geschichte der Ḥanbalitisichen Bewegungen," *Zeitschrift der Deutschen Morgenländischen Gesellschaft* 62 (1908): 1–28; Henri Laoust, *Essai sur les doctrines sociales et politiques de Takī-d-Dīn Aḥmad b. Taimīya* (Cairo: PIFAO, 1939); Laoust, "Le hanbalisme sous le califat de Baghdad," *Revue das Études Islamiques* (1959): 67–128; George Makdisi, "L'Islam Hanbalisant," *Revue des Études Islamiques* 42 (1974): 211–244, 43 (1975): 45-76 [="Hanbalite Islam," in *Studies on Islam,* trans. and ed. Merlin L. Swartz (Oxford: Oxford University Press, 1981), pp. 216–174].

2. On the relationship of the written and oral aspects of the canon, see Geo Widengren, "Holy Book and Holy Tradition in Islam," in *Holy Book and Holy Tradition: International Colloquium held in the Faculty of Theology, University of Manchester,* ed. F. F. Bruce and E. G. Rupp (Grand Rapids, Mich.: William B. Eerdmans, 1968), pp. 210–236.

3. As a caveat on the historicity of these authorities' opinions as they are extant, see the critical work of Norman Calder, *Studies in Early Muslim Jurisprudence* (Oxford: Oxford University Press, 1993). In short, it is necessary to be acknowledged that the whole enterprise of later fiqh scholarship is an attempt to use these early opinions to formulate a definition of practice. Although many of Calder's specific conclusions cannot be accepted yet, it is difficult to determine which information from later texts is from the second century. In what follows, the dating of relevant material is indicated.

4. For a sampling of some of the more recent attempts to isolate and date these developments, see Fazlur Rahman, "Sunnah and Hadith," *Islamic Studies* 1 (1962): 33–35; Rahman, "Origins and Development of the Tradition," in *Islam* (Chicago: University of Chicago Press, 1966; reprint, 1979), pp. 43–67; Michael Cook, "The Dating of Tradition," in *Early Muslim Dogma: A Source-Critical Study* (Cambridge: Cambridge University Press, 1981), pp. 107–116; G. H. A. Juynboll, *Muslim Tradition: Studies in Chronology, Provenance and Authorship of Early Ḥadīth* (Cambridge: Cambridge University Press, 1983).

5. See Rahman, "Origins and Development of the Tradition," p. 57.

6. For a summary of this position, see the succint discussion in Joseph Schacht, *Origins of Muhammadan Jurisprudence,* 2d ed. (Oxford: Oxford University Press, 1953), pp. 58–81.

7. This dating follows the conclusions in Schacht, "A revaluation of Islamic Tradition," *Journal of the Royal Asiatic Society* 49 (1949): 143–154; Schacht, *Origins of Muhammadan Jurisprudence,* pp. 190–213.

On the content of this traditional practice, see al-Wakīʿ, *Akhbār al-quḍāt,* ed. ʿAbd al-ʿAzīz Muṣṭafā al-Marāghī (Cairo: Maṭbaʿat al-Istiqāmah, 1947), pp. 1–10; al-Kindī, *The Governors and Judges of Egypt,* ed. R. Guest (Leiden: E. J. Brill, 1912); Ignaz Goldziher, *Muhammedanische Studien* (Halle: S. M. Niemeyer, 1889), vol. 2, pp. 28–87; Emile Tyan, *Histoire de l'organisation judiciaire en pays d'Islam* (Paris: Librairie du Recueil Sirey, 1938), esp. vol. 1, pp. 2–99, 119–124; M. Gudefroy-Demombynes, "Sur les origines de la justice musulmane," in *Mélanges syriens offerts à M. René Dussaud* (Paris: P. Geuthner, 1939), vol. 2, pp. 819–828.

8. Of the numerous studies of pre- or non-Islamic influence on the formation of Islamic ritual, see the many works of Goldziher reprinted in his *Gesammelte Schriften,* ed. Joseph DeSomogyi, 4 vols. (Hildesheim: G. Olms, 1970). Some of the more revealing studies by other scholars include A. J. Wensinck, "Die Entstehung der muslimischen Reinheitsgesetzgebung," *Der Islam* 5 (1914); M. J. Kister, " 'A Booth like the Booth of Moses . . .': A Study of an Early Ḥadīth," *Bulletin of the School of Oriental and African Studies* (1962): 150–155; Uri Rubin, "Morning and Evening Prayers in Early Islam," *Jerusalem Studies in Arabic and Islam* 10 (1987): 40–64.

9. On this process and its immediate results, see Schacht, *Origins of Muhammadan Jurisprudence,* pp. 192–193; C. H. Becker, "Die Kanzel im Cultus des alten Islam," in *Orientalische Studien: Theodor Nöldeke zum siebzigsten Geburstag gewidmet* (Geissen: A. Töpelmann, 1906), vol. 1, pp. 331–351 [=*Islamstudien* (Leipzig: Verlag Quelle and Meyer, 1924), vol. 1, pp. 450–471]; Becker, "Zur Geschichte des Islamischen Kultus," *Der Islam* 3 (1912): 374–399 [=*Islamstudien,* vol. 1, pp. 472–500]; S. D. Goitein, "The Origin and Nature of Muslim Friday Worship," *Muslim World* 49 (1959): 183–195 [=*Studies in Islamic History and Institutions* (Leiden: E. J. Brill, 1966), pp. 111–125].

10. On these issues, see Schacht, *Origins of Muhammadan Jurisprudence,* pp. 198-210; Tyan, *Histoire de l'organisation judiciaire,* esp. vol. 1, pp. 342-645.

11. See Schacht, ibid., pp. 193-198; Schacht, "Foreign Elements in Ancient Islamic Law," *Journal of Comparative Law* 3–4 (1950): 9–16 [=*Mémoires de l'Académie Internationale de Droit Comparé* 3, no. 4 (1955): 127–141]; Schacht, "Vom babylonischen zum islamischen Recht," *Orientalistische Literaturzeitung* (1927): 664-669; Carlo Alfonso Nallino, "Considerazioni sui rapporti fra diritto romano e diritto musulmano," presented at Congresso internazionale di diritto romano, Rome, 25 April 1933 [=*Raccolta di scritti eiti e inediti* (Rome: Istituto per l'Orient, 1942), vol. 4, pp. 85–94].

12. Mālik b. Anas, *al-Muwaṭṭāʾ,* ed. Muḥammad Fuʾād ʿAbd al-Bāqī (Cairo: Dār Iḥyāʾ al-Kutub al-ʿArabīyah, 1370; reprint, Beirut: Dār al-Kutub al-ʿIlmīyah, n.d.), vol. 2, p. 662.

13. Abū Bakr b. ʿAlī al-Ḥaddād [d. 800], *Jawharat al-nayyirah* (Cairo: Maḥmūd Bey, 1301), vol. 1, p. 258. The opinion is quoted from Aḥmad b. Muḥammad al-Qudūrī, *Mukhtaṣar fī al-fiqh* (Cairo: Maṭbaʿat al-Khayyīrah, 1324), p. 36.

14. Abū Ibrāhīm Ismāʿīl b. Yaḥyāʾ b. Ismāʿīl al-Muzanī [d. 264], *Mukhtaṣar* [=al-Shāfiʿī, *Kitāb al-umm* (Cairo: Dār al-Fikr, 1403), vol. 8, p. 174]. The discussion of this in the *Kitāb al-umm* is in vol. 3, pp. 14-29.

15. For an overview of some of the notions associated with "sunnah," see M. M. Bravmann, "Sunnah and Related Concepts," in his *The Spiritual Background of Early Islam: Studies in Ancient Arab Concepts* (Leiden: E. J. Brill, 1972), pp. 123–198.

16. On the Medinese use of local practice guaranteed by consensus, see Ibn Qutaybah [d. 276], *Taʾwīl mukhtalif al-ḥadīth* (Cairo: Maktabat al-Kullīyāt al-Azharīyah, 1326), pp. 331–335. It is significant that a similar understanding of Medinese authority is repeated in fifth century Spain by the Mālikī Ibn ʿAbd al-Barr [368-463], *al-Istīʿāb fī maʿrifat al-aṣḥāb*, ed. ʿAlī Muḥammad al-Bajāwī (Cairo: Maktabat Nahḍat Miṣr wa Maṭbaʿatu-hā, 1960), esp. vol. 1, pp. 10–20.

17. What follows relies on the redaction of Yaḥyāʾ b. Yaḥyāʾ b. Kathīr al-Maṣmūdī [d. 234 in Cordoba], ed. M. F. ʿAbd al-Bāqī, 2 vols. (Cairo, 1958; reprint, Beirut, n.d.). This redaction is also the text utilized by Ibn ʿAbd al-Barr [d. 463] in his *al-Istidhkār fī sharḥ madhāhib ʿulamāʾ al-amṣār mimmā rasama-hu li Imām Mālik fī al-Muwaṭṭāʾ min al-raʾy wa al-āthār*, ed. ʿAlī al-Najdī Nasīf (Cairo, 1390) and *al-Ziyādāt allātī taqaʿ fī al-Muwaṭṭāʾ ʿinda Yaḥyāʾ b. Yaḥyāʾ ʿan Mālik* (Cairo, 1350). For the redaction of the Ḥanafī scholar al-Shaybānī, see the texts published in Ludiana, 1876; Luknow, 1880; Kazan, 1909. On these two redactions, see Schacht, "Deux éditions inconnues du Muwaṭṭāʾ," *Studia Orientalia* 2 (1956): 477–492. On these and the other major redactions, see Fuat Sezgin, *Geschichte des arabischen Schrifttums* (Leiden: E.J. Brill, 1967), vol. 1, pp. 458–460.

18. This is based on the listing of the reports used in the *Muwaṭṭāʾ* given by Muḥammad b. ʿAbd al-Bāqī al-Zurqānī [d. 1122], *Anwār kawkab anhaj al-masālik bi-mazj Muwaṭṭāʾ al-Imām Mālik* (Cairo, 1310), vol. 1, p. 8. The numbers given are 822 reports on the authority of the prophet, 613 on the authority of ṣaḥabah, and 285 on the authority of tābiʿūn. For a comparison of these with early Ḥanafī texts, see Schacht, *Origins of Muhammadan Jurisprudence*, 21–35; Calder, *Studies in Early Muslim Jurisprudence*, p. 23.

19. The discussion of killing prey in the sacred area is common in fiqh scholarship. The basic idea is that the prey of the sacred area, defined as a specific area around the Kaʿbah in Makkah, is not to be killed. Much debate has taken

place, however, over the parameters and implications of this basic idea, such as what is considered "prey" and whether or not the injunction affects the sacred area or just people in the sacred area as pilgrims and thus in a special, sacralized state.

The discussion of the issue in the Yaḥyāʾ redaction of the *Muwaṭṭāʾ* is divided into five sections, dealing with prey that can and cannot be eaten, hunting prey with a dog, determining the penalty for killing prey, and the prey that can be killed without penalty. The arrangement and the divisions may be the result of later redaction, yet it is still possible to see the type of support Mālik gave for his opinions from the way Mālik's opinions relate to the examples of traditional practice listed.

On the use of reports of traditional practice to support Mālik's opinions, see Jalāl al-Dīn al-Suyūṭī [d. 911], *Isʿāf al-mubaṭṭaʾ bi-rijāl al-Muwaṭṭāʾ* (Cairo: al-Maktabat al-Tijārīyah al-Kubra, 1969).

20. Mālik, *al-Muwaṭṭāʾ*, vol. 1, p. 353.

21. Ibid., vol. 1, pp. 351-352.

22. Ibid., vol. 1, p. 352.

23. For references to Mālik's reliance on the practices associated with ʿUmar b. al-Khaṭṭāb, see al-Shāfiʿī, *Kitāb ikhtilāf Mālik wa al-Shāfiʿī* [=*Kitāb al-umm*, vol. 7, pp. 177–249], passim. Also see the brief discussion in Schacht, *Origins of Muhammadan Jurisprudence*, pp. 25–27.

24. Mālik, *al-Muwaṭṭāʾ*, vol. 1, p. 350. For the later use of this tradition, see Muḥammad al-Bukhārī, *Ṣaḥīḥ*, ed. L. Krehl and T. W. Juynboll (Leiden: E. J. Brill, 1862), 56:88 [references to the six authoritative collections of ḥadīth are to the *kitāb* and *bāb* where the ḥadīth is located]; Muslim, *Ṣaḥīḥ*, ed. Muḥammad Fuʾād ʿAbd al-Bāqī (Cairo: Maṭbaʿah al-Fajālat al-Jadīdah, 1955), 15:8; al-Nasāʾī, *Kitāb al-sunan al-kubrā*, ed. ʿAbd al-Ṣamad Sharaf al-Dīn (Bombay: al-Dār al-Qayyimah, 1985), 42:32; Ibn Mājah, *Sunan*, ed. Muḥammad Fuʾād al-Bāqī (Cairo: Maṭbaʿah al-Tazīyah, 1952), 27:12.

25. Mālik, *al-Muwaṭṭāʾ*, vol. 1, p. 351. For the later use of this tradition, see al-Bukhārī, 72:10; Muslim, 15:8.

26. It has been remarked by earlier critics of ḥadīth scholarship that such "links" back to an earlier authority could be fabrications, added later, during the third century, to legitimate further the precedent being reported. For more recent critical analyses of the ḥadīth literature and its transmission, see in particular Juynboll, *Muslim Tradition*, passim; M. M. Azami, *Studies in Early Ḥadīth Literature: With a Critical Edition of Some Early Texts* (Beirut, 1968;

reprint, Indianapolis: America Trust Publications, 1978), trans. *Dirāsāt fī al-ḥadīth al-nabawī wa al-ta'rīkh tadwīni-hā* (Riyadh: Jāmi'at al-Riyāḍ, 1976).

27. Mālik, *al-Muwaṭṭā'*, vol. 1, p. 356. This and the following three reports are found in al-Bukhārī, 59:15, 17; Muslim 22:43–49; Abū Dā'ūd, *Sunan,* ed. Muḥammad Muḥyī al-Dīn 'Abd al-Ḥamīd (Beirut: Dār al-Kutub al-'Ilmīyah, 1980), 16:22; al-Tirmidhī, *al-Jāmi' al-ṣaḥīḥ,* ed. Aḥmad Muḥammad Shākir and others (Delhi: Kutub Khānah Rashīdīyah, 1937), 16:17; al-Nasā'ī 42:9; Ibn Mājah, 28:1–2; al-Dārimī, *Sunan* (Kawnpore, 1293), 7:2–3.

28. Mālik, *al-Muwaṭṭā'*, vol. 1, p. 356–357.

29. Ibid., vol. 1, p. 357.

30. Ibid., vol. 1, p. 357.

31. That such practice was later associated with the prophet is evident from the reports found in al-Bukhārī, 59:15, 64:12; Muslim, 39:127–132, 135, 136, 138; Abū Dā'ūd, 37:161; al-Tirmīdhī, 16:15; Ibn Mājah, 31:42; al-Nasā'ī, 25:48.

32. Mālik, *al-Muwaṭṭā'*, vol. 1, p. 357.

33. The order in which the Yaḥyā' redaction of the *Muwaṭṭā'* lists precedents reflects not a second but a third century concept of authority according to which textual references to Qur'ānic and prophetic practice are given priority over the reports of later companion or follower practice based on Qur'ānic or prophetic precedent but not verified textually. On the arrangement of this redaction, see al-Zurqānī, *Anwār kawkab,* vol. 1, pp. 4–15. Calder, *Studies in Early Muslim Jurisprudence,* pp. 21–24, argues that this organization places the Yaḥyā' redaction of the *Muwaṭṭā'* posterior to Saḥnūn's *Mudawwana,* which "foregrounds" Malik's authority rather than that of the prophet. This conclusion misses how the *Muwaṭṭā'* evaluates and uses reports of prophetic practice and citations from the Qur'ān, namely that the *Muwaṭṭā'* has Mālik interpret these "earlier" textual precedents in light of "later" practices. In the late third and fourth centuries, the authority of earlier textual precedents outweighed the authority of precedents not supported by textual evidence. This is the implication of Schacht, *Origins of Muhammadan Jurisprudence,* esp. 269–287.

34. Recent studies of early fiqh scholarship continue to contend, largely on the basis of Schacht's brief discussion of the Qur'ān in his *Origins of Muhammadan Jurisprudence,* pp. 224–227, that use of the Qur'ān in fiqh scholarship is a relatively late development. It does seem, as Schacht argues, that attempts to systematically account for later definitions of practice in terms of Qur'ānic precedents is a late, probably fourth century development. It is also evident,

however, that Qurʾānic statements were used as precedents, usually in ad hoc fashion, as early as the second century.

For the views that the use of the Qurʾān is late, see Calder, *Studies in Early Muslim Jurisprudence,* pp. 218–219; Wansbrough, *Quranic Studies: Sources and Methods of Scriptural Interpretation* (Oxford: Oxford University Press, 1977), esp. pp. 170–202; G. R. Hawting, "The Role of Qurʾan and Ḥadīth in the Legal Controversy About the Rights of a Divorced Woman During Her 'Waiting Period' (ʿidda)," *Bulletin of the School of Oriental and African Studies* 52, no. 3 (1989): 430–445. For alternative views, see John Burton, *The Collection of the Qurʾān,* passim; David Powers, *Studies in Qurʾān and Ḥadīth: the Formation of the Islamic Law of Inheritance* (Berkeley: University of California Press, 1986), esp. pp. 1–18.

35. Mālik, *al-Muwaṭṭāʾ,* vol. 1, pp. 355–356. The punctuation of the Qurʾān verse cited is a matter of contention in fiqh scholarship, regarding whether the two just people determine the value of the prey in terms of pasturing animals or if they determine whether the killer is to sacrifice, feed poor, or fast. The punctuation given here appears to agree with later Mālikī interpretations of the verse.

36. For a discussion of the prefactory formulas "I heard" or "the best I have heard" attached to Mālik's opinions, see Schacht, *Origins of Muhammadan Jurisprudence,* pp. 68, 101, 208. From an overview of the use of these phrases, Schacht concludes that they do not seem to refer to precedents but rather to the precedent the speaker finds most favorable.

37. Mālik, *al-Muwaṭṭāʾ,* vol. 1, p. 350.

38. Refer back to the discussion in ibid., vol. 1, pp. 350–353.

39. Compare this with the polemics in al-Shāfiʿī, *Kitāb ikhtilāf Mālik wa al-Shāfiʿī* [=*Kitāb al-umm,* vol. 7, pp. 177–249], passim. Schacht quotes the passage of al-Shāfiʿī characterizing the early Mālikī position by putting the words into the mouth of Mālik: "you [Mālik] reply: if something is related from ʿUmar then one does not ask why and how, and one does not counter it by interpreting the Qurʾān differently [than he did?]" in *Origins of Muhammadan Jurisprudence,* p. 25.

40. See al-Zurqānī, *Anwar kawkab,* vol. 1, p. 184. The passage is cited for different reasons in Schacht, *Origins of Muhammadan Jurisprudence,* p. 24.

41. ʿAbd al-Salām b. Saʿīd Saḥnūn, *al-Mudawwana al-kubrā* (Cairo, 1324). This passage is quoted in Schacht, *Origins of Muhammadan Jurisprudence,* p. 63. For analyses of Saḥnūn's work and its significance for this issue, see E. Amar, "Le grand Mudawwana," *Rivista degli Studia Orientalia* 24 (1949):

45–58; C. H. Bousquet, "Ibn al-Qāsim, La Moudawwana (recension de Saḥnoun) analyse," *Annales de l'Institut d'Etudes Orientales* 14 (1958): 177–206, 17 (1959): 169–211, 18 (1960): 165–173; Calder, *Studies in Early Muslim Jurisprudence,* pp. 1–19.

42. For a similar statement by Mālik in his letter to al-Layth b. Saᶜd [d. 175], see al-Qāḍī ᶜIyāḍ [d. 544], *Tartīb al-madārik li maᶜarifat aᶜlām madhhab Mālik,* ed. Muḥammad al-Tabakhī and others (Rabat: Wizārat al-Awqāf, 1983), vol. 1, pp. 41–43. This opinion is discussion in Iftikhar Zaman, "Bukharī as faqīh," unpublished paper, MESA conference, 1991, p. 15.

43. This is the critique leveled by al-Shāfiᶜī against the Medinese claims. See al-Shāfiᶜī, *Kitāb ikhtilāf Mālik wa al-Shāfiᶜī* [=*Kitāb al-umm,* vol. 7, p. 148]. For a discussion of this critique, see Schacht, *Origins of Muhammadan Jurisprudence,* 61-69.

44. See al-Qāḍī ᶜIyāḍ, passim, vols. 1–2, where it is argued that Mālik is the "summation" of Medinese tradition.

45. al-Ḥaddād, vol. 2, p. 23. The opinions are quoted from al-Qudūrī, *Mukhtaṣar fī al-fiqh,* pp. 61–62. The opinions of Zufar, although almost always at odds with the other authorities' opinions, are not frequently reported except in later texts for pedagogical purposes. For a discussion of Zufar's opinions concerning endowment [waqf] in relation to those of the other three authorities, see ᶜUbaydallāh b. ᶜUmar al-Dabūsī [d. 430], *Taʾsīs al-naẓar* (Cairo: Zakarīyā ᶜAlī Yūsuf, 1320), esp. pp. 55–60. On Zufar's opinions in the context of Ḥanafī reasoning in general, see M. Z. al-Kawtharī, *Lamaḥāt al-naẓar fī sīrat al-Imām Zufar* (Cairo: Maṭbaᶜat al-Anwār, 1368).

46. See al-Ḥaddād, vol. 2, p. 23.

47. See ibid., vol. 2, p. 23-24.

48. On Ibn Abī Laylā, see Ibn Isḥāq al-Shīrāzī [393–476], *Ṭabaqāt al-fuqahāʾ,* ed. Iḥsān ᶜAbbās (Beirut: Dār al-Rāʾid al-ᶜArabī, 1970), p. 84.

49. Abū Yūsuf, *Ikhtilāf Abī Ḥanīfah wa Ibn Abī Laylā,* ed. Abū al-Wafāʾ al-Afghānī (Cairo: Maktabat Dār al-Hidāyah, 1357), 137. The *we* mentioned in the phrase "this we accept" refers to Abū Yūsuf's opinion.

50. The discussion of this issue is amply illustrated in later chapters. Most illuminating in filling in the background to the particular opinion of Abū Yūsuf in siding with Abū Ḥanīfah, see Muḥammad b. Aḥmad al-Sarakhsī [d. 483], *al-Mabsūṭ* (Cairo: Maṭbaᶜat al-Saᶜādah, 1324–1331), vol. 2, pp. 188–191. Abū al-Wafāʾ al-Afghānī also has a broad discussion of the point in his footnote commentary on Abū Yūsuf's *Ikhtilāf,* see pp. 137–138.

51. Abū Yūsuf, *Ikhtilāf,* pp. 138–139. On al-Ḥajjāj b. Arṭāh, see Juynboll, *Muslim Tradition,* pp. 182–184.

52. For a later discussion of Abū Yūsuf's opinion, and in particular his use of istiḥsān, see al-Sarakhsī, *al-Mabsūṭ,* vol. 1, p. 104. Also see the discussion of al-Afghānī in Abū Yūsuf's *Ikhtilāf,* 138–139.

53. Abū Yūsuf, *Ikhtilāf,* pp. 139–140.

54. For al-Afghānī's remarks on these issues, see his commentary in Abū Yūsuf's *Ikhtilāf,* pp. 139–140.

55. Abū Yūsuf, *Ikhtilāf,* p. 140. For a later discussion of Abū Yūsuf's opinion and its support, see al-Sarakhsī, *al-Mabsūṭ,* vol. 4, p. 83.

56. Abū Yūsuf, *al-Radd ᶜAlā siyar al-Awzāᶜī,* ed. Abū al-Wafāʾ al-Afghānī (Cairo: Maktabat Dār al-Hidāyah, 1980), p. 76. For this statement, also see al-Shāfiᶜī, *Kitāb siyar al-Awzāᶜī* [=*Kitāb al-umm,* vol. 7, p. 24]. There is a brief discussion of this statement in Schacht, *Origins of Muhammadan Jurisprudence,* p. 75. For commentary on Abū Yūsuf's *al-Radd,* see Zafar Ishaw Ansar, "An Early Discussion on Islamic Jurisprudence: Some Notes on *al-Radd ᶜalā siyar al-Awzāᶜī,*" in *Islamic Perspectives* (1979): 147–167.

57. Abū Yūsuf, *al-Radd,* p. 11. See the discussion of this passage in Schacht, *Origins of Muhammadan Jurisprudence,* p. 74.

58. Abū Yūsuf, *al-Radd,* pp. 17–21.

59. In addition to the examples of this already cited, see the discussion and references in Schacht, *Origins of Muhammadan Jurisprudence,* pp. 22–27.

60. Of course, in the case of conflicts within the practice of later generations, the Kūfans rely on logic to choose between different practices and isolated reports of prophetic practice. For a discussion of this procedure and further references, see Schacht, ibid., pp. 27–34.

61. On the notion of consensus [ijmāᶜ] and its complicated historical development, see Ahmad Hasan, "The Classical Definition of Ijmāᶜ: The nature of Consensus," *Islamic Studies* 14 (1975): 21–27; Ahmad Hasan, *The Doctrine of Ijmāᶜ in Islam* (Islamabad: Islamic Research Institute, 1978).

62. This is not to say that the reports were fabricated to authorize opinions reflecting practices of nonprophetic origin. That reports were fabricated for such purposes is widely acknowledged. The use of reports by second century Medinese and Kūfans to support local traditions of practice, however, does not require that those reports be fabricated. For a zealous critique of

the scholarship that suggests the early fabrication of reports of prophetic practice, see Azami, *Studies in Early Ḥadīth Literature,* passim; Azami, *On Schacht's Origins of Muhammadan Jurisprudence* (Riyadh: King Saud University, 1985). More detailed criticism can be found in Harald Motzki, "The Muṣannaf of ʿAbd al-Razzāq al-Ṣanʿānī as a Source of Authentic Aḥādīth of the First Century A.H.," *Journal of Near Eastern Studies* 50, no. 1 (1991): 1-21; Motzki, *Die Anfänge der islamischen Jurisprudenz: ihre Entwicklung in Mekka bis zur mitte des 2./8. Jahrhunderts* (Stuttgart: Abhandlungen für die Kunde des Morgenlandes, 1991).

63. Calder (see esp. pp. 67–104) dates the redaction of al-Shāfiʿī's *Risālah* and his different works collected in the *Kitāb al-umm* to the beginning of the fourth century, primarily because the ideas in them seem to anticipate by a century the development of fiqh scholarship. If these works are a product of the third rather than the second century, then their use here is as an articulation of the epistemology being developed and in use during the third and fourth centuries. If these works are the product of the second century, then they are to be regarded as seminal. In either case, the use of al-Shāfiʿī's theoretical works is to exemplify the text-based epistemology upon which the classical schools of the late fourth and fifth centuries is based. The debate over the historicity of the works attributed to al-Shāfiʿī is important but not entirely relevant to how fiqh scholarship of the fifth and sixth centuries looked back on its epistemological origins.

On al-Shāfiʿī's work, and his *Risālah* in particular, see Fakhr al-Dīn al-Rāzī, *Manāqib al-Imām al-Shāfiʿī* (Cairo: Maktabat al-Kulliyāt al-Azhariyah, 1986), pp. 55–57; G. Bergsträsser, *Grundzüge des islamischen Rechts,* ed. and trans. J. Schacht (Leipzig, 1935), 8–21; Abū Zahrah, *Uṣūl al-fiqh* (Cairo: Dār al-Fikr al-ʿArabī, 1957), pp. 14–15; Ahmad Hasan, *The Early Development of Islamic Jurisprudence* (Islamabad: Islamic Research Institute, 1970), pp. 178–220; P. Rancillac, "Des origines du droit musulman à la Risala d'al-Shafiʿī," *Mélanges de l'Institut dominicain d'études orientales du Caire* 13 (1977): 147–169.

64. For an example of al-Shāfiʿī's criticism of this method of authorizing opinions as being of prophetic origins, see al-Shāfiʿī, *Kitāb ikhtilāf Mālik wa al-Shāfiʿī* [=*Kitāb al-umm,* vol. 7, p. 147]. This passage is paraphrased and briefly discussed in Schacht, *Origins of Muhammadan Jurisprudence,* p. 69.

65. For the implications of this emphasis, see the remarks in Ibn Qutaybah, *Taʾwīl mukhtalif al-ḥadīth,* esp. pp. 215–245. For examples of how this shift has been evaluated in modern scholarship, see Schacht, *Origins of Muhammadan Jurisprudence,* 77–80; L. I. Graf, *al-Shāfiʿī's Verhandeling over de*

'Wortelen' van de Fiḳh (Leiden: E. J. Brill, 1934); Emile Tyan, "Méthodologie et sources du droit en Islam," *Studia Islamica* 10 (1959): 82–84; Rahman, "The Structure of the Law," in *Islam,* pp. 68–84, esp. pp. 75–79; Ahmad Hasan, "The Sources of Islamic Law," *Islamic Studies* 7 (1968): 15–184; P. Rancillac, "Des origines du droit musulman," pp. 147–169.

66. For the origins and early development of this method of transmission and support, see Goldziher, *Muslim Studies,* vol. 2, pp. 94–125 [=*Muhammedanische Studien,* vol. 2, pp. 88–131]; J. Horovitz, "Alter und Urpsrung des Isnad," *Der Islam* 8 (1918): 39–47; J. Robson, "The Isnād in Muslim Tradition," *Glasgow University Oriental Society Transactions* 15 (1955): 15–26.

67. On this threefold categorization of prophetic sunnah, see Muṣṭafāʾ al-Sibāʿī, *al-Sunnah wa makānatu-hā fī tashrīʿ al-Islāmī* (Cairo: Maktabat Dār al-ʿUrūbah, 1961), pp. 345–351; S. Ali Raza Naqvi, "Prophetic Sunna in the Islamic Legal Framework," *Islamic Studies* 19 (1980): 120–133.

68. al-Shāfiʿī, *Kitāb ibṭāl al-istiḥsān* [=*Kitāb al-umm,* vol. 7, pp. 267–277], p. 271. This passage and al-Shāfiʿī's exegesis of the Qurʾān to support the authority of prophetic practice are discussed in Schacht, *Origins of Muhammadan Jurisprudence,* pp. 15–16.

69. For this outright claim, see al-Shāfiʿī, *al-Risālah,* pp. 77–78. For a fuller exposition of the role of the sunnah in the explication of the revelation, see al-Shāfiʿī, *al-Risālah,* pp. 31–33.

70. Qurʾān, sūrat al-jumʿah 62:2.

71. This is a portion of Qurʾān, sūrat al-nisāʾ 4:113.

72. Schacht notes that al-Shāfiʿī seems to be "non-committal" on the issue of the sunnah's authority independent of the Qurʾān, see Schacht, *Origins of Muhammadan Jurisprudence,* p. 16. This view is held by Ibn Qutaybah, *Taʾwīl mukhtalif al-ḥadīth,* pp. 246–312. See M. Zubayr Siddiqi, "The Importance of Ḥadīth as a Source of Islamic Law," *Studies in Islam* 1, no. 1 (1964): 19–25. It is important to note that the notion of the divine inspiration of the prophet does not preclude the position that the authority of the sunnah is tied to the authority of the Qurʾān. For al-Shāfiʿī's allusion to the prophet's inspiration, see al-Shāfiʿī, *al-Risālah,* pp. 84–105, based on the exegesis of the Qurʾān, 53:3.

73. For this characterization of the prophet and his sunnah, see al-Shāfiʿī, ibid., pp. 72-73.

74. For examples of this claim, see ibid., pp. 146–157. On the significance of this claim, see the comments of al-Khaṭīb al-Baghdādī [392–463], *al-Faqīh wa*

al-mutafaqqih (Beirut: Dār al-Kutub al-ʿIlmīyah, 1975), vol. 1, pp. 90–94; Abū ʿAlī al-Fārisī, *Jawāhir al-uṣūl fī ʿilm ḥadīth al-rasūl* (Medina: Maktabat al-ʿIlmīyah, 1973), p. 4.

75. al-Shāfiʿī, *al-Risālah,* pp. 94–104. The issue of the authority of the sunnah in those cases where a Qurʾānic text is "absent" is discussed at length in the following pages and chapters.

76. This discussion occurs in al-Shāfiʿī, ibid., pp. 175–176. The verses cited by al-Shāfiʿī are 4:104 [prayer], 2:40 [offering], 3:91 [pilgrimage].

77. These specifics are discussed in ibid., pp. 176–198. References to the role of the sunnah in specifying these practices are also found in al-Shāfiʿī, *Kitāb al-umm,* passim.

78. The relevant verses are cited by al-Shāfiʿī, *al-Risālah,* pp. 198-199. The verses cited by al-Shāfiʿī are 2:234, 2:228, and 65:4.

79. al-Shawkānī states that this is the opinion of Ibn ʿAbbās and ʿAlī. See Mālik, *al-Muwaṭṭāʾ,* vol. 2, p. 589; al-Nisāʿī, 27:56; al-Shawkānī, *Nayl al-awṭār* (Cairo, 1956) vol. 6, pp. 306–307. This reference is given by Khadduri in his translation of al-Shāfīʿī's *Risālah, Islamic Jurisprudence* (Baltimore: Johns Hopkins University Press, 1961), p. 168.

80. al-Shāfiʿī, *al-Risālah,* pp. 199–200.

81. For further references to this, see Mālik, *al-Muwaṭṭāʾ,* vol. 2, pp. 589–590; al-Bukhārī, 68:39; al-Nisāʿī, 27:56; Muslim, 18:8; al-Shawkānī, *Nayl al-awṭār,* vol. 6, p. 305.

82. al-Shāfiʿī, *al-Risālah,* p. 205. The verse cited by al-Shāfiʿī is Q 6:146. Further examples are found at 2:173, 5:3, 6:122, and 16:115.

83. Two reports to this effect are cited by al-Shāfiʿī, ibid., pp. 206–208. The two reports are taken from Mālik, *al-Muwaṭṭāʾ,* vol. 2, p. 496. Other references are found in al-Bukhārī, 72:29; Muslim, 34:3, 37:3.

84. See the allusion to this line of reasoning in al-Shāfiʿī, *al-Risālah,* pp. 206–208; al-Shawkānī, *Nayl al-awṭār,* 8:120. For evidence of prophetic practice regarding the killing of snakes, see al-Bukhārī, 59:15, 64:12; Muslim, 39:127–138; Abū Dāʾūd, 37:161; al-Tirmidhī, 16:15; Ibn Mājah, 31:42; al-Nasāʿī, 25:48; Aḥmad b. Ḥanbal, *al-Musnad* (Cairo, 1313), vol. 2, p. 247. It could be that fanged animals are forbidden because they fall into the category of predatory animals that, in other places, the prophet prohibits eating.

85. The classical theory of "abrogation" [naskh] and its development in the work of al-Shāfiʿī is a complicated matter. For al-Shāfiʿī's discussion of naskh, see *al-Risālah,* pp. 105–117, 241–258. Further discussion of al-Shāfiʿī's theories can be found in Muzammad b. Mūsā al-Ḥāzimī, *al-Iʿtibār fī al-nāsikh wa al-mansūkh min al-āthār* (Cairo: Idārat al-Ṭibānʿah al-Munīrīyah, 1346). On the development of the theory of naskh, see the account in Abū Jaʿfar al-Naḥḥās, *Kitāb al-nāsikh wa al-mansūkh* (Cairo, 1323).

The mention of naskh as one of al-Shāfiʿī's attempts to reconcile the sunnah and the Qurʾān follows John Burton's discusson of *naskh al-tilāwah dūnā al-ḥukm,* and in particular his discussion of the penalty for adultery, or the so-called stoning verse. For a full exposition of this use of naskh, see John Burton, *The Collection of the Qurʾān,* esp. pp. 68–104. Also, see J. Burton, *The Sources of Islamic Law: Islamic Theories of Abrogation* (Edinburgh: University of Edinburgh, 1990), passim.

86. For a discussion of these two basic types, see al-Shāfiʿī, *al-Risālah,* pp. 53–64. These types and al-Shāfiʿī's use of the Qurʾān in deriving a definition of practice is discussed in Ahmad Hasan, *The Early Development of Islamic Jurisprudence,* pp. 180–181.

87. al-Shāfiʿī, ibid., p. 313. This report can be found in Muḥammad b. ʿAlī b. Muḥammad al-Shawkānī, *Nayl al-awṭār,* vol. 5, pp. 195–196.

88. al-Shāfiʿī, ibid., pp. 312–313. The report is taken from Mālik, *al-Muwaṭṭāʾ,* vol. 2, p. 671. For another reference to this in al-Shāfiʿī's works, see al-Shāfiʿī, *Kitāb al-umm,* vol. 3, p. 3.

89. al-Shāfiʿī, *Risālah,* p. 330. The report is taken from Mālik, *al-Muwaṭṭāʾ,* vol. 2, p. 624. For the later use of this report, see al-Bukhārī, 34:82; Muslim, 21:14.

90. al-Shāfiʿī, ibid., p. 332. The report is taken from Mālik, *al-Muwaṭṭāʾ,* vol. 2, pp. 619-620. For the later use of this report, see al-Bukhārī, 34:82; Muslim, 21:14.

91. This example is mentioned to discuss the "grafting" of isnāds in Schacht, *Origins of Muhammadan Jurisprudence,* pp. 153–154.

92. See al-Shāfiʿī, *Risālah,* pp. 334–335.

93. See ibid., pp. 250–253. These three reports are taken from Mālik, *al-Muwaṭṭāʾ,* vol. 1, pp. 135–136. The three reports can also be found in al-Bukhārī, 10:15, 47; Muslim 4:19, 21.

94. See al-Shāfiʿī, ibid., pp. 252–253. The report is also mentioned in al-Shawkānī, vol. 3, p. 180.

95. al-Shāfiʿī, ibid., pp. 253–254.

96. Ibid., p. 291. This report and related ones are found in al-Bukhārī, 4:60–62; Muslim, 2:73–74; al-Tirmidhī, 1:9; al-Nasāʾī, 1:16, 23; Ibn Mājah, 1:13.

97. al-Shāfiʿī, ibid., p. 291. This report is discussed by Shākir in his commentary on al-Tirmidhī, 1:9.

98. al-Shāfiʿī, ibid., pp. 291–292. This report is also found in Mālik, *al-Muwaṭṭāʾ*, vol. 1, pp. 193–194. Also, see al-Bukhārī, 4:12; Muslim, 2:17.

99. Khadduri, in a footnote to his translation of this section, notes that Abū Dāʾūd [1:12] cites a report that Ibn ʿUmar was seen urinating in the desert, sheltered by his camel, facing Makkah. Ibn ʿUmar reports that the prophet allowed urination facing Makkah as long as there was a barrier between the person urinating and Makkah. See Khadduri, *Islamic Jurisprudence,* p. 219.

100. For this particular significance of al-Shāfiʿī's text-based epistemology, see the comments of Abū Zahrah, *Uṣūl al-fiqh,* esp. pp. 14–15; Mohammed Hashim Kamali, *Principles of Islamic Jurisprudence,* 2d ed. (Cambridge: Islamic Texts Society, 1991), pp. 1–7.

101. For an example of a clear statement of this principle, see al-Shāfiʿī, *Ikhtilāf al-ḥadīth* [=*Kitāb al-umm,* marginalia of volume 7], pp. 339–340. This principle is also briefly discussed in Ahmad Hasan, *The Early Development of Islamic Jurisprudence* (Islamabad: Islamic Research Institute, 1970), pp. 192–194.

102. Later scholarship defines the Qurʾān as having 500 verses in it which are used to define practice. On these 500 verses, see Ibn ʿAbdallāh al-Suyūrī [d. 826], *Kanz al-ʿirfān fī fiqh al-Qurʾān,* ed. M. Baqīr Sharīf Zaddah (Tehran: al-Maktabat al-Murtaḍawīyah, 1964).

103. For al-Shāfiʿī's extended discussion of qiyās and ijtihād, see *Risālah,* pp. 475–502. A fuller account of these specific types of reasoning is given in the following chapters.

104. For an example statement of this charge, see al-Shāfiʿī, *Kitāb jimāʿ al-ʿilm* [=*Kitāb al-umm,* vol. 7, pp. 250–262], p. 258. This passage is discussed in Schacht, *Origins of Muhammadan Jurisprudence,* p. 109.

105. This issue is briefly discussed in an attempt to show its detriment to the "inwardness of religion" in Goldziher, "The Development of Law," in his *Introduction to Islamic Theology and Law,* trans. Andras Hamori and Ruth

Hamori (Princeton, N.J.: Princeton University Press, 1981), pp. 31–66, esp. pp. 52–63. The issue is also discussed without explicit reference to epistemological concerns in M. Mujeeb, "Orthodoxy and the Orthodox: The Shariʿah as Law," *Islamic Culture* 38 (1964): 27–46, esp. pp. 28–29.

106. For a strong statement of this claim, see the discussion of Mālik in al-Qāḍī ʿIyāḍ [d. 544], *Tartib al-madārik li maʿarifat aʿlām madhhab Mālik,* esp. vol. 2, pp. 38–49.

107. The statement of al-Shāfiʿī, to the effect that he forbade others from following [taqlīd] his or anyone else's opinions is given in Abū Ibrāhīm Ismāʿīl b. Yaḥyāʾ b. Ismāʿīl al-Muzanī [175–264], *al-Mukhtaṣar* [=*Kitāb al-umm* (Cairo: Dār al-Fikr, 1403), vol. 8, pp. 92–679], p. 1. This passage is mentioned by Schacht, *Origins of Muhammadan Jurisprudence,* p. 6, who considers the meaning of al-Shāfiʿī's statement to be that he did not intend to found a school of fiqh scholarship.

108. The best example of this is to be found in the ṭabaqāt literature, discussed in the following pages, or in the *manāqib* literature devoted to extolling the "virtues" of the schools' founders. For the published works on Abū Ḥanīfah, see al-Muwaffaq b. Aḥmad b. Isḥāq al-Makkī al-Khwārizmī [d. 568], *Manāqib al-Imām Abī Ḥanīfah* (Hyderabad, 1321); Muḥammad b. Aḥmad b. ʿUthmān al-Dhahabī [d. 748], *Manāqib al-Imām Abī Ḥanīfah,* ed. M. Z. al-Kawtharī and Abū al-Wafāʾ al-Afghānī (Cairo, 1366). For modern examples, see ʿAbd al-ʾAwal al-Janpūrī, *al-Nawādir al-munīfah bi-manāqib al-Imām Abī Ḥanīfah* (Kawnpur, 1310); al-Sayyid ʿAfīfī, *Ḥayāt al-Imām Abī Ḥanīfah* (Cairo, 1350); Abū Zahrah, *Abū Ḥanīfah: ḥayātu-hu wa ʿaṣru-hu āraʾu-hu wa fiqhu-hu* (Cairo: Dār al-fikr al-ʿArabī, 1947); Muḥammad Yūsuf Mūsā, *Abū Ḥanīfah wa al-qiyām al-insānīyah* (Cairo: Maktabat Naḥdat Miṣr, 1957).

For published manāqib on Mālik, see al-Suyūṭī, *Tazyīn al-mamālik li-manāqib saidinat al-Imām Mālik* (Cairo, 1324). For modern examples, see Abū Zahrah, *Mālik: ḥayātu-hu ʿaṣru-hu wa fiqhu-hu* (Cairo: Maktabat al-Anjilū al-Miṣrīyah, 1952); Amīn al-Khūlī, *Mālik b. Anas,* 3 vols. (Cairo, 1951).

For published manāqib on al-Shāfiʿī, see Abū Bakr Muḥammad b. Ibrāhīm b. al-Mundhīr [d. 318], *Riḥlat al-Imām al-Shāfiʿī ilā al-Madīnat al-munawwarah* (Cairo, 1350); Ibn Abī Ḥātim [d. 327], *Adāb al-Shāfiʿī wa-manāqibu-hu,* ed. ʿA. ʿAbd al-Khāliq (Cairo, 1953); Fakhr al-Dīn Abū ʿAbdallāh Muḥammad b. ʿUmar al-Rāzī [d. 606], *Manāqib al-Imām al-Shāfiʿī* (Cairo, 1279); Aḥmad b. ʿAlī b. Muḥammad b. Ḥajar al-ʿAsqalānī [d. 852], *Tawālī al-taʾsīs bi-maʿālī Muḥammad b. Idrīs* (Būlāq, 1301). For modern examples, see Abū Zahrah, *al-Shāfiʿī: ḥayātu-hu wa ʿaṣru-hu ārāʾu-hu wa fiqhu-hu* (Cairo: Dār al-Fikr al-ʿArabī, 1948).

109. For general statements on this process, see G. Bergsträsser, *Grundzüge des islamischen Rechts,* esp. pp. 8–21; Schacht, *Origins of Muhammadan Jurisprudence,* pp. 269–282.

110. On this specific change, see Bergsträsser, ibid., pp. 108–118; Schacht, ibid., pp. 281–287; Abū al-Qāsim Gorjī, "nigāhī beh taḥawwul-e ᶜilm-e uṣūl," trans. ᶜAlī Qulī Qarāʾī, "A brief survey of the Development of ᶜilm uṣūl al-fiqh," *al-Tawḥīd* 3, no. 2 (1986): 76–78. For the evidence of the use of so-called *mursal* traditions, reports of prophetic practice that do not go all the way back to the prophet, see Ahmad Hasan, *The Early Development of Islamic Jurisprudence,* p. 188.

111. This sort of scholarship is illustrated in following chapters. For an overview of how this affected the way the opinions of the second century authorities were interpreted, see Schacht, *Origins of Muhammadan Jurisprudence,* pp. 283-328.

112. For a brief indication of the significance, to which a huge literature is devoted, of the theory of the how chains of transmission tend to "grow backward," see Juynboll, *Muslim Tradition,* pp. 96-133.

113. On the collection of the sunnah by traveling to different locations, see al-Khāṭīb al-Baghdādī, *al-Riḥlah fī ṭalab al-ḥadīth,* ed. Nūr al-Dīn ᶜItr (Beirut: Dār al-Kutub al-ᶜIlmīyah, 1975). This practice is also discussed in Goldziher, *Muslim Studies,* vol. 2, pp. 168–185 [=*Muhammedanische Studien,* vol. 2, pp. 175–193]; and Juynboll, ibid., pp. 66–70.

114. On the link between the canonization of the sunnah and this enterprise, which has enormous significance for the development of the classical Islamic "sciences," see the discussion of Goldziher, ibid., vol. 2, pp. 168–266 [=*Muhammedanische Studien,* vol. 2, pp. 175–274] and Azami, *Studies in Early Ḥadīth Literature,* passim.

115. The six authoritative collections are al-Bukhārī [194–256], *al-Jāmiᶜ al-ṣaḥīḥ,* ed. L. Krehl and T. W. Juynboll, 4 vols. (Leiden: E. J. Brill, 1862–1908); Muslim [202–261], *al-Jāmiᶜ al-ṣaḥīḥ,* ed. Muḥammad Fuʾād ᶜAbd al-Bāqī, 5 vols. (Cairo: Maṭbaᶜah al-Fajālat al-Jadīdah, 1955–1956); Ibn Mājah [209–273], *Sunan,* ed. M. F. al-Bāqī, 2 vols. (Cairo: Maṭbaᶜah al-Tazīyah, 1952–1953); Abū Dāʾūd [208–275], *Sunan,* ed. Muḥammad Muḥyī al-Dīn ᶜAbd al-Ḥamīd, 4 vols. (Beirut: Dār al-Kutub al-ᶜIlmīyah, 1980); al-Tirmidhī [210–279], *al-Jāmiᶜ al-ṣaḥīḥ,* ed. Aḥmad Muḥammad Shākir and others, 5 vols. (Delhi: Kutub Khānah Rashīdīyah, 1937–1965)

On these six books, see the work of A. J. Wensinck, *A Handbook of Early Muhammadan Tradition,* 7 vols. (Leiden: E. J. Brill, 1927); and S. Ali Raza Naqvi, "Prophetic Sunna in the Islamic Legal Framework," pp. 126–128.

116. George Makdisi, "Institutionalized Learning as a Self-Image of Islam," in *Islam's Understanding of Itself,* ed. Speros Vryonis, Jr. Presented at the eighth Giorgio Levi Della Vida Biennial Conference, UCLA (Los Angeles: University of California Press, 1983), pp. 73–85, argues, on the basis of the books' organization and inclusion of weak isnāds, that the six books were written as a pedagogic aid.

117. There is a discussion of this point in Bernard Weiss, *The Search for God's Law: Islamic Jurisprudence in the Writings of Sayf al-Dīn al-Āmidī* (Salt Lake City: University of Utah Press, 1992), pp. 256–328, esp. pp. 256–269. For the notion of a nonwritten canon, see J. Z. Smith, "Sacred Persistence: Toward a Redescription of Canon," passim.

118. On this genre, see Juynboll, *Muslim Tradition,* pp. 134–160. The earliest and most authoritative texts are al-Bukhārī, *al-Taʾrīkh al-kabīr,* 4 vols. (Hyderabad: Maṭbaʿat Jamʿīyat Dāʾirat al-Maʿārif al-ʿUthmānīyah, 1361) and Ibn Abī Ḥātim [240–327], *al-Jarḥ wa al-taʿdīl,* ed. ʿAbd al-Raḥmān b. Yaḥyāʾ al-Muʿalamī al-Yamānī, 8 vols. (Beirut: Muʾassat al-Risālah, 1371).

119. On the development of this type of literature, see Muḥammad Ḍiyāʾ al-Raḥmān Aʿḥamī, *Dirāsāt fī al-jarḥ wa al-taʿdīl* (Banaras: al-Jāmīʿah al-Salafīyah, 1983), pp. 297–434; Juynboll, *Muslim Tradition,* pp. 161–217. For a sampling of the classical companion ṭabaqat literature, see Ibn Saʿd [168–230], *Kitāb al-ṭabaqāt al-kabīr,* ed. Iḥsān ʿAbbās (Beirut, 1968); Ibn ʿAbd al-Barr, *al-Istīʿāb fī maʿrifat al-aṣḥāb;* Ibn Ḥajar [773–852], *al-Iṣābah fī tamyīz al-ṣaḥābah,* ed. ʿAlī Muḥammad al-Bajāwī, 8 vols. (Cairo: Dār al-Naḥdat Miṣr li al-Itibāh wa al-Nashr, 1970).

120. The main sources for this biographical information are al-Mizzī, *Tuḥfat al-ashrāf bi-maʿrifat al-aṭrāf,* ed. ʿAbd al-Ṣamad Sharaf al-Dīn, 12 vols. (Bhiwandi: al-Dār al-Qayyimah, 1965–1981); al-Dhahabī, *al-Kāshif fī maʿrifat man la-hu riwāyat fī al-kutub al-sittah,* ed. ʿIzzat ʿAlī ʿĪd ʿAṭiyyah and Mūsā Muḥammad ʿAlī al-Mawshī, 3 vols. (Cairo: Dār al-Kutub al-Ḥadīthah, 1963); Ibn Ḥajar, *Tahdhīb al-tahdhīb* (Hyderabad: Maṭbaʿah Majlis Dāʾirat al-Maʿārif al-Niḥāmīyah, 1325).

121. For the weak transmitters, see al-Bukhārī, *Kitāb al-ḍuʿafāʾ al-ṣaghir;* al-Nasāʾī, *Kitāb al-ḍuʿafāʾ wa al-matrūkīn* (Beirut: Muʾassasat al-Kutub al-Thaqāfīyah, 1985); al-ʿUqaylī, *Kitāb al-ḍuʿafāʾ al-kabīr,* ed. ʿAbd al-Muʿṭī Amīn Qalʿajī, 4 vols. (Beirut: Dār al-Kutub al-ʿIlmīyah, 1404); Ibn Ḥibbān al-Bustī, *Maʿrifat al-majrūḥīn wa al-ḍuʿafāʾ min al-muḥaddithīn,* ed. ʿAzīz Baygh al-Nawshabāndī al-Qadirī, 3 vols. (Hyderabad: Majlis Dāʾirat al-Maʿārif al-ʿUthmānīyah, 1390, vol. 1); Ibn ʿAdī, *al-Kāmil fī ḍuʿafāʾ al-rijāl,* ed. Suhayl

Zakkār, 8 vols. (Beirut: Dār al-Fikr, 1988); Ibn Ḥajar, *Lisān al-mīzān,* 6 vols. (Hyderabad: Maṭbaʿat Majlis Dāʾirat al-Maʿārif al-Niḥāmīyah, 1329–1331; reprint, Beirut: Muʾassat al-Aʿlamī, 1407).

For the trustworthy transmitters, see Aḥmad al-ʿIjlī, *Taʾrīkh al-thiqāt,* ed. ʿAbd al-Muʿṭī Amīn Qalʿajī (Beirut: Dār al-Kutub al-ʿIlmīyah, 1984); Ibn Ḥibbān, *Kitāb al-thiqāt.*

122. See Abū Isḥāq al-Shīrāzī, *Ṭabaqāt al-fuqahāʾ,* ed. Iḥsān ʿAbbās (Beirut: Dār al-Rāʾid al-ʿArabī, 1970).

123. See ibid., pp. 52–53.

124. See ibid., 43, 44, 46, 47. The numbers in brackets refer to the number of transmitters that died at that location. In the case of more than one number, al-Shīrāzī has indicated several different generations of followers dying at the same location.

125. Ibid., p. 51.

126. Ibid., pp. 49, 50.

127. Ibid., p. 47.

128. Ibid., p. 44.

129. Ibid., p. 45.

130. Ibid., p. 48.

131. Ibid., p. 50.

132. Ibid., pp. 57–63, 63–66, 66–68.

133. Ibid., pp. 69–70, 70–71, 71, 71–72.

134. Ibid., pp. 73–74.

135. Ibid., pp. 74–77.

136. Ibid., pp. 77, 77–78.

137. Ibid., pp. 79–81, 81–82, 82–86.

138. Ibid., pp. 87–89, 89–91.

139. Ibid., pp. 91–93.

140. Ibid., pp. 93–94.

141. Ibid., pp. 33–35.

142. For examples of the development of the genre of *faḍāʾil al-amṣār,* see Ibn ʿAsākir, *Taʾrīkh madīnat Dimashq* (Damascus: Majmaʿ al-Lughat al-ʿArabīyah, 1954–) [=Ibn Manẓūr, *Mukhtaṣar taʾrīkh Dimashq,* 17 vols. (Damascus: Dār al-Fikr, 1984)]; al-Khaṭīb al-Baghdādī, *Taʾrīkh Baghdād,* ʿAbd al-Raḥmān b. Yaḥyā al-Muʿallimī (Hyderabad: Dāʾirat al-Maʿārif al-ʿUthmānīyah, 1959); Abū Nuʿaim, *Dhikr akhbār Iṣbahān,* ed. ʿAbd al-Wahāb Khiljī, 2 vols. (Delhi: Dār al-ʿIlmīyah, 1405); Hamzah b. Yūsuf al-Sahmī, *Taʾrīkh Jurjān,* ed. ʿAbd al-Raḥmān Yaḥyā al-Yamanī (Hyderabad: Dāʾirat al-Maʿārif al-ʿUthmānīyah, 1967).

143. For the Ḥanbalī school, see Ibn Abī Yaʿlā, *Ṭabaqāt al-ḥanābilah;* Ibn Rajab, *Dhail ṭabaqāt al-ḥanābilah,* ed. H. Laoust and S. Dahan, 2 vols. (Damascus, 1951); Ṣalāḥ al-Dīn al-Ṣafadī, *al-Wāfī bi al-wafayāt,* ed. Sven Dedering, *Das biographische Lexikon des Ṣalāḥaddīn Ḥalīl Ibn Aibak aṣ-Ṣafadī,* Bibliotheca Islamica 6 (Wiesbaden: Franz Steiner, 1962); George Makdisi, *Ibn ʿAqīl et la résurgence de l'Islam traditionaliste au XIe siècle* (Damascus: Institut Français de Damas, 1963), 58–64.

For the Mālikī school, see al-Qāḍī ʿIyāḍ; Aḥmad Bābā al-Tunbukhtī [960–1036], *Nayl al-ibtihāj fī taṭrīz al-dībāj* (Tripoli: al-Jamāhīrīyah al-ʿArabīyah al-Lībīyah al-Shaʿbīyah al-Ishtirākīyah al-ʿUẓmā, 1989).

For the Shāfiʿī school, see al-Subkī, *Ṭabaqāt al-shāfiʿīyah al-kubrā;* Jamāl al-Dīn al-Asnawī, *Ṭabaqāt al-shāfiʿīyah,* ed. ʿAbdallāh al-Jubūrī, 2 vols. (Baghdād, 1390–1391); Makdisi, *Ibn ʿAqīl et la résurgence de l'Islam, pp.* 47-58.

For the Ḥanafī school, see Ibn Abī al-Wafāʾ, *al-Jawāhir al-muḍīyah,* ed. ʿAbd al-Fattāḥ Muḥammad al-Ḥilw, 3 vols. (Cairo, 1978); al-Qāsim b. Quṭlūbughā, *Tāj al-tarājim,* ed. Gustav Flügel, *Die Krone der Lebenscheschriebungen enthaltend die Classen der Hanefiten von Zeid-ad-dîn Ḳâsim Ibn Ḳuṭlûbugha,* in *Abhandlungen für die Kunde des Morgenlandes* 2, no. 3 (Leipzig, 1862); ed. Qāsim Muḥammad al-Rajab (Baghdād: Maktabat al-Mathannā, 1962).

144. See, for example, Shams al-Dīn al-Dhahabī, *Mīzān al-iʿtidāl,* esp. vol. 3, p. 528; Goldziher, *Introduction to Islamic Theology and Law,* p. 48.

Chapter 2. Restricting Authority to the Classical Schools

1. This is the implication of al-Shāfiʿī, *al-Risālah,* pp. 91–105. For later fiqh theorists who held al-Shāfiʿī's work to have this significance, see ʿAbd al-Wahhab al-Shaʿrānī, *Kitāb al-mīzān,* trans. Perron, *Balance de la loi Musulmane: espirit de la législation Islamique et divergences de ses quatre rites juriprudentiels,* Gouvernement générale de l'Algerie (Algiers: Imprimerie Orientale, 1898), esp. pp. 21–23; Abū Zahrah, *Uṣūl al-fiqh,* p. 15.

2. On this first dispute, see the overview given by Goldziher, *Muhammedanische Studien,* vol. 2, pp. 2:66–83; George Makdisi, "The Significance of the Schools of Law in Islamic Religious History," *International Journal of Middle East Studies* 10 (1979): 1–8. Useful insights were presented by Iftikhar Zaman, "Bukharī as faqīh," unpublished paper, presented at MESA conference, Washington, D.C., 1991.

3. For this claim, see Ibn Qutaybah, *Taʾwīl mukhtalif al-ḥadīth,* pp. 43–86; Schacht, *Origins of Muhammadan Jurisprudence,* pp. 283–328; Ahmad Hasan, "Early Modes of ijtihād: Raʾy, Qiyās and Istiḥsān," *Islamic Studies* 6 (1967): 57–62 [=*The Early Development of Islamic Jurisprudence,* pp. 127–134].

On the designations *aṣḥāb al-ḥadīth* and *aṣḥāb al-raʾy* in this period, see Ibn Qutaybah, *Kitāb al-maʿārif,* ed. Muḥammad Ismāʿīl ʿAbdallāh al-Ṣāwī (Beirut: Iḥyāʾ al-Turāth al-ʿArabī, 1390), pp. 216–229; Ibn al-Nadīm, *al-Fihrist,* ed. Gustav Flügel (Leipzig: F. C. W. Vogel, 1871–1872), vol. 1: p. 225. Both these works identify the aṣḥāb al-raʾy as the Ḥanafīs, Mālikīs, and Shāfiʿīs.

For later accounts that differ in their designations, see al-Maqdisī, *Aḥsan al-taqāsim fī maʿrifat al-aqālīm,* ed. M. J. de Goeje (Leiden: E. J. Brill, 1906), pp. 37-38; al-Shahrastānī, *al-Milal wa al-nihal* [=margins of Ibn Ḥazm, *al-Fiṣal fī al-milal wa al-ahwāʾ wa al-nihal* (Cairo: Maṭbaʿat al-Adabīyah, 1318)] vol. 2: pp. 45–46; Ibn Khaldūn, *al-Muqaddimah* (Cairo: al-Maṭbaʿat al-Amīrīyah al-Būlāq, 1274), p. 218.

4. On this second dispute, see M. Schreiner, "Beiträge zur Geschichte der theologischen Bewegungen im Islam," *Zeitschrift der Deutschen Morgenländischen Gesellschaft* 52 (1898): 486–510, 53 (1899): 51–88, 513–563; Makdisi, "The Significance of the Schools of Law," pp. 5–7.

5. The *ahl al-naẓar* are here associated with the Muʿtazilīs. Because of the fiqh rather than kalām context of the discussion, the terminology used by Ibn Qutaybah is followed. For the use of the term *ahl al-naẓar,* see Ibn Qutaybah, *Taʾwīl mukhtalif al-ḥadīth,* pp. 43–86. For the use of the term *ahl al-kalām,* see al-Shāfiʿī, *Kitāb jimāʿ al-ʿilm* [=*Kitāb al-umm,* vol. 7:], pp. 250–262.

6. For this theory, see Ibn Qutaybah, *Taʾwīl mukhtalif al-ḥadīth,* pp. 246–312; M. Zubayr Siddiqi, "The Importance of Ḥadīth as a Source of Islamic Law," pp. 19–25. Although it should be noted that this view does not preclude the position that the authority of the sunnah is tied to the authority of the revelation, the theory of divine inspiration is also suggested in al-Shāfiʿī, *al-Risālah,* pp. 84–105, based on the exegesis of the Qurʾān 53:3.

7. For this idea, that parts of the sunnah are revelatory, see the statement in Ibn Saʿd, *Kitāb al-ṭabaqāt al-kabīr,* vol. 11: p. 2. Further discussion of this idea is

found in Goldziher, "Kämpfe um die Stellung des Ḥadīt im Islam," *Zeitschrift der Deutschen Morgenländischen Gesellschaft* 61 (1907): 863–864; William A. Graham, *Divine word and prophetic word in early Islam*, esp. pp. 9–19. On the reports supposed to be revelations, see Muḥyī al-Dīn al-ᶜArabī [d. 638], *Mishkāt al-anwār* (Aleppo, 1346); Muḥammad al-Madyanī [d. 881], *al-Itḥāfāt al-saniyyah fī al-aḥādīth al-qudsiyyah* (Hyderabad, 1323); ᶜAlī b. Sulṭān Muḥammad al-Qārī [d. 1014], *al-Aḥādīth al-qudsīyat al-arbaᶜīnīyah*, ed. Muḥammad Rāghib al-Ṭabbākh (Beirut: Dār al-Kutub al-ᶜIlmīyah, 1983).

8. This is most evident in the work of Ibn Ḥazm, *al-Iḥkām fī uṣūl al-aḥkām*, ed. Aḥmad Shākir (Cairo: Maṭbaᶜat al-ᶜĀṣimah, 1968), passim. The implications of Ibn Ḥazm's use of dalālāt are discussed in Goldziher, *The Ẓāhirīs*, pp. 40–62, 117–156; Miguel Asín Palacios, *Abenházm de Córdoba: historia crítica de las ideas religiosas* (Madrid: Real Academia de la Historia, 1927), vol. 1: pp. 141–144, 173–178; Roger Arnaldez, *Grammaire et théology chez Ibn Ḥazm de Cordoue: essai sur la structure et les conditions de la pensée musulmane*, Études musulmanes 3 (Paris: Librairie Philosophique J. Vrin, 1956), pp. 219–227.

9. This contention, in light of later Ẓāhirī scholarship, is discussed in Palacios, Abenházm de Cordóba, vol. 1: pp. 106–144; Goldziher, *The Ẓāhirīs*, pp. 89–96; Arnaldez, *Grammaire et théology*, esp. pp. 217–248.

10. This is suggested from the examples cited in Ibn Qutaybah, *Taʾwīl mukhtalif al-ḥadīth*, pp. 43–86. Also, see Ibn Qutaybah, *Kitāb al-maᶜārif*, pp. 216–219.

11. The connection between these two uses of interpretive logic are laid out in al-Shāfiᶜī, *al-Risālah*, pp. 190–195; al-Shāfiᶜī, *Ikhtilāf al-ḥadīth* [=*Kitāb al-umm*, margins of vol. 7], pp. 116–121, 218–221; al-Shāfiᶜī, *Kitāb al-umm*, vol. 7, pp. 205–206, pp. 291–292. For a discussion of these examples, see Ahmad Hasan, *The Early Development of Islamic Jurisprudence*, pp. 192–194.

12. For this precedent, see al-Shāfiᶜī, *al-Risālah*, pp. 64–79, pp. 167–175. That this point is made by the aṣḥāb al-raʾy in this context is discussed in Schacht, *Origins of Muhammadan Jurisprudence*, pp. 15–16; Ahmad Hasan, "The Source of Islamic law," pp. 165–184; A. Hasan, *The Early Development of Islamic Jurisprudence*, pp. 180–194; S. Ali Raza Naqvi, "Prophetic Sunna in the Islamic Legal Framework," *Islamic Studies* 19 (1980): 120–133, esp. pp. 129–132.

13. This implication is suggested in al-Shāfiᶜī, *al-Risālah*, pp. 401–470, pp. 471–476, 476–486, 487–503. This point is spelled out in Hasan, "Early Modes of Ijtihād;" pp. 57–62 [=*The Early Development of Islamic Jurisprudence*, 127–134]; Wael Hallaq, "The Authoritativeness of Sunni Consensus," *International Journal of Middle Eastern Studies* 18(1986): 427–454.

14. See the astute remarks on this point by Bernard Weiss, "Interpretation in Islamic Law: The Theory of Ijtihad," *The American Journal of Comparative Law* 26, no. 2 (1978): 199–212, esp. pp. 199–201.

15. This position is explained in Ibn Qutaybah, *Taʾwīl mukhtalif al-ḥadīth,* pp. 43–86; M. Schreiner, "Beiträge zur Geschichte der theologischen Bewegungen im Islam," Makdisi, "The Significance of the Schools of Law," pp. 5–7.

16. For examples taken from the perspective of non ahl al-naẓar scholarship, see al-Shāfiʿī, *Kitāb jimāʿ al-ʿilm* [=*Kitāb al-umm,* vol. 7:250–262], passim, where the ahl al-naẓar are referred to as the *ahl al-kalām*; Ibn Qutaybah, *Taʾwīl mukhtalif al-ḥadīth,* pp. 43–86.

17. On this point, see the arguments in Makdisi, "The Significance of the Schools of Law," 6–7.

18. On the relation of the ahl al-naẓar to the Muʿtazilīs and the miḥnah, see W. M. Patton, *Aḥmed ibn Ḥanbal and the Miḥnah,* passim; Henri Laoust, "Le hanbalisme sous le califat de Baghdad," pp. 67–128; Laoust, *Les schismes dans l'Islam: introduction à une étude de la religion musulmane* (Paris: Payot, 1965), pp. 101–118.

19. This was taken as the implication of al-Shāfiʿī, *al-Risālah,* pp. 401–470. See Ahmad Hasan, *The Early Development of Islamic Jurisprudence,* pp. 182–183.

20. See the many examples and discussion of this shift in Schacht, *Origins of Muhammadan Jurisprudence,* pp. 98–132. The development of the use of istiḥsān is discussed in Ahmad Hasan, "The Principle of Istiḥsān in Islamic Jurisprudence," *Islamic Studies* 16 (1977): pp. 347–362.

21. These terms are found discussed in al-Shāfiʿī, *Ikhtilāf al-ḥadīth* [=*Kitāb al-umm,* in the margin of vol. 7], pp. 339–340. This terminology is discussed in Ahmad Hasan, *The Early Development of Islamic Jurisprudence,* pp. 192–194.

22. See al-Shāfiʿī, *Ikhtilāf al-ḥadīth* [=*Kitāb al-umm,* in the margin of vol. 7], pp. 339–340.

23. This point is made by D. S. Margoliouth, *The Early Development of Mohammedanism* (London: Williams and Norgate, 1914), p. 97.

24. The dating and the dynamics of this process of "Islamicization" are discussed in Bergsträsser, *Grundzüge des Islamischen Rechts,* pp. 8–21; Schacht, *Origins of Muhammadan Jurisprudence,* pp. 98–137, 269–282; Z. I. Ansari, "Islamic Juristic Terminology Before Shafiʿi," *Arabica* 19, no. 3 (1972): 288–294; Wael Hallaq, "Non-analogical Arguments in Sunni Juridical Qiyās,"

Arabica 36 (1989): esp. p. 286; W. Hallaq, "Considerations of the Function and Character of Sunni Legal Theory," *Journal of the American Oriental Society* 104 (1984): 679–689.

25. A definitive, or even wide-ranging, account of the development of ikhtilāf scholarship is yet to be available. The distinction of "classical" ikhtilāf is intended to signify those works that deal with the conflict of opinion (usually among the second century local authorities, as opposed to between the Qurʾān and sunnah or within the different reports that make up the sunnah) to demonstrate the sorts of interpretive strategies used by the prophet, as represented in the sunnah. The earlier ikhtilāf work associated with Abū Yūsuf, as shown in Chapter 1, attempts to justify Abū Ḥanīfah's choice of precedents on the basis of a largely presumed prophetic logic. The ikhtilāf work associated with al-Shāfiʿī is an attempt to demonstrate the consistency of the contents of the sunnah with the contents of the revelation but not to specify the types of interpretive reasoning the prophet used to produce the sunnah.

For general discussions of the epistemological implications of classical ikhtilāf scholarship, see the articles collected in *l'ambivalence dans la culture arabe,* ed. J. Berque and J.-P. Charnay (Paris: Editions Anthropos, 1968). There is also a general survey of ikhtilāf literature in Muḥammad Ṣaghīr Ḥasan Maʿṣūmī, *Imam Ṭaḥāwī's Disagreement of the Jurists* (Islamabad: Islamic Research Institute, 1391), esp. pp. 24–30.

For the significance of Ibn Qutaybah's work in the development of ikhtilāf scholarship and fiqh scholarship in general, see M. El Shakankiri, "Loi divine, loi humaine et droit dans l'histoire juridique de l'Islam," *Revue historique de droit français et etranger* 59 (1981): 161–182, esp. pp. 163–164; Gérard Lecomte, *Le traité des divergences du ḥadīṯ d'Ibn Qutaybah* (Damascus: Institut Français de Damas, 1962), esp. pp. vii–xliv.

26. For further examples of this, see Ibn Qutaybah, *Taʾwīl mukhtalif al-ḥadīth,* [Qurʾān//ḥadīth]; pp. 101–102, 120–121, 121–122, 174–176, 176–177, 177–181, 183–184, 219–226, 260–265; [ḥadīth//ḥadīth]: 99, 100, 100–101, 107–113, 113, 114, 114–117, 117–118, 118–119, 119–120, 123–124, 127–128, 143, 147–148, 148–149, 155–156, 156–159, 159–161, 161–162, 162–163, 163–164, 172–173, 173, 173–175, 204, 204–205, 214–216, 216, 216–217, 217, 218, 250–251, 251–253, 253–258 258–260, 265–268, 277–279, 282–286, 286–287, 287–288, 288, 293–294, 294; [part of ḥadīth/part of same ḥadīth]; 129–132, 132–134, 134–138, 185, 234–236.

27. Ibid., p. 134.

28. Ibid., pp. 134–135.

29. This principle is spelled out in ibid., p. 226.

30. Some later fiqh scholarship, although accepting the basic contention put forward by Ibn Qutaybah, maintains that the sunnah does not technically "abrogate" the Qur᾿ān. Instead, where the sunnah appears to contradict the Qur᾿ān directly, the contradiction can be resolved by resorting to the basic distinction between statements of general [ᶜāmm] and particular [khāṣṣ] precedents. This resort is based on the description of naskh given in al-Shāfiᶜī, *al-Risālah,* esp. p. 103. For further discussion of this distinction, see Ibn ᶜAbd al-Barr, *Jāmiᶜ bayān al-ᶜilm wa faḍlī-hi* (Beirut, 1398), pp. 188–192; Abū Zahrah, *Uṣūl al-fiqh,* p. 149; Kamali, *Principles of Islamic Jurisprudence,* pp. 152–154. For the claim that the prophet's only abrogation of the Qur᾿ān was that which was "inspired," see al-Ghazālī, *Kitāb al-mustaṣfā᾿* (Bulāq, 1322), vol. 1, p. 125. This is discussed in Burton, *The collection of the Qur᾿ān,* pp. 52–63.

Calder (*Studies in Early Muslim Jurisprudence,* pp. 224–225) claims that Ibn Qutaybah's allowing the sunnah to abrogate the Qur᾿ān proves that his work is less sophisticated and thus earlier than the theoretical construct outlined in the *Risālah.* It appears, however, that the more rigid injunction against the sunnah abrogating the Qur᾿ān found in the *Risālah* is an earlier concept that is later abandoned, first by Ibn Qutaybah and later by many of the classical uṣūl al-fiqh scholars. This is the jist of the argument made by Burton, ibid., pp. 52–63. That Ibn Qutaybah's use of naskh as a means to illustrate that a later interpretation transfers its meaning to the text being interpreted is evident in the Ḥanafī's outright contention that *qiyās* and *ijmāᶜ* abrogate the Qur᾿ān. This is discussed in ᶜAlī b. Muḥammad al-Āmidī, *al-Iḥkām fī uṣūl al-aḥkām,* ed. ᶜAbd al-Raqqāq ᶜAfīfī, 2d ed. (Beirut: al-Maktab al-Islāmī, 1402), vol. 3: p. 161; ᶜAbd al-Raḥmān Tāj, *al-Siyāsat al-sharīᶜah* (Cairo: Maṭbaᶜah Dār al-Ta᾿līf, 1371), pp. 14–28; Abū al-ᶜAynayn Badrān, *Uṣūl al-fiqh al-Islāmī* (Alexandria: Mu᾿assasah Shabāb al-Jāmiᶜah, 1404), p. 458.

31. For examples of this, see Ibn Qutaybah, *Ta᾿wīl mukhtalif al-ḥadīth,* pp. 103–105, 106–107, 138–141, 141–143, 164–172, 206–209, 213–214, 218–219, 226–227, 227–229, 236–238, 243–245, 245–250, 276–277, 280–282, 289–293, 295–296, 296–297.

32. The distinction Ibn Qutaybah makes between ᶜiyān and khabar suggests that the latter is used to designate what is later termed āthār, referring to the practice of the companions assumed to be consistent with prophetic precedent. There is a brief discussion of this terminological development in Azami, *Studies in Early Ḥadīth Literature,* p. 3; Kamali, *Principles of Islamic Jurisprudence,* p. 47.

33. For examples of this, see Ibn Qutaybah, *Taʾwīl mukhtalif al-ḥadīth* [ijmāʿ]; 102–103, 231–233; [ijmāʿ and Qurʾān]; 184–185, 203–204, 238–243, 279–280; [khabar]; 105–106, 182–183; [reasoning and khabar]; 124–127, 149–155; [reasoning, Qurʾān, khabar, and ʿiyān]; 122–123.

34. On this point, see the example given in ibid. pp. 149–155.

35. For this significance of Ibn Qutaybah's work, see Ibn al-Nadīm, al-Fihrist, p. 77; al-Kindī, *The Governors and Judges of Egypt,* p. 546; Lecomte, *Le traité des divergences du ḥadīṯ d'Ibn Qutaybah,* pp. vii–x.

36. On the historical context, see Lecomte, *Le traité des divergences du ḥadīṯ d'Ibn Qutaybah,* pp. viii, ix; Laoust, *Les schismes dans l'Islam;* pp. 101–118.

37. For this reference, see Mālik, *al-Muwaṭṭāʾ,* vol. 1: p. 357.

38. See Ibn Abī Ḥātim, *al-Jarḥ wa al-taʿdīl.* For a discussion of Ibn Abī Ḥātim's work, see Aʿẓamī, *Dirāsāt fī al-jarḥ wa al-taʿdīl,* esp. pp. 297–434.

39. Ibn Abī Ḥātim, ibid., vol. 1, p. 1.

40. Ibid., vol. 1, p. 2.

41. Ibid.

42. Ibid., vol. 1, p. 7.

43. Ibid.

44. Ibid.

45. For this view, see Ibn Saʿd, *Kitāb al-ṭabaqāt al-kabīr,* vol. 2, p. 135. This is briefly discussed in Goldziher, "The Development of Law," in his *Introduction to Islamic Theology and Law,* p. 38.

46. Ibn Abī Ḥātim, *al-Jarḥ wa al-taʿdīl,* vol. 1, p. 3.

47. See ibid., vol. 1, pp. 1, 2, 7.

48. Ibid., vol. 1, p. 2.

49. In particular, see Abū Yūsuf, *Ikhtilāf Abī Ḥanīfah wa Ibn Abī Laylā* and Abū Yūsuf, *al-Radd ʿalā siyar al-Awzāʿī,* passim. There is a discussion of this type of logical reasoning and the second century defense of it in Schacht, *Origins of Muhammadan Jurisprudence,* pp. 288–314, esp. pp. 294–306.

50. This important observation is pointed out in Weiss, *The Search for God's Law,* pp. 259–328, esp. pp. 259–261, on the basis of the discussion in Sayf al-Dīn al-Āmidī [d. 631], *Kitāb al-iḥkām fī uṣūl al-aḥkām* (Cairo: Dār al-Kutub al-Khidīwīyah, 1914), roughly vol. 2, pp. 1–170.

51. For this reference, see the discussion in Abū Yūsuf, *al-Radd ᶜalā siyar al-Awzāᶜī,* pp. 17–21.

52. For this statement, see al-Bukhārī, 34:44; Muslim, 21:10. The statement is also quoted and discussed in al-Shāfiᶜī, *al-Risālah,* p. 313.

53. Taken from al-Ṭabarī, *Ikhtilāf al-fuqahāʾ,* ed. Frederick Kern (Beirut: Muḥammad Amīn Ramj, n.d.), p. 123. The statement of the prophet and Mālik's discussion of it is found in Mālik, *al-Muwaṭṭāʾ,* vol. 2, p. 671.

54. Taken from al-Ṭabarī, *Ikhtilāf al-fuqahāʾ,* p. 123. The opinions of Abū Ḥanīfah, Abū Yūsuf, and al-Shaybānī are given and discussed in al-Ḥaddād, *al-Jawharat al-nayyirah,* vol. 1, pp. 233–237.

55. This glosses over the conflict of opinion, not mentioned by al-Ṭabarī, that exists among the Ḥanafī authorities. Only Abū Yūsuf and al-Shaybānī allow, like Mālik, the option of canceling the sale to continue for an indefinite period. Abū Ḥanīfah limits the period to three days. This is discussed in al-Ḥaddād, *al-Jawharat al-nayyirah,* esp. vol. 1, pp. 233–234.

56. al-Ṭabarī, *Ikhtilāf al-fuqahāʾ,* p. 123.

57. Ibid.

58. Ibid., p. 123. Note that al-Thawrī includes in his version of the prophet's statement the distinction between an "optional sale" (one which automatically has the option of cancellation), and the case when the right to an option is reserved specifically for that case. It is unclear what the significance of this distinction is for al-Thawrī.

59. Ibid., p. 123. According to al-Ṭabarī, the opinion of Abū Thawr is the same as that of al-Shāfiᶜī. For a fuller discussion of al-Shāfiᶜī's position see al-Shāfiᶜī, *al-Risālah,* pp. 313–314; al-Shāfiᶜī, *Kitāb al-umm,* vol. 3, p. 3.

60. al-Ṭabarī, *Ikhtilāf al-fuqahāʾ,* p. 124.

61. There is no formal reference to this report of prophetic practice in the context of the discussion of uncultivated land in the *Muwaṭṭāʾ,* aside from Mālik's mention that the prophet "forbade uncertain transactions" [2:706]. The claim is made by al-Ṭabarī that Mālik's opinion, in particular, is based on a report of the prophet's practice [p. 124].

This issue is complicated in the reports of prophetic practice given in the six books. The general statement that it is permitted to let land for a fixed price is given in al-Nasāʾī, 35:46. Ibn Mājah, 16:11 cites reports that allow a fixed portion of the produce to be given. There are a number of examples prohibiting the transfer of property on the basis of produce not yet harvested or ripened. For these examples, see al-Bukhārī, 34:82, 37:22, 41:7, 12, 18, 42:17, 51:35, 55:7; Muslim, 21:81–97, 99, 102–105, 107–122; Abū Dāʾūd, 22:30–31; al-Tirmidhī, 12:14, 55, 63, 72, 13:42; al-Nasāʾī, 35:45, 44:27, 32, 93; Ibn Mājah, 16:7–10.

62. al-Ṭabarī, *Ikhtilāf al-fuqahāʾ*, 124. A close version of this opinion is found in Mālik, *al-Muwaṭṭāʾ*, vol. 2, p. 707.

63. al-Ṭabarī, *Ikhtilāf al-fuqahāʾ*, p. 124. This opinion is given and discussed in al-Ḥaddād, *al-Jawharat al-nayyirah,* vol. 2, pp. 54–56. According to al-Ṭabarī, Abū Thawr agrees with the opinions of Abū Ḥanīfah and Mālik.

64. al-Ṭabarī, *Ikhtilāf al-fuqahāʾ*, p. 124. This opinion is given and discussed in al-Shāfiʿī, *Kitāb al-umm,* vol. 3, pp. 10–25.

65. Ibid., p. 124. For this opinion and its discussion, see al-Ḥaddād, *al-Jawharat al-nayyirah,* vol. 2, pp. 54–56. According to al-Ṭabarī, the opinion of al-Thawrī agrees with the opinion of Abū Yūsuf and al-Shaybānī.

66. This is building upon the interpretive concepts in al-Shāfiʿī, *al-Risālah,* esp. p. 33, and Ibn Qutaybah, *Taʾwīl mukhtalif al-ḥadīth,* pp. 246–312. See the discussion in W. Hallaq, "Considerations of the Function and Character of Sunni Legal Theory," pp. 680–681.

67. There is a great deal of confusion over the text published as *Imam Ṭaḥāwī's Disagreement of the Jurists,* ed. Muḥammad Ṣaghīr Ḥasan Maʿṣūmī (Islamabad: Islamic Research Institute, 1391). The title of the manuscript reads "the second part of the *Aḥkām al-Qurʾān* of Abū Bakr al-Rāzī, known as al-Jaṣṣāṣ," which has been taken by many to indicate that this text is in fact what is known to as al-Jaṣṣāṣ's *Ikhtiṣar ikhtilāf al-fuqahāʾ li al-Ṭaḥāwī.* For these arguments, see Seedullal Qazi, *Principles of Muslim Jurispruden[c]e: Chapters on Qiyās and Ijtihād* (Lahore: al-Maktabat al-Ilmīyah, 1401), pp. 40–43; Frederick Kern's introduction to al-Ṭabarī, *Ikhtilāf al-fuqahāʾ*, esp. p. 5; Mawlah Muḥammad Yūsuf al-Banūrī, "Tabṣirat Ikhtilāf al-fuqahāʾ al-Ṭaḥāwī," *Bayyināt* (September 1972): 28; Muḥammad Zahīd al-Kawtharī, *Maqālāt al-Kawtharī* (Cairo: Maṭbaʿat al-Anwār, 1371; reprint. Cairo: al-Maktabat al-Azharīyah li al-Turāth, 1994), p. 472. Maʿṣūmī's response is found in his "Imām Ṭaḥāwī fī Kitāb Ikhtilāf al-fuqahāʾ," *Fikr-u Naẓar* (Islamabad: Islamic Research Institute, October 1973); pp. 193–194.

It is possible that the text in question is al-Jaṣṣāṣ's *Ikhtiṣār* of al-Ṭaḥāwī's ikhtilāf works. Further, it is possible that the ikhtilāf works of al-Ṭaḥāwī that al-Jaṣṣāṣ is condensing were never redacted under the separate title of *Ikhtilāf* *al-fuqahā*ʾ, but are to be identified with al-Ṭaḥāwī's two āthār works. This latter assertion seems unlikely, however, because of the great disparity between al-Ṭaḥāwī's āthār works and the ikhtilāf manuscript available. A comparative analysis of these works would help to clarify their relationship. In any case, the text used here represents al-Ṭaḥāwī's work, whether or not it was redacted at a later date by al-Jaṣṣāṣ. For the manuscript information, see Sezgin, *Geschichte des arabischen Schrifttums,* vol. 1, p. 441.

68. This division is discussed in al-Jaṣṣāṣ, *al-Fuṣūl fī al-uṣūl,* ed. Seedulla Qazi, *Principles of Muslim Jurispruden[c]e,* p. 172.

69. For a fuller explanation of this sort of reasoning, see ibid., pp. 110–139.

70. al-Jaṣṣāṣ, *Ikhtiṣar ikhtilāf al-fuqahā*ʾ *li al-Ṭaḥāwī* [=Maʿṣūmī, *Imam al-Ṭaḥāwī's Disagreement of the Jurists*], p. 57.

71. Ibid., p. 57.

72. Ibid., p. 57. This report is also found in al-Ṭaḥāwī, *Sharḥ maʿānī al-āthār,* ed. M. S. J. al-Ḥaqq (Cairo: Maṭbaʿat al-Anwār, 1968), vol. 2, pp. 257–260.

73. al-Jaṣṣāṣ, ibid., p. 57.

74. Ibid., p. 57. Also see the discussion in al-Ṭaḥāwī, *Sharḥ maʿānī al-āthār,* vol. 2, p. 259. Other reports concerning restrictions on behavior in Madīnah are found in al-Bukhārī, 29:1; Muslim, 15:158–478; Abū Dāʾūd, 11:95.

75. al-Jaṣṣāṣ, ibid., p. 57. Also see the discussion in al-Ṭaḥāwī, *ibid., vol.* 2, p. 260.

76. al-Jaṣṣāṣ, ibid., pp. 57–58.

77. al-Ṭaḥāwī, *Ikhtilāf al-fuqahā*ʾ, pp. 57–58. There are no references in the six books to the prophet having forbade this.

78. For further discussion of the reasoning responsible for this sort of conflict, see al-Jaṣṣāṣ, *al-Fuṣūl fī al-uṣūl,* pp. 132–138.

79. al-Jaṣṣāṣ, *Ikhtiṣar ikhtilāf al-fuqahā*ʾ *li al-Ṭaḥāwī* [=Maʿṣūmī, *Imam al-Ṭaḥāwī's Disagreement of the Jurists*], p. 46. The opinion of al-Shāfiʿī is found in al-Shāfiʿī, *Kitāb al-umm,* vol. 3, p. 27. Note that either al-Ṭaḥāwī or al-Jaṣṣāṣ has glossed over a difference between the Ḥanafī position and the opinion of al-Shāfiʿī. The opinion of al-Shāfiʿī does allow that the two parties mutually take possession as long as they have not separated. But, as was made evident in al-Ṭabarī's *Ikhtilāf al-fuqahā*ʾ, al-Shāfiʿī regards separation as physically leaving the location where the sale is contracted. The opinion of al-Shāfiʿī in the *Kitāb al-umm* concerns the particular case of exchanging jewelry in the context of an unmixed sale.

80. al-Jaṣṣāṣ, ibid., p. 46. The reference to Ibn al-Qāsim is to ʿAbd al-Raḥmān b. al-Qāsim b. Khālid al-ʿUtaqī [132–191]. For his unpublished works, see Sezgin, *Geschichte des arabischen Schrifttums,* vol. 1, pp. 465–466.

81. al-Jaṣṣāṣ, ibid., p. 45.

82. Ibid., p. 46.

83. This sort of conflict is discussed in al-Jaṣṣāṣ, *al-Fuṣūl fī al-uṣūl,* p. 152.

84. al-Jaṣṣāṣ, *Ikhtiṣar ikhtilāf al-fuqahāʾ li al-Ṭaḥāwī* [=Maʿṣūmī, *Imam al-Ṭaḥāwī's Disagreement of the Jurists*], p. 46. The opinion of Abū Ḥanīfah is also found in al-Shaybānī, *al-Ḥujjah fī ikhtilāf ahl al-Kūfah wa ahl al-Madīnah* (Lucknow, 1888), p. 212. The opinion of al-Shāfiʿī is found in al-Shāfiʿī, *Kitāb al-umm,* vol. 3, p. 27.

85. al-Jaṣṣāṣ, ibid., p. 46.

86. This condition is evident from the fuller opinions of Abū Ḥanīfah and al-Shāfiʿī. The opinion of Abū Ḥanīfah is also found in al-Shaybānī, *al-Ḥujjah fī ikhtilāf ahl al-Kūfah wa ahl al-Madīnah* (Lucknow, 1888), p. 212. The opinion of al-Shāfiʿī is found in al-Shāfiʿī, *Kitāb al-umm,* vol. 3, p. 27.

87. al-Jaṣṣāṣ, *Ikhtiṣar ikhtilāf al-fuqahāʾ li al-Ṭaḥāwī* [=Maʿṣūmī, *Imam al-Ṭaḥāwī's Disagreement of the Jurists*], p. 47.

88. Ibid. For information on Abū ʿAlī al-Ḥasan b. Ziyād al-Luʾluʾī's *Musnad Abī Ḥanīfah,* see Sezgin, *Geschichte des arabischen Schrifttums,* vol. 1, p. 233.

89. al-Jaṣṣāṣ, ibid., p. 47.

90. This is discussed in al-Jaṣṣāṣ, *al-Fuṣūl fī al-uṣūl,* pp. 172–174.

91. al-Jaṣṣāṣ, *Ikhtiṣar ikhtilāf al-fuqahāʾ li al-Ṭaḥāwī* [=Maʿṣūmī, *Imam al-Ṭaḥāwī's Disagreement of the Jurists*], p. 58. This seems to be taken from Mālik, *al-Muwaṭṭāʾ,* vol. 1, p. 357.

92. On these precedents, see Mālik, ibid., vol. 2, p. 496. This is pointed out in reference to al-Ṭaḥāwī's work in al-Marghīnānī, *al-Hidāyah maʿa al-dirāyah* (Karachi, 1962), vol. 4, p. 440.

93. al-Jaṣṣāṣ, *Ikhtiṣar ikhtilāf al-fuqahāʾ li al-Ṭaḥāwī* [=Maʿṣūmī, *Imam al-Ṭaḥāwī's Disagreement of the Jurists*], p. 58.

94. Ibid.

95. Ibid., p. 59.

96. See al-Jaṣṣāṣ, *Aḥkām al-Qurʾān,* vol. 3, p. 467.

97. Qur᾿ān 5:96, quoted in Ibid.

98. Qur᾿ān 5:3, quoted and discussed in al-Jaṣṣāṣ, ibid., vol. 3, p. 467.

99. See ibid.

100. See Ibid., vol. 3, pp. 467–468.

101. Both Calder and Wansbrough cite al-Jaṣṣāṣ's work as evidence of the earliest attempt to systematically show that fiqh scholarship is derived from the Qur᾿ān. It is clear from other sources, including the scholarship discussed earlier, however, that the Qur᾿ān was used, sometimes extensively, by earlier scholars both to defend the authority of the sunnah and as a basis for the definition of practice. The work of al-Jaṣṣāṣ does appear to be the earliest attempt to demonstrate how the Qur᾿ān is to be interpreted in light of the opinions as opposed to the sunnah alone. For these views, see Calder, *Studies in Early Muslim Jurisprudence,* esp. pp. 218–219; Wansbrough, *Quranic Studies,* esp. pp. 170–202.

102. This point, although not with the same specificity, is indicated in Abū al-Qāsim Gorjī, "Nigāhī beh taḥawwul-e ᶜilm-e uṣūl," trans. ᶜAlī Qulī Qarā᾿ī, "A Brief Survey of the Development of ᶜIlm Uṣūl al-Fiqh," *al-Tawḥīd* no. 3, 2 (1986): esp. pp. 62–63.

103. It is important to note that there were scholars who were not attached exclusively to one of the classical schools. An example of this is given in Shams al-Dīn al-Dhahabī, *Mīzān al-iᶜtidāl,* vol. 3, p. 528. This phenomenon is discussed in Goldziher, *Introduction to Islamic Theology and Law,* p. 48.

Also, note that the Ẓāhirī and Ḥanbalī schools, although technically not part of the aṣḥāb al-ra᾿y movement developing this modified epistemology, in theory enjoy the same authority as the other three classical schools. Both of these schools hold a unique position in the development of the classical fiqh epistemology and methodology. Much work remains to be done on how these two schools are related to the other three, historically and theoretically. On the Ẓāhirīs, see Goldziher, *The Ẓāhirīs,* passim. The analysis of Ibn Ḥazm's work is particularly relevant. See Palacios, *Abenházm de Córdoba,* and Arnaldez, *Grammaire et theology.* On the Ḥanbalīs, see Goldziher, "Zur Geschichte der ḥanbalitischen Bewegungen," passim, and Makdisi, "Hanbalite Islam," passim.

Chapter 3. The Logic of the Opinions

1. The dating of the "authoritative" collections of local opinions is still a matter of some dispute. For the most recent views, see Calder, *Studies in Early Muslim Jurisprudence,* esp. pp. 1-104. For examples of the earliest scholarship

focusing on the opinions as a defined textual corpus, see the works of Saḥnūn [160–240], Hilāl al-Raʾy [d. 245], al-Khaṣṣāf [d. 261], al-Muzanī [175–264], and al-Abḥarī [d. 287].

2. In particular, see ʿAbdallāh b. Muḥammad al-Abharī's commentary on the *Mukhtaṣar al-kabīr fī al-fiqh* of ʿAbdallāh b. ʿAbd al-Ḥakam [d. 214]. For more information on the life and works of al-Abharī, see Sezgin, *Geschichte des arabischen Schrifttums,* vol. 1, p. 477.

3. See the monumental compendium of Ibn Abī Zayd al-Qayrawānī, *al-Risālah* (Cairo, 1296; reprint, 1304, 1314, 1319, 1323, 1324, 1338, 1340). There is an English translation of sections of this work published as *First Steps in Muslim Jurisprudence: Consisting of Excerpts from Bākūrāt as-saʿd of Ibn Abī Zayd,* ed. and trans. A. D. Russell and ʿAbdallāh al-Mamun Suhrawardy (London, 1906). For the published commentaries on this work, see that of al-Qāsim b. ʿĪsā b. Nājī [d. 837] (Cairo, 1332) and Aḥmad b. Aḥmad Zarrūq [d. 889] (Cairo, 1332). For more information on the life and works of Ibn Abī Zayd al-Qayrawānī, see Sezgin, ibid., vol. 1, pp. 478–481.

4. See Ibn ʿAbd al-Barr, *al-Istidhkār fī sharḥ madhāhib al-amṣār mimmā rasama-hu al-Imām Mālik fī al-Muwaṭṭāʾ min al-raʾy wa al-āthār.* For further information on the life and work of Ibn ʿAbd al-Barr, see Brockelmann, *Geschichte der arabischen Litteratur,* vol. 1, p. 368.

5. See al-Bājī, *al-Muntaqā sharḥ al-Muwaṭṭāʾ,* 7 vols. (Cairo, 1331–1332). For further information on the life and work of al-Bājī, see Brockelmann, ibid., vol. 1, p. 419.

6. The significance of using this redaction is discussed in Ibn ʿAbd al-Barr, *al-Ziyādāt allātī taqaʿ fī al-Muwaṭṭāʾ ʿinda Yaḥyāʾ b. Yaḥyāʾ ʿan Mālik.*

7. For the available manuscripts of al-Azharī, *Kitāb al-ẓāhir fī gharīb alfaẓ al-Shāfiʿī al-maujūdah fī Mukhtaṣar al-Muzanī allādhī yarwī-hi ʿan al-Shāfiʿī,* see Sezgin, *Geschichte des arabischen Schrifttums,* vol. 1, p. 593.

8. For the available manuscripts of Abū al-Ṭayyib al-Ṭabarī, *Sharḥ al-mukhtaṣar al-Muzanī,* see Sezgin, ibid., vol. 1, p. 493. For further information on the life and work of Abū al-Ṭayyib al-Ṭabarī, see Sezgin, ibid., vol. 1, p. 502.

9. See Ibn al-Maḥāmilī, *Kitāb al-lubāb fī al-fiqh* (Cairo, 1274; reprint, 1286, 1298, 1305–1306, 1309–1315). Also see the discussion of this work's importance in Abū Zurʿa al-ʿIrāqī [d. 826], *Tanqīh al-lubāb,* with an abridgement by Zakarīyāʾ b. Muḥammad al-Anṣārī [d. 916], entitled *Taḥrīr tanqīḥ al-lubāb,* published in the margins of his *Tuḥfat al-ṭullāb* (Cairo: Muṣṭafā al-Bābī

al-Ḥalabī, 1340). For more information on the life and work of Ibn al-Maḥāmilī, see Sezgin, ibid., vol. 1, pp. 499–500.

10. The commentary of Abū Yaʿlā al-Farrāʾ is published with Ibn Qudāmah [541–620], *Muqniʿ*, 12 vols. (Cairo, 1348).

11. See al-Khiraqī, *al-Mukhtaṣar fī al-fiqh,* ed. M. Zuhair al-Shāwīsh (Damascus, 1378; reprint, Beirut, 1384). For further information on the life and work of al-Khiraqī, see Sezgin, *Geschichte des arabischen Schrifttums,* vol. 1, pp. 512–513.

12. For the many texts attributed to Ibn Ḥanbal and the masāʾil works of subsequent centuries, see Sezgin, ibid., vol. 1., pp. 502–512.

13. The significance of al-Karkhī's *Mukhtaṣar* is discussed in what follows. For more information on his life and other works, see Sezgin, ibid., vol. 1., p. 444.

14. For the significance of this distinction for classical fiqh scholarship, see B. Weiss, *The Search for God's Law,* pp. 259–328. It is important to note, based on the manuscript evidence, that the classical schools did not "copy" collections of opinions but wrote commentaries, which included the text of that on which the commentary was being made, on certain collections of opinions.

15. There was a general agreement later, perhaps originating at the end of the sixth century, that the canonical corpus of Ḥanafī opinions was to be found in a certain collection of texts attributed to Muḥammad b. al-Ḥasan al-Shaybānī [132–189], called the *ẓāhir al-riwāyah.* On the concept of the ẓāhir al-riwāyah, see Muḥammad Iʿzāz al-ʿAlī, *Ḥāshīyat al-jalīlat al-mufīdat al-musamāh bi al-iṣbāḥ,* published in the introduction and on the margins of al-Sharranbulālī, *Nūr al-īḍāḥ* (Multan: Maktabah-i Imādīyah, 1979), esp. pp. 2–8.

The concept of the opinions being limited to a certain collection of books is late. In the context of discussing the work of al-Sarakhsī, in what follows, it is also evident that these various books attributed to al-Shaybānī are the product of much later redaction. The *Aṣl,* in particular, seems to be the result rather than the basis of al-Sarakhsī's *Mabsūṭ.* For a brief overview of this argument, see Calder, *Studies in Early Muslim Jurisprudence,* pp. 39–44.

16. See Hilāl al-Raʾy, *Kitāb aḥkām al-waqf* (Hyderabad, 1355). For further information on the life and work of Hilāl al-Raʾy, see Sezgin, *Geschichte des arabischen Schrifttums,* vol. 1, pp. 435–436.

17. See al-Khaṣṣāf, *Kitāb aḥkām al-waqf* (Cairo, 1322) and his *Kitāb al-nafaqāt,* published with the commentary of Ibn Māzah [d. 536] (Hyderabad, 1349). For further information on the life and works of al-Khaṣṣāf, see Sezgin, ibid., vol. 1, pp. 437–438.

18. See Abū al-Layth al-Samarqandī, *Khizānat al-fiqh,* partially ed. J. H. Callenberg, *Juris circa Christianos Muhammedanici particulae*... (Halae Magd., 1729). Also partially published in (Baghdād: Sharikat al-Ṭabʿ wa al-Nashr al-Ahlīyah, 1965). Also see his *ʿUyūn al-masāʾil fī al-furūʿ,* ed. ʿAbd al-Razzāq al-Qādirī (Hyderabad: Maṭbaʿat Lajnat Nashr al-ʿUlūm al-Islāmīyah, 1960). For further information on the life and works of Abū al-Layth al-Samarqandī, see Sezgin, ibid., vol. 1, pp. 445–450.

19. Later Ḥanafī scholarship claims that al-Qudūrī's work is based on the work of al-Jaṣṣāṣ, which is based on the work of al-Karkhī, which is based on the work of al-Ṭaḥāwī. The manuscript evidence for this chain of transmission is still largely unexamined. From the available information, however, it is evident that al-Qudūrī is drawing upon the same, or at least, a similar corpus of opinions as these earlier scholars. On the manuscript evidence, see Sezgin, ibid., vol. 1, 439–455.

20. See al-Ṭaḥāwī, *Mukhtaṣar,* ed. Abū al-Wafāʾ al-Afghānī (Hyderabad: Lajnat Iḥyāʾ al-Maʿārif al-Nuʿmānīyah, 1950), pp. 86–90.

21. al-Qudūrī, *Mukhtaṣar fī al-fiqh* (Cairo: Maṭbaʿat al-Khayyīrah, 1324), p. 38.

22. The citation of opinions occur in the following frequencies and locations throughout the text of al-Qudūrī's *Mukhtaṣar*. Abū Ḥanīfah ≠ Abū Yūsuf and al-Shaybānī [83 occurrences: pp. 4, 5, 7, 7, 9, 10, 11, 12, 12, 14, 14–15, 15, 15, 16, 16, 16, 18, 20, 21, 21, 22, 26, 28, 29, 31, 34, 34, 35, 39, 40, 42, 44, 46, 47, 47, 47–48, 54, 55, 55, 56, 56, 57, 58, 60, 63, 65, 65, 66, 67, 67, 67, 69, 73, 83, 86, 86, 86, 90, 92, 97, 101, 104, 105, 106, 107, 108, 108, 109, 109, 111, 111, 113, 114, 114, 116, 117, 117, 121, 123, 123, 124, 126, 127]; Abū Ḥanīfah [36 occurrences: 27, 27, 30, 30, 33, 36, 42, 42, 44, 44, 47, 55, 56, 62, 67, 69, 70, 70, 72, 73, 76, 79, 79, 80, 85, 89, 89, 94, 104, 104, 105, 118, 121, 123, 123, 123]; Abū Ḥanīfah and Abū Yūsuf ≠ al-Shaybānī [16 occurrences: 15, 15, 29, 30, 37, 37, 44, 62, 68, 70, 71, 73, 74, 77, 108]; Abū Ḥanīfah and al-Shaybānī ≠ Abū Yūsuf [12 occurrences: 4, 5, 9, 20, 23, 56, 59, 60, 61, 61, 72, 81]; Abū Yūsuf ≠ al-Shaybānī [9 occurrences: 21, 22, 50, 55, 61, 61, 65, 106–107, 119]; Abū Yūsuf and al-Shaybānī [7 occurrences: 20, 21, 22, 28, 38, 43, 81]; Abū Yūsuf [7 occurences: 22, 45, 61, 61, 88, 98, 108]; al-Shaybānī [6 occurrences: 68, 78, 82, 84, 103]; Abū Ḥanīfah ≠ Abū Yūsuf ≠ al-Shaybānī [6 occurrences: 36–37, 39, 48, 61, 61, 93]; Abū Ḥanīfah and al-Shaybānī [5 occurrences: 27, 41, 43, 50, 123]; Abū Ḥanīfah ≠ Abū Yūsuf [3 occurrences: 24, 68, 115]; Abū Ḥanīfah and Abū Yūsuf and al-Shaybānī ≠ Zufar [2 occurences: 2, 56—on the first reference, see the text in al-Qudūrī, *al-Mukhtaṣar al-Qudūrī* (Multan, 1980), 2–3 and al-Qudūrī, *Qudūrī ʿarabī fārisī afghānī* (Baluchistān, n.d.), 3]; Abū Ḥanīfah and Abū Yūsuf [1 occurrence: 91]; Abū Ḥanīfah ≠ al-Shaybānī [1 occurrence: 49]; Abū Ḥanīfah and Abū Yūsuf ≠ al-Shaybānī and Zufar [1 occurrence: 6].

23. al-Qudūrī, *Mukhtaṣar fī al-fiqh,* p. 4.

24. Ibid., p. 4.

25. There is a similar reference to purification without water using "good earth" in sūrat al-nisāʾ 4:43.

26. al-Qudūrī, *Mukhtaṣar fī al-fiqh,* 21.

27. Ibid., p. 36.

28. Ibid., p. 33.

29. Ibid., pp. 23–24.

30. Ibid., p. 11.

31. For a fuller discussion of the different interpretations of the principle in this case, see al-Ḥaddād, *al-Jawharat al-nayyirah,* vol. 1, pp. 77–78.

32. al-Qudūrī, *Mukhtaṣar fī al-fiqh,* p. 2. The Qurʾān citation is from sūrat al-baqarah, 5:6.

33. See, for example, al-Shāfiʿī, *al-Risālah,* pp. 161–162. This type of sunnah is discussed in al-Shāfiʿī, *al-Risālah,* pp. 90–91 and Kamali, *Principles of Islamic Jurisprudence,* pp. 61–65.

34. al-Qudūrī, *Mukhtaṣar fī al-fiqh,* p. 2. On al-Mughīrah b. Shuʿbah [d. 49], see Juynboll, *Muslim Tradition,* p. 58.

35. al-Qudūrī, ibid., p. 36.

36. See the discussion in al-Ṭaḥāwī, *Sharḥ maʿānī al-āthār,* vol. 4, pp. 64–77.

37. For an overview of this conflict of opinions, see al-Ḥaddād, *al-Jawharat al-nayyirah,* vol. 1, p. 258.

38. al-Qudūrī, *Mukhtaṣar fī al-fiqh,* p. 65. On ʿĀmr b. Sharāḥīl al-Shaʿbī [d. 103–110], see Juynboll, *Muslim Tradition,* pp. 19–20.

39. al-Qudūrī, ibid., p. 22. The verse is from sūrat al-tawbah, 9:60.

40. According to al-Ḥaddād, *al-Jawharat al-nayyirah,* vol. 1, p. 156, "those whose hearts are reconciled" means three types of people: those with whom the prophet formed a coalition so that they might accept Islam and convert their people to Islam by their example; those who were converted to Islam but only weakly and thus the prophet wanted them to be established in Islam; and those to whom he gave alms to keep them from doing evil like ʿAbbās b. Mirdās al-Salmī, ʿUyaynah b. Ḥisn, Safwān b. Umayyah, and Sufyān b. Ḥarb.

41. al-Qudūrī, *Mukhtaṣar fī al-fiqh,* p. 36.

42. There is further discussion of this point in ʿAbd al-Ghanī al-Maydānī, *al-Lubāb fī sharḥ al-kitāb,* ed. Muḥammad Muḥyī al-Dīn ʿAbd al-Ḥamīd (Cairo: Muḥammad ʿAlī Ṣubayḥ, 1381), vol. 1, p. 247.

43. On the theoretical backdrop to the claim that consensus [ijmāʿ] can abrogate the Qurʾān and sunnah, see al-Jaṣṣāṣ, *Aḥkām al-Qurʾān,* vol. 1, pp. 58–60; al-Sarakhsī, *al-Uṣūl,* ed. Abū al-Wafāʾ al-Afghānī (Hyderabad: Lajnat Iḥyāʾ al-maʿārif al-Nuʿmānīyah, 1986), vol. 2, p. 66; Kamali, *Principles of Islamic Jurisprudence,* pp. 150–151.

44. al-Dabūsī, *Taʾsīs al-naẓar.* On the concept of analogy [qiyās] in al-Dabūsī's work, see Brunschvig, "La théorie du qiyās juridique chez le ḥanefite al-Dabūsī (Ve/XIe siècle)," *Orientalia Hispanica* 1 (1974): 150–154.

45. al-Dabūsī, ibid., p. 65.

46. Ibid.

47. Ibid., p. 66.

48. See the statement by al-Dabūsī, ibid., p. 67, where he admits that, although only those reports that go back to the prophet are to be used in the place of analogy, some of the reports in the examples he has given do not have a chain of transmission that goes back to the prophet.

49. Ibid., p. 75.

50. Ibid.

51. Ibid., p. 81.

52. The Ḥanafī opinion is probably based on an inference from sūrat al-nisāʾ 4:23. The discussion of al-Shāfiʿīs opinions on marriage and kinship can be found in al-Shāfiʿī, *Kitāb al-umm,* vol. 5, pp. 3–133.

53. al-Dabūsī, *Taʾsīs al-naẓar,* p. 68.

54. Ibid.

55. Ibid., p. 52.

56. Ibid.

57. Ibid., p. 55.

58. Ibid., p. 60.

59. Ibid., p. 62.

60. Ibid., pp. 62–63.

61. Ibid., 15–16.

62. Ibid., p. 16.

63. Ibid., p. 13.

64. Ibid.

65. Ibid., p. 8.

66. Ibid., p. 9.

67. Ibid., p. 40.

68. For a general discussion of this claim, see al-Sarakhsī, *Uṣūl,* vol. 1, pp. 277–321.

69. For an overview of these four methods, see ibid., vol. 1, pp. 232–277.

70. On this type of reasoning and textual indication, see ibid., vol. 1, pp. 236–239.

71. On this type of textual indication, see ibid., vol. 1, pp. 239–241. For a discussion of the different types of linguistic analysis required to interpret the revelation, see pp. 11–235, esp. pp. 124–200. There is a discussion of this in Aboubekr Abdesselam Ben Choaib, "L'argumentation juridique en droit musulman," *Revue du monde musulman* 7 (1909): 70–86.

72. On this type of textual indication, see al-Sarakhsī, ibid., vol. 1, pp. 241–248.

73. It has been pointed out that qiyās is not restricted to analogical reasoning in the strict sense but more broadly to logical reasoning. This observation is affected largely by the claim that the use of "qiyās" in fifth and sixth century fiqh scholarship is influenced by Aristotelian categories of logic. See W. Hallaq, "Non-analogical Arguments in Sunni Juridical Qiyās," pp. 286–306.

74. On the qiyās al-jalī or a fortiori arguments, and qiyās al-ʿaks or reductio ad absurdum arguments, see al-Sarakhsī, *Uṣūl,* vol. 1, p. 279; vol. 2, pp. 149–158. There is a discussion of these two types of reasoning in Hallaq, ibid., pp. 289–299.

75. On this type of textual indication, see al-Sarakhsī, ibid., vol. 1, pp. 258–254. There are differences in the way the uṣūl al-fiqh scholarship of the other schools outlines the types of reasoning responsible for the derivation of practice from the revelation. The Shāfiʿīs allow neither qiyās al-ʿaks nor qiyās al-khafī because they are argued from the contrary of the principle indicated in

the text. Such forms of reasoning are still used to induce principles but are taken to be based on linguistic indications in the text [istidlāl]. On these distinctions, see al-Shīrāzī, *al-Lumaᶜ fī uṣūl al-fiqh,* ed. ᶜAbd al-Majīd Turkī (Cairo: Maṭbaᶜat al-Saᶜādah, 1347; reprint, Beirut: Dār al-Gharb al-Islāmī, 1988), p. 67; Taj al-Dīn al-Subkī, *Jamᶜ al-jawāmiᶜ* (Bombay: Mawlwī Muḥammad b. Ghulām Rasūl al-Sūrtī, 1970), vol. 2, p. 343.

Other scholars rejected the validity of these forms of reasoning because, they claim, to maintain the connection between the principle and the revelation, induction must be an extraction of "the" one point or idea indicated by the text [takhrīj al-manāṭ]. Reasoning on a contrary basis is permitted only if the text has several possible ideas or points, in which case a refinement or revision of the idea [tanqīḥ al-manāṭ] is required on the basis of linguistic but not logical expertise. On this distinction, see al-Ghazālī, *al-Mustaṣfāʾ min al-ᶜilm al-uṣūl* (Cairo: al-Maktabat al-Tijārīyat al-Kubrā, 1907), vol. 2, pp. 54–55; Ibn Qudāmah, *Rawḍat al-nāẓir wa jannat al-munāẓir* (Cairo: al-Maṭbaᶜat al-Salafīyah, 1385), pp. 146–147. Defined in this sense, the Ẓāhirīs allow for the same sorts of conclusions drawn from a contrary basis, as long as it can be shown that the conclusion was reached on the basis of a text requiring linguistic expertise for its specification. On this, see Ibn Ḥazm, *al-Iḥkām fī uṣūl al-aḥkām,* passim.

76. On the use of istiḥsān, see al-Sarakhsī, *Uṣūl,* vol. 2, 203–231. The term istiṣlāḥ is usually used by Mālikīs. For discussion of the use of both, see Tyan, "Méthodologie et sources du droit en Islam," pp. 96–101; Ahmad Hasan, "The Principle of Istiḥsān in Islamic Jurisprudence," p. 125; Hallaq, "Considerations on the Function and Character of Sunni Legal Theory," pp. 679–689, esp. pp. 681–687.

77. Similar points are made, mainly regarding the development of Shāfiᶜī uṣūl al-fiqh scholarship, by Hallaq, ibid., pp. 681–685; Hallaq, "On the Authoritativeness of Sunni Consensus," *International Journal of Middle East Studies* 18 (1986): 427–454, esp. pp. 430–433; B. Weiss, "The Primacy of Revelation in Classical Islamic Legal Theory as Expounded by Sayf al-Dīn al-Āmidī," *Studia Islamica* 59 (1984): 79-109.

78. al-Sarakhsī, *Kitāb al-mabsūṭ,* vol. 4, p. 79.

79. Ibid., vol. 4, pp. 80–81.

80. Ibid., vol. 4, p. 79.

81. Ibid., vol. 4, p. 81.

82. Ibid., vol. 4, p. 82.

83. Ibid., vol. 4, p. 85.

84. Ibid.

85. Ibid., vol. 4, p. 189.

86. Ibid., vol. 4, p. 190.

87. Ibid.

88. Ibid., vol. 4, p. 188.

89. In the pages following these examples, al-Sarakhsī discusses what happens if the hunter says something to the dog after it enters the sacred area, and what happens if a Zoroastrian rather than a Muslim says something to the dog, or if a Muslim says something to a dog sent by a Zoroastrian. See ibid., vol. 4, pp. 188–189.

90. For example, see the Ḥanafī definition of how to purify oneself for prayer, discussed in previous pages. The definition is based on a principle explicit in sūrat al-mā'idah [5:6], which requires the washing of the head, arms, and legs, but the Ḥanafīs add from the sunnah that the person must wash his hands before putting them into the vessel containing the water to be used for purification, say the bismallāh, use a toothpick, rinse the mouth, snuff water up the nose, wipe the ears, comb the beard, and repeat the washing of the limbs three times. On the discussion of this see ibid., vol. 1, pp. 44–90. An outline of the different schools' definitions of purification and how they are derived from the revelation and the sunnah is discussed in Muḥammad b. Aḥmad b. Rushd [d. 595], *Bidāyat al-mujtahid wa nihāyat al-muqtaṣid,* ed. Muḥammad Sālim Muḥaysin and Muḥammad Shaᶜbān Ismāᶜīl (Cairo: Maktabat al-Kulīyāt al-Azharīyah, 1394), vol. 1, pp. 21–63.

Chapter 4. Maintenance of Authority

1. On the Ḥanafī scholarship of the sixth and subsequent centuries, see Chehata, *Études de droit musulman: introduction générale a l'étude du droit musulman,* (Paris: Presses Universitaires de France, 1971), pp. 185-196; Meron, "The Development of Legal Thought in Hanafī Texts," *Studia Islamica* 30 (1969): 91-117; Meron, *L'obligation alimentaire entre époux en droit musulman hanéfite* (Paris: Librairie Générale de Droit et de Jurisprudence, 1971), pp. 10-12.

2. The publication of this text has a long and interesting history. See ᶜAlī b. Abī Bakr al-Marghīnānī, *al-Hidāyah: sharḥ bidāyat al-mubtadā,* 4 vols. (Cairo: Maṭbaᶜah Muṣṭafā al-Bābī al-Ḥalabī, 1975). References in what follows are to this edition. Also published as *al-Hidāyah maᶜa al-darāyah fī muntakhab takhrīj aḥādīth al-Hidāyah,* 2 vols. (Multān: Maktabah-i Shīrkat ᶜIlmīyah, 1980).

A Persian translation of the *Hidāyah* was translated into English by Charles Hamilton [1753–1792], under the direction of Warren Hastings, the governor-general of Bengal, as *The Hedàyah, or Guide: A Commentary on the Mussulman Laws,* 4 vols. (London: T. Bensely, 1791). Second edition, abridged and revised by Standish Grove Grady (London: W. H. Allen, 1879; reprint. Lahore: New Book Comapny, 1957; reprint. Delhi: Islamic Book Trust, 1982).

3. al-Qudūrī attributes the opinions to different authorities only in the case of the conflict of opinion over how to assess the penalty for the prey killed. Otherwise, he gives a straight listing of the opinions. See al-Qudūrī, *Mukhtaṣar fī al-fiqh,* p. 30.

4. For the discussion of the how the *Mukhtaṣar* defines hunting in the sacred area, see al-Marghīnānī, *al-Hidāyah,* vol. 2, pp. 255–284. The attributions are given for statements number 5, 6, 7, 10, 18, 20, 26, 27, 33, and 38.

5. See statements number 6, 10, 18, 34 and 35.

6. See statements number 1, 6, 7, and 8.

7. See statements number 6 and 10.

8. See statements number 1, 5, 6, 7, 9, 10, 32, 36, and 37.

9. See statements number 30 and 34.

10. See statement number 17.

11. al-Marghīnānī, *al-Hidāyah,* vol. 2, pp. 261-262. This passage is also found in al-Qudūrī, *Mukhtaṣar fī al-fiqh,* p. 30.

12. al-Marghīnānī, ibid., vol. 2, pp. 264–265.

13. Ibid., vol. 2, pp. 263–264.

14. See ibid., vol. 2, p. 279.

15. Ibid., vol. 2, p. 255. The passage in parentheses is found in al-Qudūrī, *Mukhtaṣar fī al-fiqh,* 30.

16. See al-Sarakhsī, *Kitāb al-mabsūṭ,* esp. vol. 4, pp. 79–190.

17. Note that in al-Sarakhsī's discussion of al-Shāfiʿī's opinions concerning pointing, the principle attributed to al-Shāfiʿī was that of property. According to al-Sarakhsī, al-Shāfiʿī required a penalty as compensation for the prey killed. See ibid., esp. vol. 4, pp. 79-85.

18. al-Marghīnānī, *al-Hidāyah,* vol. 2, p. 279. The passage in parentheses is found in al-Qudūrī, *Mukhtaṣar fī al-fiqh,* p. 30.

19. al-Marghīnānī, *al-Hidāyah,* vol. 2, p. 281. The passage in parentheses is found in al-Qudūrī, *Mukhtaṣar fī al-fiqh,* p. 30.

20. al-Marghīnānī, *al-Hidāyah,* vol. 2, p. 270. The passage in parentheses is found in al-Qudūrī, *Mukhtaṣar fī al-fiqh,* p. 30.

21. al-Marghīnānī, *al-Hidāyah,* vol. 2, p. 275. The passage in parentheses is found in al-Qudūrī, *Mukhtaṣar fī al-fiqh,* p. 30.

22. al-Marghīnānī, *al-Hidāyah,* vol. 2, p. 277. The passage in parentheses is found in al-Qudūrī, *Mukhtaṣar fī al-fiqh,* p. 30.

23. For a further discussion of the black beetle and other similar insects, see Abū Bakr b. Masʿūd al-Kāsānī [d. 587], *Kitāb badāʾiʿ al-ṣanāʾiʿ fī tartīb al-sharāʾīʿ* (Beirut: Dār al-Kitāb alʿArabī, 1328; reprint, Dār al-Kutub al-ʿIlmīyah, 1394), vol. 3, p. 196.

24. Muḥammad b. ʿAbd al-Wāḥid Ibn al-Humām, *Sharḥ fatḥ al-qadīr ʿalā al-Hidāyah* (Cairo: Muṣṭafā al-Bābī al-Ḥalabī, 1389), vol. 3, p. 74.

25. al-Zaylaʿī, *Tabyīn al-ḥaqāʾiq,* vol. 3, p. 64.

26. Ibn Nujaym, *al-Baḥr al-rāʾiq,* vol. 3, p. 29.

27. Ibn al-Humām, *Sharḥ fatḥ al-qadīr,* vol. 3, p. 74.

28. Ibid., vol. 3, p. 87. The first part of this passage, up to the mention of Abū Dāʾūd, is repeated in al-Afghānī, *Kashf al-ḥaqāʾiq,* vol. 1, p. 150.

29. al-Afghānī, ibid., vol. 1, p. 149.

30. Ibn al-Humām, *Sharḥ fatḥ al-qadīr,* vol. 3, p. 73.

31. Ibn Nujaym *al-Baḥr al-rāʾiq,* vol. 3, pp. 29–30.

32. For a list of the so-called "commentaries" or shurūḥ written on al-Qudūrī's *Mukhtaṣar,* see Sezgin, *Geschichte des arabischen Schrifttums,* vol. 1, pp. 451–455. It would be difficult, given the current state of research into the delineation of postclassical Ḥanafī scholarship along generic lines, to make viable distinctions between this sort of "sharḥī" scholarship and the "farʿī" scholarship of scholars like al-Marghīnānī.

33. ʿAbd al-Ghanī al-Maydānī [d. 1298], *al-Lubāb fī sharḥ al-kitāb,* vol. 1, p. 263.

34. al-Marghīnānī, *al-Hidāyah,* vol. 2, p. 427.

35. al-Maydānī, *al-Lubāb fī sharḥ al-kitāb,* vol. 1, p. 255.

36. al-Ḥaddād, *Jawharat al-nayyirah,* vol. 1, p. 246.

37. Ibid., vol. 1, p. 101.

38. Ibid., vol. 1, p. 102.

39. Ibid., vol. 1, pp. 59–60.

40. The relative evaluation of what things invalidate prayer according to the different authorities is discussed in al-Dabūsī, *Taʾsīs al-naẓar,* 15-18.

41. al-Ḥaddād, *Jawharat al-nayyirah,* vol. 1, p. 265.

42. Ibid., vol. 1, p. 268.

43. Ibid., vol. 1, pp. 153–154.

44. Ibid., vol. 1, p. 154.

45. Ibid., vol. 1, p. 153.

46. Ibid., vol. 1, p. 72.

47. Ibid.

48. Ibid., vol. 1, pp. 132–133.

49. al-Qudūrī, *Mukhtaṣar fī al-fiqh,* p. 35.

50. al-Ḥaddād, *Jawharat al-nayyirah,* vol. 1, p. 245. The passage in paretheses is found in al-Qudūrī, ibid., p. 35.

51. al-Ḥaddād, *Jawharat al-nayyirah,* vol. 1, p. 245.

52. Ibid.

53. Ibid.

54. See Muḥammad Muṣṭafā Ṭaba and Rajab al-ʿĀyadī, *Taysīr al-Qudūrī fī al-fiqh al-Ḥanafī* (Cairo: al-Azhar, 1402), p. 10.

55. al-Ḥaddād, *Jawharat al-nayyirah,* vol. 1, p. 245.

56. Ibid., vol. 1, p. 270. The passage in paretheses is found in al-Qudūrī, *Mukhtaṣar fī al-fiqh,* p. 39.

57. al-Ḥaddād, ibid., vol. 1, pp. 245–246.

58. See ibid., vol. 1, pp. 244–245.

59. al-Maydānī, *al-Lubāb fī sharḥ al-kitāb,* vol. 1, p. 264.

60. al-Zaylaʿī, *Tabyīn al-ḥaqāʾiq,* vol. 4, p. 111. The words in brackets added to the quotation from the *Mukhtaṣar,* are added from al-Nasafī, *Kanz al-daqāʾiq,* pp. 253-254. The full quote from al-Nasafī is "(delayed delivery of items sold by dry measure) such as wheat and barley (and the weight) of the item of value such as honey and olive oil." Also, see the same passage quoted in Ibn Nujaym, *al-Baḥr al-rāʾiq,* vol. 6, p. 155.

61. al-Ḥaddād, *Jawharat al-nayyirah,* vol. 1, p. 264.

62. On this specific point, see the larger discussion of eggs in Ibn Nujaym, *al-Baḥr al-rāʾiq,* vol. 6, p. 156.

63. al-Ḥaddād, *Jawaharat al-nayyirah,* vol. 1, p. 265.

64. Ibid., vol. 1, p. 267.

65. Ibid., vol. 1, p. 264.

66. al-Maydānī, *al-Lubāb fī sharḥ al-Kitāb,* vol. 1, p. 261.

67. Ibid.

68. Ibid.

69. al-Ḥaddād, *Jawharat al-nayyirah,* vol. 1, p. 260.

70. Ibid.

71. Ibid., vol. 1, p. 261.

72. Ibid., vol. 1, pp. 260–261.

73. Ibid., vol. 1, p. 261.

74. Ibid., vol. 1, p. 262.

75. al-Maydānī, *al-Lubāb fī sharḥ al-kitāb,* vol. 1, p. 258.

76. Ibid.

Conclusions

1. See Stephen Toulmin, *Human Understanding* (Princeton, N.J.: Princeton University Press, 1972), esp. vol. 1, pp. 96–130.

2. See Thomas S. Kuhn, *The Structure of Scientific Revolutions,* 2d ed. (Chicago: University of Chicago Press, 1970), passim.

3. The locus classicus for the theoretical discussion of the churinga and its sacred authority is Émile Durkheim, *Les formes élémentaires de la vie*

religieuse (Paris: F. Alcan, 1912). English translation by Joseph Ward Swain, *The Elementary Forms of the Religious Life* (New York: The Free Press, 1915; reprint, 1965), pp. 140–148. Durkheim's account is based largely upon the account of Baldwin Spencer and F. J. Gillen, "The Churinga or Bull Roarers of the Arunta and Other Tribes," in their *The Native Tribes of Central Australia* (London, MacMillan, 1899; reprint, 1938), pp. 128–166. Another important source for Durkheim is T. G. H. Strehlow, *Die Aranda- und Loritja-Stämme in Zentral Australien,* 2 vols. (Frankfurt: J. Baer, 1968).

4. See Spencer and Gillen, ibid., p. 133; Durkheim, ibid., pp. 141–142.

5. Strehlow remarks that the churinga he saw were often just rocks polished by being rubbed together during certain rituals or random pieces of wood or rock. See Strehlow, *Aranda traditions* (Melbourne: Melbourne University Press, 1947), pp. 54–95 passim.

6. See Spencer and Gillen, "The Churinga," pp. 140–141. As an example, Spencer and Gillen describe the contents of a small churinga storehouse of the Yarumpa or honey-ant totem. There are two stone churinga and sixty-eight churinga of the Yarumpa totem. Along with these are included several Echunpa or lizard churinga and two Achilpa or wild cat churinga.

7. See ibid., p. 143.

8. See ibid., p. 141.

9. See ibid., p. 153.

10. See ibid., 132. Even though Durkheim asserts that, in these cases, the churinga were made in plain view of the rest of the clan, he rightly points out that the churinga being made on the spot is a supposition of Spencer and Gillen. The clan elders reported to Spencer and Gillen that the churinga had been dropped by the spirit of the child when it entered the mother's womb. In any case, the churinga is certainly not made in public, but rather in the company of the elder men who go to find the churinga of the new child. The mother herself is not present.

11. See ibid., pp. 152–153. The point made by Spencer and Gillen is that the clan owns the contents of the churinga storehouse collectively. Yet, it is known that often the contents of a given clan's storehouse includes some churinga borrowed from other clans. It might be more accurate to describe the clan not as "owning" the churinga in its storehouse but as having the right to use those churinga for its own purposes and benefit. This usufructuary aspect of the clan's holding of the churinga is mentioned in Claude Lévi-Straus, *La pensée*

sauvage (Paris: Librairie Plon, 1962), trans. *The Savage Mind* (London: Weidenfeld and Nicolson, 1966), p. 241.

12. Durkheim argues that the presence of these marks, emblematic of a totem, makes a given stone or piece of wood a churinga. In support of this assertion, Durkheim claims that when drawn on stationary rocks or on people's bodies, these marks also make the rocks and people sacred. There is no reason to think, however, that the marks drawn on rocks and bodies are not themselves emblematic not of the totem directly but of the churinga. See Durkheim, *The Elementary Forms of the Religious Life*, pp. 144, 147–148. Spencer and Gillen (p. 144) point out that not all churinga are marked. Some have no markings by design and others bear no marks because original markings have been rubbed off during the use of the churinga in ritual contexts.

See J. Z. Smith, *To Take Place: Toward Theory in Ritual* (Chicago: University of Chicago Press, 1987), p. 106, where he sides with Durkheim, quoting Durkheim's restatement of Spencer and Gillen's account of the markings. Smith cites two cases from Strehlow that are supposed to explain the lack of markings on certain churinga (pp. 174–175). The first case acknowledges that stone churinga are not marked. The second refers to seashells used in the place of churinga. Neither example necessarily explains the unmarked churinga observed by Spencer and Gillen nor do they explain the examples of unmarked churinga observed by Strehlow and cited by Lévi-Strauss.

13. This point is made by Lévi-Strauss *The Savage Mind*, p. 239.

14. Spencer and Gillen ("The Churinga," pp. 158–159) explain this in terms of the desire for clans to be in possession of a large number of churinga. The clan borrowing churinga is able to claim a large number for itself, and the clan lending is able to claim that it has enough churinga to spare some for loaning. Strehlow (*Die Arand-und Loritja-Stämme*, p. 161) points to the peace-keeping function of loaning churinga. Clans entrusted with each other's churinga, so the argument goes, are less likely to engage in fighting.

15. See Spencer and Gillen, ibid., pp. 141–142. Spencer and Gillen remark that the safety of the messenger is supposed to be guaranteed by his bearing the churinga. Some of the various uses of the churinga are recounted by Durkheim, *The Elementary Forms of the Religious Life*, pp. 142–143.

16. Spencer and Gillen, ibid., 130.

17. See ibid., pp. 138–139. The term for secret name, *artina churinga* also could be translated as "churinga name" or "sacred name." This is because the term *churinga*, according to Spencer and Gillen, is used as an adjective meaning "secret" or "sacred" but also as a substantive referring to sacred objects.

The synonymous nature of "secret" and "sacred" in these contexts is suggestive for how the authority of the churinga is generated. See the discussion of the terminology in Durkheim, *The Elementary Forms of the Religious Life,* p. 141.

18. See Spencer and Gillen, ibid., p. 129.

19. See ibid., pp. 134–136, where the remark is made that within the surroundings of the churinga storehouse wild animals and plants are not allowed to be destroyed. Women are not allowed to walk in the vicinity of the storehouse. When initiated men gather near the storehouse, or a temporary storehouse erected for the purposes of certain rituals, no weapons are allowed to be present.

20. See ibid., p. 140.

21. See ibid., pp. 139–140.

22. Ibid., p. 145.

23. See ibid.

24. In this respect, it is apropos that Spencer and Gillen mention the observation of Howitt that the new initiates are told during their initiation, before they are taken to the churinga storehouse, "this afternoon we will take you and show your grandfather to you." See Spencer and Gillen, ibid., p. 137. The passage is found in A. W. Howitt, "The Jeraeil, or Initiation Ceremonies of the Kurnai Tribe," *Journal of the Anthropological Institute of Great Britain* 14 (May 1885): 301.

25. This formulation of hierarchy based on the groups' position relative to purity and impurity, or sacred and profane things, is influenced by Louis Dumont, *Homo Hierarchicus: The Caste System and Its Implications,* rev. ed., trans. Mark Sainsbury, L. Dumont, and Basia Gulati (Chicago: University of Chicago Press, 1980), esp. pp. 65–91.

26. See Lévi-Strauss, ibid., pp. 239–242, where he emphasizes this point by comparing the churinga to historical archives.

27. Spencer and Gillen, "The Churinga," p. 145. For some examples of these markings and their interpretations, see pp. 145–151. One of these examples is reproduced in Lévi-Strauss, ibid., pp. 240–241.

28. See Spencer and Gillen, ibid., pp. 137–138. Lévi-Strauss (ibid., pp. 239–241) points out that the association of the churinga with the bodies of ancestors is meant to be metaphorical in the sense that the churinga represent but are not believed to actually be the bodies of ancestors. This latter interpretation is

mentioned by Durkheim (*The Elementary Forms of the Religious Life*, p. 144), as originating in Strehlow's mention that among the Arunta the churinga are the bodies of the ancestors.

Many of the churinga also have a hole bored in one end to associate a given clan's churinga with the original churinga that the ancestors hung on a pole they carried around with them on their wanderings. See Spencer and Gillen, ibid., p. 138. One of the myths associated with this sort of a pole is discussed in Smith, *To Take Place*, pp. 1–13.

29. This same idea would hold also for the markings painted on rocks near the location of the churinga storehouse, designed to warn uninitiated clan members and non-clan members of the boundaries of the area forbidden to them. See Spencer and Gillen, ibid., pp. 134–135.

30. See the shrewd remark of Bruce Lincoln, *Authority: Construction and Corrosion* (Chicago: University of Chicago Press, 1994) that authority is best conceived as "an *effect* (and the perceived capacity to produce an effect) that is operative within strongly asymmetric relations of speaker and audience" (p. 116). The sacred authority of the ancestors is conceded to those clan members who have a relatively less restricted access to the churinga.

31. Note the intriguing analysis of a similar notion in Paul Walker, *Early Philosophical Shiism: The Ismaili Neoplatonism of Abū Yaʿqūb al-Sijistānī* (Cambridge: Cambridge University Press, 1993), p. 149. Walker argues that Ismaili literature incorporates diverse sorts of texts and ideas to provide fuel for the esoteric claims of the religious hierarchy. "The Ismaili authors required doctrines about the world and its mysteries that they could seize upon as special possessions of their own *ecclesia*." By appropriating these diverse sources, the Ismailis were able to claim access to a number of different bases of authority.

32. This does not preclude the conclusion that a text whose contents are fixed requires an intepretation to make it apply to more contemporary circumstances. See J. Z. Smith, "Sacred Persistence," p. 48.

33. Hanna Arendt, "What Was Authority?" in *Authority*, ed. Carl S. Friedrich (Cambridge, Mass.: Harvard University Press, 1958), pp. 81–112 characterizes "authorities" as those in charge of extending into the present the sacred principles evident in a society's foundation. Arendt's view of authority, especially her claim that it originated in Roman times, is criticized in Lincoln, *Authority*, p. 115. That authority is effective owing to a link between a mythical past and a present is the observation of Lévi-Strauss, *The Savage Mind*, pp. 217–244.

Bibliography

Primary Sources Cited

Abū al-ᶜAynayn Badrān. *Uṣūl al-fiqh al-Islāmī.* Alexandria: Muᵓassasah Shabāb al-Jāmiᶜah, 1404.

Abū Dāᵓūd. *Sunan,* ed. Muḥammad Muḥyī al-Dīn ᶜAbd al-Ḥamīd, 4 vols. Beirut: Dār al-Kutub al-ᶜIlmīyah, 1980. Trans. *Sunan Abu Dawud: English Translation with Explanatory Notes,* 3 vols. Lahore: S. Muḥammad Ashrāf, 1984.

[Abū Ḥanīfah]. *al-Fiqh al-akbār.* Cairo: Maṭbaᶜat al-Taqaddum, 1323.

Abū Nuᶜaim. *Dhikr akhbār Iṣbahān,* ed. ᶜAbd al-Wahāb Khiljī, 2 vols. Delhi: Dār al-ᶜIlmīyah, 1405.

Abū Yūsuf. *al-Radd ᶜalā siyar al-Awzāᶜī,* ed. Abū al-Wafāᵓ al-Afghānī. Cairo: Maktabat Dār al-Hidāyah, 1980.

———. *Ikhtilāf Abī Ḥanīfah wa Ibn Abī Laylah,* ed. Abū al-Wafāᵓ al-Afghānī. Cairo: Maktabat Dār al-Hidāyah, 1357.

———. *Kitāb al-kharāj.* Būlāq, 1302.

al-Afghānī, ᶜAbd al-Ḥakīm. *Kashf al-ḥaqāᵓiq sharḥ kanz al-daqāᵓiq.* Cairo: al-Maṭbaᶜat al-Adabīyah, 1318.

al-Āmidī, ᶜAlī b. Muḥammad. *al-Iḥkām fī uṣūl al-aḥkām,* 4 vols. 2d ed., ed. ᶜAbd al-Razzāq ᶜAfīft Beirut: al-Maktab al-Islāmī, 1402.

al-Anṣārī, Zakarīyā' b. Muḥammad. *Tuḥfat al-ṭullāb bi sharḥ matn taḥrīr tanqīḥ al-lubāb fī fiqh al-Shāfiᶜī.* Cairo: Muṣṭafā al-Bābī al-Ḥalabī, 1340.

al-Asnawī, Jamāl al-Dīn. *Ṭabaqāt al-shāfiʿīyah,* ed. ʿAbdallāh al-Jubūrī, 2 vols. Baghdād, 1390–1391.

al-Bājī, Ibn Khalaf. *al-Ḥudūd fī al-uṣūl,* ed. N. Ḥammād. Beirut: Muʾassat al-Zuʿbī li al-Tibāʿah wa al-Nashr, 1973.

———. *al-Muntaqā sharḥ al-Muwaṭṭāʾ,* 7 vols. Cairo, 1331–1332.

al-Baṣrī, Muḥammad b. ʿAlī. *al-Muʿtammad fī uṣūl al-fiqh,* ed. M. Ḥamidallāh and others, 2 vols. Damascus, 1964.

al-Bukhārī, Muḥammad. *al-Ṣaḥīḥ,* ed. L. Krehl and T. W. Juynboll, 4 vols. Leiden: E. J. Brill, 1862–1908.

———. *al-Taʾrīkh al-kabīr,* 4 vols. Hyderabad: Maṭbaʿat Jamʿīyat Dāʾirat al-Maʿārif al-ʿUthmānīyah, 1361.

———. *Kitāb al-ḍuʿafāʾ al-ṣaghir.* Allahabad: Maṭbāʿ Anwār al-Ḥamd, 1325.

al-Dabūsī, ʿAlī b. ʿUmar. *Taʾsīs al-naẓar.* Cairo: Zakarīyā ʿAlī Yūsuf, 1320.

Dāmād, ʿAbd al-Raḥmān b. Muḥammad. *Majmaʿ al-anḥur fī sharḥ multaqā al-abḥur,* 2 vols. Istanbul: Dār al-Ṭibāʿah al-ʿĀmirah, 1309.

al-Dārimī. *Sunan.* Kawnpore, 1293.

al-Dhahabī, Shams al-Dīn. *Duwal al-Islām.* Hyderabad: Maṭbaʿat Jamīyah Dāʾirat al-Maʿārifat al-ʿUthmānīyah, 1337.

———. *Mīzān al-iʿtidāl fī naqd al-rijāl,* ed. ʿAlī Muḥammad al-Bahāwī. Cairo: Maṭbaʿat al-Saʿādah, 1382.

———. *Siyar aʿlām al-nubalāʾ,* ed. Shuʿayb al-Arnʿūṭ and Muḥammad Nuʿaym al-ʿArqasawī. Beirut: Muʾassat al-Risālah, 1405.

———. *al-Kāshif fī maʿrifat man la-hu riwāyat fī al-kutub al-sittah,* ed. ʿIzzat ʿAlī ʿĪd ʿAṭiyyah and Mūsā Muḥammad ʿAlī al-Mawshī, 3 vols. Cairo: Dār al-Kutub al-Ḥadīthah, 1963.

———. *Tadhkirat al-ḥuffāẓ,* 4 vols. Hyderabad: Maṭbaʿat Majlis Dāʾirat al-Maʿārif al-Niẓāmīyah, 1334.

———. *Manāqib Abī Yūsuf,* ed. M. Z. al-Kawtharī and al-Afghānī. Karachi: Mīr Muḥammad Kutub Khānah, 1366.

———. *Manāqib Muḥammad b. al-Ḥasan al-Shaybānī,* ed. M. Z. al-Kawtharī and Abū al-Wafāʾ al-Afghānī. Karachi: Mīr Muḥammad Kutub Khānah, 1366.

al-Ghazālī, Abū Ḥamīd. *al-Mustaṣfā min ʿilm al-uṣūl,* 2 vols. Cairo: al-Maktabat al-Tijārīyat al-Kubrā, 1907.

al-Ḥaddād, Abū Bakr. b. ʿAlī. *Jawharat al-nayyirah.* Cairo: Maḥmūd Bey, 1301.

al-Ḥanafī, Jamāl al-Dīn Yūsuf b. Mūsā. *al-Muʿtaṣar min al-mukhtaṣar.* Hyderabad: Maṭbaʿah Jamʿīyah Dāʾirat al-Maʿārif al-ʿUthmānīyah, 1307. Reprint. 1362.

al-Harawī, Alī al-Qāri. *al-Manḥ al-azhar.* Cairo, 1955.

al-Ḥāzimī, Muḥammad b. Mūsā. *al-Iʿtibār fī al-nāsikh wa al-mansūkh min al-āthār.* Cairo: Idārat al-Ṭibānʿah al-Munīrīyah, 1346.

Ibn ʿAbd al-Barr, *al-Istīʿāb fī maʿrifat al-aṣḥāb,* ed. ʿAlī Muḥammad al-Bajāwī, 4 vols. Cairo: Maktabat Naḥdat Miṣr wa Maṭbaʿatu-hā, 1960-1969.

———. *al-Intiqāʾ fī faḍāʾil al-thalāthat al-aʾimmat al-fuqahāʾ Mālik wa al-Shāfiʿī wa Abī Ḥanīfah.* Cairo: Maktabat al-Qudsī, 1350.

———. *al-Istidhkār fī sharḥ madhāhib ʿulamāʾ al-amṣār mimmā rasama-hu li Imām Mālik fī al-Muwaṭṭāʾ min al-raʾy wa al-āthār,* ed. ʿAlī al-Najdī Nasīf. Cairo, 1390.

———. *al-Ziyādāt allātī taqaʿ fī al-Muwaṭṭāʾ ʿinda Yaḥyāʾ b. Yaḥyāʾ ʿan Mālik.* Cairo, 1350.

———. *Jāmiʿ bayān al-ʿilm wa faḍlī-hi.* Beirut, 1398.

Ibn Abī Ḥātim, *al-Jarḥ wa al-taʿdīl,* ed. ʿAbd al-Raḥmān b. Yaḥyā al-Muʿalamī al-Yamānī, 8 vols. Beirut: Muʾassat al-Risālah, 1371.

———. *Adāb al-Shāfiʿī wa-manāqibu-hu,* ed. ʿA. ʿAbd al-Khāliq. Cairo, 1953.

Ibn Abī al-Wafāʾ. *al-Jawāhir al-muḍīyah,* ed. ʿAbd al-Fattāḥ Muḥammad al-Ḥilw. 3 vols. Cairo, 1978.

Ibn Abī Yaʿlā. *Ṭabaqāt al-ḥanābilah,* ed. M. Ḥāmid al-Fiqī. Cairo: Maṭbaʿat al-Sunnah al-Muḥammadīyah, 1371.

Ibn ᶜĀbidīn, Muḥammad Amīn. *Radd al-muḥtār ᶜalā al-dār al-mukhtār: sharḥ tanwīr al-abṣār,* 5 vols. Quetta: Maktabah Mājidīyah, 1404.

Ibn ᶜAdī. *al-Kāmil fī ḍuᶜafāʾ al-rijāl,* ed. Suhayl Zakkār, 8 vols. Beirut: Dār al-Fikr, 1985–1988.

Ibn Anas, Mālik. *al-Muwaṭṭāʾ*, ed. Muḥammad ᶜAbd al-Bāqī. Cairo: Dār Iḥyāʾ al-Kutub al-ᶜArabīyah, 1370. Trans. Aisha Aburrahman Bewley, *Al-Muwatta of Imam Malik ibn Anas: The First Formulation of Islamic Law.* New York: Kegan Paul International, 1989.

Ibn al-ᶜArabī, Muḥyī al-Dīn. *Mishkāt al-anwār.* Aleppo, 1346.

Ibn ᶜAsākir. *Taʾrīkh madīnat Dimashq.* Damascus: Majmaᶜ al-Lughat al-ᶜArabīyah, 1954–.

———. *Tahdhīb al-taʾrīkh,* ed. Ibn Badrān, 10 vols. Damascus, 1330.

———. *Tabyīn kadhab al-muftarī fī-mā nasab ilā al-imām Abī al-Ḥasan al-Ashᶜarī.* Damascus, 1347.

Ibn al-Athīr. *Usd al-ghābah fī maᶜrifat al-ṣaḥābah,* 7 vols. Cairo: Dār al-Shaᶜb, 1970–1973.

———. *Lubāb fī tahdhīb al-ansāb.* Cairo: Maktabat al-Qudsī, 1357.

———. *Kāmil fī al-taʾrīkh.* Beirut: Dār al-Kitāb al-ᶜArabī, 1386.

Ibn Ḥajar al-ᶜAsqalānī. *al-Iṣābah fī tamyīz al-ṣaḥābah,* Ed. ᶜAlī Muḥammad al-Bajāwī, 8 vols. Cairo: Dār al-Naḥdat Miṣr li al-Itibāh wa al-Nashr, 1970.

———. *Lisān al-mīzān,* 6 vols. Hyderabad: Maṭbaᶜat Majlis Dāʾirat al-Maᶜārif al-Niẓāmīyah, 1329–1331; reprint, Beirut: Muʾassat al-Aᶜlamī, 1407.

———. *Tahdhīb al-tahdhīb.* Hyderabad: Maṭbaᶜah Majlis Dāʾirat al-Maᶜārif al-Niẓāmīyah, 1325–1327.

———. *Tawālī al-taʾsīs bi-maᶜālī Muḥammad b. Idrīs.* Būlāq, 1301.

Ibn al-Ḥājib, ᶜUthmān b. ᶜUmar. *Kitāb mukhtaṣar al-muntahā al-uṣūl,* ed. Farajallāh Zakī al-Kurdī. Cairo: Maṭbaᶜah Kurdistān al-ᶜIlmīyah, 1326.

Ibn Ḥanbal, Aḥmad. *al-Musnad.* Cairo, 1313.

Ibn Ḥazm. *al-Iḥkām fī uṣūl al-aḥkām*, ed. Aḥmad Shākir. Cairo: Maṭbaᶜat al-ᶜĀṣimah, 1968.

———. *al-Fiṣal fī al-milal wa al-ahwāʾ wa al-nihal*. Cairo: Maṭbaᶜat al-Adabīyah, 1318.

Ibn Ḥibbān al-Bustī. *Maᶜrifat al-majrūḥīn wa al-ḍuᶜafāʾ min al-muḥaddithīn*, ed. ᶜAzīz Baygh al-Nawshabāndī al-Qadirī, 3 vols. Hyderabad: Majlis Dāʾirat al-Maᶜārif al-ᶜUthmānīyah, 1390–1393.

———. *Kitāb al-thiqāt*, ed. M. ᶜAbd al-Maᶜīd Khān, 9 vols. Hyderabad: Majlis Dāʾirat al-Maᶜārif al-ᶜUthmānīyah, 1393.

Ibn al-Humām, Muḥammad b. ᶜAbd al-Wāḥid. *Sharḥ fatḥ al-qadīr ᶜalā al-hidāyah: sharḥ bidāyat al-mubtadā, maᶜa sharḥ al-ᶜināyah ᶜalā al-hidāyah,* 10 vols. Cairo: Muṣṭafā al-Bābī al-Ḥalabī, 1389.

Ibn al-ᶜImād. *Shadharāt al-dhahab fī akhbār min dhahab*. Cairo: Maktabat al-Qudsī, 1350–1351.

Ibn al-Jawzī. *Muntaẓam fī taʾrīkh al-mulūk wa al-umam*, 6 vols. Hyderabad: Dāʾirat al-Maᶜārif, 1355–1360.

Ibn Jinni, Abū al-Fatḥ ᶜUthmān. *al-Khaṣāʾiṣ*. Cairo: Maṭbaᶜat Dār al-Kutub al-Miṣrīyah, 1952–1957.

Ibn Kathīr. *al-Bidāyah wa al-nihāyah fī al-taʾrīkh*. Cairo: Dār al-Fikr al-ᶜArabī, 1358.

Ibn Khaldūn. *al-Muqaddimah*. Cairo: al-Maṭbaᶜat al-Amīrīyah bi-Būlāq, 1274.

Ibn Khallikān. *Wafayāt al-ᶜayān*, ed. Iḥsān ᶜAbbās. Beirut: Dār Assakafa, 1968–1972.

Ibn al-Maḥāmilī. *Kitāb al-lubāb fī al-fiqh*. Cairo, 1274; reprint, 1286, 1298, 1305–1306, 1309–1315.

Ibn Mājah. *Sunan*, ed. Muḥammad Fuʾād ᶜAbd al-Bāqī, 2 vols. Cairo: Maṭbaᶜah al-Tazīyah, 1952–1953.

Ibn Manẓūr. *Mukhtaṣar taʾrīkh Dimashq,* 17 vols. Damascus: Dār al-Fikr, 1984–1990.

Ibn al-Mundhīr, Abū Bakr Muḥammad b. Ibrāhīm. *Riḥlat al-Imām al-Shāfiᶜī ilā Madīnat al-munawwarah*. Cairo, 1350.

Ibn al-Nadīm. *al-Fihrist,* ed. Gustav Flügel, 2 vols. Leipzig: F. C. W. Vogel, 1871–1872.

Ibn Nujaym, Zayn al-Dīn. *al-Baḥr al-rāʾiq: sharḥ kanz al-daqāʾiq,* 8 vols. Quetta: al-Maktabah al-Mājidīyah, 1983.

Ibn Qudāmah, ʿAbdallāh b. Aḥmad. *Rawḍat al-nāẓir wa jannat al-munāẓir.* Cairo: al-Maṭbaʿat al-Salafīyah, 1385.

———. *Muqniʿ,* 12 vols. Cairo, 1348.

Ibn Qutaybah. *Taʾwīl mukhtalif al-ḥadīth.* Cairo: Maktabat al-Kullīyāt al-Azharīyah, 1326.

———. *Kitāb al-maʿārif,* ed. F. Wüstenfeld. Göttingen: Vandenhoeck and Ruprecht, 1850. Ed. Muḥammad Ismāʿīl ʿAbdallāh al-Ṣāwt. Beirut: Iḥyāʾ al-Turāth al-ʿArabī, 1390.

Ibn Quṭlūbughā, al-Qāsim. *Tāj al-tarājim,* ed. Gustav Flügel, *Die Krone der Lebenscheschriebungen enthaltend die Classen der Hanefiten von Zeid-ad-dîn Ḳâsim Ibn Ḳuṭlûbugha.* In *Abhandlungen für die Kunde des Morgenlandes* 2.3 (Leipzig, 1862). Ed. Qāsim Muḥammad al-Rajab. Baghdād: Maktabat al-Mathannā, 1962.

Ibn Rajab. *Dhail ṭabaqāt al-ḥanābila,* ed. H. Laoust and S. Dahan, 2 vols. Damascus, 1951.

Ibn Rushd, Muḥammad b. Aḥmad. *Bidāyat al-mujtahid wa nihāyat al-muqtaṣid,* ed. Muḥammad Sālim Muḥaysin and Muḥammad Shaʿbān Ismāʿīl, 2 vols. Cairo: Maktabat al-Kulīyāt al-Azharīyah, 1394.

Ibn Saʿd, Muḥammad. *Kitāb al-ṭabaqāt al-kabīr,* ed. Iḥsān ʿAbbās. Beirut, 1968.

Ibn Taghrībirdī, Yūsuf. *al-Nujūm al-zāhirah fī mulūk Miṣr wa al-Qāhirah.* Cairo, 1929–1972.

Ibn Taymīyah. *Masʾalat al-istiḥṣān.* In G. Makdisi. "Ibn Taimīya's Autograph Manuscript on Istiḥṣān: Materials for the Study of Islamic Legal Thought." In *Arabic and Islamic Studies in Honor of Hamilton A. R. Gibb,* ed. G. Makdisi, pp. 446–479. Cambridge, Mass.: Harvard University Press, 1965.

al-ʿIjlī, Aḥmad. *Taʾrīkh al-thiqāt,* ed. ʿAbd al-Muʿṭī Amīn Qalʿajī. Beirut: Dār al-Kutub al-ʿIlmīyah, 1984.

al-Isnawī, ʿAbd al-Raḥīm b. al-Ḥasan. *al-Tamhīd fī takhrīj al-furūʿ ʿalā al-uṣūl*, ed. Muḥammad Ḥasan Hītū. Beirut: Muʾassat al-Risālah, 1980.

ʿIyāḍ, al-Qāḍī. *Tartīb al-madārik li maʿrifat aʿlām madhhab Mālik*, ed. Muḥammad al-Tabakhī and others. Rabat: Wizārat al-Awqāf, 1983.

al-Jaṣṣāṣ, Aḥmad b. ʿAlī. *al-Fuṣūl al-uṣūl*, ed. Seedullal Qazi, *Principles of Muslim Jurispruden[c]e: Chapters on Qiyās and Ijtihād*. Lahore: al-Maktabat el-Ilmiyyah, 1981.

———. *Aḥkām al-Qurʾān*, ed. Kilsisli Rifʿat. Istanbul, 1335–1338; reprint, Cairo, 1347; reprint, Beirut: Dār al-Kitāb al-ʿArabī, 1978.

al-Juwaynī. *al-Burhān fī uṣūl al-fiqh*, ed. ʿAbd al-ʿAẓīm al-Dīb. Cairo, 1400.

———. *al-Kāfiyah fī al-jadal*, ed. Fawqīyah Maḥmūd. Cairo: Dār Iḥyāʾ al-Kutub al-ʿArabīyah, 1979.

Kaḥḥālah, ʿUmar Riḍā. *Muʿjam al-muʾallifīn: tarājim muṣannifi al-kutub al-ʿarabīyah*. Damascus, 1377.

al-Kāsānī, Abū Bakr b. Masʿūd. *Kitāb badāʾiʿ al-ṣanāʾiʿ fī tartīb al-sharāʾiʿ*, 7 vols. Beirut: Dār al-Kitāb al-ʿArabī, 1328; reprint, Dār al-Kutub al-ʿIlmīyah, 1394.

Khalīfah, Muṣṭafā b. ʿAbdallāh Ḥājjī. *Kashf al-ẓunūn ʿan asāmī al-kutub wa al-funūn*. Istanbul: Maṭbaʿah al-ʿIlm, 1360.

al-Khaṣṣāf, Aḥmad b. ʿUmar. *Kitāb al-ḥiyal wa al-makhārij*, ed. J. Schacht. Hildesheim: Georg Olms, 1968.

———. *Kitāb aḥkām al-waqf*. Cairo, 1322.

———. *Kitāb al-nafaqāt*. Hyderabad, 1349.

al-Khaṭīb al-Baghdādī. *Taʾrīkh Baghdād*, ed. ʿAbd al-Raḥmān b. Yaḥyā al-Muʿallimī. Hyderabad: Dāʾirat al-Maʿarif al-ʿUtmānīyah, 1959.

———. *al-Riḥlah fī ṭalab al-ḥadīth*, ed. Nūr al-Dīn ʿItr. Beirut: Dār al-Kutub al-ʿIlmīyah, 1975.

———. *al-Faqīh wa al-mutafaqqih*. Beirut: Dār al-Kutub al-ʿIlmīyah, 1975.

al-Khiraqī. *al-Mukhtaṣar fī al-fiqh*, ed. M. Zuhair al-Shāwīsh. Damascus, 1378; reprint, Beirut, 1384.

Khusraw, Menla. *Ghurar al-aḥkām wa durar al-ḥukkām*. Cairo: al-Maṭbaᶜat al-ᶜAmirah al-Sharafīyah, 1304.

al-Khwārizmī, al-Muwaffaq b. Aḥmad b. Isḥāq al-Makkī. *Manāqib al-Imām Abī Ḥanīfah*. Hyderabad, 1321.

al-Kindī. *The Governors and Judges of Egypt*, ed. R. Guest. Leiden: E. J. Brill, 1912.

al-Kutubī, Ibn Shākir. *Fawāt al-wafāyāt*, ed. M. Muḥyī al-Dīn ᶜAbd al-Ḥamīd. Cairo: Maktabat al-Naḥdat al-Miṣrīyah, 1951.

al-Madyanī, Muḥammad. *al-Ithāfāt al-saniyyah fī al-aḥādīth al-qudsiyyah*. Hyderabad, 1323.

al-Maqdisī. *Aḥsan al-taqāsim fī maᶜrifat al-aqālim*, ed. M. J. de Goeje. Leiden: E. J. Brill, 1906.

al-Marghīnānī, ᶜAlī b. Abī Bakr. *al-Hidāyah: sharḥ bidāyat al-mubtadā*, 4 vols. Cairo: Maṭbaᶜah Muṣṭafā al-Bābī al-Ḥalabī, 1975. Reprint as *al-Hidāyah maᶜa al-darāyah fī muntakhab takhrīj aḥādīth al-hidāyah*, 2 vols. Multān: Maktabah-i Shīrkat ᶜIlmīyah, 1980. Trans. Charles Hamilton, *The Hedàyah, or Guide: A Commentary on the Mussulman Laws*, 4 vols. London: T. Bensley, 1791; 2d ed. by Standish Grove Grady, London, 1870; reprint, Lahore: New Book Company, 1957.

al-Māwardī, ᶜAlī b. Muḥammad. *Iḥkām al-sulṭānīyat al-wilāyat al-dīnīyah*. Cairo, 1404.

al-Māwardī, Ibn Ḥabīb. *Adab al-qāḍī*, ed. M. Sarhan, 2 vols. Baghdad: Riʾāsat Dīwān al-Awqāf, 1971–1972.

al-Maydānī, ᶜAbd al-Ghanī. *al-Lubāb fī sharḥ al-kitāb*, ed. Muḥammad Muḥyī al-Dīn ᶜAbd al-Ḥamīd, 4 vols. Cairo: Muḥammad ᶜAlī Ṣubayḥ, 1381.

al-Mizzī. *Tuḥfat al-ashrāf bi-maᶜrifat al-aṭrāf*, ed. ᶜAbd al-Ṣamad Sharaf al-Dīn, 12 vols. Bhiwandi: al-Dār al-Qayyimah, 1965–1981.

Muslim. *al-Ṣaḥīḥ*, ed. Muḥammad Fuʾād ᶜAbd al-Bāqī, 5 vols. Cairo: Maṭbaᶜah al-Fajālat al-Jadīdah, 1955–1956.

al-Naḥḥās, Abū Jaᶜfar. *Kitāb al-nāsikh wa al-mansūkh*. Cairo, 1323.

al-Nasāʾī. *Kitāb al-sunan al-kubrā*, ed. ʿAbd al-Ṣamad Sharaf al-Dīn. Bombay: al-Dār al-Qayyimah, 1985.

———. *Kitāb al-ḍuʿafāʾ wa al-matrūkīn*. Beirut: Muʾassasat al-Kutub al-Thaqāfīyah, 1985.

al-Nasafī, ʿAbdallāh b. Aḥmad. *Kanz al-daqāʾiq*. Multān: Maktabah-ī Imādīyah, 1979.

al-Nawawī, Yaḥyā b. Sharaf. *al-Arbaʿūn ḥadīthan*, ed. ʿAbd al-Majīd al-Sharnūbī. Cairo: Maktabat al-Kullīyāt al-Azharīyah, 1300.

al-Nuʿmān, al-Qāḍī. *Ikhtilāf uṣūl al-madhāhib*, ed. S. Lokhandwalla. Simla: al-Maʿhad al-Hindī li al-Dirāsat al-Mutaqaddimah, 1972.

al-Pazdawī, ʿAbdallāh b. Muḥammad. *Kanz al-wuṣūl ilā maʿrifat al-uṣūl*. Constantinople: Şirket-i Sahafiye-ʾi Osmaniye, 1370. Reprint. Beirut: Dār al-Kitāb al-ʿArabī, 1974.

al-Qārī, ʿAlī b. Sulṭān Muḥammad. *al-Aḥādīth al-qudsīyat al-arbaʿīnīyah*, ed. Muḥammad Rāghib al-Ṭabbākh. Beirut: Dār al-Kutub al-ʿIlmīyah, 1983.

al-Qayrawānī, Ibn Abī Zayd. *al-Risālah*. Cairo, 1296. Ed. and trans. A. D. Russell and ʿAbdallāh al-Mamun Suhrawardy, *First Steps in Muslim Jurisprudence: Consisting of Excerpts from Bākūrāt as-saʿd of Ibn Abī Zayd*. London, 1906.

al-Qazwīnī, Aḥmad b. Fāris. *Ḥulīyat al-fuqahāʾ*, ed. ʿAbdallāh b. ʿAbd al-Muḥsin al-Turkī. Beirut, 1403.

———. *Muʿajam māqayīs al-lughah*, ed. ʿAbd al-Salām Muḥammad Hārūn, 6 vols. Cairo, 1389–1392.

al-Qudūrī, Aḥmad b. Muḥammad. *Mukhtaṣar fī al-fiqh* or *Matn al-Qudūrī fī fiqh madhhab al-Imām al-Aʿẓam Abī Ḥanīfah al-Nuʿmān*. Cairo: Maṭbaʿat al-Khayyīrah, 1324.

al-Qurayshī, Ibn Abī al-Wafāʾ. *al-Jawāhir al-muḍīyah*, ed. ʿAbd al-Fattāḥ Muḥammad al-Ḥilw, 3 vols. Cairo: Dār Iḥyāʾ al-Kutub al-ʿArabīyah, 1978.

al-Rāzī, Aḥmad b. Muḥammad. *Ḥujaj al-Qurʾān*, ed. Aḥmad ʿUmar al-Maḥmaṣānī. Cairo: Maṭbaʿat al-Mawsūʿāt, 1320.

al-Rāzī, Fakhr al-Dīn. *Manāqib al-Imām al-Shāfiʿī*. Cairo: Maktabat al-Kullīyāt al-Azharīyah, 1986.

al-Ṣafadī, Ṣalāḥ al-Dīn. *al-Wāfī bi al-wafayāt,* ed. Sven Dedering, as *Das biographische Lexikon des Ṣalāḥaddīn Ḥalīl Ibn Aibak aṣ-Ṣafadī.* Bibliotheca Islamica 6. Wiesbaden: Franz Steiner, 1962.

al-Sahmī, Hamzah b. Yūsuf. *Taʾrīkh Jurjān,* ed. ʿAbd al-Raḥmān Yaḥyā al-Yamanī. Hyderabad: Dāʾirat al-Maʿārif al-ʿUthmānīyah, 1967.

Saḥnūn, ʿAbd al-Salām b. Saʿīd. *al-Mudawwana al-kubrā.* Cairo: Maṭbaʿat al-Saʿādah, 1324, reprint, Beirut: Dār Sādir, 19–.

al-Sakhāwī, Muḥammad b. ʿAbd al-Raḥmān. *al-Ḍawʾ al-lāmiʿ li-ahl al-qarn al-tāsiʿ.* Cairo: Maktabat al-Qudsī, 1353–1355.

al-Samʿānī, ʿAbd al-Karīm. *Kitāb al-ansāb,* ed. ʿAbd al-Raḥmān b. Yaḥyā. Hyderabad: Maṭbaʿah Majlis Dāʾirat al-Maʿārif al-ʿUthmānīyah, 1399.

al-Samarqandī, ʿAlā al-Dīn. *Tuḥfat al-fuqahāʾ,* ed. Muḥammad al-Muntaṣar al-Kitābī and Wahbah al-Zuḥaylī, 3 vols. Damascus: Dār al-Fikr, 1964.

al-Samarqandī, Abū al-Layth Naṣr b. Muḥammad. *Bayān ʿaqīdat al-uṣūl,* ed. A. W. Juynboll. *Tijdschrift voor de Taal-, Land en Volkenkunde von Nederland Indië,* series 4, no. 4 (1881): 215–231, 267–274.

———. *ʿUyūn al-masāʾil fī al-furūʿ,* ed. ʿAbd al-Razzāq al-Qādirī. Hyderabad: Maṭbat Lajnat Nashr al-ʿUlūm al-Islāmīyah, 1960.

———. *Khizānat al-fiqh,* partially ed. J. H. Callenberg, *Juris circa Christianos Muhammedanici particulae . . .* Halae Magd., 1729; Baghdād: Sharikat al-Ṭabʿ wa al-Nashr al-Ahlīyah, 1965.

al-Sarakhsī, Muḥammad b. Aḥmad. *Uṣūl,* ed. Abū al-Wafāʾ al-Afghānī. Hyderabad: Lajnat Ihyāʾ al-maʿārif al-Nuʿmānīyah, 1986.

———. *al-Nukat: sharḥ li-zīyādāt al-zīyādāt,* ed. Abū al-Wafāʾ al-Afghānī, with commentary by Aḥmad b. Muḥammad al-Bukhārī. Hyderabad: al-ʿUlūm al-Islāmīyah, 1378.

———. *Kitāb al-mabsūṭ,* 30 vols. Cairo: Maṭbaʿat al-Saʿādah, 1324–1331.

al-Shāfiʿī, Muḥammad b. Idrīs. *al-Risālah,* ed. Muḥammad Shākir. Cairo: Maktabat Ḥalabī, 1358. Trans. Majid Khadduri, *Islamic Jurisprudence.* Baltimore: Johns Hopkins University Press, 1961.

———. *Kitāb al-umm,* 7 vols. Bulāq, 1329.

al-Shahrastānī. *al-Milal wa al-nihal.* Cairo: Maṭbaᶜat al-Abadīyah, 1318.

al-Shaʾrānī, ᶜAbd al-Wahhab. *Kitāb al-mīzān,* 2 vols. Cairo: Qasṭallī, 1279. Trans. Perron, *Balance de la loi Musulmane: esprit de la législation Islamique et divergences de ses quatre rites jurisprudentiels.* Algiers: Imprimerie Orientale, 1898.

al-Sharranbulālī. *Nūr al-īḍāḥ.* Multān: Maktabh-ī Imādīyah, 1979.

al-Shawkānī, Muḥammad b. ᶜAlī. *Irshād al-fuḥūl ilā taḥqīq al-ḥaqq min ᶜilm al-uṣūl.* Cairo: Maṭbaᶜat al-Saᶜādah, 1909.

———. *Nayl al-awṭār,* 8 vols. Cairo, 1952.

Shaybah, Abū Bakr. *Rudūd ᶜalā Abī Ḥanīfah,* ed. M. Z. al-Kawtharī. Cairo, 1365.

al-Shaybānī, Muḥammad b. al-Ḥasan. *Kitāb al-aṣl fī al-furūᶜ,* ed. Chafik Chehata. Cairo, 1954. Ed. al-Afghānī, 4 vols. Hyderabad: Maṭbaᶜah Majlis Dāʾirat al-Maᶜārif al-ᶜUthmānīyah, 1966–1973.

———. *al-Jāmiᶜ al-ṣaghīr.* Karachi: Idārat al-Qurʾān wa al-ᶜUlūm al-Islāmīyah, n.d.

———. *al-Jāmiᶜ al-kabīr.* Hyderabad: Lajnat Iḥyāʾ al-Maᶜārif al-Nuᶜmānīyah, 1937; reprint, Pakistan: Dār al-Maᶜārif al-Nuᶜmānīyah, 1981.

———. *Kitāb al-athār,* ed. M. ᶜAbd al-Ḥayy Laknawī. Lucknow, 1883; reprint, Lahore, 1309.

———. *al-Ḥujjah fī ikhtilāf ahl al-Kūfah wa ahl al-Madīnah.* Lucknow, 1888.

———. *Kitāb al-makhārij fī al-ḥiyal ᶜan Abī Ḥanīfah bi-riwāyat Abī Yūsuf,* partially ed. J. Schacht. Leipzig: J.C. Hinrichs'sche Buchhandlung, 1930

al-Shīrāzī, Abū Isḥāq. *Ṭabaqāt al-fuqahāʾ,* ed. Iḥsān ᶜAbbās. Beirut: Dār al-Rāʾid al-ᶜArabī, 1970.

———. *al-Lumaᶜ fī uṣūl al-fiqh,* ed. ᶜAbd al-Majīd Turkī. Cairo: Maṭbaᶜat al-Saᶜādah, 1347; reprint, Beirut: Dār al-Gharb al-Islāmī, 1988.

al-Subkī, Tāj al-Dīn. *Ṭabaqāt al-shāfiᶜīyah al-kubrā,* ed. ᶜAbd al-Fattāḥ Muḥammad al-Ḥilw and Maḥmūd Muḥammad al-Ṭināḥī. Cairo: ᶜĪsā al-Bābī al-Ḥalabī, 1964.

———. *Jamᶜ al-jawāmiᶜ,* 2 vols. Bombay: Mawlwī Muḥammad b. Ghulām Rasūl al-Sūrtī, 1970.

al-Suyūrī, Ibn ᶜAbdallāh. *Kanz al-ᶜirfān fī fiqh al-Qurʾān,* ed. M. Baqīr Sharīf Zaddah. Tehran: al-Maktabat al-Murtaḍawīyah, 1964.

al-Suyūtī, Jalāl al-Dīn. *Bughyat al-wuᶜāh fī ṭabaqāt al-lughawīyīn wa al-nuḥāh.* Cairo: Maṭbaᶜat ᶜĪsā al-Bābī al-Ḥalabī, 1326.

———. *Isᶜāf al-mubaṭṭaʾ bi rijāl al-Muwaṭṭāʾ.* Cairo: al-Maktabat al-Tijārīyah al-Kubrā, 1969.

———. *Tazyīn al-mamālik li-manāqib saidinat al-Imām Mālik.* Cairo: al-Maṭbaᶜah al-Khayrīyah, 1324.

Ṭabaᶜ, Muḥammad Muṣṭafā and Rajab al-ᶜĀyadī. *Taysīr al-Qudūrī fī al-fiqh al-Ḥanafī.* Cairo: al-Azhar, 1402.

al-Ṭabarī, Muḥammad b. Jarīr. *Ikhtilāf al-fuqahāʾ,* ed. Frederick Kern. Beirut: Muḥammad Amīn Ramj, n.d.

Tahānawī. *Kashshāf iṣṭilāḥāt al-funūn,* ed. Aloys Sprenger and others, 2 vols. Calcutta: Asiatic Society of Bengal, 1862.

al-Ṭaḥāwī, Aḥmad b. Muḥammad. *Sharḥ maᶜānī al-āthār,* ed. Muḥammad Sayīd Jādd al-Ḥaqq, 4 vols. Cairo: Maṭbaᶜat al-Anwār al-Muḥammadīyah, 1968.

———. *Ikhtilāf al-fuqahāʾ.* Trans. as *Imam Ṭaḥāwiʾs Disagreement of the Jurists,* ed. Muḥammad Ṣaghīr Ḥasan Maᶜṣūmī. Islamabad: Islamic Research Institute, 1391.

———. *Bayān muskhil al-aḥādīth,* 4 vols. Hyderabad, 1333.

Tāj, ᶜAbd al-Rahmān. *al-Siyāsat al-sharīᶜah.* Cairo: Maṭbaᶜah Dār al-Taʾlīf, 1371.

al-Tirmidhī. *al-Jāmiᶜ al-ṣaḥīḥ,* ed. Aḥmad Muḥammad Shākir, Muḥammad Fuʾād ᶜAbd al-Bāqī, and Ibāhīm ᶜAṭwah ᶜIwaḍ, 5 vols. Delhi: Kutub Khānah Rashīdīyah, 1937–1965.

al-Tunbukhtī, Abmad Bābā. *Nayl al-ibtihāj fī taṭrīz al-dībāj.* Tripoli: al-Jamāhīrīyah al-ᶜArabīyah al-Lībīyah al-Shaᶜbīyah al-Ishtirākīyah al-ᶜUẓmā, 1989.

al-ᶜUqaylī. *Kitāb al-ḍuᶜafāʾ al-kabīr*, ed. ᶜAbd al-Muᶜṭī Amīn Qalᶜajī, 4 vols. Beirut: Dār al-Kutub al-ᶜIlmīyah, 1404.

al-Wakīᶜ. *Akhbār al-quḍāt*, ed. ᶜAbd al-ᶜAzīz Muṣṭafā al-Marāghī. Cairo: Maṭbaᶜat al-Istiqāmah, 1947–1950.

al-Yāfiᶜī, ᶜAbdallāh b. Asᶜad. *Mirāt al-jinān wa ᶜibrat al-yaqẓān fī maᶜrifat mā yuᶜtabar min ḥawādith al-zamān*. Beirut: Muʾassat al-Risālah, 1338.

Yāqūt. *Irshād al-arīb ilā maᶜrifat al-adīb*, ed. D. S. Margoliouth, *Dictionary of the Learned Men of Yāqūt*. Gibb Memorial Series 6. Leiden: E. J. Brill, 1924.

al-Zaylaᶜī, ᶜUthmān b. ᶜAlī. *Tabyīn al-ḥaqāʾiq: sharḥ kanz al-daqāʾiq*, 6 vols. Būlāq: al-Maṭbaᶜat al-Kubrā al-Amīrīyah, 1313–1315.

al-Ziriklī, Khayr al-Dīn. *al-Aᶜlām: qāmūs tarājim li-ashar al-rijāl wa al-nisāʾ min al-ᶜarab wa al-mustaᶜribīn wa al-mustashriqīn*. Cairo: al-Ṭabᶜat al-ᶜArabīyah, 1374.

al-Zurqānī, Muḥammad b. ᶜAbd al-Bāqī. *Anwār kawkab anhaj al-masālik bi-mazj Muwaṭṭāʾ al-Imām Mālik*. Cairo, 1310.

Secondary Works Cited

Abdelrahman, H. "La place du syllogisme juridique dans la méthode exégétique chez Gazali." In *Proceedings of the World Congress for Legal and Social Philosophy*, ed. H. Hubien, pp. 184–194. Louvain: Editions Nauwelaerts, 1971.

———. "L'argument *a maiori* et l'argument par analogie dans la logique juridique musulmane." *Rivista Internazionale di Filosofia del Diritto* 98 (1971): 127–148.

Abū Zahrah, Muḥammad. *Uṣūl al-fiqh*. Cairo: Dār al-Fikr al-ᶜArabī, 1957.

———. *Abū Ḥanīfah: ḥayātu-hu wa ᶜaṣru-hu āraʾu-hu wa fiqhu-hu*. Cairo: Dār al-Fikr al-ᶜArabī, 1947.

———. *Mālik: ḥayātu-hu ᶜaṣru-hu wa fiqhu-hu*. Cairo: Maktabat al-Anjilū al-Miṣrīyah, 1952.

———. *al-Shāfiᶜī: ḥayātu-hu wa ᶜaṣru-hu āraʾu-hu wa fiqhu-hu*. Cairo: Dār al-Fikr al-ᶜArabī, 1948.

Adams, C. C. "Abū Ḥanīfah: Champion of Liberalism and Tolerance in Islam." *Muslim World* 36 (1946): 217–227.

ʿAfīfī, al-Sayyid. *Ḥayat al-Imām Abī Ḥanīfah.* Cairo: al-Maṭbaʿah al-Salafīyah, 1350.

Amar, E. "Le grand Mudawwana." *Rivista degli Studia Orientalia* 24 (1949): 45–58.

Ansar, Zafar Ishaw. "Islamic Juristic Terminology Before Shafiʿi." *Arabica* 19, no. 3 (1972): 288–294.

———. "An Early Discussion on Islamic Jurisprudence: Some Notes on *al-Radd ʿalā siyar al-Awzāʿī." Islamic Perspectives* (1979): 147–167.

Antoun, Richard T. *Muslim Preacher in the Modern World: a Jordanian Case Study in Comparative Perspective.* Princeton, N.J.: Princeton University Press, 1989.

Arendt, Hanna. "What Was Authority?" In *Authority,* ed. Carl S. Friedrich, pp. 81–112. Cambridge, Mass.: Harvard University Press, 1958.

Arnaldez, Roger. *Grammaire et théology chez Ibn Ḥazm de Cordoue: essai sur la structure et les conditions de la pensée musulmane.* Études musulmanes 3. Paris: Librairie Philosophique J. Vrin, 1956.

Aʿẓamī, Muḥammad Ḍiyāʾ al-Raḥmān. *Dirāsāt fī al-jarḥ wa al-taʿdīl.* Benaras: al-Jāmiʿah al-Salafīyah, 1983.

Azami, M. M. *Studies in Early Ḥadīth Literature: With a Critical Edition of Some Early Texts.* Beirut, 1968; reprint, Indianapolis: American Trust Publications, 1978. Trans. *Dirāsāt fī al-ḥadīth al-nabawī wa al-taʾrīkh tadwīni-hā.* Riyadh: Jāmiʿat al-Riyāḍ, 1976.

———. *On Schacht's "Origins of Muhammdan Jursiprudence."* Riyadh: King Saud University, 1985.

al-Banūrī, Mawlah Muḥammad Yūsuf. "Tabṣirat Ikhtilāf al-fuqahāʾ al-Ṭaḥāwī." *Bayyināt* (September 1972): 28.

Becker, C. H. "Die Kanzel im Cultus des alten Islam." In *Orientalische Studien: Theodor Nöldeke zum siebzigsten Geburtstag gewidmet,* ed. Carl Bezold, vol. 1, pp. 331–351. Geissen: A. Töpelmann, 1906.

———."Zur Geschichte des Islamischen Kultus." *Der Islam* 3 (1912): 374–399.

———. *Islamstudien.* Leipzig: Verlag Quelle and Meyer, 1924.

Ben Choaib, Aboubekr Abdesselam. "L'argumentation juridique en droit musulman." *Revue de monde musulman* 7 (1909): 70–86.

Bergsträsser, G. *Grundzüge des islamischen Rechts,* ed. and trans. J. Schacht. Leipzig, 1935.

Bernand, Marie. *L'accord unanime de la communauté comme fondement des status légaux de l'Islam: d'après Abū l-Ḥusayn al-Baṣrī.* Études Musulmanes 11. Paris: Librairie Philosophique J. Vrin, 1970.

Bijlefeld, Willem A. "Islamic Studies Within the Perspective of the History of Religion." *Muslim World* 62 (1972): 1–11.

Bourdieu, Pierre. *Outline of a Theory of Practice,* trans. Richard Nice. Cambridge: Cambridge University Press, 1977.

Bousquet, C. H. "Ibn al-Qāsim, La Moudawwana (recension de Saḥnoun) analyse." *Annales de l'Institute d'Etudes Orientales* 14 (1958): 177–206; 17 (1959): 169–211; 18 (1960): 165–173.

Bravmann, M. M. *The Spiritual Background of Early Islam: Studies in Ancient Arab Concepts.* Leiden: E. J. Brill, 1972.

Brockelmann, Carl. *Geschichte der arabischen Litteratur,* 5 vols. Leiden: E. J. Brill, 1937.

Brooks, Douglas Renfrew. *The Secret of the Three Cities: An Introduction to Hindu Śākta Tantrism.* Chicago: University of Chicago Press, 1990.

Brunschvig, R. "Logic and Law in Classical Islam." In *Logic in Classical Islamic Culture,* ed. G. E. von Grunebaum, pp. 9–20. First Giorgio Levi Della Vida biennial conference. Wiesbaden: Otto Harrassowitz, 1970.

———. "La théorie du qiyās juridique chez le ḥanefite al-Dabūsī (Ve/XIe siècle)." *Orientalia Hispanica* 1 (1974): 150–154.

———. "Argumentation Fatimide contre le raisonnement juridique par analogie (qiyās)." In *Recherches d'Islamologie: recueil d'articles offerts à Georges ᶜAnawati et Louis Gardet par leurs Collègues et amis,* ed. R. Arnaldez and S. van Riet, pp. 75–84. Louvain: Peeters, 1977.

Burton, John. *The Collection of the Qurʾān.* Cambridge: Cambridge University Press, 1977.

———. *The Sources of Islamic Law: Islamic Theories of Abrogation.* Edinburgh: University of Edinburgh, 1990.

Calder, Norman. *Studies in Early Muslim Jurisprudence.* Oxford: Oxford University Press, 1993.

Charnay. "Pluralisme normatif et amibuïté dans le fiqh." In *L'ambivalence dans la culture arabe,* ed. J. Berque and J.-P. Charnay, pp. 382–396. Paris: Editions Anthropos, 1968.

Chehata, Chafik. *Théorie générale de l'incapacité en droit musulman.* Doctoral thesis, Faculté de Droit. Paris 1965.

———. "Logique juridique et droit musulman." *Studia Islamica* 23 (1965): 5–25.

———. *Le concept de contrat en droit musulman.* Extract des Archives de Philosophie du Droit 13. Paris: Sirey, 1968.

———. "L'ikhtilāf et la conception musulman du droit." In *L'ambivalence dans la culture arabe,* ed. J. Berque and J.-P. Charnay, pp. 258–266. Paris: Editions Anthropos, 1968.

———. *Essai d'une théorie générale de l'obligation en droit musulman.* Cairo, 1966; reprint. Paris 1969.

———. *Études de droit musulman: introduction générale a l'étude du droit musulman.* Travaux et recherces de la faculté de droit et des sciences économiques de Paris, série Afrique 7. Paris: Presses Universitaires de France, 1971. Reprint of *Introduction générale au droit musulman.* Faculté de Droit de Paris. Cours de 4e année de Licence, 1966–1967.

———. *Études de droit musulman: la notion de responsabilité contractuelle, le concept de propriété.* Travaux et recherches de l'Université de droit d'éconimie et de sciences sociales de Paris, série Afrique 1. Paris: Presses Universitaires de France, 1973.

Cook, Michael. *Early Muslim Dogma: A Source-Critical Study.* Cambridge: Cambridge University Press, 1981.

Dimitroff, I. "al-Shaybānī und sein corpus juris ᶜal-Ǧāmiᶜ aṣ-Ṣagīr." *Mitteilungen des Seminars für orientalische Sprachen zu Berlin: Westasiatische Studien* 11 (1908): 60–206.

Dumont, Louis. *Homo Hierarchicus: The Caste System and Its Implications,* rev. ed., trans. Mark Sainsbury, L. Dumont, and Basia Gulati. Chicago: University of Chicago Press, 1980.

Durkheim, Émile. *Les formes élémentaires de la vie religieuse.* Paris: F. Alcan, 1912. Trans. Joseph Ward Swain, *The Elementary Forms of the Religious Life.* New York: Free Press, 1915; reprint, 1965.

Elwakil, Chams Eldine. *Terminologie juridique: a l'usage des étudiants de la première année de licence.* Alexandria, 1963.

d'Emilia, A. "Il Ḫiyār aṣ-šarṭ nel Aṣl di Šaibānī." Scritti in onore di G. Furlani. *Revista degli studi orientalia* 32 (1957): 633–640.

al-Fārisī, Abū ᶜAlī. *Jawāhir al-uṣūl fī ᶜilm ḥadīth al-rasūl.* Medina: al-Maktabah al-ᶜIlmīyah, 1973.

Fraade, Steven D. *From Tradition to Commentary: Torah and Its Interpretation in the Midrash Sifre to Deuteronomy.* Albany: State University of New York Press, 1991.

Fyzee, A. A. A. *Outlines of Muhammadan Law,* ed. D. Pearl. Oxford: Oxford University Press, 1983.

Gaudefroy-Demombynes, M. "Sur les origines de la justice musulmane." In *Mélanges syriens offerts à M. René Dussaud,* vol. 2, pp. 819–828. Paris: P. Geuthner, 1939.

Geertz, Clifford. *Local Knowledge.* New York: Basic Books, 1983.

Goiten, S. D. "The Origin and Nature of Muslim Friday Worship." *Muslim World* 49 (1959): 183–195.

Goldziher, Ignaz. *Die Ẓâhiriten: Ihr Lehrsystem und ihre Geschichte. Beitrag zur Geschichte der muhammedanischen Theologie.*

[Leipzig, 1884] trans. Wolfgang Behn. *The Ẓāhirīs: Their Doctrine and Their History: A Contribution to the History of Islamic Theology.* Leiden: E. J. Brill, 1971.

———. "Kämpfe um die Stellung des Ḥadīṯ im Islam." *Zeitschrift der Deutschen Morgenländischen Gesellschaft* 61 (1907): 863–864.

———. "Zur Geschichte der ḥanbalitischen Bewegungen." *Zeitschrift der Deutschen Morgenländischen Gesellschaft* 62 (1908): 1–28.

———. "Katholische Tendenz und Partikularismus im Islam." *Beiträge zur Religionswissenschaft* 1 (1913): 115–142. Reprint, "Catholic Tendencies and Particularism in Islam." In *Studies on Islam,* trans. and ed. Merlin L. Swartz, pp. 123–139. Oxford: Oxford University Press, 1981.

———. "Iǧmāᶜ," *Nachrichten von der königlichen Gesellschaft der Wissenschaften zu Göttingen, Phil.-historische Klasse* 1 (1916): 81–85.

———. *Muhammedanische Studien* [Halle: S. M. Niemeyer, 1889], trans. and ed. S. M. Stern, *Muslim Studies.* London: Allen and Unwin, 1967.

———. *Gesammelte Schriften,* ed. Joseph DeSomogyi. Hildesheim: G. Olms, 1970.

———. *Introduction to Islamic Theology and Law,* trans. Andras Hamori and Ruth Hamori. Princeton, N.J.: Princeton University Press, 1981.

Goody, Jack. *Domestication of the Savage Mind.* Cambridge: Cambridge University Press, 1977.

Gorjī, Abū al-Qāsim. "Nigāhī beh taḥawwul-e ᶜilm-e uṣūl." Trans. ᶜAlī Qulī Qarāʾī, "A Brief Survey of the Development of ᶜIlm Uṣūl al-Fiqh." *al-Tawḥīd* 3, no. 2 (1986): 76–78; 3, no. 3 (1986): 95–111.

Graf, L. I. *al-Shāfiᶜīʾs Verhandeling over de 'Wortelen' van den Fiḳh.* Leiden: E. J. Brill, 1934.

Graham, William A. *Divine Word and Prophetic Word in Early Islam: A Reconsideration of the Sources, with Special Reference to the Divine Saying or Ḥadīth Qudsī.* Religion and Society 7. The Hague: Mouton, 1977.

Hallaq, Wael. "Was the gate of ijtihad closed?" *International Journal of Middle East Studies* 16 (1984): 3–41.

———. "Considerations of the Function and Character of Sunni Legal Theory." *Journal of the American Oriental Society* 104 (1984): 679–689.

———. "On the Authoritativeness of Sunni Consensus." *International Journal of Middle East Studies* 18 (1986): 427–454.

———. "The Development of Logical Structure in Sunni Legal Theory." *Der Islam* 64 (1987): 42–67.

———. "Non-analogical Arguments in Sunni Juridical Qiyās." *Arabica* 36 (1989): 286–306.

Hamidullah, M. "Codification of Muslim Law by Abū Ḥanīfah." *Z.V. Togan'a Armajan* (1950–1955): 369–378.

Hasan, Ahmad. "Early Modes of Ijtihād: Raʾy, Qiyās and Istiḥsān." *Islamic Studies* 6 (1967): 57–62.

———. "The Sources of Islamic Law." *Islamic Studies* 7 (1968): 15–184.

———. *The Early Development of Islamic Jurisprudence.* Islamabad: Islamic Research Institute, 1970.

———. "The Classical Definition of Ijmāʿ: The nature of Consensus." *Islamic Studies* 14 (1975): 21–270.

———. "The Principle of Istiḥsān in Islamic Jurisprudence." *Islamic Studies* 16 (1977): 347–362.

———. *The Doctrine of Ijmāʿ in Islam.* Islamabad: Islamic Research Institute, 1978.

———. "The Legal Cause in Islamic Jurisprudence: An Analysis of ʿIllat al-Ḥukm." *Islamic Studies* 19 (1980): 247–270.

———. "Modes of Reasoning in Legal Cause: al-Ijtihād fiʾl-ʿIllah." *Islamic Studies* 22, no. 1 (1983): 71–90.

Hawting, G. R. "The Role of Qurʾan and Ḥadīth in the Legal Controversy About the Rights of a Divorced Woman During Her 'Waiting Period' (ʿidda)." *Bulletin of the School of Oriental and African Studies* 52, no. 3 (1989): 430–445.

Hefner, Robert. *Hindu Javanese: Tengger Tradition and Islam.* Princeton, N.J.: Princeton University Press, 1985.

Henderson, John B. *Scripture, Canon, and Commentary: A Comparison of Confucian and Western Exegesis.* Princeton, N.J.: Princeton University Press, 1991.

Horovitz, J. "Alter und Ursprung des Isnad." *Der Islam* 8 (1918): 39–47.

Howitt, A. W. "The Jeraeil, or Initiation Ceremonies of the Kurnai Tribe." *Journal of the Anthropological Institute of Great Britain* 14 (May 1885): 301–328.

Ḥusaynī, ᶜAbd al-Fattāḥ. *al-Ijmāᶜ maṣdar thālith min maṣādir al-tashrīᶜ al-islāmī.* Cairo: Dār al-Ittiḥād al-ᶜArabī li al-Tibāᶜah, 1979.

Jakobson, Roman. "Langue and Parole: Code and Message." In his *On Language,* ed. Linda R. Waugh and Monique Monville-Burston, pp. 80–109. Cambridge, Mass.: Harvard University Press, 1990.

al-Janpūrī, ᶜAbd al-ʾAwal. *al-Nawādir al-munīfah bi-manāqib al-Imām Abī Ḥanīfah.* Kawnpur, 1310.

Junod, H. A. *Life of a South African Tribe.* London: Macmillan, 1927.

Juynboll, G. H. A. *Muslim Tradition: Studies in Chronology, Provenance and Authorship of Early Ḥadīth.* Cambridge: Cambridge University Press, 1983.

Kamali, Mohammed Hashim. *Principles of Islamic Jurisprudence,* 2d ed. Cambridge: Islamic Texts Society, 1991.

al-Karakī, al-Muḥaqqiq. "The Method of Derivation of the Rules of the Sharīᶜah." *al-Tawḥīd* 2, no. 3 (1985): 42–55.

al-Kawtharī, M. Zāhid. *al-Ḥāwī fī sīrat al-Imām Abī Jaᶜfar al-Ṭaḥāwī.* Cairo: Maṭbaᶜat al-Anwār al-Muḥammadīyah, 1368.

———. *Ḥusn al-taqāḍī fī sīrat al-Imām Abī Yūsuf al-qāḍī.* Ḥoms: R. Hākimī, 1968.

———. *Bulūgh al-amānī fī sīrat al-Imām Muḥammad ibn Ḥasan al-Shaybānī.* Cairo: Dār al-Hidāyah, 198–.

———. *Lamaḥāt al-naẓar fī sīrat al-Imām Zufar.* Cairo: Maṭbaᶜat al-Anwār, 1368.

———. *Maqālāt al-Kawtharī.* Cairo: Maṭbaᶜat al-Anwār, 1371. Reprint. Cairo: al-Maktabat al-Azharīyah li al-Turāth, 1994.

Khadeer, Mohammed Abdul. *Ijma and Legislation in Islam.* Secunderabad: Shivaji Press, 1974.

Khallāf, ʿAbd al-Wahhāb. *ʿIlm uṣūl al-fiqh.* Kuwait: Dār al-Qalam, 1972.

al-Khūlī, Amīn. *Mālik b. Anas,* 3 vols. Cairo, 1951.

Kister, M. J. "'A Booth Like the Booth of Moses . . .': A Study of an Early Ḥadīth." *Bulletin of the School of Oriental and African Studies* (1962): 150–155.

Kruse, H. "Al-Shaibānī on International Instruments." *Pakistan Historical Society Journal* 1 (1953): 90–100.

———. "Die Begründung der islamischen Völkerrechtslehre, Muḥammad aš-Šaybānī, Hugo Grotius der Moslimen." *Saeculum* 5 (1954): 221–241.

Kuhn, Thomas S. *The Structure of Scientific Revolutions,* 2d ed. Chicago: University of Chicago Press, 1970.

Laoust, Henri. *Essai sur les doctrines sociales et politiqes de Takī-d-Dīn Aḥmad b. Taimīya.* Cairo: Institut Français d'Archeologie Orientale, 1939.

———. "Le hanbalisme sous le califat de Baghdad." *Revue des Études Islamiques* (1959): 67–128.

———. *Les schismes dans l'Islam: introduction à une étude de la religion musulmane.* Paris: Payot, 1965.

———. "La pédagogie d'al-Ġazālī dans le mustaṣfā." *Revue des Études Islamique* 44 (1976): 71–79.

Layish, Aharon. "Notes on Joseph Schacht's Contribution to the Study of Islamic Law." *British Society for Middle Eastern Studies Bulletin* 9 (1982): 132–140.

Lecomte, Gérard. *Le traité des divergences du ḥadīṯ d'Ibn Qutaybah.* Damascus: Institut Français de Damas, 1962.

Levering, Miriam, ed. *Rethinking Scripture: Essays from a Comparative Perspective.* Albany: State University of New York Press, 1989.

Lévi-Strauss, Claude. *La pensée sauvage.* Paris: Librairie Plon, 1962. Trans. *The Savage Mind.* London: Weidenfeld and Nicolson, 1966.

Lincoln, Bruce. *Authority: Construction and Corrosion.* Chicago: University of Chicago Press, 1994.

Makdisi, George. *Ibn ᶜAqīl et la résurgence de l'Islam traditionaliste au XIe siècle.* Damascus: Institut Français de Damas, 1963.

———. "The Scholastic Method in Medieval Education: An Inquiry into Its Origins in Law and Theology." *Speculum* 49 (1974): 640–661.

———. "L'Islam Hanbalisant." *Revue des Études Islamiques* 42 (1974): 211–244, 43; (1975): 45–76 Reprinted. "Hanbalite Islam." In *Studies on Islam,* trans. and ed. Merlin L. Swartz, pp. 216–174. Oxford: Oxford University Press, 1981.

———. *The Rise of Colleges: Institutions of Learning in Islam and the West.* Edinburgh: Edinburgh University Press, 1981.

———. "Institutionalized Learning as a Self-Image of Islam." In *Islam's Understanding of Itself,* ed. Speros Vryonis, Jr., pp. 73–85. Los Angeles: University of California Press, 1983.

Margoliouth, D. S. *The Early Development of Mohammedanism.* London: Williams and Norgate, 1914.

Masud, K. *Islamic Legal Theory.* Islamabad: Islamic Research Institute, 1977.

Maᶜṣūmī, Muḥammad Ṣaghīr Ḥasan. "Imām Ṭaḥāwī fī Kitāb Ikhtilāf al-fuqahāᵓ." In *Fikr-u Naẓar,* pp. 193–194. Islamabad: Islamic Research Institute, 1973.

Meron, Yaᶜakov. "The Development of Legal Thought in Hanafi Texts." *Studia Islamica* 30 (1969): 73–118.

———. *L'obligation alimentaire entre époux en droit musulman Hanéfite.* Bibliothèque de droit privé 114. Paris: Librairie Générale de Droit et de Jurisprudence, 1971.

Mez, Adam. *The Renaissance of Islam.* London: Luzac, 1937.

Motzki, Harald. "The Muṣannaf of ᶜAbd al-Razzāq al-Ṣanᶜānī as a Source of Authentic Aḥādīth of the First Century A.H." *Journal of Near Eastern Studies* 50, no. 1 (1991): 1–21.

———. *Die Anfänge der islamischen Jurisprudenz: ihre Entwicklung in Mekka bis zur mitte des 2./8. Jahrhunderts.* Stuttgart: Abhandlungen für die Kunde des Morgenlandes, 1991.

al-Muḥmaṣānī, Ṣubḥī. "qāḍī quḍāt Baghdād wa atharuhū fī al-fiqh al-Islāmī." *Majallat majma*ᶜ *al-lughat al-*ᶜ*arabīyah bi Dimashq* 40 (1965): 117–136.

Mujeeb, M. "Orthodoxy and the Orthodox: The Shariᶜah as Law." *Islamic Culture* 38 (1964): 27–46.

Mūsā, M. Yūsuf. *Abū Ḥanīfah wa al-qiyām al-insānīyah.* Cairo: Maktabat Naḥdat Miṣr, 1957.

Muṭahharī, Murtaḍā. "The Role of Ijtihād in Legislation." *al-Tawḥīd* 4, no. 2 (1986–87): 21–41.

———. "The Role of Reason in Ijtihād." *al-Tawḥīd* 4, no. 2 (1986–87): 42–52.

Nallino, Carlo Alfonso. "Considerazioni sui rapporti fra diritto romano e diritto musulmano." In *Raccolta di scritti editi e inediti,* vol. 4, pp. 85–94. Rome: Istituto per l'Orient, 1942.

Naqvi, A. Ali Raza. "Prophetic Sunna in the Islamic Legal Framework." *Islamic Studies* 19 (1980): 120–133.

Palacios, Miguel Asín. *Abenházm de Córdoba: historia crítica de las ideas religiosas,* 5 vols. Madrid: Real Academia de la Historia, 1927.

Patton, Laurie L., ed. *Authority, Anxiety, and Canon: Essays in Vedic Interpretation.* Albany: State University of New York Press, 1994.

Patton, W. M. *Aḥmed ibn Ḥanbal and the Miḥna: A Biography of the Imām Including an Account of the Mohammedan Inquisition Called the Miḥna 218–234 A.H.* Leiden: E. J. Brill, 1897.

Peltrier, Frédéric. *Le livre des ventes du Mouwaṭṭā de Mālik ben Anas, traduction avec éclaircissements.* Algiers: Typographie A. Jourdan, 1911.

Powers, David. *Studies in Qurʾān and Ḥadīth: The Formation of the Islamic Law of Inheritance.* Berkeley: University of California Press, 1986.

al-Qāḍī, Waḍāḍ. "The Islamic Book in the Form of Biographical Dictionaries: Inner Structure and Cultural Significance." In *The Book in the Islamic World: The Written Word and*

Communication in the Middle East, ed. George N. Atiyeh, 93–122. Albany: State University of New York Press, 1995.

Rahman, Fazlur. "Sunnah and Hadith." *Islamic Studies* 1 (1962): 33ff.

———. *Islam.* Chicago: University of Chicago Press, 1966; reprint, 1979.

———. *Islam and Modernity: Transformation of an Intellectual Tradition.* Publications of the Center for Middle Eastern Studies 15. Chicago: University of Chicago Press, 1982.

Rancillac, P. "Des origines du droit musulman à la Risala d'al-Shafiᶜi." *Mélanges de l'Institut dominicain d'études orientales du Caire* 13 (1977): 147–169.

Robson, J. "Muslim Traditions: The Question of Authenticity." *Memoirs and Proceedings: Manchester Literary Philosophical Society* 93 (1951–52): 84–102.

———."The Isnād in Muslim Tradition." *Glasgow University Oriental Society Transactions* 15 (1955): 15–26.

Rubin, Uri. "Morning and Evening Prayers in Early Islam." *Jerusalem Studies in Arabic and Islam* 10 (1987): 40–64.

Sachau, Eduard. "Zur älteste Geschichte des muhammedanischen Rechts." *Akademie der Wissenschaften, Wien. Philosophisch-historische Klasse. Sitzungsberichte* 65 (1870): 99–723.

———. "Die Schulfächer und die Scholastik der Muslime." *Zeitschrift der Deutschen moregneländischen Gesellschaft* 32 (1878): 1–20.

al-Ṣadr, Muḥammad Ṣādiq. *al-Ijmāᶜ fī al-tashrīᶜ al-islāmī: dirāsah mawḍūᶜīyah li al-rukn al-thālith min adillat al-ijtihād muqāranatan biᶜarā al-madhāhib al-Islāmīyah kaffah.* Beirut: Manshūrāt ᶜUwaydāt, 1969.

Schacht, Joseph. "Vom babylonischen zum islamischen Recht." *Orientalistische Literaturzeitung* (1927): 664–669.

———. "A revaluation of Islamic tradition." *Journal of the Royal Asiatic Society* 49 (1949): 143–154.

———. "Foreign Elements in Ancient Islamic Law." *Journal of Comparative Law* 3–4 (1950): 9–16.

———. *Origins of Muhammadan Jurisprudence,* 2d ed. Oxford: Oxford University Press, 1953.

———. "Deux éditions inconnue du Muwaṭṭā'." *Studia Orientalia* 2 (1956): 477–492.

Schreiner, M. "Beiträge zur Geschichte der theologischen Bewegungen im Islam." *Zeitschrift der Deutschen Morgenländischen Gesellschaft* 52 (1898): 486–510; 53 (1899): 51–88, 513–563.

Sezgin, Fuat. *Geschichte des arabischen Schrifttums,* vol. 1. Leiden: E. J. Brill, 1967.

El Shakankiri, M. "Loi divine, loi humaine et droit dans l'histoire juridique de l'Islam." *Revue historique de droit français et etranger* 59 (1981): 161–182.

al-Sibā'ī, Muṣṭafā'. *al-Sunnah wa makānatu-hā fī al-tashrī' al-Islāmī.* Cairo: Maktabat Dār al-'Urūbah, 1961.

Siddiqi, M. Zubayr. "The Importance of Ḥadīth as a Source of Islamic Law." *Studies in Islam* 1, no. 1 (1964): 19–25.

Smith, Jonathan Z. *Imagining Religion.* Chicago: University of Chicago Press, 1982.

———. *To Take Place: Toward Theory in Ritual.* Chicago: University of Chicago Press, 1987.

Smith, Wilfred Cantwell. "The Study of Religion and the Study of the Bible." *Journal of the American Academy of Religion* 39 (1971): 131–140.

Spencer, Baldwin, and F. J. Gillen. *The Native Tribes of Central Australia.* London: Macmillan, 1899; reprint, 1938.

Spies, O. "Un grand juriste musulman Muḥammad b. al-Ḥasan al-Shaybānī." In *Rapports Génerale au Congress internationale de droit comparé,* pp. 125–129. Brussels: E. Bruylant, 1960.

———. "Instanbuler Handschriften zu dem Rechtswerk Badā'i' aṣ-Ṣanā'i' des Kāsānī." *Islam* 41 (1965): 18–26.

Sprenger, Aloys. "On the Origin and Progress of Writing Down Historical Facts Among the Musulmans." *Journal of the Asiatic Socity of Bengal* 25 (1856): 303–329.

Strehlow, T. G. H. *Die Aranda- und Loritja-Stämme in Zentral Australien,* 2 vols. Frankfurt: J. Baer, 1968.

———. *Australian Traditions.* Melbourne: Melbourne University Press, 1947.

Tāj, ʿAbd al-Raḥmān. *al-Siyāsah al-sharīʿah.* Cairo: Maṭbʿah Dār al-Taʾlīf, 1371.

Toulmin, Stephen. *Human Understanding.* Princeton, N.J.: Princeton University Press, 1972.

Turner, Victor. *Ndembu Divination.* Rhodes-Livingstone papers 31. Manchester: Manchester University Press, 1961.

———. *Forest of Symbols.* Ithaca, N.Y.: Cornell University Press, 1967.

———. *Revelation and Divination in Ndembu Ritual.* Ithaca, N.Y.: Cornell University Press, 1975.

Tyan, Emile. *Histoire de l'organisation judiciaire en pays d'Islam,* 2 vols. Paris: Librairie du Recueil Sirey, 1938–1943, 2d ed. Leiden: E. J. Brill, 1960.

———."Méthodologie et sources du droit en Islam." *Studia Islamica* 10 (1959): 82–84.

Waldman, Marilyn R. "Primitive Mind/Modern Mind: New Approaches to an Old Problem Applied to Islam." In *Approaches to Islam in Religious Studies,* ed. Richard C. Martin, pp. 91–105. Tucson: University of Arizona Press, 1985.

Walker, Paul. *Early Philosophical Shiism: The Ismaili Neoplatonism of Abū Yaʿqūb al-Sijistānī.* Cambridge: Cambridge University Press, 1993.

Wansbrough, John. *Quranic Studies: Sources and Methods of Scriptural Interpretation.* Oxford: Oxford University Press, 1977.

Weiss, Bernard. "Interpretation in Islamic Law: The Theory of Ijtihad." *The American Journal of Comparative Law* 26, no. 2 (1978): 199–212.

———."The Primacy of Revelation in Classical Islamic Legal Theory as Expounded by Sayf al-Dīn al-Āmidī." *Studia Islamica* 59 (1984): 79–109.

———. *The Search for God's Law: Islamic Jurisprudence in the Writings of Sayf al-Dīn al-Āmidī.* Salt Lake City: University of Utah Press, 1992.

Wensinck, A. J. "Die Entstehung der muslimischen Reinheitsgesetzgebung." *Der Islam* 5 (1914).

———. *A Handbook of Early Muhammadan Tradition,* 7 vols. Leiden: E. J. Brill, 1927.

White, C. M. N. *Witchcraft, Divination and Magic.* Northern Rhodesia: Lusaka Government Printer, 1947.

Widengren, Geo. "Holy Book and Holy Tradition in Islam." In *Holy Book and Holy Tradition: International Colloquium Held in the Faculty of Theology, University of Manchester,* ed. F. F. Bruce and E. G. Rupp, pp. 210–236. Grand Rapids, Mich.: William B. Eerdmans, 1968.

Wiedensohler, G. "Der Rechtsirrtum im islamischen Recht nach as-Saraḫsī." *Zeitschrift für vergleichenden Rechtswissenschaft* 70 (1968): 97–109.

Young, M. J. L. "Arabic Biographical Writing." In *Religion, Learning and Science in the ʿAbbasid Period,* ed. M. J. L. Young and others, pp. 169–187. Cambridge History of Arabic Literature. Cambridge: Cambridge University Press, 1990.

Index